*Discovering
North Carolina*

Discovering

North Carolina

A Tar Heel Reader

Edited by

Jack Claiborne and

William Price

The University of North Carolina Press

Chapel Hill and London

© 1991 The University of North Carolina Press
Manufactured in the United States of America

The paper in this book meets the guidelines for permanence and
durability of the Committee on Production Guidelines for Book
Longevity of the Council on Library Resources.

95   94   93   92   91   5   4   3   2   1

Library of Congress Cataloging-in-Publication Data

Discovering North Carolina : a Tar Heel reader / edited by Jack
  Claiborne and William Price.
        p.   cm.
    Includes bibliographical references.
    ISBN 0-8078-1931-X (cloth : alk. paper)
      1. North Carolina—History.   I. Claiborne, Jack.   II. Price,
  William S. (William Solomon), 1941–
  F254.5.D57   1991
  975.6—dc20   90-50009
                                                        CIP

A complete list of the sources from which the pieces included in
this book are reprinted can be found at the end of the book.

To our favorite discoverers of North Carolina,

our children,

Jack E. Claiborne, Jr.

Margaret L. Claiborne

Marie Elizabeth Price

Katherine Reynolds Price

Contents

❧ *People*

❧ *Events*

❧ *Social Fabric*

⁊ *Preface*

This anthology is intended to help all North Carolinians, newcomers as well as longtime residents, explore the traditions that have marked the mind and character of their state. It is, of necessity, a sampler, a beginning.

Many elements go into defining North Carolina, and one could spend a lifetime browsing among them, learning from them. There are several solid, informative histories of the state. There are hundreds of biographies and scores of useful guides to historic and natural sites. There are varied cultural activities and institutions to participate in. There are also cities and towns, country stores and family farms, mountains and seascapes, great universities and tiny private schools, symphonies and satellite dishes. Above all, there are people: rich and poor, proud and humble, racially diverse and interbred, sophisticated and simple.

As an introduction to all that makes North Carolina what it is, we have tried to put together a collection of writings that will acquaint readers with the richness and variety of our state's past and present and aid them in developing a more informed sense of its future. Many of the pieces we have chosen are short; many others have been condensed. Our goal was to span more than 400 years with a diversity of readable, representative material.

One of the special joys of compiling this book has been our own discovery of new things about a place we thought we knew pretty well. The joint effort enlarged our experience of the state. While both of us are native Tar Heels, we come from different backgrounds. Jack Claiborne is a journalist; William Price, a historian. Claiborne was reared in Charlotte, our largest city; Price in Warrenton, a small town. We grew up on opposite ends of the Piedmont; Claiborne on the southwest edge, Price on the northeast. The historian has always been drawn to our prehistory and early history; the journalist to the Civil War and the rich story of its aftermath.

Both of us live in North Carolina by choice and have sought to serve its needs. We have watched our children grow up amidst its beauty and opportunity, have seen the hatefulness of segregation and the hope of equality, have wanted to leave our state better than we found it.

In compiling the anthology, we made a conscious effort to use Tar Heel writers whenever possible. This is, after all, an effort to define the character of North Carolina, and its own native sons and daughters seem to know that character best. However, the occasional "outsider" drops in with an observation all the keener for its objectivity.

We also have chosen material from a wide variety of sources, in hopes of acquainting readers with the wealth of waiting histories, biographies, essays, and reference works about North Carolina. We hope to stimulate interest in those resources too.

The selections we offer are personal choices, often containing our favorite stories about the state. We read thousands of pages before including the hundreds that follow. There are omissions that will bother some students of North Carolina's past; there are also inclusions that will puzzle some people living in the present. We don't apologize for that!

We know, too, that not all that we have included portrays North Carolina in a favorable light. Nor do we apologize for that. The book is a collaboration between men who love this state—who love it so much that they are not hesitant to criticize it. Our parents lived here, we were married here, our children were born and reared here. North Carolina is home.

And like a good home, it has its own personality, its own character. We've enjoyed discovering that character. We hope you will too.

ᴄᴇᴎ Acknowledgments

This book got started in the late spring of 1985 when Matthew Hodgson and David Perry of the University of North Carolina Press approached William Price about compiling a volume of readings on North Carolina that would help many newcomers to the state understand it better. Price suggested that his training as a historian might lead to a book that lacked the liveliness to entice newcomers to pick up such a volume, much less to read it. He suggested that Jack Claiborne be approached about joining the enterprise. Hodgson and Perry agreed enthusiastically.

Claiborne and Price had worked together earlier in the 1980s as members of the North Carolina Humanities Council, had shared an occasional glass of refreshment and story with one another, and knew that together they made a more interesting person than either of them did by himself! Thus was born the collaboration that has produced *Discovering North Carolina*.

That collaboration would not have succeeded without the help, advice, counsel, and occasional skepticism of the following people: Freda Brittain, Jerry Cashion, Jeff Crow, and Suellen Hoy of the North Carolina Division of Archives and History; Brent Glass, formerly executive director of the North Carolina Humanities Council; H. G. Jones and his staff, especially Robert Anthony, Alice Cotten, and Harry McKown, of the North Carolina Collection in the Wilson Library at the University of North Carolina at Chapel Hill; and Pat Ryckman and her staff, including Sheila Bumgardner, Joan Carothers, Ann Dugger, and Lew Herman, at the Carolina Room of the Charlotte-Mecklenburg Public Library.

Profound thanks for their support and encouragement also go to our wives, Margaret Claiborne and Pia Price, both of whom teach young Tar Heels about their state and teach their husbands about strength. We are grateful to them for that and for their considerable role in creating the discoverers named in the dedication.

Jack Claiborne
William Price

Environment:
Physical, Historical,
Attitudinal

"View of the Black Mountains," *Harper's New Monthly Magazine*, August 1880, W. H. Morse, illustrator. Courtesy North Carolina Collection, Wilson Library, University of North Carolina at Chapel Hill.

A Sailor's First Impressions

Arthur Barlowe

In 1584 Walter Raleigh equipped two ships and commissioned Captains Philip Amadas, about nineteen years old, and Arthur Barlowe to sail them to the New World. Threading the Outer Banks at Ocracoke Inlet, they became the first Englishmen to set foot on what is now North Carolina. Later they established a base at Roanoke Island and explored much of the surrounding land.

Some of the excitement of that venture—and the wonder of North Carolina's Outer Banks—is reflected in this excerpt from Captain Barlowe's report to Walter Raleigh about the voyage. It was taken from Richard Hakluyt's 1589 *Principal Navigations*, but the original spelling has been modernized and some of the punctuation regularized. Notice that the Englishmen smelled the land before they saw it. Notice too the welcome they received from the Indians.

The 27th day of April, in the year of our redemption 1584, we departed the west of England, with two barks well furnished with men and victuals, having received our last and perfect directions by your letters, confirming the former instructions and commandments delivered by yourself at our leaving the river of Thames. . . .

The second of July, we found shoal water, which smelled so sweetly, and was so strong a smell, as if we had been in the midst of some delicate garden, abounding with all kind of odoriferous flowers, by which we were assured that the land could not be far distant; and keeping good watch and bearing but slack sail, the fourth of the same month, we arrived upon the coast, which we supposed to be a continent and firm land, and we sailed along the same a hundred and twenty English miles before we could find any entrance or river issuing into the sea. The first that appeared unto us we entered, though not without some difficulty, and cast anchor about three harquebus shot within the haven's mouth, on the left hand of the same; and after thanks given to God for our safe arrival thither, we manned our boats and went to view the land next adjoining and to "take possession of the same in the right of the Queen's Most Excellent Majesty as rightful Queen and Princess of the same," and after delivered the same over to your use, according to Her Majesty's grant and letters patent under Her Highness's great seal. Which being performed, according to the ceremonies used in such enterprises, we viewed the land about us, being whereas we first landed very sandy and low towards the water side, but so full of grapes as the very beating and surge of the sea overflowed them, of which we found such plenty, as well there as in all places else, both on the sand and on the green soil on the hills, as in the plains, as well on every little shrub as also climbing towards the tops of the high cedars, that I think in all the world the like abundance is not to be found. . . .

We passed from the sea side towards the tops of those hills next adjoining, being but of mean height, and from thence we beheld the sea on both sides to the north and to the south, finding no end any of both ways. This land lay stretching itself to the west, which after we found to be but an island of twenty leagues long, and not above six miles broad. Under the bank or hill whereon we stood we beheld the valleys replenished with goodly cedar trees and, having discharged our harquebus shot, such a flock of cranes (the most part white) arose under us, with such a cry redoubled by many echoes, as if an army of men had shouted all together.

This island had many goodly woods full of deer, conies, hares, and fowl, even in the midst of summer, in incredible abundance. The woods are . . . the highest and reddest cedars of the world. . . . We remained by the side of this island two whole days before we saw any people of the country. The third day we espied one small boat rowing towards us, having in it three persons; this boat came to the land's side, four harquebus shot from our ships, and there, two of the people remaining, the third came along the shore side towards us and, we being then all within-board, he walked up and down upon the point of the land next unto us. Then the master and the pilot of the admiral, Simon Ferdinando, and the Captain, Philip Amadas, myself, and others rowed to the land, whose coming this fellow attended, never making any show of fear or doubt. And after he had spoken of many things not understood by us, we brought him with his own good liking aboard the ships and gave him a shirt, a hat, and some other things and made him taste of our wine and our meat, which he liked very well. And after having viewed both barks, he departed and went to his own boat again, which he had left in a little cove or creek adjoining. As soon as he was two bowshots into the water, he fell to fishing, and in less than half an hour, he had laden his boat as deep as it could swim, with which he came again to the point of the land, and there he divided his fish into two parts, pointing one part to the ship and the other to the pinnace, which, after he had (as much as he might) requited the former benefits received, he departed out of our sight. . . .

When we first had sight of this country, some thought the first land we saw to be the continent, but after we entered into the haven, we saw before us another mighty long sea, for there lies along the coast a tract of islands two hundred miles in length, adjoining to the ocean sea, and between the islands two or three entrances. When you are entered between them (these islands being very narrow for the most part, as in most places six miles broad, in some places less, in few more), then there appears another great sea, containing in breadth in some places forty, and in some fifty, in some twenty miles over, before you come unto the continent, and in this enclosed sea there are about a hundred islands of divers bigness, whereof one is sixteen miles long, at which we were, finding it to be a most pleasant and fertile ground, replenished with goodly cedars and divers other sweet woods full of currants, of flax, and many other notable commodities, which we at that time had no leisure to view. Besides this island, there are many, as I have said, some of two, of three, of four, or five miles, some more, some less, most beautiful and pleasant to behold, replenished with deer, conies, hares, and divers beasts, and about them the goodliest and best fish in the world and in greatest abundance.

Thus, sir, we have acquainted you with the particulars of our discovery, made this present voyage, as far north as the shortness of the time we there continued would afford us to take view of; and so contenting ourselves with this service at this time, which we hope hereafter to enlarge as occasion and assistance shall be given, we resolved to leave the country and to apply ourselves to return for England, which we did accordingly and arrived safely in the west of England about the midst of September.

❧ The Legacy of the Lost Colony

❧ Though blessed with good looks, stylish manners, and powerful friends, Sir Walter Raleigh had rotten luck. As a young soldier he caught the eye of Queen Elizabeth, was invited to join her court, and launched a series of enterprises to parlay her favor into personal wealth. All his schemes failed, including an effort to colonize the New World and reap riches for himself and England. His colonial ventures were dogged by bad timing and natural disaster. But they left a lasting imprint on North Carolina and a mystery to haunt imaginations for more than 400 years.

News of the Amadas and Barlowe expedition—and the appearance of two Indian boys, Manteo and Wanchese, who accompanied the explorers back to England—created a sensation in London. Queen Elizabeth knighted Raleigh, named the new land Virginia after herself, the Virgin Queen, and joined Sir Walter and his friends in financing an even larger expedition.

In 1585 Lieutenant Ralph Lane led a military company of 107 men to Roanoke Island in an effort to establish an English colony there. The company included Philip Amadas; artist John White, whose watercolor sketches of plants and Indians would later delight English eyes; and scientist-surveyor Thomas Harriot, whose descriptions of animals, vegetables, trees, and other wildlife would excite the interest of future explorers.

Arriving in Roanoke in August, Lane's soldiers erected a fort, sent Sir Richard Grenville back to England for more supplies, and began charting the territory. Their surveying parties ranged as far north as Chesapeake Bay and as far inland as the Roanoke River. After exploring the mainland west of Roanoke, Ralph Lane declared it "the goodliest soile under the cope of heaven," a vision to stir the blood of any real estate promoter and one that North Carolina orators still invoke to touch the hearts of their hearers.

The description occurs in a letter Lane wrote to lawyer Richard Hakluyt back in England. The letter said, in part:

> In the meantime while you shall understand that since Sir Richard Grenvils departure from us, as also before, we have discovered the main to bee the goodliest soile under the cope of heaven, so abounding with sweete trees, that bring such sundry rich and most pleasant gummes, grapes of such sweetnes, yet wild, as France, Spaine nor Italy hath no greater, so many sortes of Apothecarie drugs, such severall kindes of flaxe, and one kinde like silke, the same gathered of a grasse, as comon there as grasse is here. And now within these few dayes we have found here a Guinie wheate, whose eare yeeldeth corne for bread, 400. upon one eare, and the Cane maketh very good and perfect suger. . . . Besides that, it is the goodliest and most pleasing territorie of the world (for the soile is of a huge unknowen greatnesse, and very wel peopled and towned, though savagelie) and the climate so wholesome, that we have not had one sicke, since we touched land here. . . .

As winter came and then spring, the colonists ran low on food and grew anxious when Sir Richard Grenville's ships failed to return with fresh supplies. Their fears of being stranded were eased when Sir Francis Drake stopped by in June 1586 after raiding Spanish shipping off Florida and the West Indies. Drake offered them supplies and a small ship, but after a three-day storm, the entire company leaped at the chance to accompany him to England. Drake departed so hastily that he left behind three explorers and several slaves.

Within days a ship arrived at Roanoke with provisions, and a fortnight later Sir Richard Grenville returned also. It was typical of Raleigh's luck. Had the supplies arrived a few days earlier, the Lane colony might have survived and changed the course of North Carolina history and English fortunes in America. Failing to find the departed colonists, Grenville left fifteen men with two years' provisions and went back to England.

Lane's return was a disappointment to Walter Raleigh, who was running out of time and treasure. He had spent £40,000 and still had nothing to show for it. But the summaries of Lane, the drawings of White, and the reports of Harriot stirred widespread interest and helped recruit investors in another venture, one that would include 91 men, 17 women, and 9 boys in a company governed by John White.

They arrived at Roanoke in 1587, found a skeleton and some personal effects of Grenville's men, and began building a new colony. In August, nineteen-year-old Eleanor Dare, daughter of Governor White, gave birth to a daughter, Virginia, the first child born of English parents in America. It was an auspicious start, but more bad luck lay ahead.

The settlers had arrived in midsummer, too late to plant crops, and as provisions ran low the wary colonists persuaded Governor White to return to England for more. Reluctantly he left in late 1587 and arrived home just as England was declaring war against Spain. The first ships he could outfit were diverted from their mission by a captain who was more interested in piracy among Spanish shipping. Three anxious years passed before Governor White could return to Roanoke; in March of 1590 he sailed aboard a vessel appropriately named the *Hopewell*. In his journal he described what he found:

> The 15 of August towards Evening we came to an anker at Hatorask, in 36 degr. and on[e] third, in five fadom water, three leagues from shore, At our first comming to anker on this shore we saw a great smoke rise on the Ile Roanoke nere the place where I left our Colony in the year 1587, which smoake put us in good hope that some of the Colony were there expecting my return out of England.

The next morning he started ashore with two boats, having instructed the ship's gunners to fire the cannon at regular intervals "to the end that their reportes might be heard to the place where wee hoped to finde some of our people."

When another plume of smoke appeared on the horizon, they hurriedly made for it instead, but arrived to find no sign that anyone had recently been there. Wearied, they rowed to Hatteras, rested the night on shore, and the next day set out again for Roanoke.

But before we could get to the place where our planters were left, it was so exceeding darke, that we overshot the place a quarter of a mile: there we espied towards the North end of the Iland ye light of a great fire thorow the woods, to which we presently rowed: when we came right over against it, we let fall our Grapnel neare the shore, & sounded with a trumpet a Call & afterward many familiar English tunes of Songs, and called to them friendly; but we had no answer.

In departing from the colonists three years earlier, Governor White had instructed that if they moved their settlement they should carve on their doors or the trunks of trees their new location. If the move was made in distress, they were to embellish the carving with a cross.

After a night of unanswered trumpet calls and songs, Governor White and his sailors went ashore to the place he had left the colonists and found carved in the bark of a tree the letters CRO. Moving on to the site of the settlement, he found the houses torn down and in their place a fort. At an entrance to the fort he found carved the word CROATOAN, the place where the Indian Manteo was born and where Governor White knew the Indians to be friendly. The word was not accompanied by a cross or other sign of crisis.

Before he could sail to Croatoan, believed to be modern-day Hatteras, a storm blew his ship out to sea and left it too damaged to navigate the currents that swirl around the Outer Banks. The ship limped south to Trinidad and from there to England.

What happened to White's daughter, granddaughter, and the rest of the colonists? Nobody knows. Some say they moved north and were killed by Indians. Some say they moved inland to live with Indians. Some say their descendants survive today in Robeson County as the Lumbee or "Croatan" Indians.

Whatever happened to them, the story of the Lost Colony remains a compelling source of myth and a challenge to historians. In July 1937, in a specially built amphitheater on Roanoke Island, Pulitzer Prize–winning playwright Paul Green's symphonic drama *The Lost Colony* began reenacting the mystery. The play has stirred Tar Heel imaginations ever since.

ஐ *The First Permanent Colony*

John Lawson

After the Lost Colony, more than seventy years passed before a permanent settlement was made in North Carolina. During that time nine of America's original thirteen colonies were established, beginning with Virginia in 1607. Only three of the thirteen—New Jersey, South Carolina, and Georgia—were settled later than North Carolina.

Actually, North Carolina owes its lasting settlement to a spillover from Virginia. Beginning about 1653, settlers moving south along the Chowan River began to filter down to the western edge of the Albemarle Sound and later established what became the town of Edenton.

In this excerpt from *A New Voyage to Carolina*, published in 1709, explorer, surveyor, and historian John Lawson describes that migration. Lawson was an Englishman who traveled the Carolinas from 1700 to 1711, often living among the Indians. He counts the Lost Colony as the first attempt at a North Carolina settlement and the Albemarle infiltration as the second.

ஐ A second Settlement of this Country was made about fifty Years ago, in that part we now call *Albemarl*-County, and chiefly in *Chuwon* Precinct, by several substantial Planters, from *Virginia*, and other Plantations; Who finding mild Winters, and a fertile Soil, beyond Expectation, producing every thing that was planted, to a prodigious Increase; their Cattle, Horses, Sheep, and Swine, breeding very fast, and passing the Winter, without any Assistance from the Planter; so that every thing seem'd to come by Nature, the Husbandman living almost void of Care, and free from those Fatigues which are absolutely requisite in Winter-Countries, for providing Fodder and other Necessaries; these Encouragements induc'd them to stand their Ground, altho' but a handful of People, seated at great Distances one from another, and amidst a vast number of *Indians* of different Nations, who were then in *Carolina*. Nevertheless, I say, the Fame of this new-discover'd Summer-Country spread thro' the neighbouring Colonies, and, in a few Years, drew a considerable Number of Families thereto, who all found Land enough to settle themselves in, (had they been many Thousands more) and that which was very good and commodiously seated, both for Profit and Pleasure. And indeed, most of the Plantations in *Carolina* naturally enjoy a noble Prospect of large and spacious Rivers, pleasant Savanna's, and fine Meadows, with their green Liveries, interwoven with beautiful Flowers, of most glorious Colours, which the several Seasons afford; hedg'd in with pleasant Groves of the ever-famous Tulip-tree, the stately Laurel, and Bays, equalizing the Oak in Bigness and Growth; Myrtles, Jessamines, Wood-bines, Honeysuckles, and several other fragrant Vines and Ever-greens, whose aspiring Branches shadow and interweave themselves with the loftiest Timbers, yielding a pleasant Prospect, Shade and Smell, proper Habitations for the Sweet-singing Birds, that melodiously entertain such as travel thro' the Woods of *Carolina*.

The Planters possessing all these Blessings, and the Produce of great Quantities of Wheat and *Indian* Corn, in which this Country is very fruitful, as likewise in Beef, Pork, Tallow, Hides, Deer-Skins, and Furs; for these Commodities the *New-England*-Men and *Bermudians* visited *Carolina*, in their Barks and Sloops, and carry'd out what they made, bringing them, in Exchange, Rum, Sugar, Salt, Molosses, and some wearing Apparel, tho' the last at very extravagant Prices.

As the Land is very fruitful, so are the Planters kind and hospitable to all that come to visit them; there being very few House-keepers, but what live very nobly, and give away more Provisions to Coasters and Guests who come to see them, than they expend amongst their own Families.

∾ Early Settlement

∾ As Virginians streamed south into the Albemarle region, other settlements were being made in a leapfrog pattern along river basins farther down the Carolina coast. In the 1690s settlers moved from the Chowan area into the Pamlico basin where in 1706 they founded Bath, the state's first town. About 1707, French Huguenots from the Richmond area of Virginia moved into the Neuse and Trent river basins. In 1710 German and Swiss palatines arrived from England to establish the town of New Bern at the confluence of the Trent and the Neuse. In 1725, settlers moving up from South Carolina spilled over into the lower Cape Fear Valley to start a settlement near the town of Brunswick.

Each of these outposts was separate, isolated, and distant from the others. It was about fifty miles from the Chowan to the Pamlico, about thirty miles from the Pamlico to the Neuse, and about 100 miles from the Neuse to the Cape Fear. There were no north-south waterways to connect them and no roads overland, so there was little travel among the remote settlements and little trade, communication, or sense of unity.

Adding to the problem of isolation was a stream of settlers who began trickling into the Piedmont backcountry in the 1730s and reached a flood tide in the 1750s. The reason: cheap land. In 1729 King George II regained control of the Carolina territory from heirs of the Lords Proprietors and sent his land agents north into Maryland and Pennsylvania, alerting crowded farmers to the inviting tracts available in the Carolinas' backwoods. The Scotch-Irish and German yeomen responded in great numbers, but on their arrival they felt little kinship with their fellows to the east.

As a result of all these actions, plus England's defeat of the Scots in the Battle of Culloden, which sent Highlanders fleeing into the upper Cape Fear Valley around modern Fayetteville, North Carolina was growing rapidly. In 1730 it contained only 30,000 whites and 6,000 blacks, ranking as one of the least settled of the American colonies. By 1755 the population had doubled; by 1765 it had quadrupled; and by 1775, on the eve of the American Revolution, it included 265,000 whites and 80,000 blacks to make North Carolina the fourth largest of the thirteen colonies.

Yet it would take many years and much effort to mold these disparate, often fractious communities into one commonwealth. Much of their regional rivalry and suspicion persists to this day.

❧ *Hereditary Nobility in the Carolinas*

C. Wingate Reed

If the Lords Proprietors had had their way, North Carolina would have been organized as a feudal society, with hierarchies of nobility reigning over the common people and each nobleman bearing an exalted title—like something from a modern Elks lodge.

In 1663, as a reward for assisting his restoration to the throne following the Cromwellian interlude, Charles II gave the territory including both Carolinas to eight men of wealth and power who became known as the Lords Proprietors.

Some of the lords' names or titles are preserved in Carolina place names: Hyde County, N.C., and Clarendon County, S.C., named for Edward Hyde, earl of Clarendon; the Albemarle Sound and city of Albemarle, N.C., for George Monck, duke of Albemarle; Craven County, N.C., for William, earl of Craven; Berkeley County, S.C., for John, Baron Berkeley; Carteret County, N.C., for Sir George Carteret; the Ashley-Cooper River in

South Carolina for Anthony Ashley-Cooper, earl of Shaftesbury; and Colleton County, S.C., for Sir John Colleton.

To promote settlement and protect property rights, the eight proprietors instructed the English philosopher John Locke, then their secretary, to draw up a plan of government, "The Fundamental Constitutions of Carolina." Locke's plan is described in the following article taken from the *State* magazine of May 27, 1961. It was written by C. Wingate Reed of Washington, N.C., a West Point graduate and retired U.S. Army colonel who also wrote *Beaufort County: Two Centuries of Its History*.

ᐴ Two hundred and ninety years ago [in 1669], the "true and absolute" Lords Proprietors of Carolina conceived and attempted to spawn a government of landed aristocracy in the sparsely populated wilderness of Carolina.

To judge fairly the grandiose plans of those eight Earls, Lords, Dukes, and Baronets, one must consider the political climate and human relations of England at that time. After their success in restoring Charles II to the throne of England, the creation of a Palatinate of Carolina must have seemed a relatively easy project. They saw nothing wrong in a privileged class of nobility, nor an underprivileged class of leetmen and serfs, subject to the will of their masters. Both were accepted by all Englishmen.

In addition to the vast area of land, the King's charter included the "jurisdiction and privileges of a County Palatine of Durham." This included the right to create an order of nobility in Carolina, provided the titles used were not those common to England. "Only God could create a King, with divine rights, and only a King could create a Lord."

Inspired by visions of a principality in Carolina as great as the German Palatinate on the Rhine, the Lords Proprietors borrowed the title or *dignity* of *Palatine* for the ruler of their domain. *Landgrave*, also a German title, borrowed from the ruler of Hesse-Kassel, was next in *dignity* to the *Palatine*. *Cacique*, the Spanish equivalent of a Count, and a title used by Spaniards to designate a native chief or ruler of their American possessions, was selected as the third *dignity*. For each *Landgrave*, there were to be two *Caciques*.

The eldest member of the Lords Proprietors was to be the *Palatine* of Carolina, the pinnacle of this pyramid of nobility. He, with the seven other Lords Proprietors, each having a resounding, but empty title, such as Admiral, Chancellor, or Chamberlain of Carolina, formed the *Palatine* Court, which was to rule the Province or Palatinate of Carolina. Upon his death, the *Palatine* was to be succeeded by the next older Proprietor.

Initially, Carolina was to be divided into twelve counties of 480,000 acres each. Each county was divided into seignories, baronies, and colonies. A barony consisted of 12,000 acres, "in one single piece." A seignory was one or more baronies. A provision was made for "manors" of from 3,000 to 12,000 acres, so designated by grant, for commoners.

For each county, there would be one, and only one *Landgrave*, and two *Caciques*. These *dignities* were to be bestowed upon "such of the inhabitants of the said Province," as the Lords Proprietors thought deserving of the honor.

Within each county, each Proprietor was to have a seignory of 12,000 acres. The *Landgrave* was to have four baronies, totaling 48,000 acres. Each *Cacique* was to have two baronies, totaling 24,000 acres. This accounted for two-fifths of the land area of the county. The remaining three-fifths, or 288,000 acres, was to be divided into four colonies (precincts), for the use of freeholders. The possession of land was a legal requirement for the holder of any *dignity* or office within the Province.

Disregarding the provisions of their "sacred and unalterable" Fundamental Constitutions, the first *Landgrave* appointed was John Locke, author of the constitutions. He, and a half dozen other *Landgraves*, and a number of *Caciques*, never saw Carolina.

Landgrave Able Kettleby, Agent of the Province before the Board of Trade, lived in London. *Landgrave* Thomas Amy, a London grocer, was appointed and granted a barony, for "meeting and treating (prospective colonists) in the Carolina Coffee House in London." Thomas Eastchurch was made a *Landgrave* and appointed Governor of Albemarle, but died before taking office. Captain Henry Wilkenson of London, was appointed a *Cacique*, and Governor of Albemarle, and like Eastchurch, never took office.

The nobility provisions of the constitutions rested lightly on the shoulders of the settlers of Albemarle, later North Carolina. For years before the constitutions were issued, they had an organized, and satisfactory government, consisting of a Governor, Council, and Assembly. When their Governor proved worthless, as so many appointed by the Proprietors did, the Council and Assembly got rid of him, be he proprietor, nobleman, or commoner.

Seth Sothel bought the proprietary shares of the Earl of Clarendon, and was appointed Governor of Albemarle. He arrived in 1682, and established a seignory on the Pasquotank River. For seven years he misruled the county, until impeached by the Assembly. Banned from Albemarle for a year, and the government forever, Sothel went to Charles Town. There, under his proprietary rights, he assumed the government of that county until removed by the *Palatine* Court.

Colonel Robert Daniel was the first *Landgrave* to reside in North Carolina. Appointed while serving on the Governor's council in Charles Town, Daniel came to North Carolina as deputy Governor. He received no barony in North Carolina, but purchased a plantation on the Pamlico, now known as Archbell's Point, across Bath Creek from Bath Town. Later, Daniel returned to Charles Town, as deputy to Governor Craven. After Craven returned to England, Daniel assumed the Governorship.

The Swiss Baron Christopher von Graffenried, who founded New Bern, was the second *Landgrave* to reside in North Carolina. He wrote that during the Cary Rebellion, while Governor Hyde was in Virginia, "a small crowd of North Carolina inhabitants offered the government to me, . . . as in the absence of a Governor, the *Landgrave* occupied the first rank and held the presidial. . . ." Graffenried declined, explaining, "I had been an ocular witness to his (Hyde's) election by the Lords Proprietors, and had congratulated him . . . far more, he was a near relative of the Queen."

Governor Charles Eden was the third, and last, *Landgrave* to live in North Carolina.

Colonel Philip Ludwell was appointed deputy Governor of "That Part of the Province of Carolina That Lies North and East of the Cape Fear." Two years later, he was promoted to be Governor of Carolina. He moved to Charles Town, and was appointed a *Cacique*. . . .

The only North Carolina manor of record, was that of John Bland, "fronting on Albemarle Sound." Several "manor plantations" are recorded in wills.

In South Carolina, under the influence of Sir Peter Colleton, who succeeded Sir John as Proprietor, the nobility provisions of the constitutions received greater impetus. . . .

Between the years 1671 and 1726, at least twenty-six *Landgraves* and thirteen *Caciques* were appointed. . . .

Actually, the *dignity* of *Landgrave*, in most cases, expired with the original holder. There were exceptions, . . . where a *dignity* descended to the second or third generation.

After more than a quarter of a century of trying to get the "assent and approbation of the Freemen," or their Assemblies, to the Fundamental Constitutions, the Proprietors abandoned the hope and directed the Governor to "come as nigh as possible," in the laws passed by the Assembly.

This failure was not because the constitutions created class distinction in Carolina. Such distinctions were there. The bell tolled for hereditary nobility in Carolina because the constitutions threatened the two things the Freemen of Carolina prized most; their freedom and "good bottom land."

They had no intention of surrendering the "liberties, franchises, and privileges of the King's subjects resident within the realm of England," guaranteed them by the charter. Their greatest objection was the grant of vast tracts of 12,000 to 48,000 acres of choice land to a single individual. These land-hungry Freemen saw this as the greatest threat to their future, and that of Carolina.

Over half a century elapsed before the Lords Proprietors finally abandoned their hope of creating a *Palatinate* in Carolina, and surrendered their charter to the Crown, leaving their hereditary nobility in Carolina to wither on the vine.

This desire for "nobility" did not expire easily. Forty years after the Revolution, a lady in South Carolina, whose husband was a descendant of Sir John Colleton, signed herself; "Baroness of Fairlawn and *Landgravine* of Colleton."

How North Carolina Got Its Name

If North Carolina started out being called Virginia, after Elizabeth, the Virgin Queen, how did it become North Carolina? Ask Tar Heels that question and you're likely to get a variety of answers.

Some will tell you, accurately, that "Carolina" is derived from the Latin for "Charles," which is "Carolus." They might go on to say, less accurately, that the "Charles" in question was the rakish monarch Charles II, who issued the Charter of 1663 to eight of his loyal supporters, the Lords Proprietors. After all, it was during the proprietary period in the reign of Charles II that the Carolina colony was permanently settled.

In point of fact, the "Charles" for whom the colony was first named was Charles I, who tried to rule England as an absolute monarch and was beheaded in 1649. He was the father of Charles II.

In 1629 Charles I issued a charter to his attorney general, Sir Robert Heath, for territory in America stretching from the Atlantic shores of Albemarle Sound southward nearly to the boundary of northern Florida and westward to the Pacific Ocean! The king named the territory "Carolana" after himself, but Heath was unsuccessful in his efforts to raise enough money to settle his grant.

In 1663, after regaining the throne lost by his father, Charles II renamed the province "Carolina" in his charter to the Lords Proprietors, and so it has remained ever since. The change from "Carolana" to "Carolina" was in part to honor the new king.

From the beginning of permanent settlement of the Carolina territory, colonists gathered around Albemarle Sound in the north and (from 1670 on) around Charleston in the south. Of course the area was too vast and sparsely populated to be governed from one location, and each settlement tended to manage its own affairs.

It was not until 1689 that the Lords Proprietors commissioned Philip Ludwell as governor of "that part of our Province that lyes north and east of Cape Feare." Before Ludwell, all who had held that job were referred to as governors of the "County of Albemarle."

For a while, "northern" colonists still clung to the name "Albemarle," but as settlement expanded southward toward Pamlico Sound, the name "North Carolina" began to come into use. Finally, in 1712 Edward Hyde was appointed "Governor of North Carolina" as the Lords Proprietors came to acknowledge what was indeed already fact.

From the creation of the name "Carolana" in 1629 to the proprietors' confirmation of the name "North Carolina" in 1712, a period of eighty-three years passed and a lot of things happened. Any other effort to explain the derivation of the name gets at least as complicated as this one.

The main thing to remember, though, is that Latin for "Charles" is "Carolus" and that England's first "Carolus" was Charles I.

∽ A Land of Opportunity

William Tryon

William Tryon (1729–88) arrived in North Carolina late in 1764 from his native England. The following year he succeeded Arthur Dobbs as governor of the colony. A professional soldier, Tryon was a keen student of the resources of the colony and sought to learn all he could about the province King George III had placed in his trust.

In the excerpt below, Tryon writes to a relative in England about North Carolina's natural resources and populace. Notice his concentration on fruit, deerskins, beeswax, and other articles we rarely associate with modern North Carolina. Notice too that he neglects to mention tobacco. His comments about tar, turpentine, and deck planking were especially meaningful to the world's greatest maritime power of that day—Great Britain. Finally, his equating slave ownership with wealth provides evidence that slaveholding had become a measure of social status even before the American Revolution.

Sℛ

North Carolina
Brunswick on Cape Fear River
July ye 26th, 1765

My Dear Sir:

I most gratefully received the happiness you conferred on me the 5th Ins:t by your letter bearing date the 12th of Feby last, accompanied with a most acceptable present, a Gold Box with the Picture of an invariable friend, as well to my family, as myself. You could not have sent me a more acceptable present; and for which you have my most sincere acknowledgements.

Your particular detail of your affectionate and steady conduct in adjusting the intricate state of the affairs of my Mother, and the agreement she has entered into with my Brother for the sale of my Hobby Horse Norbury, gives me great satisfaction from the evident necessity of such a proceeding. Your good offices on this, and every other occasion claim as they merit, more than I am able to repay you. . . .

The garden has nothing to Boast of except Fruit Trees. Peaches, Nectrs Figgs and Plumbs are in perfection and of good Sorts. I cut a Musk Melon this week which weighed 17½ Pounds. Apples grow extremely well here I have tasted excellent Cyder the Produce of this Province. Most if not all kinds of garden greens and Pot herbs grow luxuriant with us. We are in want of nothing but Industry & skill, to bring every Vegetable to a greater perfection in this Province. Indian Corn, Rice, and American Beans (Species of the Kidney Bean) are the grain that is Cultivated within a hundred and fifty Miles of the Sea Board at which distance to the Westward you begin to perceive you are approaching high ground, and fifty Miles farther you may get on tolerable high Hills. The Blue Mountains that Cross our Province I imagine lay three Hundred Miles from the Sea. Our Settlements are carried within one Hundred Miles of them. In less than twenty years or perhaps in half the time inhabitants may Settle at the foot of these Mountains. In the Back or Western Counties, more industry is observed than to the Eastward, the White People there to, are more numerous than the Negroes. The Calculation of the Inhabitants in this Province is one hundred and twenty Thousand White & Black, of which there is a great Majority of White People. The Negroes are very numerous I suppose five to one White Person in the Maritime Counties, but as you penetrate into the Country few Blacks are employed, merely for this Simple reason, that the poorer Settlers coming from the Northward Colonies sat themselves down in the back Counties where the land is the best but who have not more than a sufficiency to erect a Log House for their families and procure a few Tools to get a little Corn into the ground. This Poverty prevents their purchasing of Slaves, and before they can get into Sufficient affluence to buy Negroes, their own Children are often grown to an age to work in the Field. not but numbers of families in the back Counties have Slaves from three to ten, Whereas in the Counties on the Sea Coast Planters have from fifty to 250 Slaves. A Plantation with Seventy Slaves on it, is esteemed a good property. When a man marries his Daughters he never talks of the fortune in Money but 20 30 or 40 Slaves is her Portion and possibly an agreement to deliver at stated Periods, a Certain Number of Tarr or Turpentine Barrels, which serves towards exonerating the charges of the Wedding which are not grievous here.

I suppose you will expect to be informed what return is Made for the expence of Supporting such a Number of Slaves in the Province. Their chief employ is in the Woods & Fields, Sowing, and attending and gathering in the Corn. Making of Barrels, Hoops, Staves, Shingles, Rails, Posts and Pails, all which they do to admiration, Boxing of Pine Trees to draw off the Turpentine, Making of Tarr kills [kilns] which is a good deal after our Manner of making a Charcoal Pitt, excepting they have a Subterraneous passage to draw off the Tarr as the fire forces it from the Lightwood in the Kiln. Lightwood I understand to be as follows. When a Tree has been blown down or Cut. The Turpentine that is in the tree, in a few years retires to all the knotty parts of the said Tree. These they Cut up in small strips and will form a Tarkiln so large that when set on Fire, will run from 6, 7, 8 or 1000 Barrels of Tar. These splinters are so loaded with Bitumen that they will burn like a Candle; it is a usual thing to carry a Torch of Light Wood at night as you Europeans do flam beaus. The above are the articles we export Beside Deer Skins, Barrels of Pork, Beef, Bees Wax, Tallow &tc. Great Quantity of Lumber is Shipped to the West Indies. We have in the Creeks and Branches of this River of Cape Fear from 36 to 40 Saw mills, each with two Saws, and upon an honest Medium, each Mill saws two hundred Thousand feet of Timber. They could do a thousand more but most of them in the Summer Months are obliged to lay Still for want of Water. This Article would make a fine remittance to Great Britain if a Bounty was allowed on the importation. The Pine (as Mr Hawks the Master Builder I took over with me from England, and who is a very able Worthy man) says is Vastly Superior to the Norway Pine, for the Decking of Ships, as it is more Solid and filled with Turpentine which makes it very durable. He is Positive that a Ship's Deck laid of the yellow Pine of this Province will last at least as long as two decks of the Norway Pine. The Shingles made for

Exportation are made of Cypress, and are Sold the best at 9ˢ Sterling per Thousand.

⟋ *Benighted in the Wilds of America*

Janet Schaw

This account of North Carolina on the eve of the American Revolution comes from the pen of Janet Schaw, a native of Scotland. Then about forty years old and a self-acclaimed woman of "good breeding," Miss Schaw was visiting her younger brother at his plantation, Schawfield, a few miles north of Wilmington only weeks before the 1775 Battles of Lexington and Concord.

The excerpt below, taken from her book, *The Journal of a Lady of Quality*, gives the modern reader a vivid sense of travel before the days of trains, automobiles, and electric lights. Her closing reference is to the action of the Continental Congress in discouraging "expensive diversions and entertainments" in the face of impending war.

⟋

Schawfield March 22ᵈ 1775.

We have been these three or four days here, but this is the first time it has been in my power to write, but I have now sat down to bring up my Journal from leaving Brunswick; which we did last Friday, under the care of a Mʳ Eagle, a young Gentleman just returned from England and who owns a very considerable estate in this province. The two brothers were to follow and be up with us in a few miles, which however they did not. We were in a Phaeton and four belonging to my brother, and as the roads are entirely level, drove on at good speed, our guide keeping by us and several Negro servants attending on horse back. During the first few miles, I was charmed with the woods. The wild fruit trees are in full blossom; the ground under them covered with verdure and intermixed with flowers of various kinds made a pleasing Scene. But by and by it begins to grow dark, and as the idea of being benighted in the wilds of America was not a pleasing circumstance to an European female, I begged the servant to drive faster, but was told it would make little difference, as we must be many hours dark, before we could get clear of the woods, nor were our fears decreased by the stories Mr Eagle told us of the wolves and bears that inhabited that part of the country.

Terrified at last almost to Agony, we begged to be carried to some house to wait for day-light, but we had drove at least two miles in that situation before Mr Eagle recollected that a poor man had a very poor plantation at no great distance, if we could put up with it and venture to go off the road amongst the trees. This was not an agreeable proposition; however it was agreed to, and we soon found ourselves lost in the most impenetrable darkness, from which we could neither see sky, nor distinguish a single object. We had not gone far in this frightful state, when we found the carriage stopt by trees fallen across the road, and were forced to dismount and proceed thro' this dreary scene on foot. All I had ever heard of lions, bears, tigers and wolves now rushed on my memory, and I secretly wished I had been made a feast to the fishes rather than to those monsters of the woods. With these thoughts in my head, I happened to slip my foot, and down I went and made no doubt I was sinking into the centre of the earth. It was not quite so deep however, for with little trouble Mr Eagle got me safe up, and in a few minutes we came to an opening that showed us the sky and stars, which was a happy sight in our circumstances.

The carriage soon came up, and we again got into it. I now observed that the road was inclosed on both sides, and on the first turning the carriage made, we found ourselves in front of a large house from the windows of which beamed many cheerful tapers, and no sooner were we come up to the gate than a number of black servants came out with lights. Mr Eagle dismounted, and was ready to assist us, and now welcomed us to his house and owned that the whole was a plan only to get us to it, as he feared we might have made some objections; he having no Lady to receive us. I had a great mind to have been angry, but was too happy to find myself safe, and every thing comfortable. We found the Tea-table set forth, and for the first time since our arrival in America had a dish of Tea. We passed the evening very agreeably, and by breakfast next morning, the two brothers joined us. Mr Eagle was my brother Bob's ward, and is a most amiable young man. We stayed all the forenoon with him, saw his rice mills, his indigo works and timber mills. The vast command they have of water makes those works easily conducted. Before I leave the country, I will get myself instructed in the nature of them, as well as the method of making the tar and turpentine, but at present I know not enough of them to attempt a description.

We got to Schawfield to dinner, which is indeed a fine plantation, and in the course of a few years will turn out such an estate, as will enable its master to visit his native land, if his wife who is an American will permit him, which I doubt. This plantation is prettily situated on the northwest branch of the river Cape Fear. Every thing is on a large Scale, and these two great branches of water come down northeast and northwest, and join at Wilmingtown. They are not less in breadth than the Tay at Newburgh, and navigable up a vast way for ships of pretty large burthen.

Mr Eagle, who is still here, appears every day more worthy of esteem. He is not yet Major, yet has more knowledge than most men I have met with at any age. He left his country a child, and is just returned, so is entirely English, as his father and mother were both of that part of our Island and his relations all there. He very justly considers England as the terrestrial paradise and proposes to return, as soon as he is of age. I would fain hope his good sense will prevent his joining in schemes, which I see plainly are forming here, and which I fear you at home are suffering to gain too much ground from mistaken mercy to a people, who have a rooted hatred to you and despise your mercy, which they View in a very different light. We have an invitation to a ball in Wilmingtown, and will go down to it some day soon. This is the last that is to be given, as the congress has forbid every kind of diversion, even card-playing.

A Visit by President Monroe

Lemuel Sawyer

President James Monroe's visits to the swamps and canals of the Albemarle region were not always pleasures for members of his entourage, as the Pickwickian humor in this anecdote indicates. Written by Congressman Lemuel Sawyer, the account reflects the casual quality of presidential travel and Albemarle hospitality, in contrast to the lavish arrangements for presidential journeys today.

Born near Elizabeth City in 1777, Lemuel Sawyer was a 1799 graduate of the University of North Carolina, studied law in Pennsylvania, and was elected to Congress from the Albemarle region eight times between 1807 and 1829, in a period when his Jeffersonian Democrats were often defeated by Whigs.

The Mr. Calhoun cited in the account was John C. Calhoun of South Carolina, who had served in the House with Congressman Sawyer and at this time was President Monroe's secretary of war. The account was excerpted from Sawyer's *Auto-Biography*, published in 1844.

The session closed in May, and I returned home and made the usual tour of the district. Whether it was from my invitation in my speech on the internal improvement resolution, or from a laudable desire to make a tour of inspection personally, as Mr. Monroe afterwards stated, in June he did us the honor of paying us a visit. He came out with about twenty gentlemen as an escort, besides four or five as a part of his family, among whom was his and his wife's nephews, James Monroe and Samuel Gouverneur, Esqrs., of New York. We received them as they reached us from Norfolk, by the Dismal Swamp road, they having passed a part of the day in visiting Lake Drummond, and spent that night at a public house on the Canal, about sixteen miles from Elizabeth City. In returning from the lake in a yawl boat, furnished from the Navy Yard at Gosport, and manned by four of the seamen, she struck on a stump, and canting to one side, threw a greater part of the passengers overboard. The water was not over four feet deep, but was plentifully intermixed with mud, and several gentlemen, among them Com. Elliot got a due proportion of both. When they arrived at the hotel, in the carriage, the Commodore hastened to divest himself of his muddy garments and to invest himself with those of a lighter complexion. His mind, however, was ill at ease with the accident, and in giving vent to his discontent, did not spare even his Excellency himself, who happened to be standing near the carriage at the time. The Commodore in loud terms cursed the folly of a President of the United States in attempting such puerile trips in such a place, and throwing his friends into such a ridiculous plight.

In the midst of his soliloquy, Mr. Monroe put his head into the door of the carriage, and saluted the abashed Commodore with the question, "What is the matter, friend Elliot?" The Commodore laid an injunction of secrecy upon the cause of his complaints, and hastened his toilet in perfect silence. We heard of their approach; and in the afternoon I rode a few miles out to meet the cortege, the dust of which, for near a mile off, gave signs of their approach. The President's carriage, surrounded by a dozen attendants on horseback, was in the van, and Mr. Crowninshield and Calhoun followed, and I fell into the rear, and joined them at the City Hotel. Here I introduced a large number of the citizens, and at their motion I invited Mr. Monroe and his party to remain over the next day, to give our constituents the opportunity of tendering to him the hospitalities of the town, and to become their guest at a dinner the next day. He and his numerous escort accepted the invitation; and accordingly a large number of the citizens united on the occasion, and sat down with them to an excellent repast, in which a fine green turtle presented the most inviting dish.

My brother Enoch was Collector of the port, and with the other brother, Wilson, composed a part of the company at dinner. My brother's (the Collector's) residence, a spacious mansion, was three miles distance, across his toll-bridge, in Camden County. He invited Mr. Monroe, and all his escort, to spend the evening with him at his house. Upon his assenting, he merely wrote three lines, and sent a messenger to his wife, notifying her of the honor of the intended visit. Had the President come, like Lear with his hundred knights, he could have accommodated them. I took Mr. Calhoun in my barouche, and all the rest of the company followed in their carriages and on horseback. Among the number I may mention the Secretary of the Navy, Mr. Crowninshield; Mr. Basset, a member of Congress from York district; Mr. Newton, from Norfolk; Col. James Monroe, and Mr. Samuel Gouverneur, the President's private Secretary, and ten or a dozen private gentlemen, that joined the suite at Norfolk. My niece Mary, a beautiful and accomplished young maiden, entertained the party, after early tea, till bedtime, by some of her best airs on the harp, an instrument on which she excelled, accompanied by a sweet well-trained voice. Col. Swift was the gentleman, usher and cashier to the President. Before tea, it being the month of roses, Mary went to the flower garden, to prepare a bouquet for the President. Col. Swift watched her; and as soon as she came through the gate with a beautiful bunch of flowers, declaring that he must have it, gave chase to her: they had a hard race for it, but she reached the President first and put it in his hands. We passed an agreeable evening. The President appeared highly gratified at his reception, and always made it a point to inquire particularly into the welfare of the family upon meeting me afterwards. The next morning the President took his leave, and the whole cavalcade departed, on their return to Norfolk, and thence on their route homewards.

North Carolina's Languishing Condition

James Seawell

In achieving statehood at the outbreak of the Revolution, North Carolina adopted a narrow, restrictive Constitution that all but prohibited internal improvements and discouraged political and economic opportunity among the masses. As a result many people left the state for better opportunities elsewhere.

Among those who left were Andrew Jackson, James K. Polk, and Andrew Johnson, each of whom became president of the United States, and William Rufus de Vane King, who in 1852 became vice president. Also leaving were nine men who later became Cabinet members, two who became speakers of the U.S. House, more than twenty who became members of Congress (including Senator Thomas Hart Benton of Missouri), seven who became governors of other states, five who founded universities in other states, and Hiram R. Revels, the first black elected to Congress.

For more than fifty years, reformers struggled to liberalize the Constitution and open up North Carolina for greater economic development, but all efforts failed until 1835. The next selection, a product of that struggle, is an excerpt from an 1833 report to the state legislature by James Seawell of Fayetteville, a member of the Committee on Internal Improvements.

ᴄᴥ Upon comparing the present languishing condition of the agricultural resources of North Carolina with the improved and prosperous conditions of even the most inconsiderable member of the Union, the picture portrays the contrast, characteristic of a community worn down by the hand of adversity, in colours too strong to be concealed. That in North Carolina, it is apparent the reward of labor has ceased to be a stimulus to industry and enterprise; that agriculture has ceased to yield to the land owner a compensation equivalent to the expense attending the transportation of his surplus produce to market. The consequent result of this state of things is, that real estate throughout the country has so depreciated in the hands of farmers, as to be considered not to possess a fixed value estimated upon its products. Hence our citizens are daily abandoning the places of their birth for situations in other States less healthy, and often not superior in fertility of soil; but which, by the improvement of those States, rendered so by the fostering aid of Legislative patronage, the facilities to wealth and the means of acquiring the necessaries of life, the profits of labor hold out stronger inducements to agricultural pursuits than is to be found in North Carolina. Nor does the evil stop here. The tide of emigration, which never ebbs, not only carries with it a great portion of the enterprise and prime of our youth, but much of the productive and most valuable description of the State's wealth. These are facts of "ominous import," which should admonish us to guard against the fatal issue with which they are pregnant. Can it be our interest so to shape our policy as to render our State the mere nursery for the Western and Southwestern States? Surely not. We not only thereby lessen the political influence of the State in the councils of the General Government, but we evidently weaken the ties of patriotism of our citizens to the land of their nativity.

The social relations of family connections evidently constitute the most lasting cement of the political permanency of any country. Indeed, what else is it but the social ties of family connections, when rendered happy and prosperous by their own industry, that stamps a value upon society? Or will it be contended that the present scattered condition of the family connections of North Carolina has a tendency to increase either the happiness or the devotion of its inhabitants to the interest of the State? Go into any neighborhood, and inquire of the seniors or heads of families, "how many children they have raised, and in what State do they reside?" and in nine cases out of ten, the answer will be, "I have raised some six or eight children; but the major portion of them have migrated to some other State;" and adds the parent, "I am anxious to sell my lands, to enable me to follow them." Thus, it will appear that the lands of nine-tenths of the farmers of the State are actually in market; and what does it arise from? Evidently from the fact, that the distance to, and expense of sending the staple products of the soil to market, so far lessen the profits upon agricultural labor, that the farmer has no inducements to effort. Therefore, it is that all our farmers are land sellers, and not land buyers.

⮧ The Poorest State in the Union

Frances Anne Kemble

The excerpt below, taken from *The Journal of a Residence on a Georgia Plantation*, describes North Carolina's rude transportation facilities and dreary travel accommodations in the early days of railroads. The journal was written by Frances Anne Kemble, who was traveling with her children, including a nursing infant, from Philadelphia to Georgia in December 1838.

⮧ To describe to you the tract of country through which we now passed would be impossible, so forlorn a region it never entered my imagination to conceive. Dismal by nature, indeed, as well as by name, is that vast swamp, of which we now skirted the northern edge, looking into its endless pools of black water, where the melancholy cypress and juniper trees alone overshadowed the thick-looking surface, their roots all globular, like huge bulbous plants, and their dark branches woven together with a hideous matting of giant creepers, which clung round their stems, and hung about the dreary forest like a drapery of withered snakes.

It looked like some blasted region lying under an enchanter's ban, such as one reads of in old stories. Nothing lived or moved throughout the loathsome solitude, and the sunbeams themselves seemed to sicken and grow pale as they glided like ghosts through these watery woods. Into this wilderness it seems impossible that the hand of human industry, or the foot of human wayfaring should ever penetrate; no wholesome growth can take root in its slimy depths; a wild jungle chokes up parts of it with a reedy, rattling covert for venomous reptiles; the rest is a succession of black ponds, sweltering under black cypress boughs—a place forbid.

The wood which is cut upon its borders is obliged to be felled in winter, for the summer, which clothes other regions with flowers, makes this pestilential waste alive with rattlesnakes, so that none dare venture within its bounds, and I should even apprehend that, traveling as rapidly as one does on the railroad, and only skirting this district of dismay, one might not escape the fetid breathings it sends forth when the warm season has quickened its stagnant waters and poisonous vegetation.

After passing this place, we entered upon a country little more cheerful in its aspect, though the absence of the dark swamp water was something in its favor—apparently endless tracks of pine forest, well called by the natives, Pine Barrens. The soil is pure sand; and, though the holly, with its coral berries, and the wild myrtle, grow in considerable abundance, mingled with the pines, these preponderate, and the whole land presents one wearisome extent of arid soil and gloomy vegetation. Not a single decent dwelling did we pass: here and there, at rare intervals, a few miserable Negro huts squatting round a mean framed building, with brick chimneys built on the outside, the residence of the owner of the land, and his squalid serfs, were the only evidences of human existence in this forlorn country.

Toward four o'clock, as we approached the Roanoke, the appearance of the land improved; there was a good deal of fine soil well farmed, and the river, where we crossed it, although in all the naked unadornment of wintry banks, looked very picturesque and refreshing as it gushed along, broken by rocks and small islands into rapid reaches and currents. Immediately after crossing it, we stopped at a small knot of houses, which, although christened Weldon, and therefore pretending to be a place, was rather the place where a place was intended to be. Two or three rough pine warerooms, or station houses, belonging to the railroad; a few miserable dwellings, which might be either not half built up, or not quite fallen down, on the banks of a large millpond; one exceedingly dirty-looking old wooden house, whither we directed our steps as to the inn; but we did not take our ease in it, though we tried as much as we could.

However, one thing I will say for North Carolina—it has the best material for fire, and the noblest liberality in the use of it, of any place in the world. Such a spectacle as one of those rousing pine-wood chimneyfuls, is not to be described, nor the revivification it engenders even in the absence of every other comfort or necessary of life. They are enough to make one turn Gheber—such noble piles of fire and flame, such hearty brilliant life—full altars of light and warmth. These greeted us upon our entrance into this miserable inn, and seemed to rest and feed, as well as warm us. We (the women) were shown up a filthy flight of wooden stairs, into a dilapidated room, the plastered walls of which were all smeared and discolored, the windows begrimed, and darkened with dirt. Upon the three beds, which nearly filled up this wretched apartment, lay tattered articles of male and female apparel; and here we drew round the pine-wood fire, which blazed up the chimney, sending a ruddy glow of comfort and cheerfulness even through this disgusting den. We were to wait here for the arrival of the cars from a branch railroad, to continue our route; and in the meantime a so-called dinner was provided for us, to which we were presently summoned. Of the horrible dirt of everything at this meal, from the eatables themselves to the tablecloth, and the clothes of the Negroes who waited upon us, it would be impossible to give any idea. The poultry, which formed here, as it does all through the South, the chief animal part of the repast (except the consumers always understood), were so tough that I should think they must have been alive when we came into the house, and certainly died very hard. They were swimming in black grease, and stuffed with some black ingredient that was doubt and dismay to us uninitiated; but, however, knowledge would probably have been more terrible in this case than ignorance. We had no bread, but lumps of hot dough, which reminded me forcibly of certain juvenile creations of my brothers, yclept dumps. I should think they would have eaten very much alike.

I was amused to observe that while our tea was poured out, and handed to us by a black girl of most disgustingly dirty appearance, no sooner did the engine drivers, and persons connected with the railroads and coaches, sit down to their meal, than the landlady herself, a portly dame, with a most dignified carriage, took the head of the table, and did the honors with all the grace of a most accomplished hostess. Our male fellow travelers no sooner had dispatched their dinner, than they withdrew in a body to the other end of the apartment, and large rattling folding doors being drawn across the room, the separation of men and women so rigidly observed by all traveling Americans, took place. This is a most peculiar and amusing custom, though sometimes I have been not a little inclined to quarrel with it, inasmuch as it effectually deprives one of the assistance of the men under whose protection one is traveling, as well as all the advantages or pleasure of their society. Twice during this southward

trip of ours my companion has been most peremptorily ordered to withdraw from the apartment where he was conversing with me, by colored
cabin girls, who told him it was against the rules for any gentleman to
come into the ladies' room. This making rules by which ladies and gentlemen are to observe the principles of decorum and good breeding, may be
very necessary, for aught I can tell, but it seems rather sarcastical, I think,
to have them enforced by servant girls. . . .

Our sole resource on the present occasion was to retire again to the
horrible hole above stairs, where we had at first taken refuge, and here we
remained until summoned down again by the arrival of the expected train.
My poor little children, overcome with fatigue and sleep, were carried, and
we walked from the *hotel* at Weldon to the railroad, and by good fortune
obtained a compartment to ourselves.

It was now between eight and nine o'clock, and perfectly dark. The
carriages were furnished with lamps, however, and, by the rapid glance
they cast upon the objects which we passed, I endeavored in vain to guess
at the nature of the country through which we were traveling; but, except
the tall shafts of the ever-lasting pine trees which still pursued us, I could
descry nothing, and resigned myself to the amusing contemplation of the
attitudes of my companions, who were all fast asleep.

Between twelve and one o'clock [in the early morning of Sunday,
December 23, 1838], the engine stopped, and it was announced to us that
we had traveled as far upon the railroad as it was yet completed, and that
we must transfer ourselves to stagecoaches; so in the dead middle of the
night we crept out of the train, and taking our children in our arms,
walked a few yards into an open space in the woods, where three four-
horse coaches stood waiting to receive us. A crowd of men, principally
Negroes, were collected here round a huge fire of pinewood, which,
together with the pine torches, whose resinous glare streamed brilliantly
into the darkness of the woods, created a ruddy blaze, by the light of which
we reached our vehicles in safety, and, while they were adjusting the
luggage, had leisure to admire our jetty torchbearers, who lounged round
in a state of tattered undress, highly picturesque—the staring whites of
their eyes, and glittering ranges of dazzling teeth, exhibited to perfection
by the expression of grinning amusement in their countenances, shining in
the darkness almost as brightly as the lights which they reflected.

We had especially requested that we might have a coach to ourselves,
and had been assured that there would be one for the use of our party. It
appeared, however, that the outside seat of this had been appropriated by
someone, for our coachman, who was traveling with us, was obliged to
take a seat inside with us; and though it then contained five grown persons

and two children, it seems that the coach was by no means considered full. The horrors of that night's journey I shall not easily forget. The road lay almost the whole way through swamps, and was frequently itself under water. It was made of logs of wood (a corduroy road), and so dreadfully rough and unequal, that the drawing a coach over it at all seemed perfectly miraculous. I expected every moment that we must be overturned into the marsh, through which we splashed, with hardly any intermission, the whole night long. Their drivers in this part of the country deserve infinite praise both for skill and care; but the roadmakers, I think, are beyond all praise for their noble confidence in what skill and care can accomplish.

You will readily imagine how thankfully I saw the first whitening of daylight in the sky. I do not know that any morning was ever more welcome to me than that which found us still surrounded by the pine swamps of North Carolina, which, brightened by the morning sun, and breathed through by the morning air, lost something of their dreary desolateness to my senses. . . .

As we alighted from our coach, we encountered the comical spectacle of the two coachloads of gentlemen who had traveled the same route as ourselves, with wristbands and coat cuffs turned back, performing their morning ablutions all together at a long wooden dresser in the open air, though the morning was piercing cold. Their toilet accommodations were quite of the most primitive order imaginable, as indeed were ours. We (the women) were all shown into one small room, the whole furniture of which consisted of a chair and wooden bench: upon the latter stood one basin, one ewer, and a relic of soap, apparently of great antiquity. Before, however, we could avail ourselves of these ample means of cleanliness, we were summoned down to breakfast; but as we had traveled all night, and all the previous day, and were to travel all the ensuing day and night, I preferred washing to eating, and determined, if I could not do both, at least to accomplish the first. There was neither towel, nor glass for one's teeth, nor hostess or chambermaid to appeal to. I ran through all the rooms on the floor, of which the doors were open; but though in one I found a magnificent veneered chest of drawers, and large looking glass, neither of the above articles [was] discoverable. Again the savage passion for ornament occurred to me as I looked at this piece of furniture, which might have adorned the most luxurious bedroom of the wealthiest citizen in New York—here in this wilderness, in a house which seemed but just cut out of the trees, where a tin pan was brought to me for a basin, and where the only kitchen, of which the window of our room, to our sorrow, commanded an uninterrupted prospect, was an open shed, not fit to stable a well-kept horse in.

As I found nothing that I could take possession of in the shape of towel or tumbler, I was obliged to wait on the stairs, and catch one of the dirty black girls who were running to and fro serving the breakfast room. Upon asking one of these nymphs for a towel, she held up to me a horrible cloth, which, but for the evidence to the contrary which its filthy surface presented, I should have supposed had been used to clean the floors. Upon my objecting to this, she flounced away, disgusted, I presume, with my fastidiousness, and appeared no more. As I leaned over the banisters in a state of considerable despondency, I espied a man who appeared to be the host himself, and to him I ventured to prefer my humble petition for a clean towel. He immediately snatched from the dresser where the gentlemen had been washing themselves a wet and dirty towel, which lay by one of the basins, and offered it to me. Upon my suggesting that that was not a *clean* towel, he looked at me from head to foot with ineffable amazement, but at length desired one of the Negroes to fetch me the unusual luxury.

Of the breakfast at this place no words can give any idea. There were plates full of unutterable-looking things, which made one feel as if one should never swallow food again. There were some eggs, all begrimed with smoke, and powdered with cinders; some unbaked dough, cut into little lumps, by way of bread; and a white hard substance, calling itself butter, which had an infinitely nearer resemblance to tallow. The mixture presented to us by way of tea was absolutely undrinkable; and when I begged for a glass of milk, they brought a tumbler covered with dust and dirt, full of such sour stuff that I was obliged to put it aside, after endeavoring to taste it. Thus *refreshed*, we set forth again through the eternal pinelands, on and on, the tall stems rising all round us for miles and miles in dreary monotony, like a spell-land of dismal enchantment, to which there seemed no end. . . .

North Carolina is, I believe, the poorest state in the Union: the part of it through which we traveled should seem to indicate as much. From Suffolk to Wilmington we did not pass a single town—scarcely anything deserving the name of a village. The few detached houses on the road were mean and beggarly in their appearance; and the people whom we saw when the coach stopped had a squalid, and at the same time fierce air, which at once bore witness to the unfortunate influences of their existence. Not the least of these is the circumstance that their subsistence is derived in great measure from the spontaneous produce of the land, which yielding without cultivation the timber and turpentine, by the sale of which they are mainly supported, denies to them all the blessings which flow from labor.

Here the gentlemen of our party informed us that they observed, for the first time, a custom prevalent in North Carolina, of which I had myself frequently heard before—the women chewing tobacco, and that, too, in a most disgusting and disagreeable way, if one way can be more disgusting than another. They carry habitually a small stick, like the implement for cleaning the teeth, usually known in England by the name of a root—this they thrust away in their glove, or their garter string, and, whenever occasion offers, plunge it into a snuffbox, and begin chewing it. The practice is so common, that the proffer of the snuffbox, and its passing from hand to hand, is the usual civility of a morning visit among the country people; and I was not a little amused at hearing the gentlemen who were with us describe the process as they witnessed it in their visit to a miserable farm house across the fields, whither they went to try to obtain something to eat.

☙ Early Industries

Porte Crayon

Nearly two decades after Frances Anne Kemble's journey through eastern North Carolina, another visitor covered much of the same territory but described the state differently. He was a writer and illustrator who used the name Porte Crayon in narratives written for *Harper's* magazine.

The following pieces, excerpted from *Harper's* March and April 1857 editions, reflect the fishing industry that still supports much of the state's coastal economy and the tar and turpentine industries that gave North Carolina its nickname "the Tar Heel State."

☙ The glimpse that our traveler had obtained of the fisheries in coming down the Chowan had so excited his imagination on the subject, that he deferred his intended exploration of the town of Edenton next morning, and shouldering his knapsack, started on foot in quest of a fishing-beach, of which he had received information from his landlord.

Pursuing the beaten road for some distance, he at length turned into a by-way, which seemed to lead toward the point which had been indicated to him. Like all the by-ways treated of in moral allegories, this soon led our pilgrim into serious difficulties. Too perverse to turn back, and, in truth, being rather attracted by the gloomy grandeur of the swamp forest, he pushed boldly into a wilderness of reeds, tangled green briar, and cypress-knees. After half an hour of plunging and tearing, he was at length brought up on the shore of the Albemarle Sound. The scene which here presented itself was unique and beautiful, one peculiarly Southern in its features, and more easily pictured than described. In fact, Porte Crayon was decidedly blown, and here was an opportunity of resting for half an hour, without acknowledging his condition even to himself. When he had completed the sketch to his satisfaction, he re-commenced his walk, skirting the Sound for the distance of a mile or more, and, issuing from the swamp, at length gladly found himself on *terra firma*, in full view of the Belvidere Fishery.

Fatigue, hunger, and mud were all forgotten in the animated scene which here met his eye. In the foreground was the landward boat moored to the beach, while her swarthy crew were actively engaged in piling up the seine as it was drawn in by the exertions of four lively mules at the windlass hard by. In the centre, upon a bank a little elevated above the water, rose a group of sheds and buildings, alive with active preparation. Beyond these the seaward boat appeared, while upon the surface of the water, inclosing the whole beach in a grand semicircle, swept the dotted cork line of the seine. To complete this scene of bustle and animation on land and water, the air furnished its legions of fierce and eager participants. Numerous white gulls, fish-hawks, and eagles hovered or sailed in rapid circles over the narrowing cordon of the seine, at times uttering screams of hungry impatience, then darting like lightning to the water and bearing away a struggling prize in beak or talons.

It was wonderful to observe the brigand-like audacity with which these birds followed up the nets and snatched their share of the prey, sometimes almost within arm's-length of their human fellow-fishermen and fellow-robbers.

Our hero hastily unslung his knapsack, whipped out his pencil, and, seating himself upon the outer windlass, made a note of this busy and picturesque scene; and having thereby partially gratified his artistic yearnings, he lost no time in introducing himself at head-quarters. Here he was received with that frank hospitality which characterizes the region, and ere long was seated at the dinner-table, where boiled rock, stewed cat-fish, white perch, and broiled shad disputed the claim on his taste and attention. Unable to decide by the eye, he tried them all twice round, swearing with devout sincerity at each dish that it was the most delicious morsel he had ever tasted. . . .

But we must not tarry too long at table. The approaching cries of the mule-drivers at the windlasses warn us that the seine is gathering in, and on sallying forth we perceive that the dotted semicircle of cork line is narrowed to the diameter of fifty paces. Both boats are at hand, their platforms piled high with the enormous masses of netting, like great stacks of clover hay. The windlasses have done their part, and the mules discharged from their labors, as they are led away by their conductors, celebrate the event with cheerful brayings. All hands now leave the boats, and, at a signal from the chief, dash into the water waist deep to man the rope. A train of women, armed with knives and bearing large tubs, is seen hastening down the bank. Within the circuit of the net one may already see a thousand back fins skimming rapidly over the surface of the water. Every eye is lighted with excitement. "Hard cork!" shouts the captain. "Mind your leads thar!" yells the lieutenant. "Hard cork! mind lead! ay, ay, Sir!" roar the fifty black, dripping tritons as they heave the heavy net upon the beach. Behind the cork line where the seine bags the water now is churned to foam by the struggling prey, and the silvery sides of the fish may be seen flashing through the strong meshes. The eager gulls shriek at the sight, and sweep unheeded over the busy fishermen. One more hurrah, and the haul is landed, a line of wide planks is staked up behind, the net withdrawn, and the wriggling mass is rolled upon the beach—ten or fifteen thousand voiceless wretches, whose fluttering sounds like a strong rushing wind among the leaves.

"To the boats! to the boats!" and away go the men; now the boys and women rush knee-deep into the gasping heap. The shad are picked out, counted, and carried away to the packing-house. The rock are also sorted, and then the half-savage viragoes seat themselves in line, and begin their bloody work upon the herring. With such unmerciful celerity they work, that the unhappy fish has scarcely time to appreciate the new element into which he has been introduced ere he is beheaded, cleaned, and salted away.

If you now raise your eyes to look for the boats, you will see them already far on their way out in the Sound, the voice of their captain mingling with the cries of the disappointed gulls. In the operations of the fisheries there are no delays. Success is in proportion to the promptitude and energy displayed in every department, and from the beginning of the season to the end they are driving day and night without intermission. The powers of endurance are as heavily taxed as in the life of a soldier campaigning in an enemy's country.

After a delicious supper on various dishes of fish, washed down with yeopon tea, our traveler retired to bed, blessing the man that invented sleep.

About midnight he was aroused by the hand of the manager on his shoulder: "If you wish to see a night haul, now is your time, Sir; we will land the seine in fifteen or twenty minutes."

Mr. Crayon sprung to his feet, and hastily donning his vestments, repaired to the beach. Here was a scene similar to that which he had witnessed during the day, except that the picturesque effect was greatly enhanced by the glare of the fires that illuminated the landing. The wild swart figures that hurried to and fro carrying pine torches, the red light flashing over the troubled waters, the yelling and hallooing suggested the idea that these might be Pluto's fishermen dragging nets from the Styx, or maybe a dance of demons and warlocks on a Walpurgis Night.

But such half-drowsy fancies were contradicted by the dark quiet background, where one could see faint twinkling lights marking the spot where some vessel rode at anchor, and the dim unbroken line of the horizon, from whence sprung, high over all, the vaulted arch of heaven studded with stars. How calmly and solemnly they looked down upon this scene of midnight turmoil! . . .

The product of these fishers constitutes a most important item in the wealth of this region, and during the fishing season (which begins about the middle of March, and lasts until the middle of May) their success is a subject of as general conversation and all-absorbing interest to the inhabitants as is the yearly overflow of the Nile to the Egyptians.

There is scarcely an estate bordering on the Sound furnishing a practicable beach where there is not a fishery established. The number is limited, however, by the fact that these natural advantages are less frequently afforded than one might suppose. The water is often too shallow, bordered by extensive tracts of swamp, or filled with obstacles which prevent the proper dragging of the nets. . . .

Nearly the whole of the eastern part of North Carolina is covered with pine forests, extending from the swampy country bordering the sea-board as far back as Raleigh, the capital of the State. This section is sparsely populated, but little improved, and although it furnishes the greater portion of the resinous matter used in ship-building in the United States, it has hitherto been little known. It is called by the Carolinians "The Piny Woods," and we must prepare to follow our persevering traveler, Porte Crayon, in his wanderings through this primitive and lonely region.

At Plymouth we find him seated on the porch, at Enoch Jones's Hotel, looking as lazy and listless as if he were a citizen of the place. Plymouth, we believe, is the county town of Washington, situated on the opposite side of the Sound from Edenton, a short distance up the Roanoke, and contains a thousand or twelve hundred inhabitants.

It is the successful commercial rival of Edenton, and plumes itself on its business activity, not without reason, for Crayon reports that its wharves were crowded with six or seven sloops; and during the day he staid there, no less than three vessels loaded with lumber hauled up to take in grog and then passed on their way. The shores of the Roanoke in the vicinity are low and swampy, and although the village is not unpleasing to the eye, it contains nothing of sufficient interest to detain the traveler long. . . .

From Plymouth to Washington the road is generally good, and the coaches make very fair speed. Nevertheless, the leisurely habits of the people during the necessary stoppages for watering and changing teams, give ample time to note the peculiarities of the country. Its features are monotonous in the extreme, varied only by alternate swamp and piny woods; the former bordering the water-courses, the latter covering the sandy ridges between.

These forests are of the long-leafed pine, the *Pinus palustris* of the Southern States. From them is gathered one of the great staples of North Carolina—the turpentine. And although this product and its derivatives are, in our country, almost in as common use as bread and meat, very little is known of the manner of procuring them. We will therefore endeavor to describe it accurately, relying upon such sketches and observations as Crayon was enabled to make during his tour.

These trees at maturity are seventy or eighty feet high, and their trunks eighteen or twenty inches in diameter near the base. They grow close together, very straight, and without branches to two-thirds of their height. Overhead, their interlocking crowns form a continuous shady canopy; while beneath, the ground is covered with a thick, yellow matting of pine-straw, clean, dry, level, and unbroken by undergrowth. The privilege of tapping the trees is generally farmed out by the landowner, at a stated price per thousand, say from twenty to thirty dollars. Under this privilege the laborer commences his operations. During the winter he chops deep notches in the base of the tree, a few inches from the ground, and slanting inward. Above, to the height of two or three feet, the surface is scarified by chipping off the bark and outer wood. From this surface the resinous sap begins to flow about the middle of March, at first very slowly, but more rapidly during the heat of summer, and slowly again as winter approaches. The liquid turpentine runs into the notches, or boxes, as they are technically called, each holding from a quart to half a gallon. This, as it gathers, is dipped out with a wooden spoon, barreled, and carried to market, where it commands the highest price. That which oozes out and hardens upon the scarified surface of the tree is scraped down with an iron instrument into a sort of hod, and is sold at an inferior price. Every year the process of scarifying is carried two or three feet higher up the trunk, until it reaches the height of twelve or fifteen feet—as high as a man can conveniently reach with his long-handled cutter. When this ceases to yield, the same process is commenced on the opposite side of the trunk. An average yield is about twenty-five barrels of turpentine from a thousand trees, and it is estimated that one man will dip ten thousand boxes.

The produce is carried to market on a sort of dray or cart which holds but two barrels, consequently the barrels are always seen setting about in the woods in couples. The trees at length die under these repeated operations. They are then felled, split into small sticks, and burned for tar. The dead trees are preferred for this purpose, because when life ceases the resinous matter concentrates in the interior layers of the wood. In building a tar-kiln a small circular mound of earth is first raised, declining from the circumference to the centre, where a cavity is formed, communicating by a conduit with a shallow ditch surrounding the mound. Upon this foundation the split sticks are stacked to the height of ten or twelve feet.

The stack is then covered with earth as in making charcoal, and the fire applied through an opening in the top. As this continues to burn with a smouldering heat, the wood is charred, and the tar flows into the cavity in the centre, and thence by the conduit into the ditch, or into vessels sunk to receive it.

In a country endowed by nature with such unlimited plantations, yielding their valuable products for so small an amount of labor, one might expect to see some signs of wealth and prosperity; yet here all appearances seem to indicate the reverse. Human habitations are few and far between; and when found, are but little better in appearance than the huts of our Western borderers.

‿ A Tight Boot

Charles W. Chesnutt

On the eve of the Civil War, North Carolina's 992,622 inhabitants included 362,307 blacks, most of whom were slaves. This fictitious account of slave life was written by Charles W. Chesnutt, one of North Carolina's first black writers.

The son of free blacks, Chesnutt was born in Ohio but grew up in Fayetteville and clerked in his father's store after the Civil War. There he met many former slaves and listened to their stories, perhaps including this one.

He later taught school in Charlotte and at the State Colored Normal School (now Fayetteville State University), the first institution of its kind in the South. When post-Reconstruction conditions in North Carolina became oppressive, he moved to New York and then to Cleveland, where he worked as a journalist and clerk and later as a professional writer.

In the 1890s and 1910s his short stories and novels, most of them written in dialect and dealing with racial themes he recalled from his North Carolina boyhood, won him a place in the first rank of black writers of his day.

❧ Some years before the war Squire Mirabeau MacKinnon kept the Jefferson House at Macedonia, the county seat of one of the up-country counties of North Carolina. The hotel was a big two-story frame house, fronting on the Court House Square, with broad piazzas running along both stories, front and rear. A row of big elms along the sidewalk made a pleasant shade for loiterers on the front piazza, and sheltered from the summer heat the horses that were fastened to the dozen or more hitching-posts. Beyond the sidewalk a well and a watering-trough furnished additional facilities for the accommodation of the public. Back of the house, and separated from it by the clean-swept yard, stood the big red kitchen. The yard was perfectly innocent of grass or herbage of any kind—unless the elms and china trees might be included under that head—and by constant trampling was as hard and white as an ancient threshing-floor.

During the greater part of the year the Jefferson House did not do a very large business. The farmers on their way down to the larger towns on the navigable rivers or near the coast, with wagon-loads of cotton and tobacco, would stop at the Jefferson overnight, settling their bills when they came back with plenty of money and supplies of sugar, coffee, calico and other luxuries which were not produced on their plantations. A few town folks came up to Macedonia to spend a few weeks of the hot summer; and unquestionably it was a pleasant place.

Court week was the busy season at the Jefferson House. Court was in session for a week or ten days several times a year, and on these occasions the hotel was filled to overflowing, and in summer hammocks were swung on the piazzas and in winter pallets were made on the floor for those whom there were not beds to accommodate. The judges, the lawyers, and the county dignitaries who came in from their plantations to attend court all put up at the Jefferson House and kept Squire and Mrs. MacKinnon and their corps of servants very busy.

The duty of blacking the boots for the guests devolved upon a colored man by the name of "Bob." Under ordinary circumstances Bob enjoyed a sinecure, and was only consoled for his hard lot during the court week by the numerous dimes and quarters which he extorted from the good-natured gentlemen whose boots were the objects of his gentle ministrations.

One evening during the summer term Bob went around about ten o'clock to the rooms of such guests as had retired, and collected the boots for cleaning. He took them to the kitchen, and in order to lessen his work in the morning, blacked about half the lot. He wanted to attend a colored dance at a cabin a mile from the hotel, and while his orders were to stay at home, he thought he might slip away an hour or two without his absence being noticed.

While he was reveling in the anticipation of the fine time he would have, and keeping time with the blacking brush to the strains of an imaginary banjo, he took up a remarkably neat boot. It was a big boot, but made of fine leather, and quite new. It struck Bob that that boot was just about his size, and it looked so neat he thought he would try it on. It went on without difficulty, though it was a little tight about the hollow of the foot and the heel. Then it occurred to Bob that those boots would look nice on him at the ball. He drew on the other, and jumping over the back fence, made his way to the house where the ball was in progress.

The laws forbade any assemblage of the slaves, and when they had their balls, prayer meetings, etc., it was customary to station sentinels along the roads and paths which led to the meeting place to watch for the patrol—or "patterole," as the natives called it—a sort of mounted police, whose special duty it was to keep the slaves under surveillance at night. Bob avoided the patrol by going through the woods, passed the sentinels, and was soon swinging the girls around, and displaying the new boots, to the inspiring strains of "Camptown Races" and "Old Dan Tucker" as rendered by the combined exertions of a banjo, a fiddle, and a pair of bones.

The fun was at its height when someone dashed up to the door and yelled "Patterole!" Instantly the candles were blown out, a bucket of water was thrown on the fire, and the crowd rapidly dispersed through the various openings of the cabin—one frightened fellow going out through the big chimney. It was a false alarm, given by some ill-natured darky who had not been invited to the ball; but Bob did not know this, so he dodged into the bushes, and by cutting across the plantations, kept clear of the patrol and reached the hotel at about two o'clock in the morning.

He tried to pull the boots off, but either the peculiar conformation of his heel prevented it, or his feet were so swollen by his recent exertions that the boot would not come off. As Bob was very tired and sleepy, he spread a quilt on the kitchen floor and went to sleep, confident that in the morning the boot would come off without difficulty.

The cook, Aunt Lyddy, went in the kitchen in the morning to begin preparations for breakfast and there Bob was asleep on the floor. She called him, but got only a grunt in response. Finally a gourd of water thrown into his face brought about the desired result, and Bob got up, rolled up his pallet and put it away, grumbling at Aunt Lyddy's cruelty.

"Better g'long an' black dem boots," said Aunt Lyddy, who was a woman of few words.

"Wait till I git dis boot off, Aun' Lyddy," replied Bob; he had pulled off one boot, and as he began an account of the ball the night before, he took hold of the other with the confident expectation that it would slip off easily. His confidence was somewhat shaken when the boot showed no sign of yielding. He had no better success with a bootjack, and Bob began to get just a little anxious. Breakfast time was drawing near and the gentlemen would want their boots. One of them came to the top of the stairs and called:

"Boy!"

Squire MacKinnon, who was not yet dressed himself, heard the call and came to his bedroom door.

"Well, what is it, Colonel?" he asked.

"Tell that boy to bring my boots, if you please, Squire."

Squire MacKinnon went to the back door and called across the yard in his sharp way:

"Bob, you Bob!"

"S-s-s-s-ah!" replied Bob, who labored under a slight impediment in his speech, which came out strong when he was excited.

"Colonel Tyson wants his boots!"

"Y-a-a-s, s-s-s-ah!" replied Bob, tugging away desperately. The sweat had collected in great beads on his forehead and rolled in dirty streams down his cheeks.

"Fur de Lawd' sake, Aun' Lyddy, he'p me git dis boot off," he said imploringly.

"I can't take my han's out'n de dough," said Aunt Lyddy, who was filling a big pan with biscuits. But she called in another servant from the yard—Isham—and he added his efforts to those of Bob; but all in vain. The boot stuck—closer than a porous plaster—closer than poor relations—closer than Sinbad's Old Man of the Sea—as closely as though it were glued to his foot.

The Colonel was growing impatient. He came to the door again, and called:

"Boy, I want them boots right off!" The Colonel was more anxious about his boots than his grammar.

Squire MacKinnon, in shirt and trousers, came to the back door again.

"Bob, Bob, you Bob!"

"Ya-a-a-s, Marse!" came from the kitchen in anxious tones.

"Bring Colonel Tyson's boots right away!"

Bob was now in despair. He knew his master's disposition, and trembled for the probable consequences if he did not get that boot off very soon. His shirt was wet with perspiration, and his eyes stood out like a couple of dinner plates. Aunt Lyddy, who had finished the biscuits, Phyllis, Chloe, Isham, and another boy who had come in from the stable—all united in the fruitless attempt to get that boot off. Isham had hold of the boot in front and Aunt Lyddy had Bob by the waist; the others were ranged behind her and Isham respectively, all pulling hard, but with no success. The stubborn boot would not come off.

The Colonel came out on the upper floor of the piazza and thundered out:

"I want them boots, blacked or not blacked, and I want 'em quick!"

"Wha-a-at!" said the Squire, as he heard the Colonel's loud tones, and ran out, still half-dressed upon the lower floor piazza.

The other gentlemen had begun to come for their boots, and Squire MacKinnon, fearful of offending his guests, walked quickly across the yard to the kitchen to see what was the matter. Bob and his friends were still pulling away in sheer desperation. The sweat had accumulated in little puddles on the floor, and the boot had begun to rip a little at the heel. Squire MacKinnon was puzzled for a moment, and then the full meaning of the situation dawned upon him.

"What the d——l does this mean?" demanded he.

"I j-j-j-is' put the boot on to black it better, Marse, and it won't come off no mo'," replied the trembling Bob.

The Squire pushed the others aside, caught the boot by the heel, and jerking the unfortunate Bob from the chair, dragged him around the kitchen. As he went around Bob caught at whatever came in his way; he overturned several chairs; he caught the leg of the table, and the dishes came down with a crash; and as the Squire, in his mad career, whirled him around again, he caught Aunt Lyddy by the ankle, causing that amiable woman and accomplished cook to lose her balance and sit down in the big pot of hot water on the hearth. It is needless to say that she lost no time in getting up again.

As the angry Squire made more circuits of the kitchen, Bob caught by the door frame and held on like grim death. The Squire gave one "long, last, last, long lingering" pull, and off came the boot!

The said boot continued to play an important part in the scene that followed for a few minutes, and Bob had ample time, while recovering from his bruises, to reflect on the sin of vanity, of the evil consequences of which his experience had certainly qualified him to think intelligently. He stayed at the Jefferson House until near the end of the war, when he drifted off in the wake of Sherman's army. Up to that time, however, he was not known to indulge again in the luxury of wearing other men's boots.

❧ The Civil War on the Home Front

Catherine Ann Devereaux Edmondston

In terms of broad-scale impact on every facet of society, economy, and everyday life, the Civil War (or War between the States or War for Southern Independence, or whatever the conflict was called where you grew up) was the single most important event in the history of North Carolina. In some measure it touched the life of every man and woman, high and low, black and white, in the state.

The entries below, from *"Journal of a Secesh Lady": The Diary of Catherine Ann Devereaux Edmondston, 1860–1866*, are the work of a remarkable resident of Halifax County. Mrs. Edmondston lived through the war with all the fierce pride and increasing deprivation experienced by many of the planter class. Her words reflect the depth of feeling on the home front.

❧

November 6, 1860

Election day. No fears in my mind that Lincoln & that half blooded Hanibal Hamlin will be elected, tho' Patrick feels gloomy about it. Brother John is enough to depress anyone he talks so gloomily about debts, politics, etc—*"ruin"* is a house hold word with him. I have no patience with him. If we are to die, let it be but once, not daily! As to Politics, Peter is worse than brother. He thinks us on the eve of Civil War. Father hoots at it and so abuses S C for her ultra views, & particularly for sending commissioners to Va after the John Brown Raid last fall to consult about a uniform policy for the South, that I dread to hear him! . . .

November 25, 1860

Sunday, I left off on Election day when I could not be persuaded that Lincoln would be elected, but how greviously was I disappointed. He is our President Elect, having received every Northern vote but three of New Jersey's, but not one single Southern one. We were divided between Bell, Breckenridge & Douglas. Ah! would that we as a people had studied old Esop to better purpose! But the lesson in the fable of the old man & the bundle of sticks has been lost to us. A sectional President! Pray God his Administration may not be so also. . . .

December 22, 1860

Between Wilmington & Florence met Dr Tennant & Mr Gregg who told us of the Secession of South Carolina. The Ordinance was signed upon the 20th of December. So South Carolina is no longer one of the United States! One link is missing! One pearl lost from the glorious string! Pray God that it be not the beginning of Evils as Patrick predicts. As the cars started he heaved a sigh and said it is the beginning of the end. . . .

At Florence we unexpectedly met our friends Mr & Mrs John Witherspoon of Society Hill. They gave us an account of their adventures on the night when the news of the Secession of S.C. reached their village, which to show the bitterness of party politics I will set down here. In the dead hour of the night they heard guns, first at one neighbors then at another. Whilst they were speculating as to the cause, came a message from Mrs. W's father Col Williams who was alone in his own house, that persons were firing around his house, that he had returned it & desired their immediate presence. They sprang out of bed, Mr Witherspoon taking his gun, Mrs W her pistol, whilst their servant Stephen brought up the rear with the carving knife. On the way Mrs Witherspoon stumbled &, not having stayed to put on her Hoop, became entangled in her skirts & rolled over with the loaded Pistol in her hand! Fortunately it did not explode! . . .

March 5, 1861

Went to Hascosea. Straightened Asparagus beds. Sowed Beets, Carrots, Salsafy, Onions, Leeks, & turnips. Mr. Edmondston & I set out 22 Dwarf Pears from Philadelphia & 4 Dwarf Apples. Brought 2 pears & 2 Apples to Looking Glass.

Patrick is dreadfully despondant and enough to take the heart out of one. Whilst we were planting the Trees—I holding it & he throwing in the Earth—he suddenly stopped & said "where is the use? We may be doing this for the Yankees! Before this tree bears fruit the Yankees may have over run our whole country." On my remonstrating he continued, "Yes before a year has gone over our heads a rascally Yankee may pull this identical tree up." It cast a damper upon me & I said, "O Patrick, dont talk so; you distress me." "Well" he said as he resumed his spade, "I wont! But depend on it before this tree bears fruit—we shall be in the midst of the most desperate War the world ever saw!" Pray God he prove a false prophet. . . .

April 17, 1861

Heard last night that Lincoln had issued his Proclamation calling for 75,000 troops to compel South Carolina to obedience. Set to the Gov of N C. for [————] that being the quota required from N Carolina. Thank God! that we had a governor who had spirit to refuse, which he did most decidedly & firmly. Think of the insult the man puts on us!—call upon us to subdue our Sister! . . .

April 23, 1861

Came brother John, full of news about the action of the State & preparations for war; told of us a shocking thing that himself & another gentleman, a slaveholder, had the greatest difficulty in preventing yesterday at Weldon. The actual hanging of a man by the mob, for the suspicion even of Abolitionism. Mama & Sue were in the cars, & he had to use every endeavour to keep concealed from them the actual state of affairs. He intends to join the SNMR [Scotland Neck Mounted Reserves]. So Patrick will have some one he can confide in with him in case of actual War. With him came Mr John Whitaker, & they had a long & earnest conversation with Mr E which resulted in his determining to go to Raleigh with Brother tomorrow. Ah this absence—how hard it will be to bear, but courage! "As thy days—so shall thy Strength be"!

April 24, 1861

Mr E. left for Raleigh. Frank & I went to Hascosea on a gardening expedition. How lonely it is without Mr Edmondston! Gardening is no longer the same occupation. Planted my Dahlia Roots. As I worked Mrs Hemans Lines "Bring Flowers to strew in the Conquerer's path" recurred again & again to me. Yes! I will plant flowers for the Conquerer's—for our own path! A short time of conflict & the day is ours—ours for Freedom, for Right, for Self Government! They can never overcome, never conquer us, for we fight for our Birthright—Freedom! Let them try their boasted *Blockade! Who cares?* Who will be most hurt—us? themselves? or England? Not us, for we make the necessaries of Life. But what will England do for Cotton when her looms are idle? what her starving population for bread? King Cotton will raise his own blockade in his own time in spite of the Yankee vessels.

A heavy & sudden thunderstorm came up about dark. As I sat in the still silent house alone with little Frank, almost in utter darkness, as the storm caught the servants out of the house, & I could not find a match, he asked me if I was afraid. I said "No! my child, God will take care of us, even tho Uncle is gone. Are you afraid?" "No Aunt Kate not with you," & then waxing bold he continued "I am not afraid of Thunder, and I know I am not of old Lincoln & the Yankees. I hate Yankees!" I could feel his little fist clench in my hand & his pulses quicken as he said it! Can they nourish so insane an idea as reconstruction when the very children feel it so? And as for subjugation, annihilation first! . . .

May 3, 1861

Sewed all day on Patrick's fatigue Uniform, Grey trimmed with Green. The change in Sue is most delightful & pleasant to me. She is really a pleasant companion now, & one does not feel obliged to keep continually "turning corners" to prevent discussions. Her Southern feelings are thoroughly aroused. . . .

Brought home yesterday another tent on which my forces are busily engaged. The Cloth for these Uniforms & Tents is purchased by individual subscription, not waiting for the State to equip its men, & this thing is going on all over the whole South. Thousands of Ladies who never worked before are hard at work on coarse sewing all over our whole country. . . .

May 22, 1861

Heard today that on the 20th, it being the anniversary of the Signature of the Mecklenburg Dec of Independence, the Convention of NC signed the ordinance of Secession. The scene is said to have beggared description. So soon as the Ordinance had been signed & the Speaker had announced that North Carolina "abjured her allegiance to the U S" & solemnly "assumed her own Sovereignty," Ramseur's Battery stationed outside fired a Salute of a hundred Guns! This seemed a signal for men, women & children to flock to the State House. The men shook hands, the women rushed into each other's arms, every body congratulated every body else. Persons who had not spoken for years exchanged the most cordial & fraternal greeting. When quiet was restored after a brief interval, the President put the Question as to whether North Carolina should join the Southern Confederacy, which was carried by acclaim first, then by individual vote without one dissentient! So now we are under Mr Davis rule! "Hurrah for Jeff Davis!" On that day we good people of N C were under three distinct Governments. We woke up members of the U S; then having resumed our own sovreignty North Carolina claimed our allegiance. But she like a wise and careful custodian deposited the jewel in the

Casket by the side of her Southern Sisters & gave the Key to President Davis! . . .

April 15, 1862

. . . Beauregard's call for Plantation Bells to be cast into canon is most cheerfully responded to by every one. Church bells are freely & gladly tendered by the congregations throughout the land. Preserving Kettles are joyfully given to the government to make into Caps & all the old copper is eargly sought after & rumaged out by the housewifes all over the country. One little child asked plaintively as she saw the Preserving Kettle going, "but what shall we do for preserves?" "My child," said the father, "we think now only of preserving our country." . . .

June 28, 1862

Went to Evans Spruill's funeral, the first victim to the war whose funeral I have attended. His poor Mother, the accounts of her greif are terrible; her friends fear for her reason. She does nothing but walk up & down & repeat his last letter. It seems, poor lady, that she thought him recovering and was expecting him home when she received the telegram announcing his death. . . .

July 13, 1862

Sunday—Yesterday came home Patrick & to my great sorrow quite sick. He gives a most moving account of the suffering in Richmond. He says it is fearful—the hot weather, the crowded Hospitals, the stench, the want of attendance, the filthy muddy James River water, tepid at that, the actual want of proper food—altogether make an amount of human suffering difficult to conceive of & then add to that the desolation of heart, the anguish endured by those who have lost friends, or have them suffering unable to alleviate their pain, and it makes a picture of War from which one turns appalled! . . .

September 9, 1862

Details of the late great battle come in so slowly that the heart sickens at the delay! God help those who have friends, husbands, sons in the army. Their suspense must be cruel! We fought on three successive days, Thursday, Friday, & Saturday, the 28th, 29th, and 30th of Aug. On Friday night the enemy acknoledged a loss of 17,000 & several entire batteries of cannon & yet that shameless liar Gen Pope, altho in full retreat, sent a dispatch to his Government claiming a victory and at the same time wrote to Gen Lee requesting a suspension of hostilities & leave for his ambulances to pass through our lines to attend his wounded. We have killed & taken many officers, several Generals amongst them. . . .

March 5, 1863

Have been riding on horseback with Mr E. every afternoon for a week past & find much benefit from it. Yesterday saw the first Plumb blossom fully expanded. Spring will soon be upon us. We have planted a larger crop of Irish Potatoes than we ever did before, in view of the need of our Army & the high prices they command. We were fortunate in being able to buy good seed. A letter from brother to father yesterday fills us with alarm on account of the supplies of food for our Army in Va. He says the Sec of War has written to Gov Vance that unless supplies of provisions come in faster for the next five weeks than they have done for the past five that our *Army in Va will be out of food.* . . .

June 10, 1863

Today came Sue on horseback to see Rachel who left this afternoon for Raleigh with her Uncle John. She brought news received through one of her husband's relatives of my sister Nora, about whom we have long been anxious, living as she does within the Federal lines, & so near to that den of oppression—Memphis. She has suffered severely for the Tories came to her house whilst she was sick in bed, ransacked it from top to bottom, took her silver, such of her clothes as they wished, her husband's instruments & horses & carried him off a prisoner & threw him into Jail. After some little time, however, they released him & he was again at home. She says that as yet they have food sufficient, but know not how long it will be the case, for there are neither mules nor horses in the country & in consequence no crop has been planted & they are exposed to depredations, thefts, & seizures at any moment. Poor child, brought up as she has been in the lap of luxury, what will become of her and her four little children? I weep when I think of her! Ah! that she could get here where bread at least is certain. . . .

I lead so different a life, so calm, so quiet, so peaceful that my heart overflows with thankfulness & praise to the Giver of all my good gifts who hath made me to differ?!

My house is now in perfect order. Every one of my possessions, every book, paper, piece of cloth, Linen, China, & Glass has been inspected & compared with the muster roll of my little possessions. The Store Room, the Pantry, the bed chambers, all have been routed out & put to rights again. I beleive it only remains for me to examine the Kitchen ware & take an account of stock. When I have done & can tell all about everything I own & when I compare the quiet, the repose, the happiness which results from a well ordered home with the anxiety, the distress, the heart crushing misery, which those under the Federal rule endure—I feel almost ashamed that I suffer so little for the Cause, the glorious Cause of our Country's freedom! Something I may do for my distressed country women & that I will set about speedily. Nora has lost all her servants & has no one to do anything for her four little ones. . . .

July 10, 1863

Grant me patience with the news! I know not what to beleive! I hate to fill my Journal with rumours & yet it will be no truthful expositor of our lives if I fail to relate the state into which these uncertain Telegrams have brought us. One tells us that the fight was not renewed on Sunday, consequently the 40,000 men whom it reported as refusing parole were *not* captured & Lee is not pressing Meade who is not falling back to Baltimore, but per contra *Lee* it is who is falling back to Hagerstown. Now which is true? But our perplexities do not end here. A Dispatch which freezes the marrow in our bones, signed, too, Joseph E Johnston, tells Mr Seddon that Vicksburg has capitulated, that the garrison march out with the honours of war, officers wearing their side arms. This no one seems to beleive tho it is countersigned by one of Johnson's staff. The impression is that the wires have been tampered with by sugar speculators. . . .

July 19, 1863

Johnston will, it is said, fall back from Jackson so as to draw Grant from his base of supplies, so we may hear of the abandonment of Jackson at any day. Had Vicksburg held out two days more, Johnston would have attacked Grant, with what success who can tell? Hope fills the cup with a tempting draught which disappointment turns to [illegible] in our grasp! Ah Pemberton! Pemberton!—why did not you remain in Penn with your own blood & ruin your own nation instead of ours. We have found out, that is the papers have, that Bragg falling back was "a masterly movement." It looks to us uninitiated folks like "a *change of base—a la McClellan*," but we were not born Brigadiers General!

Commander Cook came up from the River yesterday afternoon & brought us the cheering news that Clingman's Brigade had attacked & driven the enemy back from Morris island, but as this was not confirmed by the papers we know not what to think of it. Passengers by R R brought the rumour, adding that the Brigade was terribly cut up in the assault. We have a nephew, George Miller, a private in the 31st Regt in that brigade, so we are uneasy on his account. From Lee's army we hear nothing, but that he has crossed the river safely, the Yankees attacking his rear guard, but were repulsed without much loss to us. Gen Pettigrew, who had been wounded in the wrist at Gettysburg but who has not left the field being severly wounded & at Winchester, per contra the enemy says that they captured 2000 men, killed Gen Pettigrew, & have possession of his body. God pity his friends exposed to the torture of statements so opposite. Time only will show the truth.

Yesterday was published the President's Proclamation calling out the men between 40 & 45—a sad thing but it is necessary in the face of the draft of 300 000 ordered by Mr Lincoln. Mr Edmondston has just passed his 44 birthday. I know not whether or not his Major's Commission will exempt him. If not, God's will be done! Brother is not yet 44 & with the large business which rests on his shoulders & his numerous little children, I cannot see how he can be spared. . . .

March 22, 1864

Snowing fast & furiously all day & today, which was not the case yesterday, the snow lies where it falls, & the earth is wrapped in a winding sheet. My Hyacinths peep out from their white envelope & make one sad to look at them. They remind me of fair young girls who have just taken the White Veil & are not yet dead to all of Earth's enjoyments. The brilliant yellow of Forsythia now in magnificent bloom shows in sickly contrast to the pallor of all around it. White does not bring out its beauty as strongly as does a green carpet. Ah! for the Peaches! We breath a sigh over, I fear now extinct, hopes of a harvest. No dawdling through the "fragrant orchard" this summer, no flitting from tree to tree in search of new beauties, and, fie, Mrs Edmondston, for so sublunary a thought, no luscious desserts which cost the pleasure only of gathering. . . .

June 17, 1864

Inexpressibly shocked last night by the news by Telegraph of Uncle Polk's death! He was killed instantly by a cannon ball. Gens Johnston, Hardee, & Hood were with him when he fell. My poor Aunt! God be with & comfort her! Contrary to many anticipations, Gen Polk has proved himself an excellent officer, "a good fighting General," handling his men well & commanding the confidence as well as the affection of his men. He leaves children none of whom, however, are of tender age. . . .

October 29, 1864

Afternoon—Just at home from the plantation where I dined with Mr E, a lovely day, the perfection of a dreamy autumn day! Every thing so still that you could almost hear the graceful fall of the many tinted leaves as they wavered down. The solitary chirp of the grasshopper, that note so associated with the fall & which he never uses until September, alone broke the intense silence. It is as tho nature is hushed into repose. Before closing her eyes for her winter's sleep she prepares for it by a season of meditation and prayer. Her ripened fruits, her matured grain stand forth a silent thank offering of Praise to Almighty God. One can scarcely beleive on such a day as this that a bloody and cruel war devastates our land, that men's pride & passion are making a ruin, yea a hell, of a land so calm, so quiet, so beautiful, but yet so it is. . . .

December 27, 1864

Last night came tidings of the fall of Savannah! The Telegram tells us that it was "successfully evacuated" on Tuesday the 20th, nothing more. So fall all our hopes, all our boasts of "crushing" Sherman. How empty they now seem! We know nothing of the state of affairs, nothing of the force we had, nothing of our casualties, so form no judgment even or opinion of the event. It stands before us in sorrow only, a sad fact which has others sadder in its train. We have Yankee news of a great Victory by Thomas over Hood, but we try not to allow it to discourage or cast us down. We remember that Cretan character and know how to estimate their paper victories, but coming as it does on the fall of Savannah, it instills another drop of bitterness into our cup! . . .

February 27, 1865

Mr E off this morning for Raleigh. His departure was much saddened by tidings brt by Mr Brinkley before breakfast to the effect that "Charlotte was in Sherman's hands and that we had evacuated Goldsboro." This was the rumour which lengthened the faces of the "quid nuncs" at Clarksville last night; it shall not lengthen mine for I do not beleive it. . . .

April 16, 1865

How can I write it? How find words to tell what has befallen us? *Gen Lee has surrendered*! Surrendered the remnant of his noble Army to an overwhelming horde of mercenary Yankee knaves & foreigners. On Sat as Mr E & I sat at what has been for the past few days our constant employment, i.e., burning our private papers, came a note from Mr McMahon telling us that the news had been brought by a Courier in search of that drunken Gen Baker. . . .

Since we heard of our disaster I seem as tho' in a dream. I go about in a kind of *"drowsy dream."* I sleep, sleep, sleep endlessly; if I sit in my chair for ten minutes, I doze. I think of it, but I cannot grasp it or its future consequences. I sit benumbed. It is to me like the idea of eternity. . . .

It is an odd state to which I have reduced myself, to an utterly paperless condition. I am entirely without a record of my life up to July 60 & what I reserved, my Journal, since then is secreted where perhaps I may never see it again. As I said before, I am utterly paperless. Every letter I possessed, letters which I had cherished as my heart's blood, mementos of those I had loved & lost years ago, literary memoranda, excerpts, abstracts, records of my own private self examinations, poetry—all, all destroyed & as I look at my empty cabinets & desks & feel the void that their emptiness causes within my heart, a hatred more bitter than ever rises within me as I think of the "*loathed Yankee*" whose vulgar curiosity & unbounded barbarity has rendered the destruction of these private papers a matter of self preservation. I never thought to shed such tears as the burning of Mr Edmondston's letters to me, letters written both before & since our marriage, wrung from my eyes. As the packet consumed scarce could I refrain from snatching it from the flames & at least keeping *one*, one of those precious sheets which seemed to me transcripts of our young hearts & young love; but the thought of seeing them in Yankee hands, of hearing them read in vile Yankee drawl amidst peals of vulgar Yankee laughter, or worse still, of knowing them heralded abroad in Yankee sensational newspapers, restrained me! This has been the fate of thousands of my fellow countrywomen, for the Northern journals teem with private papers stolen from Southern Households & published to a vulgar curious world as specimens of Southern thought, Southern feeling, & Southern composition. When I thought of all this, I say, I restrained my hands, but turning to Mr Edmondston, I buried my face in his lap and fairly wept aloud! . . .

ᕦ *On the Eve of Reconstruction*

Jonathan Worth

As the last southern state to secede before the Civil War, North Carolina sought to be the first to rejoin the Union after the war. It elected Unionists as governor and members of Congress, rewrote its Constitution, and adopted the Thirteenth Amendment abolishing slavery, all in compliance with the plan of reunion put forward by President Andrew Johnson, a native son. But Radicals in Congress rejected President Johnson's program, denied North Carolina's statehood, and established a Joint Committee on Reconstruction that sent federal troops into the South to occupy the former Confederacy.

In that atmosphere, Governor Jonathan Worth of Asheboro, a Unionist who had opposed secession and a man honored for his judgment and unflinching honesty, wrote the following letter expressing the mood of many white North Carolinians in the uncertain hours before Reconstruction.

☙
To E. M. Gibson
Raleigh, Aug. 23, 1867.

Your inquiry, as you served in the U.S. army in the late war, whether it would be wise for you to make your home in this State discloses the fact that you believe in the absurd conclusion which Northern demagogues have fostered in the minds of the Northern people; to-wit, that we are a semi-savage and lawless people. How a people claiming to be so much more virtuous and civilized and christianized than we are, can honestly indulge in such sentiments, excites among us combined wonder and [*illegible*]. The fact ought to be known to every body having *any* access to sources of correct information that there is no place in Christendom when a man behaves himself with decorum, is safer than in any part of N.C., no odds what may be his opinions, political or religious. Even if he come among us, prepossessed with the notion and continually making this notion prominent—odiously prominent—that he claims superiority over us in patriotism—virtue—learning—everything noble in the nature of our species, you are still "*safe*" from personal harm—but we have not yet been reduced to the debasement generally (a few who seek favor by fawning pretend to love and respect those who thus revile us) to lick the hand which inflicts stripes upon us. The great body of our people were forced to elect between Secessionists and Abolitionists—thus forced they took up arms in favor of their home and section:—when conquered they desired to be allowed to participate in a restored Union: When the North demands of them that the future government of the State shall be committed to the recently emancipated slave in order to maintain the continued ascendency of a party which despises the forgiving spirit taught by the religion we profess, and delights to trample on a vanquished people and throw obstacles in the way of their recuperation, they submit as the vanquished must submit to a conqueror, but they are not so meek and so stultified as to *love* such a people. But every body is "*safe*" here who behaves with decorum— and any of our people respect a Union soldier, who, when the fight was over, treats his vanquished foeman, as genuine courage always treats the vanquished.

‏‏‎ *A Blackjack Bargainer*

O. Henry

William Sydney Porter was born in Greensboro in 1862 and grew up working in his uncle's pharmacy. At eighteen he went to Texas where he knocked about as a ranch hand, draftsman, cartoonist, journalist, and bank teller. While working as a teller, he was charged with embezzlement and fled to Honduras but returned to stand trial in Austin. Though professing innocence, he was convicted and served three years in a federal prison. There he began writing short stories under a variety of pseud-onyms, finally settling on O. Henry, the name of a French pharmacist whose articles often appeared in pharmaceutical journals that arrived at his uncle's drugstore.

The following story was written in prison and published in 1901, when O. Henry went to New York to establish himself as a writer. Of his 250 stories, only two have a North Carolina setting. This is one of those. Like all O. Henry stories, it reflects the manners, values, language, dress, and landscape of its locale, in this instance the upper reaches of North Carolina's Catawba Valley in the 1880s and 1890s. Many surnames in the story—Settle, Goforth, and Galloway, for instance—are familiar in north-western North Carolina.

‏‏‎ The most disreputable thing in Yancey Goree's law office was Goree himself, sprawled in his creaky old armchair. The rickety little office, built of red brick, was set flush with the street—the main street of the town of Bethel.

Bethel rested upon the foot-hills of the Blue Ridge. Above it the mountains were piled to the sky. Far below it the turbid Catawba gleamed yellow along its disconsolate valley.

The June day was at its sultriest hour. Bethel dozed in the tepid shade. Trade was not. It was so still that Goree, reclining in his chair, distinctly heard the clicking of the chips in the grand-jury room, where the "court-house gang" was playing poker. From the open back door of the office a well-worn path meandered across the grassy lot to the courthouse. The treading out of that path had cost Goree all he ever had—first inheritance of a few thousand dollars, next the old family home, and, latterly the last shreds of his self-respect and manhood. The "gang" had cleaned him out. The broken gambler had turned drunkard and parasite; he had lived to see this day come when the men who had stripped him denied him a seat at the game. His word was no longer to be taken. The daily bout at cards had arranged itself accordingly, and to him was assigned the ignoble part of the onlooker. The sheriff, the county clerk, a sportive deputy, a gay attorney, and a chalk-faced man hailing "from the valley," sat at table, and the sheared one was thus tacitly advised to go and grow more wool.

Soon wearying of his ostracism, Goree had departed for his office, muttering to himself as he unsteadily traversed the unlucky pathway. After a drink of corn whiskey from a demijohn under the table, he had flung himself into the chair, staring, in a sort of maudlin apathy, out at the mountains immersed in the summer haze. The little white patch he saw away up on the side of Blackjack was Laurel, the village near which he had been born and bred. There, also, was the birthplace of the feud between the Gorees and the Coltranes. Now no direct heir of the Gorees survived except this plucked and singed bird of misfortune. To the Coltranes, also, but one male supporter was left—Colonel Abner Coltrane, a man of substance and standing, a member of the State Legislature, and a contemporary with Goree's father. The feud had been a typical one of the region; it had left a red record of hate, wrong, and slaughter.

But Yancey Goree was not thinking of feuds. His befuddled brain was hopelessly attacking the problem of the future maintenance of himself and his favourite follies. Of late, old friends of the family had seen to it that he had whereof to eat and a place to sleep, but whiskey they would not buy for him, and he must have whiskey. His law business was extinct; no case had been intrusted to him in two years. He had been a borrower and a sponge, and it seemed that if he fell no lower it would be from lack of opportunity. One more chance—he was saying to himself—if he had one more stake at the game, he thought he could win; but he had nothing left to sell, and his credit was more than exhausted.

He could not help smiling, even in his misery, as he thought of the man to whom, six months before, he had sold the old Goree homestead. There had come from "back yan'" in the mountains two of the strangest creatures, a man named Pike Garvey and his wife. "Back yan'," with a wave of the hand toward the hills, was understood among the mountaineers to designate the remotest fastnesses, the unplumbed gorges, the haunts of lawbreakers, the wolf's den, and the boudoir of the bear. In the cabin far up on Blackjack's shoulder, in the wildest part of these retreats, this odd couple had lived for twenty years. They had neither dog nor children to mitigate the heavy silence of the hills. Pike Garvey was little known in the settlements, but all who had dealt with him pronounced him "crazy as a loon." He acknowledged no occupation save that of a squirrel hunter, but he "moonshined" occasionally by way of diversion. Once the "revenues" had dragged him from his lair, fighting silently and desperately like a terrier, and he had been sent to state's prison for two years. Released, he popped back into his hole like an angry weasel.

Fortune, passing over many anxious wooers, made a freakish flight into Blackjack's bosky pockets to smile upon Pike and his faithful partner.

One day a party of spectacled, knickerbockered, and altogether absurd prospectors invaded the vicinity of the Garveys' cabin. Pike lifted his squirrel rifle off the hooks and took a shot at them at long range on the chance of their being revenues. Happily he missed, and the unconscious agents of good luck drew nearer, disclosing their innocence of anything resembling law or justice. Later on, they offered the Garveys an enormous quantity of ready, green, crisp money for their thirty-acre patch of cleared land, mentioning, as an excuse for such a mad action, some irrelevant and inadequate nonsense about a bed of mica underlying the said property.

When the Garveys became possessed of so many dollars that they faltered in computing them, the deficiencies of life on Blackjack began to grow prominent. Pike began to talk of new shoes, a hogshead of tobacco to set in the corner, a new lock to his rifle; and, leading Martella to a certain spot on the mountain-side, he pointed out to her how a small cannon—doubtless a thing not beyond the scope of their fortune in price—might be planted so as to command and defend the sole accessible trail to the cabin, to the confusion of revenues and meddling strangers forever.

But Adam reckoned without his Eve. These things represented to him the applied power of wealth, but there slumbered in his dingy cabin an ambition that soared far above his primitive wants. Somewhere in Mrs. Garvey's bosom still survived a spot of femininity unstarved by twenty years of Blackjack. For so long a time the sounds in her ears had been the scaly-barks dropping in the woods at noon, and the wolves singing among the rocks at night, and it was enough to have purged her of vanities. She had grown fat and sad and yellow and dull. But when the means came, she felt a rekindled desire to assume the perquisites of her sex—to sit at tea tables; to buy inutile things; to whitewash the hideous veracity of life with a little form and ceremony. So she coldly vetoed Pike's proposed system of fortifications, and announced that they would descend upon the world, and gyrate socially.

And thus, at length, it was decided, and the thing done. The village of Laurel was their compromise between Mrs. Garvey's preference for one of the large valley towns and Pike's hankering for primeval solitudes. Laurel yielded a halting round of feeble social distractions comportable with Martella's ambitions, and was not entirely without recommendation to

Pike, its contiguity to the mountains presenting advantages for sudden retreat in case fashionable society should make it advisable.

Their descent upon Laurel had been coincident with Yancey Goree's feverish desire to convert property into cash, and they bought the old Goree homestead, paying four thousand dollars ready money into the spendthrift's shaking hands.

Thus it happened that while the disreputable last of the Gorees sprawled in his disreputable office, at the end of his row, spurned by the cronies whom he had gorged, strangers dwelt in the halls of his fathers.

A cloud of dust was rolling slowly up the parched street, with something travelling in the midst of it. A little breeze wafted the cloud to one side, and a new, brightly painted carryall, drawn by a slothful gray horse, became visible. The vehicle deflected from the middle of the street as it neared Goree's office, and stopped in the gutter directly in front of his door.

On the front seat sat a gaunt, tall man, dressed in black broadcloth, his rigid hands incarcerated in yellow kid gloves. On the back seat was a lady who triumphed over the June heat. Her stout form was armoured in a skin-tight silk dress of the description known as "changeable," being a gorgeous combination of shifting hues. She sat erect, waving a much-ornamented fan, with her eyes fixed stonily far down the street. However Martella Garvey's heart might be rejoicing at the pleasures of her new life, Blackjack had done his work with her exterior. He had carved her countenance to the image of emptiness and inanity; had imbued her with the stolidity of his crags, and the reserve of his hushed interiors. She always seemed to hear, whatever her surroundings were, the scaly-barks falling and pattering down the mountainside. She could always hear the awful silence of Blackjack sounding through the stillest of nights.

Goree watched this solemn equipage, as it drove to his door, with only faint interest; but when the lank driver wrapped the reins about his whip, awkwardly descended, and stepped into the office, he rose unsteadily to receive him, recognizing Pike Garvey, the new, the transformed, the recently civilized.

The mountaineer took the chair Goree offered him. They who cast doubts upon Garvey's soundness of mind had a strong witness in the man's countenance. His face was too long, a dull saffron in hue, and immobile as a statue's. Pale-blue, unwinking round eyes without lashes added to the singularity of his gruesome visage. Goree was at a loss to account for the visit.

"Everything all right at Laurel, Mr. Garvey?" he inquired.

"Everything all right, sir, and mighty pleased is Missis Garvey and me with the property. Missis Garvey likes yo' old place, and she likes the neighbourhood. Society is what she 'lows she wants, and she is gettin' of it. The Rogerses, the Hapgoods, the Pratts, and the Troys hev been to see Missis Garvey, and she hev et meals to most of thar houses. The best folks hev axed her to differ'nt kinds of doin's. I cyan't say, Mr. Goree, that sech things suits me—fur me, give me them thar." Garvey's huge, yellow-gloved hand flourished in the direction of the mountains. "That's whar I b'long, 'mongst the wild honey bees and the b'ars. But that ain't what I come fur to say, Mr. Goree. Thar's somethin' you got what me and Missis Garvey wants to buy."

"Buy!" echoed Goree. "From me?" Then he laughed harshly. "I reckon you are mistaken about that. I reckon you are mistaken about that. I sold out to you, as you yourself expressed it, 'lock, stock, and barrel.' There isn't even a ramrod left to sell."

"You've got it; and we 'uns want it. 'Take the money,' says Missis Garvey, 'and buy it fa'r and squar'.' "

Goree shook his head. "The cupboard's bare," he said.

"We've riz," pursued the mountaineer, undeflected from his object, "a heap. We was pore as possums, and now we could hev folks to dinner every day. We been reco'nized, Missis Garvey says, by the best society. But there's somethin' we need we ain't got. She says it ought to been put in the 'ventory ov the sale, but tain't thar. 'Take the money, then,' says she, 'and buy it fa'r and squar'.' "

"Out with it," said Goree, his racked nerves growing impatient.

Garvey threw his slouch hat upon the table, and leaned forward, fixing his unblinking eyes upon Goree's.

"There's a old feud," he said distinctly and slowly, "'tween you 'uns and the Coltranes."

Goree frowned ominously. To speak of his feud to a feudist is a serious breach of the mountain etiquette. The man from "back yan' " knew it as well as the lawyer did.

"Na offense," he went on, "but purely in the way of business. Missis Garvey hev studied all about feuds. Most of the quality folks in the mountains hev 'em. The Settles and the Goforths, the Rankins and the Boyds, the Silers and the Galloways, hev all been cyarin' on feuds f'om twenty to a hundred year. The last man to drap was when yo' uncle, Jedge Paisley Goree, 'journed co't and shot Len Coltrane f'om the bench. Missis Garvey and me, we come f'om the po' white trash. Nobody wouldn't pick a feud with we 'uns, no mo'n with a fam'ly of tree-toads. Quality people everywhar, says Missis Garvey, has feuds. We 'uns ain't quality, but we're buyin' into it as fur as we can. 'Take the money, then,' says Missis Garvey, 'and buy Mr. Goree's feud, fa'r and squar'.' "

The squirrel hunter straightened a leg half across the room, drew a roll of bills from his pocket, and threw them on the table.

"Thar's two hundred dollars, Mr. Goree; what you would call a fa'r price for a feud that's been 'lowed to run down like yourn hev. Thar's only you left to cyar' on yo' side of it, and you'd make mighty po' killin'. I'll take it off yo' hands, and it'll set me and Missis Garvey up among the quality. Thar's the money."

The little roll of currency on the table slowly untwisted itself, writhing and jumping as its folds relaxed. In the silence that followed Garvey's last speech the rattling of the poker chips in the court-house could be plainly heard. Goree knew that the sheriff had just won a pot, for the subdued whoop with which he always greeted a victory floated across the square upon the crinkly heat waves. Beads of moisture stood on Goree's brow. Stooping, he drew the wicker-covered demijohn from under the table, and filled a tumbler from it.

"A little corn liquor, Mr. Garvey? Of course you are joking about—what you spoke of? Opens quite a new market, doesn't it? Feuds, prime, two-fifty to three. Feuds, slightly damaged—two hundred, I believe you said, Mr. Garvey?"

Goree laughed self-consciously.

The mountaineer took the glass Goree handed him, and drank the whiskey without a tremor of the lids of his staring eyes. The lawyer applauded the feat by a look of envious admiration. He poured his own drink, and took it like a drunkard, by gulps, and with shudders at the smell and taste.

"Two hundred," repeated Garvey. "Thar's the money."

A sudden passion flared up in Goree's brain. He struck the table with his fist. One of the bills flipped over and touched his hand. He flinched as if something had stung him.

"Do you come to me," he shouted, "seriously with such a ridiculous, insulting, darned-fool proposition?"

"It's fa'r and squar'," said the squirrel hunter, but he reached out his hand as if to take back the money; and then Goree knew that his own flurry of rage had not been from pride or resentment, but from anger at himself, knowing that he would set foot in the deeper depths that were being opened to him. He turned in an instant from an outraged gentleman to an anxious chafferer recommending his goods.

"Don't be in a hurry, Garvey," he said, his face crimson and his speech thick. "I accept your p-p-proposition, though it's dirt cheap at two hundred. A t-trade's all right when both p-purchaser and buyer are s-satisfied. Shall I w-wrap it up for you, Mr. Garvey?"

Garvey rose, and shook out his broadcloth. "Missis Garvey will be pleased. You air out of it, and it stands Coltrane and Garvey. Just a scrap ov writin', Mr. Goree, you bein' a lawyer, to show we traded."

Goree seized a sheet of paper and a pen. The money was clutched in his moist hand. Everything else suddenly seemed to grow trivial and light.

"Bill of sale, by all means. 'Right, title, and interest in and to' . . . 'forever warrant and—' No, Garvey, we'll have to leave out that 'defend,' " said Goree with a loud laugh. "You'll have to defend this title yourself."

The mountaineer received the amazing screed that the lawyer handed him, folded it with immense labour, and placed it carefully in his pocket.

Goree was standing near the window. "Step here," he said, raising his finger, "and I'll show you your recently purchased enemy. There he goes, down the other side of the street."

The mountaineer crooked his long frame to look through the window in the direction indicated by the other. Colonel Abner Coltrane, an erect, portly gentleman of about fifty, wearing the inevitable long, double-breasted frock coat of the Southern lawmaker, and an old high silk hat, was passing on the opposite sidewalk. As Garvey looked, Goree glanced at his face. If there be such a thing as a yellow wolf, here was its counterpart. Garvey snarled as his unhuman eyes followed the moving figure, disclosing long, amber-colored fangs.

"Is that him? Why, that's the man who sent me to the pen'tentiary once!"

"He used to be district attorney," said Goree carelessly. "And, by the way, he's a first-class shot."

"I kin hit a squirrel's eye at a hundred yard," said Garvey. "So that thar's Coltrane! I made a better trade than I was thinkin'. I'll take keer ov this feud, Mr. Goree, better'n you ever did!"

He moved toward the door, but lingered there, betraying a slight perplexity.

"Anything else to-day?" inquired Goree with frothy sarcasm. "Any family traditions, ancestral ghosts, or skeletons in the closet? Prices as low as the lowest."

"Thar was another thing," replied the unmoved squirrel hunter, "that Missis Garvey was thinkin' of. 'Tain't so much in my line as t'other, but she wanted partic'lar that I should inquire, and ef you was willin', 'pay fur it,' she says, 'fa'r an' squar'.' Thar's a buryin' groun', as you know, Mr. Goree, in the yard of yo' old place, under the cedars. Them that lies thar is yo' folks what was killed by the Coltranes. The monyments has the names on 'em. Missis Garvey says a fam'ly buryin' groun' is a sho' sign of quality. She says ef we git the feud, thar's somethin' else ought to go with it. The names on them monyments is 'Goree,' but they can be changed to ourn by—"

"Go! Go!" screamed Goree, his face turning purple. He stretched out both hands toward the mountaineer, his fingers hooked and shaking. "Go, you ghoul! Even a Ch-Chinaman protects the g-graves of his ancestors—go!"

The squirrel hunter slouched out of the door to his carryall. While he was climbing over the wheel Goree was collecting, with feverish celerity, the money that had fallen from his hand to the floor. As the vehicle slowly turned about, the sheep, with a coat of newly grown wool, was hurrying, in indecent haste, along the path to the court-house.

At three o'clock in the morning they brought him back to his office, shorn and unconscious. The sheriff, the sportive deputy, the county clerk, and the gay attorney carried him, the chalk-faced man "from the valley" acting as escort.

"On the table," said one of them, and they deposited him there among the litter of his unprofitable books and papers.

"Yance thinks a lot of a pair of deuces when he's liquored up," sighed the sheriff reflectively.

"Too much," said the gay attorney. "A man has no business to play poker who drinks as much as he does. I wonder how much he dropped to-night."

"Close to two hundred. What I wonder is whar he got it. Yance ain't had a cent fur over a month, I know."

"Struck a client, maybe. Well, let's get home before daylight. He'll be all right when he wakes up, except for a sort of beehive about the cranium."

The gang slipped away through the early morning twilight. The next eye to gaze upon the miserable Goree was the orb of day. He peered through the uncurtained window, first deluging the sleeper in a flood of faint gold, but soon pouring upon the mottled red of his flesh a searching, white, summer heat. Goree stirred, half unconsciously, among the table's débris, and turned his face from the window. His movement dislodged a heavy law book, which crashed upon the floor. Opening his eyes, he saw, bending over him, a man in a black frock coat. Looking higher, he discovered a well-worn silk hat, and beneath it the kindly, smooth face of Colonel Abner Coltrane.

A little uncertain of the outcome, the colonel waited for the other to make some sign of recognition. Not in twenty years had male members of these two families faced each other in peace. Goree's eyelids puckered as he strained his blurred sight toward this visitor, and then he smiled serenely.

"Have you brought Stella and Lucy over to play?" he said calmly.

"Do you know me, Yancey?" asked Coltrane.

"Of course I do. You brought me a whip with a whistle in the end."

So he had—twenty-four years ago; when Yancey's father was his best friend.

Goree's eyes wandered about the room. The colonel understood. "Lie still, and I'll bring you some," said he. There was a pump in the yard at the rear, and Goree closed his eyes, listening with rapture to the click of its handle, and the bubbling of the falling stream. Coltrane brought a pitcher of the cool water, and held it for him to drink. Presently Goree sat up—a most forlorn object, his summer suit of flax soiled and crumpled, his discreditable head tousled and unsteady. He tried to wave one of his hands toward the colonel.

"Ex-excuse—everything, will you?" he said. "I must have drunk too much whiskey last night, and gone to bed on the table." His brows knitted into a puzzled frown.

"Out with the boys a while?" asked Coltrane kindly.

"No, I went nowhere. I haven't had a dollar to spend in the last two months. Struck the demijohn too often, I reckon, as usual."

Colonel Coltrane touched him on the shoulder.

"A little while ago, Yancey," he began, "you asked me if I had brought Stella and Lucy over to play. You weren't quite awake then, and must have been dreaming you were a boy again. You are awake now, and I want you to listen to me. I have come from Stella and Lucy to their old playmate, and to my old friend's son. They know that I am going to bring you home with me, and you will find them as ready with a welcome as they were in the old days. I want you to come to my house and stay until you are yourself again, and as much longer as you will. We heard of your being down in the world, and in the midst of temptation, and we agreed that you should come over and play at our house once more. Will you come, my boy? Will you drop our old family trouble and come with me?"

"Trouble!" said Goree, opening his eyes wide. "There was never any trouble between us that I know of. I'm sure we've always been the best friends. But, good Lord, Colonel, how could I go to your home as I am—a drunken wretch, a miserable, degraded spendthrift and gambler—"

He lurched from the table into his armchair, and began to weep maudlin tears, mingled with genuine drops of remorse and shame. Coltrane talked to him persistently and reasonably, reminding him of the simple mountain pleasures of which he had once been so fond, and insisting upon the genuineness of the invitation.

Finally he landed Goree by telling him he was counting upon his help in the engineering and transportation of a large amount of felled timber from a high mountain-side to a waterway. He knew that Goree had once invented a device for this purpose—a series of slides and chutes—upon which he had justly prided himself. In an instant the poor fellow, delighted at the idea of his being of use to any one, had paper spread upon the table, and was drawing rapid but pitifully shaky lines in demonstration of what he could and would do.

The man was sickened of the husks; his prodigal heart was turning again toward the mountains. His mind was yet strangely clogged, and his thoughts and memories were returning to his brain one by one, like carrier pigeons over a stormy sea. But Coltrane was satisfied with the progress he had made.

Bethel received the surprise of its existence that afternoon when a Coltrane and a Goree rode amicably together through the town. Side by side they rode, out from the dusty streets and gaping townspeople, down across the creek bridge, and up toward the mountain. The prodigal had brushed and washed and combed himself to a more decent figure, but he was unsteady in the saddle, and he seemed to be deep in the contemplation of some vexing problem. Coltrane left him in his mood, relying upon the influence of changed surroundings to restore his equilibrium.

Once Goree was seized with a shaking fit, and almost came to a collapse. He had to dismount and rest at the side of the road. The colonel, foreseeing such a condition, had provided a small flask of whiskey for the journey but when it was offered to him Goree refused it almost with violence, declaring he would never touch it again. By and by he was recovered, and went quietly enough for a mile or two. Then he pulled up his horse suddenly, and said:

"I lost two hundred dollars last night, playing poker. Now, where did I get that money?"

"Take it easy, Yancey. The mountain air will soon clear it up. We'll go fishing, first thing, at the Pinnacle Falls. The trout are jumping there like bullfrogs. We'll take Stella and Lucy along, and have a picnic on Eagle Rock. Have you forgotten how a hickory-cured-ham sandwich tastes, Yancey, to a hungry fisherman?"

Evidently the colonel did not believe the story of his lost wealth; so Goree retired again into brooding silence.

By late afternoon they had travelled ten of the twelve miles between

Bethel and Laurel. Half a mile this side of Laurel lay the old Goree place; a mile or two beyond the village lived the Coltranes. The road was now steep and laborious, but the compensations were many. The titled aisles of the forest were opulent with leaf and bird and bloom. The tonic air put to shame the pharmacopaeia. The glades were dark with mossy shade, and bright with shy rivulets winking from the ferns and laurels. On the lower side they viewed, framed in the near foliage, exquisite sketches of the far valley swooning in its opal haze.

Coltrane was pleased to see that his companion was yielding to the spell of the hills and woods. For now they had but to skirt the base of Painter's Cliff; to cross Elder Branch and mount the hill beyond, and Goree would have to face the squandered home of his fathers. Every rock he passed, every tree, every foot of the roadway, was familiar to him. Though he had forgotten the woods, they thrilled him like the music of "*Home Sweet Home.*"

They rounded the cliff, descended into Elder Branch, and paused there to let the horses drink and splash in the swift water. On the right was a rail fence that cornered there, and followed the road and stream. Inclosed by it was the old apple orchard of the home place; the house was yet concealed by the brow of the steep hill. Inside and along the fence, pokeberries, elders, sassafras, and sumac grew high and dense. At a rustle of their branches, both Goree and Coltrane glanced up, and saw a long, yellow, wolfish face above the fence, staring at them with pale, unwinking eyes. The head quickly disappeared; there was a violent swaying of the bushes, and an ungainly figure ran up through the apple orchard in the direction of the house, zigzagging among the trees.

"That's Garvey," said Coltrane; "the man you sold out to. There's no doubt but he's considerably cracked. I had to send him up for moonshining once, several years ago, in spite of the fact that I believed him irresponsible. Why, what's the matter, Yancey?"

Goree was wiping his forehead, and his face had lost its colour. "Do I look queer, too?" he asked, trying to smile. "I'm just remembering a few more things." Some of the alcohol had evaporated from his brain. "I recollect now where I got that two hundred dollars."

"Don't think of it," said Coltrane cheerfully. "Later on we'll figure it all out together."

They rode out of the branch, and when they reached the foot of the hill Goree stopped again.

"Did you ever suspect I was a very vain kind of fellow, Colonel?" he asked. "Sort of foolish proud about appearances?"

The colonel's eyes refused to wander to the soiled, sagging suit of flax and the faded slouch hat.

"It seems to me," he replied, mystified, but humouring him, "I remember a young buck about twenty, with the tightest coat, the sleekest hair, and the prancingest saddle horse in the Blue Ridge."

"Right you are," said Goree eagerly. "And it's in me yet, though it don't show. Oh, I'm as vain as a turkey gobbler, and as proud as Lucifer. I'm going to ask you to indulge this weakness of mine in a little matter."

"Speak out, Yancey. We'll create you Duke of Laurel and Baron of Blue Ridge, if you choose; and you shall have a feather out of Stella's peacock's tail to wear in your hat."

"I'm in earnest. In a few minutes we'll pass the house up there on the hill where I was born, and where my people have lived for nearly a century. Strangers live there now—and look at me! I am about to show myself to them ragged and poverty-stricken, a wastrel and a beggar. Colonel Coltrane, I'm ashamed to do it. I want you to let me wear your coat and hat until we are out of sight beyond. I know you think it a foolish pride, but I want to make as good a showing as I can when I pass the old place."

"Now, what does this mean?" said Coltrane to himself, as he compared his companion's sane looks and quiet demeanour with his strange request. But he was already unbuttoning the coat, assenting, readily, as if the fancy were in no wise to be considered strange.

The coat and hat fitted Goree well. He buttoned the former about him with a look of satisfaction and dignity. He and Coltrane were nearly the same size—rather tall, portly, and erect. Twenty-five years were between them, but in appearance they might have been brothers. Goree looked older than his age; his face was puffy and lined; the colonel had the smooth, fresh complexion of a temperate liver. He put on Goree's disreputable old flax coat and faded slouch hat.

"Now," said Goree, taking up the reins, "I'm all right. I want you to ride about ten feet in the rear as we go by, Colonel, so that they can get a good look at me. They'll see I'm no back number yet, by any means. I guess I'll show up pretty well to them once more, anyhow. Let's ride on."

He set out up the hill at a smart trot, the Colonel following, as he had been requested.

Goree sat straight in the saddle, with head erect, but his eyes were turned to the right, sharply scanning every shrub and fence and hiding-place in the old homestead yard. Once he muttered to himself, "Will the crazy fool try it, or did I dream half of it?"

It was when he came opposite the little family burying ground that he saw what he had been looking for—a puff of white smoke, coming from the thick cedars in one corner. He toppled so slowly to the left that Coltrane had time to urge his horse to that side, and catch him with one arm.

The squirrel hunter had not overpraised his aim. He had sent the bullet where he intended, and where Goree had expected that it would pass—through the breast of Colonel Abner Coltrane's black frock coat.

Goree leaned heavily against Coltrane, but he did not fall. The horses kept pace, side by side, and the Colonel's arm kept him steady. The little white houses of Laurel shone through the trees, half a mile away. Goree reached out one hand and groped until it rested upon Coltrane's fingers, which held his bridle.

"Good friend," he said, and that was all.

Thus did Yancey Goree, as he rode past his old home, make, considering all things, the best showing that was in his power.

ᴄᴧ *Charlotte and Her Neighbors*

Isaac Erwin Avery

With the end of Reconstruction in 1876, North Carolina, like other southern states, began abandoning its Old South economy and developing the industry and commerce of a New South. One of the leaders in that movement was Charlotte, which between 1880 and 1920 became the heart of a cotton-manufacturing region and North Carolina's largest city.

This sketch reflects the civic pride and boosterism that accompanied that New South enterprise. Published in the *Charlotte Observer* about 1902, the sketch appeared in a weekly column by Isaac Erwin Avery, then the paper's city editor.

ᴄᴧ The thing to do for the stranger within the gates is to betake him to the tower of the D. A. Tompkins Company building. The citizen of Charlotte who thinks he has kept pace with its growth and knows how big the town is ought to go up there and have his eyes opened. The big, square structure, with observatory platform under its very roof, holds its head above all the steeples and domes in the city. It looks high from the street, but a realization of its loftiness is to be gained only by a trip to its top, and really the ascent to the Tompkins tower is one of the treats of Charlotte.

The tower is equal in height to a fourteen-story building and the ascent up to within four floors of the top is made by an electric elevator. All visitors desiring to make the ascent are met by a polite official in the store room on the first floor, where they register their names. There an attendant is assigned them, who accompanies them to the elevator and to the top and designates all the interesting objects in the landscape.

The view from the tower is an extraordinarily fine one. North, south, east and west, it covers every street and house in Charlotte, and the suburban towns are as plain as pictures on canvas. Out over the town on all sides the range of vision extends for distances, varying according to topography, from twelve to thirty miles. One building near Davidson College is clearly indicated, as are also farmhouses about Sharon church. The view of the mountains is surprisingly fine. Not only are a dozen or more individual peaks clearly outlined, but back of them and towering high, but in a paler blue, is seen the Blue Ridge range. The peaks and the range are visible to the naked eye.

The best view of the mountains is to be obtained in the forenoon, when the sun shines upon them, but at any hour of the day the view from the Tompkins tower is an interesting one. At first the visitor is struck with the oddity of the roof effect of Charlotte, and next with the intensified volume of the roar of traffic. The bang and rattle of a loaded truck passing in the street below seems tenfold greater at this height than it does on the street level. The clatter of horses' hoofs and the exhaust of steam engines come up with piercing keenness.

The charm of the view, however, is the picture of moving life, the living current of people and vehicles, the smoke from the factories and the exhaust of the railroad engines on the four sides of the town. The long, curved trestle from Fourth street to Mint street, with the shifting engines going to and fro over it, is strikingly like a section of elevated railroad. In whatever direction one looks, the horizon is blotted with factory smoke. Closer in on the north, south, east and west the black puffs from railroad engines is pierced by the ascending columns of exhaust steam. A beautiful picture of a busy and thrifty city is framed in the white and black of the steam and smoke of industry.

This view of Charlotte and surrounding country is entrancing in itself, but if the visitor happens to be in the tower in the late afternoon, there is injected in the landscape to the south something that is worth looking at. It is the coming of the local train from Atlanta. If the afternoon is still, there will be seen on the western horizon, rounding King's Mountain, a puff of black smoke which slowly rises, spreads and hangs in the air. Then another will rise in front of it, and a short distance nearer still another. That is the trail of the incoming train. The black smoke is emitted as the train is coming up the grades, and when it is first seen the cars are perhaps two miles in front of it. The course of the train can be outlined by the overhanging clouds of smoke until suddenly the engine darts into view through the deep cut on the Dowd farm two miles distant. It is down grade there, and the train comes flying into sight with black smoke and white steam streaming back like ribbons over the roofs of the cars. In a few seconds the whole train comes into view as it crosses the big trestle to the west of the city, then it is alternately hidden as it goes through cuts and under the foliage of trees, until three blocks away it is seen creeping into the train yard. For many minutes after it has reached the depot the route of the train is outlined in the western skies by a lazily rising, sinuous cloud of smoke. The Charlotte citizen who has not been on top of the Tompkins tower does not know Charlotte at all.

ᔫ The Downfall of Fascism in Black Ankle County

Joseph Quincy Mitchell

Though the Ku Klux Klan and other night riders were significant factors in rural North Carolina politics until the twentieth century, their stature was later diminished and often became comic, as in this short story by Joseph Mitchell.

In 1925 Joseph Quincy Mitchell left a Robeson County tobacco farm near Fairmont to attend the University of North Carolina at Chapel Hill. He later went on to New York as a reporter for the *Herald-Tribune* and the *World-Telegram* and eventually joined the staff of *New Yorker* magazine. There he specialized in short stories and amusing sketches of Greenwich Village characters. This story was taken from a 1943 collection of his writings, *McSorley's Wonderful Saloon*.

ᔫ Every time I see Mussolini shooting off his mouth in a newsreel or Göring goose-stepping in a rotogravure, I am reminded of Mr. Catfish Giddy and my first encounter with Fascism. In 1923, when I was in the ninth grade in Stonewall, North Carolina, Mr. Giddy and Mr. Spuddy Ransom organized a branch of the Knights of the Ku Klux Klan, or the Invisible Empire, which spread terror through Black Ankle County for several months. All the kids in town had seen "The Birth of a Nation," and they were fascinated by the white robes and hoods worn by the local

Klansmen, and by the fiery crosses they burned at midnight on Saturdays in the vacant lot beside the Atlantic Coast Line depot. On Tuesday and Friday, the Klan's meeting nights, the kids would hide in the patch of Jerusalem-oak weeds in the rear of the Planters Bank & Trust Company and watch the Klansmen go up the back stairs to their meeting hall above the bank. Sometimes they reappeared in a few minutes, dressed in flowing white robes, and drove off mysteriously. I spent so many nights hiding in the weed patch that I failed my final examinations in algebra, the history of North Carolina, English composition, and French, and was not promoted, which I did not mind, as I had already spent two years in the ninth grade and felt at home there.

Now, when I look back on that period and reflect on the qualities of Mr. Giddy, Mr. Ransom, and their followers, I wonder why the people of Black Ankle County, particularly the people of Stonewall, stood for the Ku Klux Klan as long as they did. Traditionally, the people of Stonewall are sturdy and self-reliant. In fact, the town was named General Stonewall Jackson, North Carolina, when it was founded right after the Civil War; later the name was shortened to Stonewall. There was certainly nothing frightening about Mr. Giddy, the Führer of the local Klan. His full name was J. Raymond Giddy, but he had a mustache on his plump face which he treated with beeswax and which stuck out sharply on both sides, and consequently he was almost always referred to as Mr. Catfish Giddy, even in the columns of the weekly *Stonewall News*. He was rather proud of the nickname. He used to say, "I may not be the richest man in Black Ankle County, but I sure am the ugliest; you can't take that away from me." Mr. Giddy was a frustrated big businessman. Before he got interested in the Klan, he had organized the Stonewall Boosters and a Stonewall Chamber of Commerce, both of which died after a few meetings. He was always making speeches about big business, but he was never much of a big businessman himself. At the time he and Mr. Ransom organized the Klan he was a travelling salesman for a chewing-tobacco concern. When he returned from a trip he would never brag about how many boxes of cut plugs he had sold. Instead, he would brag that the cut plug manufactured in North Carolina in one year, if laid end to end, would damn near reach to Egypt, or Australia, or the moon, or some other distant place.

"In the manufacture of chewing tobacco, my friends," he would boast, "the Tar Heel State leads the whole civilized world."

He was the town orator and the town drunk. In his cups, he would walk up and down Main Street, singing. He had a bass voice and his favorite songs were "Old Uncle Bud," new verses for which he would make up as he went along, and a song about Lydia Pinkham's vegetable compound and its effect on the human race, a song he had learned when he was a young man attending a business college in Atlanta. The high-school boys and girls, drinking Coca-Colas in the Stonewall Drug Company, would run to the door and stare and giggle when Mr. Giddy got drunk and marched up Main Street. "Old Uncle Bud," he would sing, "is the jelly-roll king. Got a hump on his back from shaking that thing."

Mr. Ransom was far more frightening than Mr. Giddy. He was a gaunt, wild-eyed farmer. He was a religious fanatic, always screaming about wickedness. Even when he was dressed in his Ku Klux Klan outfit, he could easily be identified because he walked with a peculiar, hobbledehoy gait. He was a deacon in the Stonewall Jackson Baptist Church, the church I went to, and he used to ring the bell before services until he got a little too impassioned one Sunday morning and pulled the rope so hard the bell came unscrewed and fell out of the loft, landing on his left shoulder. After that accident he always walked as if his next step would be his last. Like Mr. Giddy, he had a nickname. He was christened John Knox Ransom, but he was called Mr. Spuddy because he habitually argued that the Southern farmer should quit planting cotton and tobacco and plant Irish potatoes. "Something you can eat," he would argue, smacking his palms together for emphasis. "Goodness gracious, my friends, if you can't sell your crop, you can put it on the table and eat it." One winter he tried to live on Irish potatoes and got so thin his belt wouldn't hold his pants up. His worried wife would urge him to eat some meat to get his strength back, and he would shout, "Is a mule strong? Does a mule eat meat?" His wife, who was a sensible woman, would ask meekly, "Does a mule eat Irish potatoes?"

I don't think Mr. Giddy, the drunken drummer, and Mr. Ransom, the fanatical deacon, thought very highly of each other until Mr. Giddy returned from a selling trip in the winter of 1923 with some booklets about the Klan he had picked up in Atlanta. Mr. Giddy discreetly distributed the booklets among some of the loafers in Stonewall, and Mr. Ransom got one. After reading it, he came to the conclusion that the best way to fight wickedness, the best way to drive corn-whiskey distillers, loose women, gypsy mule traders and fortune tellers, chautauquas, and Holy Roller preachers out of Black Ankle County was to organize the Klan there.

He and Mr. Giddy got together, hired the hall over the bank, painted the windows black for the sake of secrecy, and enrolled seventeen men in the Klan. They included a tobacco auctioneer, an undertaker, a grocery clerk, an indolent house painter, and a number of farmers. The farmers were all like Mr. Ransom in that they spent less time in their fields than they did around the pot-bellied stove of the Stonewall Hardware & General Merchandise Company, arguing about religion and politics. Most of the men joined the Klan because it gave them an excuse to get away from their wives at night and because it seemed to them to have even more mystery and ceremony than the Masons or the Woodmen of the World. The undertaker and Mr. Ransom were the only "respectable" men in it; most of the others, according to the standards of Stonewall, were either "common" or "sorry." Some were both—the house painter, for example. I once heard him summed up by an old woman in Stonewall, who said, "He's common. Fishes in the summer and hunts in the winter, and when it rains he sits by the stove and plays checkers. He sure is one sorry man."

The fathers of some of my friends joined the Klan and gradually I learned many of the Klan secrets. I learned that the initiation fee was ten dollars and that the robe and hood cost six-fifty. A friend of mine swiped his father's Klan books. One was called "The Platform of the Invisible Empire." I persuaded him to let me have it in exchange for Zane Grey's "Riders of the Purple Sage." I still have it. On the cover is this declaration: "The Ku Klux Klan stands on a platform of 100-per-cent Americanism, white supremacy in the South, deportation of aliens, purity of womanhood, and eradication of the chain store." In the book are a number of denunciations of Catholics, Jews, Negroes, and labor unions. The kids in Stonewall spied on the Klan much as kids now play G-men and gangsters; it was a game. We were frightened by the Klansmen, but not too frightened to hide in the weed patch and watch them come and go. I remember one kid, lying beside me in the weeds, pointing to a robed figure and hoarsely whispering, "There goes Pa."

Mules are used almost exclusively instead of horses in the tobacco and cotton fields of Black Ankle County, and during the first weeks of the Klan's existence in Stonewall the members rode plough mules on their night rides about the countryside. They preferred to ride cross-country, probably because that made them feel invincible, and they couldn't use automobiles because they would quickly bog down in the sticky mud of the bottom fields and the sloblands, the black mud which gives the county its name. The mules were supplied by Mr. Ransom and by other members who were farmers. That lasted until Mr. Giddy and Mr. Ransom, as the leaders, sent to Klan headquarters in Atlanta for some white horse-robes. They draped the robes over their mules one dark night and rode out to a sawmill in a swamp to keep a rendezvous with their followers. When they galloped up on their shrouded steeds the mules of the other Klansmen got frightened; they let out angry neighs, reared back on their heels, and stampeded into the swamp with their riders. One Klansman was thrown from his mule and suffered a broken leg and three fractured ribs. After that the Klansmen gave up cross-country riding. They stuck to the highways and used automobiles. Fat Mr. Giddy undoubtedly felt out of place on the sharp back of a plough mule, anyway.

The Klansmen began their terrorism by burning fiery crosses, huge crosses made of fence rails sprinkled with kerosene, in the yards of all the Negro churches in the lower part of the county. Then they kidnapped an aged, irritable blacksmith who was celebrated for his profanity. They covered him with tar. They sprinkled chicken feathers over the tar. Then they tossed him into Bearcat Millpond. I have heard that the old black-smith crawled out of the millpond with ten brand-new oaths. A few nights later the Klansmen went after a mentally defective woman who used to wander about the county with her fatherless children, sleeping in tobacco barns and haylofts. They flogged her, clipped her hair close to her scalp, and branded a "K" on her head. Next day a rural policeman found the bleeding, frantic woman on a ditch bank beside a country road and took her to a hospital. Later she was sent to an asylum. One night, a few weeks later, they broke into a chain grocery in Stonewall, the A. & P., and wrecked it. The same night they went to a Negro café in the Back Alley, the Negro section of Stonewall, and smashed a big, loud Edison phonograph, which the proprietor of the café had mortgaged her home to buy. Then they began threatening a quiet, lonesome Jew who lived above his dry-goods store on Main Street. Some of the members of the Klan had charge accounts, long unpaid, at his store. At the post office one night, waiting around for the evening mail to be sorted, I heard Mr. Giddy talking about him. He said, "He sits up there all night long, reading books. No telling what he's plotting." The dry-goods merchant went to the hardware store one morning at a time when some of the Klan members were sitting around the stove and bought a double-barrelled shotgun and three boxes of twelve-gauge shells. He was not threatened any more.

Late that spring it was rumored in Stonewall that the Klan had decided to do something about the corn-whiskey-distilling situation. The biggest distiller was Mr. Sledge MacKellar; he employed four men at his copper still in Pocahontas Swamp. We knew he was immune from the Klan because he was Mr. Giddy's personal bootlegger, because he was fabulously expert with a shotgun, and because he had publicly served notice on the Klan. Mr. MacKellar came out of the swamp one afternoon and said he was prepared for "the Bed-Sheets." By that time Klansmen were called "the Bed-Sheets." He said, "I'm a Democrat and I got my rights. The first time one of them Bed-Sheets sticks his head in my front gate, I'm going to take his head right off. I got a shotgun and I got it loaded and I'm just aching to pull the trigger."

We knew the distillers the Klan had in mind were the Kidney boys, and we were not surprised when we heard that a date had been set on which they were to be tarred and feathered. The Kidney boys were three drunken Irish brothers who lived in a house about two and a half miles out from Stonewall and operated a still in Big Cherokee Swamp, behind their house. Their names were Patrick, Pinky, and Francis. They drank about half the whiskey they manufactured. When they came to town that week for supplies, the clerks in the stores kidded them. "I hear the Bed-Sheets are going to call on you boys for a pot of tea Friday night," one clerk said.

The Kidney boys had a hired man, an aged Negro named Uncle Bowleg, who later worked for a relative of mine. One time Uncle Bowleg told me how the Kidney boys brought about the downfall of the Invisible Empire in Black Ankle County. There were three entrances to the Kidney house—a front door, a back door, and a side door. When they heard the Klan was planning a call on Friday night, the brothers rented three dynamite outfits from a man who made his living blasting out tree stumps. They swapped him a gallon of charcoal-cured corn whiskey for the use of the outfits. They buried three great charges of dynamite in the yard, under the three paths leading to the entrances of the house. Wires led from the buried dynamite to batteries, to which switches were attached. The Kidney boys placed the batteries in the house, beneath three windows where they could sit and watch for approaching Klansmen. They planned to throw a switch the moment the Klansmen walked up one of the paths.

That night the Kidney boys turned off all the lights and took places at the windows with the dynamite batteries and switches in their laps. Uncle Bowleg was in the house with them. The Kidneys soon got tired of staring out into the yard, waiting for Klansmen, and ordered Uncle Bowleg to fetch them a jug of whiskey and a pitcher of water. Uncle Bowleg said he was kept busy running from one Kidney to another with the whiskey. The whiskey made them happy and they began to talk, speculating on how much noise their blasts would make. "We'll blow those Bed-Sheets to Kingdom Come," said Pinky.

About ten o'clock, when the moon was high, Francis Kidney, who was guarding the side door, decided he could wait no longer. The whiskey had given him an irresistible desire to throw the switch on his battery.

"Get ready!" he shouted suddenly. "I just can't wait no longer. I'm going to test this dynamite. The Bed-Sheets won't come in by the side door, anyway."

He threw the switch and there was a blast that shook the entire lower half of Black Ankle County. It caused people to leap out of their beds. We heard the blast in my home, and I remember that my grandmother said she thought that Judgment Day or the Second Coming was at hand.

Uncle Bowleg said the blast tore up a massive longleaf pine tree in the yard of the Kidney house and threw it into the highway. Uncle Bowleg was so frightened he jumped under a bed and hid. The Kidneys ran to the front porch and looked at the great tree lying in the highway. It pleased them. They laughed and slapped each other's shoulders. They came in and poured themselves some drinks. Then Patrick and Pinky took their places again, but Francis had thrown his switch, so he lost interest and went to sleep in his chair. In about half an hour, Patrick Kidney, who was guarding the rear door, heard a rustle out in back of the house. He knew it was the wind rustling the leaves on the chinquapin bushes, but all he wanted was an excuse to throw his switch.

"I think I hear them coming!" he shouted to Pinky, who was sitting at the front door with his hand on his switch. "Get ready. I'm going to let go."

Pinky needed some excitement, too. "Throw the switch!" he yelled.

Patrick threw his switch. The blast rattled Pinky and he threw his switch, too. The blasts were almost simultaneous. The slats fell out of the bed under which Uncle Bowleg was hiding and bruised him all over. A big framed picture of the mother of the Kidney brothers fell off the wall and hit Francis on the head. The legs dropped off the kitchen range and it fell apart. The entire back porch was torn loose from the house. The blast blew up the chicken house and a barrel in which the two hounds slept. All the chickens were killed, except an old rooster, and he never crowed again. Next morning there were six dead hens on the roof of the house and dead hens and ducks were scattered all over the yard. The South Carolina line runs near the rear of the Kidney house, and Uncle Bowleg swears that the hounds landed in South Carolina and were so shocked and outraged they never crossed back into North Carolina again. The mule's stall fell in.

"The roof fell down on that old plug," Uncle Bowleg told me, "and he bolted out into the road with the roof on his back like a saddle and galloped two miles before he felt safe enough to slow down and look around. And there was a rocking chair on the back porch and the dynamite set it to rocking. Next morning it was still rocking."

When the noise died down that night, and when things stopped falling apart, the Kidney brothers looked at each other. They were shame-faced. Suddenly they felt frightened. Without their dynamite, they felt naked and defenceless. "If the Bed-Sheets come now, we're sure done for," Francis said. His mother's picture was raising a bump on his head. All of a sudden the Kidney boys ran out of the house and made a dash for Big

Cherokee Swamp, with Uncle Bowleg following. Early next morning Uncle Bowleg got hungry and went back to the house for something to eat but the Kidney boys stayed in the swamp until noon.

As a matter of fact, they would have been just as safe in their wrecked house as they were in the swamp, because the Ku Klux Klan never did show up. The Klan had postponed its scheduled call because Mr. Giddy had arrived at the hall over the bank too drunk to take any interest in Klan matters. However, while the Kidneys were still snoring in the swamp, Mr. Ransom, who hadn't been able to get any sleep because of the three strange blasts, drove into Stonewall in his Ford and picked up Mr. Giddy. Mr. Ransom was sleepy and irritable and Mr. Giddy had a bad hangover, and they were not a happy pair. They drove out to the Kidney house to see what had happened during the night. When they arrived, Uncle Bowleg was sitting in the rocking chair on the front porch, eating a plate of corn bread and molasses. Mr. Giddy and Mr. Ransom walked into the yard and looked into the three gaping holes. Uncle Bowleg watched them like a hawk.

"Spuddy," said Mr. Giddy as he peered into the hole out of which the longleaf pine had come, "that sure is a damned big hole. I sure am glad I wasn't around when those holes were dug."

"Catfish," said Mr. Ransom in a frightened voice, "somebody might of got murdered last night. It's a good thing the Klan didn't ride last night."

Uncle Bowleg said they both stared into the holes and shuddered. Then they got into the Ford and drove away rapidly. During the day all the members of the Invisible Empire took occasion to drive by the Kidney house. They also shuddered when they saw the dynamite pits.

Late that afternoon Mr. Giddy showed up on Main Street. He was drunk again. He walked down Main Street, but he didn't sing. He stopped each person he met and said, "Friend, I have resigned." "Resigned from what, Mr. Catfish?" people asked. "Don't make no difference what I resigned from," he answered. "I just want you to know I resigned." The Ku Klux Klan never held another meeting in Stonewall. In a week or two the black paint was scraped off the windows in the hall above the bank and a "For Rent" sign was hung out. One woman ripped up her husband's Klan robe and made a pillowcase out of the cloth. Others heard about it and did the same. Mrs. Catfish Giddy ripped up her husband's robe and told her friends he was so fat she found enough material in it for two pillowcases, an apron, and a tablecloth.

🐾 *Greensboro, or What You Will*

Gerald W. Johnson

New South boosterism marked the spirit of other Carolina communities besides Charlotte, as this jeering essay by Gerald W. Johnson makes clear. It was published in 1924, while Johnson was editor of the *Greensboro Daily News*. He went on to earn a national reputation as an essayist, historian, and social critic.

A native of Scotland County, Johnson was educated at Wake Forest College; worked as a newspaperman from 1910 to 1924; taught journalism at the University of North Carolina at Chapel Hill from 1924 to 1926; and, as an editorialist for the *Sun* papers in Baltimore from 1926 to 1943, became an associate of H. L. Mencken. In twenty-five years he wrote more than twenty-five books. The following was taken from *South-Watching*, a 1983 collection of his essays.

🐾 This is a chant of the city that is to be, and you may name it what you please—Charlotte, or Raleigh, or Winston-Salem in North Carolina, Greenville or Spartanburg if you go south, Danville or Roanoke if you go north, or any one of a hundred other names of a hundred other towns precisely like it scattered from the Potomac to Mobile Bay, from Hatteras to the Rio Grande. I name it Greensboro, North Carolina, because I am a citizen of Greensboro, and our muezzins summon us to prayer with the sacred formula, "There is no God but Advertising, and Atlanta is his prophet." Nevertheless, we are resolutely broad-minded. We gulp, and admit that there are other towns in our class known to some people besides Mr. Rand and Mr. McNally. Therefore, if it pleases you to strike out Greensboro and write in another name, by all means proceed to do so; we of Greensboro shall be secretly outraged but just to prove that we are no Mainstreeters we shall smile from the teeth out and acquiesce too heartily.

But from one thing, I pray you, refrain. Do not curl your lip because Alias Greensboro comes shouldering its way into the grave and dignified company of its elders. If the reviewer's ambition is to present a complete series of Southern types, this one cannot be neglected. The word "city" does not mean in the South Richmond, Baltimore, Charleston, New Orleans, Louisville and no more. Nor may the collection be regarded as complete if Atlanta be added. By a merciful dispensation of Providence Greensboro has never been able to imitate Atlanta as closely as it would like. It is still distinctly different, still of an independent type, and to many hundreds of thousands of Southerners the word "city" means just such a

town as Greensboro. A town that may be identified by so many Southerners as their own certainly is of right to be included in any gallery of pictures
of Southern cities.

O. Henry once wrote that he was born in "a somnolent little Southern
town," and in so doing a man to whose nature malevolence was foreign left
to his city a legacy of bitterness. A considerable portion of Greensboro's
stock in the advertising trade is O. Henry. It earnestly desires not to be
ungrateful to him, but how those words "somnolent" and "little" do rankle!
Greensboro is enormous, and so wide-awake that it is pop-eyed. Why, did
we not have a special officer of the census bureau down last year to count
us after the cotton mill villages had been taken in, and did he not report a
total population of 43,525? Everyone knows it. None can escape the
knowledge, except the wholly illiterate, for both the morning and evening
newspapers still print the magic figures in large, black type every day. And
as for alert modernity, does not a seventeen-story office building spurt up
suddenly and unreasonably from the middle of town, like Memnon among
the dunes singing the glory of its creators when the rays of the rising sun
touch it in the morning? It is really too bad that O. Henry wrote that line,
for his worshippers still come here in numbers, expecting to find a quaint
Southern village, with the scent of honeysuckle and the sound of guitars
filling the suave air at dusk. And they generally fail to appreciate at its true
worth the progress that Greensboro has made. Some have been known to
go away peevish.

Nevertheless, Greensboro is more representative of the present South
than would be the somnolent little town for which these pilgrims seek in
vain. Change is the breath of its nostrils, indeed the very texture of its soul.
It was created by the sudden transition into an industrial region of the vast
plateau that parallels the Blue Ridge from Atlanta to Lynchburg, Virginia.
Here is established headquarters of one division of the new invasion of the
South, which has occurred since O. Henry was a boy, and which has
relegated the South that he knew to the pages of romance. Where Sherman
came up and Grant came down to grind the Confederate armies between
them, now Cotton and Tobacco have established their armies of occupation, and Greensboro and a long line of towns like it have sprung up with a
speed comparable to the speed with which the cantonments grew in 1917.

But while the cantonments have already vanished, Greensboro will
remain and nothing is more important to the South at the moment than to
examine it, to inquire what manner of thing this is which has been thrust
upon it, and which threatens to dominate its future. Inspection of its
material phases is only too painfully easy. But whisper your inquiry, and
our Chamber of Commerce will fall upon you ecstatically, snowing you

under with pamphlets, casting recklessly into the air handfuls of popping statistics like Chinese firecrackers, hustling you into a motor car to exhibit to you endless miles of asphalt and endless rows of unlovely skeletons of houses in process of construction.

It is a subtler and more difficult thing to catch a glimpse of the spirit of the place. It is not the business of the Chamber of Commerce to know that such a thing exists, and such things as it is not its business to know it painstakingly forgets. It cannot possibly remember, for instance, that Greensboro has only one railroad; why even inquire of it whether or not the city has a soul?

If the inquiry were made, the inquirer would almost certainly be misdirected. He would doubtless be sent to look at one of the suburban developments, which would be pleasant, but not profitable. They are merely additions to the pamphlets, the statistics, the automobile trip about the city. True, they are delightful to visit, all smooth-shaven lawns, broad streets with parkways running along them, and handsome homes all new and shiny inside. Some of them contain books and flowers and music as well as velours and mahogany and Oriental rugs; but they all have concealed plumbing, electric washing machines and vacuum cleaners. In other words, they are both new and complete. They have arrived, and the only story connected with them is a story of achievement. Greensboro, on the other hand, is new, but it is not complete; and the only story connected with it that is worth the telling must be a story of aspiration, a story of hopes hardly formulated, of ideals dimly perceived.

They wandered down Elm street on Saturday afternoon, when the mill villages on the outskirts of the town pour their populations into Greensboro's main thoroughfare. The inadequate sidewalk swarmed with people in a hurry, but they were untroubled by the incessant bumps and shoves of speeding pedestrians on business bent. They had obviously come to take in the town, and they were taking it in, leisurely and with immense satisfaction.

He carried in his arms a child of some eighteen months. She wheeled a perambulator. First one, then the other, grasped the hand of a toddler of three and slung it along, its feet rapping the pavement staggeringly and ineffectually. His suit certainly had been purchased, some time ago, at a fire sale in New Jerusalem, down by the railroad station. His shirt might have been the cause of the fire. Her shapeless shoes, cotton lisle stockings, and dress of neutral tint were topped by a hat that reminded one of a startled hen balancing on a board fence and ready to fly at the slightest alarm. The characteristic pallor of the cotton mill operative lay upon them both. Their faces were equally vacant, but hers was pinched by a hunger not of physical food.

Their direction carried them into the stream of traffic nearest the curb, but suddenly before a shop window she turned at right angles, thrust the perambulator straight through the line of people going in the other direction without the slightest interest in the ensuing disturbance of traffic, and brought it to a halt before the sheet of plate glass. Languidly he joined her, and they stood at gaze.

The window advertised a sale of silks, and the decorator had followed the custom of fixing bolts on high and permitting the fabric to cascade to the floor in shimmering streams. The window was a riot of colour blended with artful carelessness, a debauch of loveliness, voluptuous, enticing, exquisite. It fairly cried aloud for great ladies, imperiously it demanded wonderful bodies, soft and flawless skins, perfect contours, dignity and utter grace, for which these wonderful and costly things might furnish a worthy setting.

Outside he and she stood, not enraptured, but calmly and judicially admiring; indefinitely far from suspecting the irony that might have set Olympus a-roaring; and when they soon tired of it, they moved on, having spoken only a harsh word or two to the squirming toddler.

Yet for a moment there had been a gleam in her eyes.

Greensboro is the Master Key to the South's Best Markets. If you don't believe it, ask the Chamber of Commerce. It has published a booklet saying so, and it ought to know, for that is one of the things it is supposed to know about. Perhaps you may have been deluded into believing that the master key is Danville, or Roanoke, or Winston-Salem, or Charlotte, or Raleigh, or Greenville, or Spartanburg, or Macon, or Augusta, or some other of those Southern towns that are always making preposterous claims. But it isn't. It's Greensboro. Greensboro thought of the phrase first and can prove it.

Greensboro has the biggest denim mills, and—and—and, oh, well it's all in the pamphlet. The point to remember is that Greensboro has the biggest.

Greensboro has a proud list of illustrious sons. She has named a cigar and a mattress and a hotel after O. Henry, and if Wilbur Daniel Steele ever gets a big enough reputation she will doubtless name a cigar and a mattress after him. We have no new hotel to name just now.

Greensboro has many varied industries employing many thousands of workmen and the payroll amounts to so much monthly, and twelve times that in the course of a year.

Greensboro, as was said of Cedar Rapids, Iowa, is equidistant from all points of the horizon and is therefore a natural distribution center.

Greensboro has practically the same climate as North Carolina, but being thirty miles east of Winston-Salem, and ninety miles north of Charlotte, and eighty miles west of Raleigh, and fifty miles south of Danville, she is protected on all sides from blizzards, sand-storms and beating rains.

Greensboro has the absolutely unique distinction of being the third city in size in North Carolina.

Greensboro is infinitely preferable as a place of residence to New York, London, Paris, Berlin, or Vienna. I forget why, but you can find that and many more such absorbing items of information in the pamphlet.

No, that is inexact—I forget the reason given in the pamphlet, but I am well aware of many reasons for living in Greensboro that the pamphlet curiously omits. For instance, a good business man has served this city for three years as mayor without stealing a cent and without getting anything for his labour but a prolific crop of enemies. A big lawyer has spent $50,000 worth of his time trying to get—and getting—decent school-houses for the city's children, including the negro children. An insurance man for years has lived on half the income he might have made because half his time was taken up in a heart-breaking struggle to keep real estate brigands from putting garages in people's front yards, and in securing parks and playgrounds for the city. I might multiply instances of the kind, but these are suggestion enough.

Why do they do these difficult and profitless things? Well, they seem somehow to see, as through a glass darkly, a shimmer of magnificence in the future of this commonplace little town. They have the impression that somewhere beyond their reach, but within sight, there is such splendor, such grace and dignity and beauty as the town has never dreamed of; and arrested by the vision they stand spellbound. They allow themselves to be jostled and pushed aside by hurrying passers-by without protest, rather than turn away from the loveliness they expect never to touch. And he who strives to create unattainable beauty, regardless of his medium, has he not the artist's soul?

The irony of it is not subtle. He must be humourless indeed who fails to perceive the incongruity of Greensboro's critical appraisal of the apparel of queenly cities. I do not challenge your right to laughter who have seen her only as you passed by and have had time barely to note that she is well fed and musicless, dramaless, destitute of painting and sculpture and scantily endowed with architecture meriting a second glance. Languidly

chewing gum and inspecting rich brocades woven for mistresses of em-
pires and broad seas, she is perhaps justly an object of derision. But I pray
you pardon me if I do not join in your mirth, for I am somehow not in the
mood for laughter. I have seen the gleam in her eyes.

✎ *Half across the Mighty State*

Thomas Wolfe

Few writers have portrayed the majesty and mystery of the North Carolina
mountains as well as Thomas Wolfe, one of their most famous sons. Born
in Asheville in 1900, he was educated at the University of North Carolina
at Chapel Hill and at Harvard, taught six years at New York University, and
in the decade before his death in 1938 turned out a torrent of fiction,
beginning with *Look Homeward, Angel*, about life in his hometown.

This excerpt, describing a train ride down the mountains and across
the Piedmont to the Virginia line, is from the second of his novels, *Of Time
and the River*, published in 1935.

✎ The journey from the mountain town of Altamont to the tower-masted
island of Manhattan is not, as journeys are conceived in America, a long
one. The distance is somewhat more than 700 miles, the time required to
make the journey a little more than twenty hours. But so relative are the
qualities of space and time, and so complex and multiple their shifting
images, that in the brief passage of this journey one may live a life, share
instantly in 10,000,000 other ones, and see pass before his eyes the infinite
panorama of shifting images that make a nation's history.

First of all, the physical changes and transitions of the journey are
strange and wonderful enough. In the afternoon one gets on the train and
with a sense of disbelief and wonder sees the familiar faces, shapes, and
structures of his native town recede out of the last fierce clasp of life and
vision. Then, all through the waning afternoon, the train is toiling down
around the mountain curves and passes. The great shapes of the hills,
embrowned and glowing with the molten hues of autumn, are all about
him: the towering summits, wild and lonely, full of joy and strangeness and
their haunting premonitions of oncoming winter soar above him, the
gulches, gorges, gaps, and wild ravines, fall sheer and suddenly away with
a dizzy terrifying steepness, and all the time the great train toils slowly
down from the mountain summits with the sinuous turnings of an enor-

mous snake. And from the very toiling slowness of the train, together with the terrific stillness and nearness of the marvellous hills, a relation is established, an emotion evoked, which it is impossible to define, but which, in all its strange and poignant mingling of wild sorrow and joy, grief for the world that one is losing, swelling triumph at the thought of the strange new world that one will find, is instantly familiar, and has been felt by every one.

The train toils slowly round the mountain grades, the short and powerful blasts of its squat funnel sound harsh and metallic against the sides of rocky cuts. One looks out the window and sees cut, bank, and gorge slide slowly past, the old rock wet and gleaming with the water of some buried mountain spring. The train goes slowly over the perilous and dizzy height of a wooden trestle; far below, the traveller can see and hear the clean foaming clamors of rock-bright mountain water; beside the track, before his little hut, a switchman stands looking at the train with the slow wondering gaze of the mountaineer. The little shack in which he lives is stuck to the very edge of the track above the steep and perilous ravine. His wife, a slattern with a hank of tight drawn hair, a snuff-stick in her mouth, and the same gaunt, slow wondering stare her husband has, stands in the doorway of the shack, holding a dirty little baby in her arms.

It is all so strange, so near, so far, so terrible, beautiful, and instantly familiar, that it seems to the traveller that he must have known these people forever, that he must now stretch forth his hand to them from the windows and the rich and sumptuous luxury of the pullman car, that he must speak to them. And it seems to him that all the strange and bitter miracle of life—how, why, or in what way, he does not know—is in that instant greeting and farewell; for once seen, and lost the moment that he sees it, it is his forever and he can never forget it. And then the slow toiling train has passed these lives and faces and is gone, and there is something in his heart he cannot say.

At length the train has breached the last great wall of the soaring ranges, has made its slow and sinuous descent around the powerful bends and cork-screws of the shining rails (which now he sees above him seven times) and towards dark, the lowland country has been reached. The sun goes down behind the train a tremendous globe of orange and pollen, the soaring ranges melt swiftly into shapes of smoky and enchanted purple, night comes—great-starred and velvet-breasted night—and now the train takes up its level pounding rhythm across the piedmont swell and convolution of the mighty State.

Towards nine o'clock at night there is a pause to switch cars and change engines at a junction town. The traveller, with the same feeling of wild unrest, wonder, nameless excitement and wordless expectancy, leaves the train, walks back and forth upon the platform, rushes into the little station lunch room or out into the streets to buy cigarettes, a sandwich—really just to feel this moment's contact with another town. He sees vast flares and steamings of gigantic locomotives on the rails, the seamed, blackened, lonely faces of the engineers in the cabs of their great engines, and a little later he is rushing again across the rude, mysterious visage of the powerful, dark, and lonely earth of old Catawba.

Toward midnight there is another pause at a larger town—the last stop in Catawba—again the feeling of wild unrest and nameless joy and sorrow. The traveller gets out, walks up and down the platform, sees the vast slow flare and steaming of the mighty engine, rushes into the station, and looks into the faces of all the people passing with the same sense of instant familiarity, greeting, and farewell,—that lonely, strange, and poignantly wordless feeling that Americans know so well. Then he is in the pullman again, the last outposts of the town have slipped away from him and the great train which all through the afternoon has travelled eastward from the mountains half across the mighty State, is now for the first time pointed northward, worldward, towards the secret borders of Virginia, towards the great world cities of his hope, the fable of his childhood legendry, and the wild and secret hunger of his heart, his spirit and his life.

Already the little town from which he came in the great hills, the faces of his kinsmen and his friends, their most familiar voices, the shapes of things he knew seem far and strange as dreams, lost at the bottom of the million-visaged sea-depth of dark time, the strange and bitter miracle of life. He cannot think that he has ever lived there in the far lost hills, or ever left them, and all his life seems stranger than the dream of time, and the great train moves on across the immense and lonely visage of America, making its great monotone that is the sound of silence and forever. And in the train, and in ten thousand little towns, the sleepers sleep upon the earth.

Then bitter sorrow, loneliness and joy come swelling to his throat—quenchless hunger rises from the adyts of his life and conquers him, and with wild wordless fury horsed upon his life, he comes at length, in dark mid-watches of the night, up to the borders of the old earth of Virginia.

✒ In Defense of North Carolina

Clyde R. Hoey

After the Civil War, the manufacture of cotton, tobacco, and furniture enabled North Carolina to rise as one of the nation's most industrial states. But low wages, small farms, and a lagging per capita income also kept it among the nation's poorest, a fact that its corporate and political plutocracy often chose to ignore, at least publicly.

That attitude is reflected in this excerpt from a 1939 speech by Governor Clyde R. Hoey in response to a federal report that southern poverty was a major impediment to the nation's recovery from the Great Depression. With flowing gray locks, a wing collar, and a swallowtail coat, Clyde Hoey was the epitome of a southern orator in the 1930s and 1940s, when he served his native state as a governor and U.S. senator.

✒ A recent survey classified the South as the Nation's economic problem No. 1. With full admission of all our shortcomings and needs, I must insist that North Carolina does not fit into that classification. During the whole period of the depression, North Carolina has maintained fourth place in her total contributions by way of taxes to the Federal Government. Only New York, Pennsylvania, and Illinois exceeded this State in the sums paid annually. Of course tobacco taxes accounted for a large proportion of the total sum, but automobile purchases throughout the country help pay Michigan's, the users of all nationally sold products contribute to the home state of manufacture, and then all of us help New York pay hers by our losses on the stock exchange.

During the depression period North Carolina has received less from the Federal Government per capita than any state in the Union and we have paid more per capita than any state save Delaware. In 1938 there were only two states whose income from cash crops was greater than North Carolina—California and Texas. We grow and manufacture more tobacco than any other state, we have attained the primacy in textiles and stand second in the manufacture of furniture. Last year the total manufactured products of North Carolina reached the grand total of one billion and three hundred million dollars. And the laborer in North Carolina received as high a percentage of the manufacturer's dollar as in any other state. There has not been a bank failure in North Carolina in more than seven years. This State stands fifth in the development of hydro-electric power. Briefly, upon this showing I regard my State as a stalwart, supporting member of the family rather than a problem child.

ᐳ *A Piece of Luck*

Frances Gray Patton

Durham is one of North Carolina's most diverse urban centers. It has sophisticated academic communities around Duke and North Carolina Central universities. It has a vigorous laboring class employed in tobacco and textile plants. And it has a wealthy corporate community that includes the North Carolina Mutual Insurance Company, one of the nation's most successful black-owned enterprises. Somehow those varied elements, some very rich and some very poor, manage to accommodate one another with civility and respect, as exemplified in this story by Frances Gray Patton.

The daughter of a Raleigh newspaperman, Frances Gray Patton attended Trinity College (now Duke University) and the University of North Carolina at Chapel Hill. She married a Duke professor of English and was a wife and mother before she began to write fiction. This story, which won the 1935 Sir Walter Raleigh Award for the year's best North Carolina fiction, shows off her subtle humor, her eye for vivid detail, and her deft characterization.

ᐳ About three o'clock one nice Thursday afternoon, I was waiting for a city bus at Five Points, here in Durham, North Carolina, and I chanced to witness a little street scene, a comedy of manners, in which a man who was cast by Nature in a mob role, without business or lines, ad-libbed and walked off with the honors of the piece.

Five Points is the transfer junction for most bus riders in town, but especially for those who arrive by the bus coming west from Fayetteville Street, the main thoroughfare of Haiteye, which is a large section of town populated by colored people. That bus comes up Pettigrew Street on the south side of the railroad tracks, turns north to Five Points through the Chapel Hill Street underpass, loops back east down Main, and eventually returns to its starting place in Haiteye. Passengers who wish to continue their westward journey have to change at Five Points and on my particular Thursday there were a dozen or more people waiting with me on the sidewalk, all of them Negroes.

Thursday is a Colored Clinic day at Duke Hospital, and I guessed that most of the crowd were on their way out there. They came from various stations in life. There were several spruce, buxom young matrons with dressed-up babies in their arms, who stood clustered together, complimenting one another's offspring, as any group of mothers will. There was a twisted old crone—the sort of woman my nurse used to scare me with when I was a child—with hands like prehensile claws, and snuff juice seeping through the crack between her sunken lips. There was a great yellow buck of a fellow, with an alarmingly amoral expression, engaged in laconic conversation with a hoarse, rouged woman who must, surely, have had "something wrong with her blood," as the accepted euphemism would put it. And I saw, standing near the curb, aloof from *hoi polloi*, two persons whom I recognized as a retired Duke University janitor—called Ducky by the students and faculty—and his wife.

In common with all who knew Ducky (and since he is a powerful preacher and a shrewd speculator in rental-housing property as well as an ex-janitor, his acquaintance is legion), I respect him. He is a sawed-off man, with very short legs—the "duck legs" that give him his nickname— but he has the gift of presence. His skin is the color of a good Havana cigar. His large, round head, bald except for a bristle of gray hair on either temple, his pouter-pigeon chest, the elegance of his dress—for he invariably wears a wing collar, a dark coat and waistcoat, and the sort of striped trousers that ordinary men hold in reserve for weddings—give him a presence that any giant might envy. That Thursday he wore, also, a black Homburg and, in gracious acknowledgment of the season, a daffodil in his buttonhole. He was not looking in my direction and I was about to go and speak to him, but I thought better of it. The sad truth was that I couldn't recollect his real name.

I observed his wife, a portly woman, much taller and younger than he, who carried herself with dignity and poise. I noticed the reverential glances that the other Negroes shot in his direction and the way they all— even the yellow buck and his friend—assumed a decorous air whenever he happened to glance around at them, and I decided that I wouldn't address this gentleman of substance and distinction as "Ducky." I leaned against the plate-glass window of a furniture store and passed my time in idle speculation as to which section of Haiteye each of my fellow travelers hailed from.

Haiteye is a region of some mystery to me, but in a superficial way I know it pretty well. I have been there to take oranges to sick cooks, to ferret out cleaning men, and to attend concerts in the auditorium of the Negro college, which is far and away the pleasantest concert hall in Durham. I know Lincoln Heights, where the dwellings are likely to have fluted porch pillars, cut-glass fanlights, and lace curtains in their windows, and to preserve on their lawns, like symbols of stubborn gentility, the iron deer that once graced the grass of the original tobacco magnates of Durham. I know Booker T. Place, a new real-estate development of brick cottages that boast Heatrolas and indoor plumbing. I have seen the listing frame tenements with the broken windowpanes, the refuse—egg shells, wet coffee grounds, and dirty pork-and-beans cans—littering their entrance halls, and the obscenities chalked on their steps, and I've driven down the narrow, lumpy roads that soon dwindle out into the clay fields and scrub-pine patches of the countryside, and are known, for some reason, as alleys. Kingpin Alley, Husband's Alley, Little Jones Alley—they are all alike. Among them, dingy, two-room houses perch on stilts, with torn green shades drawn over their front windows; in the air is the faint, pervading odor of a sewer ditch and an uneasy kind of quietness. A white stranger in one of those alleys has the feeling that his approach has been sensed a long way off and that people are hiding, waiting for him to pass. He feels that they are compelled to hide not by fear, or by any emotion so definite as fear, but by an instinct for retreat. It is as if they ask nothing of life but anonymity, as if they admit themselves to be without real consequence, living, by sufferance, on the fringe of the world.

Well, I thought, Mr. and Mrs. Ducky are swells from Lincoln Heights; the yellow man and the painted woman hang out in one of the tenements that are raided by the police every week end, and I have doubtless read their names in a Monday newspaper among the list of offenders fined by the County Recorder for such misdemeanors as disturbing the peace, shooting crap, or using rooms for immoral purposes; the girls with the babies come from Booker T. or some neighborhood just as wholesome if not so modern; and the crone—for all her evil aspect—probably lives with respectable relatives who treat her with exquisite consideration and subscribe piously to a burial association that will someday provide her with suitable obsequies. I was peering down the street, hoping to glimpse my bus in the offing, when I saw two more Negroes, a man and a woman, strolling toward me from the corner. I couldn't put the woman in any residential category—she had a country look, really, with her long, bony shanks and her hair that was "wropped" and parted in sections, like a map—but I was instantly certain about the man. Husband's Alley, I said to myself.

He was a slack, unsubstantial-looking man with the dull complexion that members of his race despise. He wore khaki pants that weren't very clean and a blue serge coat with its collar turned up, and he had an enormous swath of bandage over his left eye. There was nothing vicious in his face, but there was nothing in it to recommend him, either. He was what we Durhamites, white or black, would be likely to dismiss as a "harmless, no-count nigger"—a man born to be the victim of circumstance. If you hired him to chop wood, he would either whack his toe off with the ax or, coming into your kitchen for a glass of water, accidentally find your liquor and get drunk. I decided that not only was he from

Husband's Alley; he was, even there, merely somebody's roomer. And I was surprised to note that his companion looked at him with a certain deference.

The two of them stopped beside me. There was a perceptible stir among the other Negroes—that is, among all of them except Ducky and his wife, who were still looking the other way. Everyone else cast furtive, half-fearful glances at the bandaged eye (there is that about an eye injury that touches the imagination on the quick), and then politely glanced away again. The two were talking in the animated fashion of casual acquaintances who have met up by accident.

"I can't tell how you done it!" the woman declared. "Me—I'd go down, down, down!"

"It had to be did, like the Book say," the man said. He laughed in a foolish, spuriously modest way, but there was an undertone of happiness in his laughter, as if he were wondering at himself. "Where your baby brother at now?" he asked.

"My baby brother? He in New York City, workin' in a café."

"Is that a fact! How it suit him up yonder?"

"It suit him and it don't suit him," the woman said. "He allow the work ain't hard, it just too steady."

"I ain't been workin' since Liggett's & Myers' turn me off," the man said. "My boss say come see him when the green season start, but I don't know now." He sighed resignedly, as if idleness were not his notion of an unmitigated evil. "I gets thirteen dollars ev'y Saddy from the Unemployment. My conversation money."

"Thirteen dollar don't last out, the way sump'n't'eat cost now," the woman said, "but it he'p." She shook her head. "Boy, you is purely got the nerve. I gonna set down this evenin', if'n it the last thing I do, and write a letter to my baby brother 'bout you!"

The man looked gratified. "Tell him I say 'hey,' " he said.

Suddenly, I noticed that Ducky and his wife had turned and were trying to hear what the two were saying, and were looking at the man's bandaged eye with the same interest that the others had shown. Ducky, being a man of authority, is not one to suffer curiosity in silence. He took a step toward the newcomers. But his wife laid a hand on his arm. Obviously, she thought her husband had grown childish in his old age and she intended to prevent his making a spectacle of himself.

There was a brief silence. Ducky pulled out a gold sea biscuit of a watch, clicked up its lid, and, with the air of a man to whom minutes mean money, went through the pantomime of comparing its time with that of the clock on the Amoco Service Station across the street. One of the babies said, "Tick-tick." The crowd laughed tenderly and the young mothers resumed their chatter.

The man with the bandaged eye spoke to me.

"Lady," he said, "could you kindly direct me which bus carry you to Duke's Hospital?"

I knew that his inquiry was in the nature of an opening wedge—a preparation, probably, for the request of a handout. The way to Duke Hospital is not complicated, and I was fairly confident that this man had been there before. His bandage had not been folded by an amateur.

"The Duke Hospital bus," I said.

"Is that right? The Duke's Hospital bus!" He turned to his companion. "She say it the Duke's Hospital bus carry you to Duke's Hospital!"

"Well—t'be sure!" the woman exclaimed.

The man took a greasy wallet from his inside breast pocket. He shook its contents—a little silver, some pennies, and a blue clinic card—into his palm. He regarded these resources sadly with his unbandaged eye. "I reckon I can make out till Saddy, when I gets my conversation," he said, ostensibly to his friend.

I opened my purse. I thought I'd give him a quarter if he asked for it. I have principles about encouraging beggars, but I have superstitions about refusing them.

The man pretended not to notice what I was doing, and I felt justly rebuked. I hadn't gone through the amenities the situation required.

"Does your eye cause you much pain?" I asked.

"No, ma'am," he said. "It don't pain me none. Not now."

The woman had been standing somewhat in the background, like a supporting actor who doesn't presume to share the spotlight with the lead. Suddenly, she thrust her long neck forward. She said, close to my ear, in an awed, low voice, "He had it removed!"

"Oh, I'm sorry!" I said, shocked. "That's terrible!"

The man assumed the noble, important expression of chief mourner at a funeral. He was a man whom God had singled out.

"They didn't put him to sleep," the woman said. "He laid on a table, wide awake, and had it removed. I couldn't bring myself to do it. I'd go down, down, down!" She let her legs sag at the knees to illustrate what she meant.

"Them Duke's doctors froze it," the man said, unwilling to take more credit than was his due.

"They froze his eye!" the woman said. Her own eyes, very white around the irises, gleamed with horror.

"A local anesthetic's said to be best, if the patient's brave enough," I said. I fumbled in my purse. This called for a dollar.

"I'm too tender-hearted. I can't stand nothin' like that," the woman said. "When the health-apartment lady give my little boy the typhoid shots, I went down, down, down!"

"How did you hurt your eye?" I asked the man.

"I didn't for to say hurt it," he said. "It hurt me. It commenced inflamin' and infectin' and doin' ev'ything, seems like, 'cep'n what it oughta been doin'! So I had it removed."

During this time, Ducky had been restive under restraint. He had kept fidgeting, cocking his head in a plain effort to overhear what we were saying, and making an occasional tentative move in our direction; but his wife had always pulled him up with a quiet word, as though she had him on a short leash. Now he caught my eye. I smiled. My smile was the means of his escape.

"Bless the Lord, it's Miss Rowena!" Ducky ejaculated, bustling up to me. He lifted his Homburg with a flourish and bowed from the waist. "Howdy-do, ma'am? Howdy-do?"

My name is not Rowena or anything like it, but I understood why Ducky had called me that. He had been unable quite to place me; he knew I was an old friend, once a Duke student and now a faculty wife, and he could gauge my approximate age from my appearance, but exactly who I was he couldn't remember, so he had addressed me by a name that he was satisfied I wouldn't resent. Rowena Allen was the beauty of my college generation, a never-to-be-forgotten girl with raven hair and eyes like water on a starry night. Any woman who had ever seen her would be delighted to be mistaken for her. Marveling at Ducky's diplomatic genius, I again sought his name in my mind. Happily, I found it.

"How are you, Buchanan?" I said.

"I'm not complaining, Miss Rowena," Ducky said. "Of course, I've put on some age. Some Anno Domini, as the Caesars would say."

"You don't show it," I said.

"I've lived right," Ducky said, "and the Lord loves even unto the third and fourth generation them as keep His commandments." He looked sharply at the man with the bandage. "I'm ready to meet my Maker when He calls. Meantimes, I continue working in His vineyard. In other words, Heaven is my home, but I'm not homesick for it."

This sally drew an appreciative titter from the crowd. Ducky's wife, looking anxious and maternal, joined us. "How do you do, Mrs. Patton?" she said to me.

"How do you do?" I said. "Your husband's wonderful."

"He does fairly well, considering," she said. "He misses the intellectual atmosphere of the Duke campus."

Ducky ignored her. Having done his devoirs to convention, he now attacked the matter he had in mind. He cleared his throat in a series of commanding "hrmph, hrmph, hrmph's," and faced the man from Husband's Alley. "What seems to be wrong with your eye, fellow?" he said.

The whole crowd of Negroes inched closer to us. The woman, the yellow buck, and even the babies seemed to hold their breath in admiration for this resident of Lincoln Heights who had peremptorily challenged the mystery that troubled them.

The alley man hesitated. He folded his hands in a meek, self-deprecatory way. "I had it removed," he said demurely.

Ducky jumped backward as if he'd heard a shot. "You had it *removed!*" he gasped.

The crowd gasped, too. No one was looking at Ducky now.

"They didn't put him to sleep. They *froze* it," the country woman said.

"Sweet Jesus!" said the buck.

Ducky pulled himself together. He frowned, pursing his lips like a judge who is about to cite courtroom spectators for contempt. He glared accusingly at the man with the bandage. "What made you do a thing like that?" he asked.

The man raised his remaining orb to heaven. "If thine eye offend thee, pluck it out," he said.

Ducky let his mouth fall open. He stood there staring and licking his lips. He said nothing, because there was nothing further to say. This poor creature from the alleys of society—a figure insignificant in church or state or savings bank—had said it all and had said it on the highest possible plane of expression. I had heard of men being "deflated," but I hadn't known what the word could mean until then, as I watched Ducky. He appeared to grow smaller under my eyes; his tight, shiny skin seemed to loosen and to hang in folds from his jaws. His kind wife put an arm across his shoulders.

A Duke Hospital bus drew to the stop. The crowd stood aside until the one-eyed man and his companion had climbed aboard. Ducky was the last to enter the bus.

"Now you be calm, Buchanan, and don't talk," I heard his wife advise him. "You know the doctor says talking too much is bad for your high blood." As if to salve his pride, she added, "We'll return to Lincoln Heights in a cab."

Left alone, waiting for the Hillsboro Road bus, I realized that I still held a dollar bill in my hand. At first, I was distressed, thinking that even so small an amount of cash might have tided the poor man over the rest of that day and Friday, until, on Saturday, he could collect his compensation money. But, on further reflection, I was glad I'd forgotten to give it to him. That man had had a piece of luck. He had enjoyed a moment of self-esteem, which is a rarer thing than one ordinarily supposes. He had risen above his natural element. Charity from a white stranger, and one who was the friend—the *property*, in a manner of speaking—of Ducky, would have plopped him back where he belonged.

A dollar is a dollar, of course, and it will—in Durham, at least—buy considerable sustenance for the body. It is good for ten hot dogs in rolls with mustard and onion sauce, or twenty cups of coffee, or five cans of beer. But if you happened to live in Husband's Alley, it might be that you could use another kind of sustenance. The recollection of success—of being a hero among your own people at Five Points, of scripture falling trippingly off your tongue to stupefy a citizen of Lincoln Heights, of a brute who could have broken you in his hands, a witch who could have hexed you, comely young women whose husbands would have beaten you if you'd spoken to them, all standing aside to let you get on a Duke Hospital bus—that recollection might be a bauble of great sentimental value. It wouldn't change your life, of course—for once a genuine alley man, always an alley man. But you could play with it and fondle it, turning its several pretty facets to the light on chilly mornings while you held your glass eye in your mouth to warm it up a little.

◌ In the Great Pine Forest

Jack Kerouac

The flat, loamy fields around Rocky Mount, at the start of North Carolina's boundless coastal plain, offer some of the state's most desolate landscapes, places where the earth seems raw, empty, and vast. It was to those fields that Jack Kerouac came in 1955 to live with his mother and sister, where he gathered material for *The Dharma Bums*, the second of his books that defined the "beat generation" in America.

Jack Kerouac was a native of Lowell, Massachusetts, who attended Horace Mann School for Boys in New York City, won a football scholarship to Columbia University, but grew disinterested in both football and college and joined the Merchant Marine during World War II. After the war he roamed the country, living as a drifter and defying bourgeois values. *On the Road*, his 1957 novel based on those experiences, made him a hero to a rising generation of rebellious youth. The next year he wrote *The Dharma Bums* as a sequel. The following is an excerpt from that book.

🙠 They all wanted me to sleep on the couch in the parlor by the comfortable oil-burning stove but I insisted on making my room (as before) on the back porch with its six windows looking out on the winter barren cottonfield and the pine woods beyond, leaving all the windows open and stretching my good old sleeping bag on the couch there to sleep the pure sleep of winter nights with my head buried inside the smooth nylon duck-down warmth. After they'd gone to bed I put on my jacket and my earmuff cap and railroad gloves and over all that my nylon poncho and strode out in the cottonfield moonlight like a shroudy monk. The ground was covered with moonlit frost. The old cemetery down the road gleamed in the frost. The roofs of nearby farmhouses were like white panels of snow. I went through the cottonfield rows followed by Bob, a big bird dog, and little Sandy who belonged to the Joyners down the road, and a few other stray dogs (all dogs love me) and came to the edge of the forest. In there, the previous spring, I'd worn out a little path going to meditate under a favorite baby pine. The path was still there. My official entrance to the forest was still there, this being two evenly spaced young pines making kind of gate posts. I always bowed there and clasped my hands and thanked Avalokitesvara for the privilege of the wood. Then I went in, led moonwhite Bob direct to my pine, where my old bed of straw was still at the foot of the tree. I arranged my cape and legs and sat to meditate.

The dogs meditated on their paws. We were all absolutely quiet. The entire moony countryside was frosty silent, not even the little tick of rabbits or coons anywhere. An absolute cold blessed silence. Maybe a dog barking five miles away toward Sandy Cross. Just the faintest, faintest sound of big trucks rolling out the night on 301, about twelve miles away, and of course the distant occasional Diesel baugh of the Atlantic Coast Line passenger and freight trains going north and south to New York and Florida. A blessed night. I immediately fell into a blank thoughtless trance wherein it was again revealed to me "This thinking has stopped" and I sighed because I didn't have to think any more and felt my whole body sink into a blessedness surely to be believed, completely relaxed and at peace with all the ephemeral world of dream and dreamer and the dreaming itself. All kinds of thoughts, too, like "One man practicing kindness in the wilderness is worth all the temples this world pulls" and I reached out and stroked old Bob, who looked at me satisfied. "All living and dying things like these dogs and me coming and going without any duration or self substance, O God, and therefore we can't possibly exist. How strange, how worthy, how good for us! What a horror it would have been if the world was real, because if the world was real, it would be immortal." My nylon poncho protected me from the cold, like a fitted-on tent, and I stayed a long time sitting crosslegged in the winter midnight woods, about an hour. Then I went back to the house, warmed up by the fire in the living room while the others slept, then slipped into my bag on the porch and fell asleep.

The following night was Christmas Eve which I spent with a bottle of wine before the TV enjoying the shows and the midnight mass from Saint Patrick's Cathedral in New York with bishops ministering, and doctrines glistering, and congregations, the priests in their lacy snow vestments before great official altars not half as great as my straw mat beneath a little pine tree I figured. Then at midnight the breathless little parents, my sister and brother-in-law, laying out the presents under the tree and more gloriful than all the Gloria in Excelsis Deos of Rome Church and all its attendant bishops. "For after all," I thought, "Augustine was a spade and Francis my idiot brother." My cat Davey suddenly blessed me, sweet cat, with his arrival on my lap. I took out the Bible and read a little Saint Paul by the warm stove and the light of the tree, "Let him become a fool, that he may become wise," and I thought of good dear Japhy and wished he was enjoying the Christmas Eve with me. "Already are ye filled," says Saint Paul, "already are ye become rich. The saints shall judge the world." Then in a burst of beautiful poetry more beautiful than all the poetry readings of all the San Francisco Renaissances of Times: "Meats for the belly, and the belly for meats; but God shall bring to naught both it and them."

"Yep," I thought, "you pay through the nose for shortlived shows. . . ."

That week I was all alone in the house, my mother had to go to New York for a funeral, and the others worked. Every afternoon I went into the piney woods with my dogs, read, studied, meditated, in the warm winter southern sun, and came back and made supper for everybody at dusk. Also, I put up a basket and shot baskets every sundown. At night, after they went to bed, back I went to the woods in starlight or even in rain sometimes with my poncho. The woods received me well. I amused myself writing little Emily Dickinson poems like "Light a fire, fight a liar, what's the difference, in existence?" or "A watermelon seed, produces a need, large and juicy, such autocracy."

"Let there be blowing-out and bliss forevermore," I prayed in the woods at night. I kept making newer and better prayers. And more poems, like when the snow came, "Not oft, the holy snow, so soft, the holy bow," and at one point I wrote "The Four Inevitabilities: 1. Musty Books. 2. Uninteresting Nature. 3. Dull Existence. 4. Blank Nirvana, buy that boy." Or I wrote, on dull afternoons when neither Buddhism nor poetry nor wine nor solitude nor basketball would avail my lazy but earnest flesh, "Nothin to do, Oh poo! Practically blue." One afternoon I watched the ducks in the pig field across the road and it was Sunday, and the hollering preachers were screaming on the Carolina radio and I wrote: "Imagine blessing all living and dying worms in eternity and the ducks that eat 'em . . . there's your Sunday school sermon." In a dream I heard the words, "Pain, 'tis but a concubine's puff." But in Shakespeare it would say, "Ay, by my faith, that bears a frosty sound." Then suddenly one night after supper as I was pacing in the cold windy darkness of the yard I felt tremendously depressed and threw myself right on the ground and cried "I'm gonna die!" because there was nothing else to do in the cold loneliness of this harsh inhospitable earth, and instantly the tender bliss of enlightenment was like milk in my eyelids and I was warm. And I realized that this was the truth Rosie knew now, and all the dead, my dead father and dead brother and dead uncles and cousins and aunts, the truth that is realizable in a dead man's bones and is beyond the Tree of Buddha as well as the Cross of Jesus. *Believe* that the world is an ethereal flower, and ye live. I knew this! I also knew that I was the worst bum in the world. The diamond light was in my eyes.

My cat meowed at the icebox, anxious to see what all the good dear delight was. I fed him.

∿ *Warrenton Was a One-Street Town*

Reynolds Price

Though North Carolina is one of the nation's ten most populous states, it remains one of the most rural. Without a dominant metropolitan city, its population is distributed rather evenly across the landscape, mostly in small towns and cities, where residents know each other, each other's families, and each other's frailties. Much of the fiction of Duke University author Reynolds Price is drawn from his experiences in several North Carolina towns. This excerpt from *Kate Vaiden*, his 1986 best-seller, portrays the life and values in Warrenton, where he spent much of his boyhood.

◆ . . . Early next morning I called Swift's house and asked could I catch a ride in to town with him. He sounded enthused and said he'd come get me. I gritted my teeth but said I'd be ready. Since my parents died I'd shunned Swift Porter every chance I got, without acting mean. And even though he and his scared-squirrel wife lived in sight of our house, he seldom came by. Sometimes weeks would pass before Holt would say "Anybody seen Swift?" And Caroline would call him to stop by for breakfast. So I knew that morning I was hell-bent on something if I'd stooped to call Swift.

Swift was usually asleep till noon. He'd rise and drive to work but be sluggish till everybody else was fine. So on the way to town, I barely had to speak. Yes, I'd turned a new corner, shopping alone. Yes, I'd go to the show that afternoon. Then I'd meet him at five o'clock to head on home. Otherwise we were quiet. Back then nobody that far from a city ever had to warn you of any human danger. The place wasn't Heaven. There were killings and rapes but never by strangers, always family members. A sixteen-year-old girl like me—no stunner but nothing to ruin your lunch—could drift through the streets and never pass a thing more harmful than wishes.

Holt had given me four five-dollar bills; and I bought the clothes first, everything as dark as possible except a white blouse. That was partly in mourning and partly because I'd already seen how much finer everybody looks in deep blue. Then I bought some school shoes and had my feet X-rayed to prove they fit (everybody my age took hours of sizzling foot-rays, but we're mostly still upright). I left those boxes in Swift's department and figured I'd wander.

Warrenton then was a one-street town, far as sights were concerned. Down at one end were the grocery stores and clothiers—high dim old places where an ancient clerk would hand you every can from closed shelves behind him or a lady with a goiter could make you a hat to match your shape and color exactly. Then the bank and the courthouse square with the library. Then the one white cafe and theater, then the Hotel Warren with salesmen on the porch, and then just houses. On a Saturday morning the sidewalks would be choked solid with black people in from the country. The county was seventy-percent black in those days, and a stranger driving through might well have thought he'd stumbled on Africa—dressed-up blacks all swapping the news. That was well before the local whites had heard blacks were miserable, and even now I'll have to say nothing ever gave a better imitation of relishing life than those shining faces.

But this was Friday and, though a few farmers were already lined up with trucks of tobacco ready to sell, I cut a clear path to the library door. In the years right after my parents died, that one bright room of worn shellacked books had been a real rescue-ship for me. Miss Mabel Davis, the spinster librarian, was deaf as a biscuit but had the knack of knowing what book you needed on any given day and leading you to it, with no grins or cooing. Right as she always was in her choice, her face and tight body also served notice that this long job of improving your mind and bracing your soul against oncoming life was no daisy hunt for rich white sissies but rough steady labor. (I recall her with even more gratitude now whenever I see a television culture-host, all oiled and alluring, promising easy profit from books. No wonder nobody reads more than drug labels or whore's revelations.)

That day when she saw me, Miss Mabel just said "I thought you'd quit" and turned back to mending torn pages with tape that her long tongue licked in slow frowning stripes.

In the years with Gaston, I'd slacked off here and at the bookmobile. You didn't abandon Miss Mabel but once. I was on my own now, to find my cure like a dog in the woods. So I went toward *Fiction*, the dangerous aisle. Miss Mabel was liable to veto you there. *Forever Amber* was still a few years down the road, but there were already plenty of novels you'd better not try to check out until you were married. She'd refused *Grapes of Wrath* to a girl in my grade the year before. I searched the historical novels first but had read most of those more than once already. In a few more minutes, I'd begun to believe I could never sit still long enough to read again. Just the sour-milk smell of old paper and glue made me think books were one more comfort ruined by Gaston. I turned to leave and there was Miss Mabel, bearing down on me fast with a big green book.

She held it out in both hands. "You've never had this" (she always spoke of *having* a book). Her eyes were bright as icepicks.

I took it—*Moll Flanders* by Daniel Defoe. I'd had *Robinson Crusoe* half a dozen times but had never known of this. I said "No ma'm" and checked it out to please her. It was still by my bed unopened when I left. Not till twenty years later did I find another copy, and by then it was too late to ask Miss Mabel if she'd offered me consolation or a warning that hot clear day.

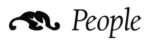 *People*

Jonathan Daniels

The contrasts and contradictions among North Carolina's landscapes are surpassed by those among its people. As this essay by Raleigh editor and author Jonathan Daniels asserts, North Carolinians are humble but also proud, poor but also rich, riven by regional loyalties yet unified.

Daniels himself was one of North Carolina's more fascinating citizens. A vigorous critic, he was also a staunch defender of his native state and exerted a strong influence on its politics and race relations. Born in Raleigh, he grew up on the *News and Observer*, a newspaper edited by his father, Josephus Daniels, and in time succeeded his father as editor. He also served as administrative assistant and press secretary to President Franklin Roosevelt. In addition, he was the author of more than fifteen books.

This essay appeared as the preface to *North Carolina: A Guide to the Old North State*, published by the Writers' Project of the Works Progress Administration and reissued by the University of North Carolina Press in 1939.

✑ As old William Byrd of Virginia told it, the line between North Carolina and Virginia was drawn across the map with much bickering and boozing. And when the line between the two Carolinas was drawn, legend insists that the South Carolina commissioners, being low-country gentlemen, were concerned with little more than keeping Charleston in South Carolina. Between the lines, between William Byrd's aristocratic contempt and the Charleston gentlemen's aristocratic unconcern, was left an area which for years on end rejoiced in the generalization that it was a vale of humility between two mountains of conceit. The generalization is useful, as most generalizations are. A modicum of truth lies in it, a persisting modicum, borne out in the report of a modern North Carolinian that among his State's neighbors there were only two classes of people, those who never had worn shoes and those who made you feel that you never had. His report is important as reflecting, in a North Carolina recently more proud than humble, a continuing conviction that one man is as good as another and that if you don't believe it he'll show you he's a damn sight better. . . .

Such a generalization certainly can indicate nothing about the fact that between the fishermen of Manteo and the men in the coves beyond Murphy there are at least three areas, different not only in the geography of Coastal Plain, Piedmont, and Mountain Regions, but different in the men and their preoccupations within them. Over roads and taxes, representation and offices, they have fought and quarreled and still fight and quarrel. The East, which once angrily insisted on political preference because it paid most of the taxes, now resists the Piedmont, which today does most of the paying. The greater part of the tobacco crop is raised in the East but all tobacco is manufactured in the Piedmont, and growers have shouted in anger both at tobacco prices and corporation politics. The East, conventional old agricultural plantation South of cash crops, Negro labor, and a straight Democratic ticket, remains socially conservative while it grows politically liberal. The Piedmont is the New South, up-and-coming, in which the cleavages of industry have flung up, out of the same small farmer class, the class-conscious worker and the property-conscious millionaire. And beyond them both the Mountain Region, still politically divided in memory of Union and Confederate division in the War between the States, remains more divided too in its desire for industry like the Piedmont's and preoccupation with its precipitate earth—rich, if sometimes difficult, for farming for living, and magnificent in its appeal to those able to come up from the physically undramatic lowlands. . . .

The East remains expansive, leisurely, interminably and excellently conversational, concerned with good living, devoted to pleasure, politically fixed but also politically philosophical. Perhaps the absence of any large cities has contributed to the fact that the easterner's neighborliness is little short of Gargantuan. Gregarious in an area not thickly settled, he finds it a trifle to go a hundred miles for a dance—and found it a trifle even when traveling meant trains and not the simplicity of automobile movement. His social life is restricted to no county or town. His "social set" is a whole population. . . .

The Piedmont is another land. It has always been a more serious-minded land. Somehow, the Episcopalians, though they are relatively few in number, seem to have marked the East, not as a church but as a people. In contrast, the Piedmont seems more directly to have grown from the stern spirits of the Quakers of Guilford, the Moravians of Forsyth, the Calvinists of Mecklenburg, the ubiquitous Baptists, and that practical Methodism from which the Dukes emerged. The plantation disappeared at the fall line. Labor became increasingly white. Leisure was less highly regarded, and practical concerns were paramount above philosophy, even above pleasure. Furthermore, where there was little Negro labor, there was water falling in the streams. And, long before the hydroelectric plants of Duke, it did not fall in vain. Hard-working, hard-headed men, with no foreknowledge of the inevitable change in relationship from money and land to money and machinery, attached themselves and their region to the change. Doing so long ago, they took the Carolina Piedmont into the direct stream of modern mechanical America and built the Piedmont in North Carolina into an area less distinguished for its differences from than its similarities to American industrial areas elsewhere. Its people are stirring or struggling. Wealth here has more sharply stratified society than in the older and more aristocratic East. But unlike some other industrial areas, its people are homogeneous. There are more foreign corporations than there are foreign workers. . . .

Perhaps the mountains meet the Piedmont in those towns where folk have come from the difficulties of scratching a living out of the steep sides of tough hills to the promised ease and regularity and generosity of the mills. The meeting has not always been a happy one. Sometimes it has been as violent as might be expected in the collision of the Elizabethan and electricity. The mountain man is by no means so quaint as some of the novelists have made him. His isolation is seldom so complete as it has been pictured; indeed, some sentimentalists spend themselves weeping over its disappearance. There are movies in every mountain town. Good roads run into a great many mountain coves. The boys and girls have gone out of the valleys to the schools. And now a good many simple mountaineers are waiting in hopefulness for some simple tourists. But the characteristics of the mountaineer remain. An individual may emerge from isolation swiftly, but a people does not immediately lose the characteristics created by long dwelling apart. The tourist is now to be welcomed, but to come to trust the stranger wholly is a more gradual process. . . . The divided mountaineers in the War between the States received the undivided and indistinguishable attentions of undisciplined bands of soldiers on both sides. . . . The antagonism . . . was more personal and immediate than elsewhere. There the division between the Union and the Confederacy might be no wider than the creek between two men's houses. A man learned to trust in himself, to share his deeper thinking slowly, to welcome warily, to mind his own business, and to vote as his granddaddy fought. He still does.

But to reduce the North Carolinian to three North Carolinians is only the first step in the reduction of generalization to particular fact. There are diverse men among mountaineers. Certainly there are plenty of different types and classes and people in the Piedmont. In the East they are a different folk who fish on Harkers Island from those who plant peanuts in Bertie. . . .

There are, however, in North Carolina interesting groups which, without losing the characteristics of section, yet create a unity that—beyond the uniformity of taxes and laws—may very well be called North Carolina. Strongest of all, perhaps, is the alumni of the University of North

Carolina. This of course does not mean the body of enthusiasts articulate over football. Far more importantly it means a group of men in every section of the State who have something more than a provincial's sense of the meaning of his native land. From Battle and Winston through Alderman and Venable and Graham and Chase to another Graham, a series of able presidents has made the institution in a very real sense the center for an aristocracy of intelligence that in half a century has transformed the State. In no sense are these men everywhere in North Carolina steadily agreed on the directions that the State should take. Personal and sectional interests move them as they do other men. But in a broad and diverse State they know each other and have together a sense of the importance of their university and the schools that lead to its doors. They were chiefly responsible for North Carolina's educational advance. They are responsible now for their university's high integrity in freedom. And that institution, more than the capital at Raleigh, is the center for the progressive idealism of the State.

The university at Chapel Hill serves as a symbol for unity in aspiration as do few other institutions in the country. Sometimes regarded with suspicion, sometimes attacked with bitterness, the university nevertheless is more often held in an almost pathetic affection by the State. North Carolina was so long in ignorance, so long in poverty! Its people today are restless in the consciousness of their former stagnation. Chapel Hill, no longer remote, embodies their aspiration that the vale may become the mountain (if, indeed, already it has not!)—that the inconsiderable people between the two aristocracies may yet accomplish a greater destiny than either.

A Well-Shaped, Clean-Made People

John Lawson

Explorer-historian John Lawson's observations of Indians in colonial North Carolina are keenly written and full of interesting detail. This account, excerpted from his 1709 book, *A New Voyage to Carolina*, reminds us that the Indians' use of tobacco predated the coming of white settlers. Like many Europeans in the New World, Lawson viewed Indians as "noble savages." In an ironic twist of fate, Lawson was killed by the Tuscarora tribe in the early days of their war against whites in 1711.

🔗 The *Indians* of North-*Carolina* are a well-shap'd clean-made People, of different Staturies, as the *Europeans* are, yet chiefly inclin'd to be tall. They are a very streight People, and never bend forwards, or stoop in the Shoulders, unless much overpower'd by old Age. Their Limbs are exceeding well-shap'd. As for their Legs and Feet, they are generally the handsomest in the World. Their Bodies are a little flat, which is occasion'd, by being laced hard down to a Board, in their Infancy. This is all the Cradle they have, which I shall describe at large elsewhere. Their Eyes are black, or of a dark Hazle; The White is marbled with red Streaks, which is ever common to these People, unless when sprung from a white Father or Mother. Their Colour is of a tawny, which would not be so dark, did they not dawb themselves with Bears Oil, and a Colour like burnt Cork. This is begun in their Infancy, and continued for a long time, which fills the Pores, and enables them better to endure the Extremity of the Weather. They are never bald on their Heads, although never so old, which, I believe, proceeds from their Heads being always uncover'd, and the greasing their Hair (so often as they do) with Bears Fat, which is a great Nourisher of the Hair, and causes it to grow very fast. Amongst the Bears Oil (when they intend to be fine) they mix a certain red Powder, that comes from a Scarlet Root which they get in the hilly Country, near the Foot of the great Ridge of Mountains, and it is no where else to be found. They have this Scarlet Root in great Esteem, and sell it for a very great Price, one to another. The Reason of its Value is, because they not only go a long way for it, but are in great Danger of the *Sinnagars* or *Iroquois*, who are mortal Enemies to all our *Indians*, and very often take them Captives, or kill them, before they return from this Voyage. The *Tuskeruros* and other *Indians* have often brought this Seed with them from the Mountains; but it would never grow in our Land. With this and Bears Grease they anoint their Heads and Temples, which is esteem'd as ornamental, as sweet Powder to our Hair. Besides, this Root has the Virtue of killing Lice, and suffers none to abide or breed in their Heads. For want of this Root, they sometimes use *Pecoon* [probably Pecan]-Root, which is of a Crimson Colour, but it is apt to die the Hair of an ugly Hue.

Their Eyes are commonly full and manly, and their Gate sedate and majestick. They never walk backward and forward as we do, nor contemplate on the Affairs of Loss and Gain; the things which daily perplex us. They are dexterous and steady both as to their Hands and Feet, to Admiration. They will walk over deep Brooks, and Creeks, on the smallest Poles, and that without any Fear or Concern. Nay, an *Indian* will walk on the Ridge of a Barn or House and look down the Gable-end, and spit upon the Ground, as unconcern'd, as if he was walking on *Terra firma*. In Running, Leaping, or any such other Exercise, their Legs seldom miscarry, and give them a Fall; and as for letting any thing fall out of their Hands, I never yet knew one Example. They are no Inventers of any Arts or Trades worthy mention; the Reason of which I take to be, that they are not possess'd with that Care and Thoughtfulness, how to provide for the Necessaries of Life, as the *Europeans* are; yet they will learn any thing very soon. I have known an *Indian* stock Guns better than most of our *Joiners*, although he never saw one stock'd before; and besides, his Working-Tool was only a sorry Knife. I have also known several of them that were Slaves to the *English*, learn Handicraft-Trades very well and speedily. I never saw a Dwarf amongst them, nor but one that was Hump-back'd. Their Teeth are yellow with Smoaking Tobacco, which both Men and Women are much addicted to. They tell us, that they had Tobacco amongst them, before the *Europeans* made any Discovery of that Continent. It differs in the Leaf from the sweet-scented, and *Oroonoko*, which are the Plants we raise and cultivate in *America*. Theirs differs likewise much in the Smell, when green, from our Tobacco, before cured. They do not use the same way to cure it as we do; and therefore, the Difference must be very considerable in Taste; for all Men (that know Tobacco) must allow, that it is the Ordering thereof which gives a Hogoo [relish] to that Weed, rather than any Natural Relish it possesses, when green. Although they are great Smokers, yet they never are seen to take it in Snuff, or chew it.

☙ An Unquieted Passion for Adventure

Robert E. Lee

North Carolina's jagged coast, treacherous ocean currents, and shifting channels made its hidden inlets a perfect refuge for eighteenth-century pirates. Not every coastal resident thought the pirates were evil, as this profile of Blackbeard reveals. A century and a half later, the pirates' elusive seamanship would be a model for southern sailors trying to run the Union blockade and keep the Confederacy alive.

This account of Blackbeard's life was taken from the *Dictionary of North Carolina Biography* and was written by Dr. Robert E. Lee, a law professor at Wake Forest University who also authored a 1975 biography of Blackbeard.

☙ Blackbeard the Pirate, picturesque colonial pirate, is usually said to have been born in Bristol, England. The circumstances of his early life are not known. Pirates rarely wrote about themselves or their families: each hoped to acquire a vast fortune and return to his former home without having tarnished his family name.

Because pirates tended to adopt one or more fictitious surnames while engaging in piracy, there is no absolute certainty of Blackbeard's real surname. In all the records made during the period in which he was committing his sea robberies, he was identified as either Blackbeard or Edward Teach. Numerous spellings of the latter name include Thatch, Thack, Thatche, and Theach, but Teach is the form most commonly encountered, and most historians have identified him by that name.

Captain Charles Johnson (recently thought to be a pseudonym for Daniel Defoe), a recognized authority on the pirates of the era, states emphatically in *A General History of the Robberies and Murders of the Most Notorious Pyrates*, originally published in 1724, that Edward Teach sailed for some time out of Jamaica on the ships of privateers during Queen Anne's War and that "he had often distinguished himself for his uncommon boldness and personal courage."

Sometime in 1716, Teach transferred the base of his operations from Jamaica to New Providence in the Bahama Islands. He served an apprenticeship under Captain Benjamin Hornigold, who was the fiercest and ablest of all pirates regularly operating out of the island of New Providence. Jointly they captured and looted a number of large merchant vessels. Having amassed a sizeable fortune and recognizing that the profitable days of piracy were nearing an end, Hornigold in early 1718 retired from piracy and took up the honest life of a planter on New Providence. He took full advantage of the king's pardon when Woodes Rogers arrived in Nassau on 27 July 1718 as the newly appointed governor of the Bahama Islands.

Teach converted a large French ship, *Concord*, which he and Captain Hornigold had captured, into a pirate ship of his own design. He renamed her the *Queen Anne's Revenge* and mounted upon her forty guns. The vessel was eventually manned by a crew of three hundred, some of whom had been members of her crew when she sailed under the French flag.

Most men of this period did not wear beards, but Teach discovered that he could grow a coarse, coal-black beard that covered the whole of his face. He allowed his monstrous mane to grow to an extravagant length, and he was accustomed to braiding it into little pigtails, tied with ribbons of various colors. As a finishing touch before a battle, he tucked under the brim of his hat fuses that would burn at the rate of a foot an hour, the curling wisps of smoke from which added to the frightfulness of his appearance. Across his shoulders he wore a sling with two or three pistols hanging in holsters, like a bandolier. In the broad belt strapped around his waist was an assortment of pistols and daggers and an oversized cutlass. Teach's deliberately awesome appearance in battle array had its effect. When ferociously attacked, the crews of many merchant ships surrendered without any pretense of a fight.

Near the end of May 1718, when Teach was at the high tide of his piratical career, he and his armed flotilla of five or six vessels appeared outside the entrance to the harbor of Charleston, S.C., and blockaded the busiest and most important port of the southern colonies. All vessels, inbound or outbound, were stopped and looted. Teach demanded and received from the governor of South Carolina and his council a chest of medicine. Without the firing of a single gun, the pirate king reduced to total submission the proud and militant people of South Carolina.

After the daring and bizarre blockade of Charleston, Teach and his small fleet sailed northward up the Atlantic into what is today commonly known as Beaufort Inlet, for a general disbanding of the crew of about four hundred men: Teach knew the "golden age of piracy" was nearing its end.

Sometime in June 1718, Blackbeard and at least twenty members of his crew passed through Ocracoke Inlet, N.C., entered Pamlico Sound, and headed for the town of Bath on the Pamlico River fifty-odd miles from the Atlantic Ocean. There they received from Governor Charles Eden a "gracious pardon" pursuant to proclamation from the king of England, intended to suppress piracy.

Teach acquired a home in Bath and, for a while, lived the life of a gentleman of leisure. He lost little time in selecting his fourteenth bride, a girl who was about sixteen years of age and the daughter of a Bath County planter. Governor Eden performed the marriage ceremony. But Teach had an unquieted passion for adventure. He was soon, once again, pirating on the high seas and bringing back to Bath his spoils.

Ocracoke Inlet was Blackbeard's favorite anchorage. All oceangoing vessels bound for or leaving settlements in northeastern North Carolina passed through this inlet, and he was usually to be found on the sound side of the southern tip of Ocracoke Island. His crew, however, was greatly reduced; his experienced officers and fighting men of former days were no longer with him, because there was no profit in associating with him unless he was actively engaged in looting vessels. It was here that Blackbeard's death occurred in a famous hand-to-hand battle with Lieutenant Robert Maynard, who had been sent by Governor Alexander Spotswood of Virginia to capture the pirate and his treasure.

Maynard ordered Blackbeard's head severed from his body and suspended from the bowsprit of one of Maynard's two armed vessels. The rest of Blackbeard's corpse was thrown overboard. The head of Blackbeard would be proof irrefutable that Maynard and his crew had slain the pirate chieftain, enabling them to collect the reward of one hundred pounds sterling offered by the Colony of Virginia.

～ *Tar on Daniel Boone's Heels*

Joe Knox

We usually don't think of Indian fighter Daniel Boone as a pacifist Quaker, but he was raised as one. His family came south from Pennsylvania to settle in the Yadkin River basin of North Carolina about 1751, when Daniel was seventeen years old. Many people think of him as a Kentucky explorer and Missouri frontiersman but not as a Tar Heel, though he lived in North Carolina longer than he lived anywhere else. This account of his North Carolina days appeared in the *Greensboro Daily News* of February 29, 1976, as part of a report by Joe Knox on citizen efforts to have North Carolina's Daniel Boone Trail designated as historic.

～ North Carolina claims a number of notable firsts in our nation's history, but one that has been all but overlooked is the "first" accounted for by Daniel Boone.

More than any other single person, he moved young America's frontier west of the Appalachian Mountains with his pioneering exploratory probes into the wilderness.

By most popular reckoning, Boone belongs to Kentucky. He "discovered" Kentucky, and Kentuckians won't let you forget it. They have preserved Daniel Boone by community name, artifacts, memorabilia and monuments such that you cannot very well escape his 200-year-old presence.

But in North Carolina we seem to have ignored the Daniel Boone who grew to manhood in the Yadkin River Valley near Statesville. He spent nearly half of his life here, and in fact did not settle west of the mountains until he was 41.

Daniel Boone was a North Carolinian long before he was a Kentuckian.

He was born in 1734 near what is now Reading, Pa., and came south with his English Quaker family in 1751 during a general resettlement of English, Germans, Scotch and Irish from the north into the Yadkin and Catawba Valleys of North Carolina.

He grew up on Bear Creek, a western tributary of the Yadkin, and in

1756 married Rebecca Bryan, daughter of Morgan Bryan, who had founded a colony of Pennsylvania Quakers on banks of the Yadkin.

In time he was to count Rebecca as being one-third of his recipe for happiness: "A good gun, a good horse, and a good wife." She was known to be a courageous pioneering woman, an ideal mate for her wanderlusting husband.

But early in the marriage, she upset one of his plans and thereby may have altered the course of American history. Soon after Florida became a British territory in 1756, Boone went down there to look at the warm country, and he liked it so well he decided to settle there.

He reckoned without Rebecca. She would not budge from the Boone homestead in the Yadkin Valley, and Daniel looked elsewhere for his Promised Land.

He did a little farming in the decade to follow, but his great love was hunting, and on one of his longer hikes, in 1767, he wandered into the Kentucky territory. In a better organized expedition in 1769–71, he explored the new country thoroughly and, in 1773, attempted to establish a colony there but was driven away by Indian attacks.

Then just two years later, his credentials as a frontiersman well established, Boone left his Yadkin Valley home for the trip that was forever to imprint his name on American history. Employed by Judge Richard Henderson and the Transylvania Land Company, he led a band of 30 armed men on a trail-blazing expedition across the Blue Ridge Mountains into Tennessee and Kentucky over a route to become famed as the Wilderness Road.

Boone and his little band founded the community of Boonesborough on the Kentucky River. Within weeks they were joined by Henderson and more pioneers in search of fortunes west of the mountains. Before the year had ended, Boone returned to North Carolina for his family, and this time Rebecca was persuaded to move.

Now in the prime of life, Boone was famous all over the land. A book about his exploits, "Discovery, Settlement and Present State of Kentucky," (1784) by John Filson was widely read. He became an international celebrity from verses written about him by Lord Byron in the epic poem, "Don Juan."

Boone was to go on to many more pioneering adventures and make other contributions toward the building of America, but nothing he did later matched the significance of carving the Wilderness Road across the mountains.

In North Carolina it followed roughly what is now Highway 115 from a point north of Statesville to what is now Wilkesboro. From there it went nearly along the route now taken by U.S. 421 up the mountain to Deep Gap, then to Boone and on beyond the continental divide. Traces of the Wilderness Road are now evident only to the most diligent history buffs.

Boone showed the way, and over the decades to follow, thousands of pioneers used the trail to find a new life in country drained by the Mississippi River.

They were Anglo-Saxon settlers of Tennessee, Arkansas, Texas, Missouri, southern Ohio, Illinois, Indiana and Kentucky, and their names are intimately familiar to residents of present-day Western Piedmont North Carolina—Daniel Boone country—because this is where they came from.

Carl W. Ramsey, historian of Hillsborough, . . . says there is good evidence that . . . some of the North Carolinians who followed the Daniel Boone Trail to Kentucky, went on to settle in territories just to the west, (Indiana and Illinois) and were forebears of Thomas Hart Benton, William Jennings Bryan and Adlai Stevenson.

Ramsey's son, the late Robert W. Ramsey, professor of history at Appalachian State University, wrote his doctoral dissertation on pioneer settlers of the Yadkin and Catawba River basin. Published in 1964 by the University of North Carolina Press under the title, "Carolina Cradle," it is an exhaustive study of people who migrated from northern colonies between 1747 and 1762 in search of cheap, abundant, fertile land.

The book tells exactly who these people were and where they settled, often on lands granted by the King of England. . . .

Many of these settlers stayed put in this Carolina Cradle; but families were broken as sons and daughters and other relatives, seeking ever-more open space, not wanting to wait out inheritances, took to the Wilderness Road to seek fortunes west of the mountains.

The fact that so many of them not only settled in Middle America but were influential in eventually bringing these new territories into the United States, makes the Boone Trail of national importance.

❧ A Roaring, Rollicking Fellow

Robert V. Remini

Though controversy continues over whether Andrew Jackson was born in North Carolina or South Carolina, there is no dispute over the fact that he spent much of his youth in North Carolina, studied law in Salisbury, and practiced law in the state before moving to Tennessee. This account of his

North Carolina days was condensed from *Andrew Jackson*, a 1966 biography by Robert V. Remini.

🔊 The election had been as filthy as presidential elections are ever likely to get. It set a record for character assassination, scurrility, and unspeakable vulgarity. Both men seeking the high office paid a fearful price for their ambition. One of them, the sixty-year-old Andrew Jackson, watched in agony as his wife reeled under the assaults upon her character that daily spewed forth from the public prints. One day, as he sat in his home in Tennessee reading a newspaper, he spotted a paragraph that had a neatly-drawn hand pointing to the opening words. As he scanned the first line he paled; then, in a sudden, uncontrolled burst of emotion he broke down in tears, and his body shook with grief. His wife, Rachel, entered the room at that moment and, seeing his distress, asked him what was wrong. Jackson pointed to the offending newspaper. "Myself I can defend," he said. "You I can defend; but now they have assailed even the memory of my mother." Rachel picked up the paper and stared at the incredible words. "General Jackson's mother was a COMMON PROSTITUTE," it read, "brought to this country by the British soldiers! She afterward married a MULATTO MAN, with whom she had several children, of which number General JACKSON IS ONE!!!"

It may seem strange that General Andrew Jackson, hero of the War of 1812 and the courageous soldier boy of the American Revolution, could respond with tears to the lying words of a vicious newspaper editor. It would have been more characteristic had he stood up and roared his rage, summoned the vile penman to the field of honor, and there avenged his mother's name with a well-placed bullet; for Jackson did have a monumental temper, which when roused could hurl itself with fearful fury against those who displeased him. . . .

Some said the temper was to be expected in a redheaded man who had "so much genuine Irish blood in his veins;" except that it was not Irish exactly; it was Scotch-Irish. His father and mother had come from Carrickfergus, an old town on the northeastern coast of Ireland, about ten miles from Belfast. His father, also named Andrew, was the son of a well-to-do linen weaver, and had migrated to America in 1765, with his wife, Elizabeth Hutchinson, and two sons: Hugh, who was two years old, and Robert, who was six months old. On arrival, the family headed straight for the Waxhaws, a settlement approximately 160 miles northwest of Charleston, South Carolina, where Elizabeth's sisters were living with their husbands. This region straddled North and South Carolina and was watered by the Waxhaw Creek, a branch of the Catawba River that ran through the fertile land. The settlement was ringed by a jungle of piny woods. Near the edge of this waste, the Jacksons settled on a tract of two hundred acres, and for two years the father struggled to improve the sour land. He cleared some fields, brought in a late crop the first year, and built a cabin—to no avail. He died suddenly in February 1767 at the age of twenty-nine, leaving two boys and a pregnant wife.

A rude farm wagon ferried the body to the Waxhaw churchyard where it was buried. Elizabeth, in no condition to return to her own house after the funeral, went to the house of her sister, Mrs. Jane Crawford, whose husband was the most prosperous of the inlaws. A few days later, the shock of her husband's death brought on labor pains, and Elizabeth gave birth to her third son on March 15, 1767. She named him Andrew after her dead husband.

A controversy of sorts exists about whether Andrew Jackson was born in North or South Carolina. (It has also been suggested that he was born either abroad or at sea, but there is no validity to these theories.) The argument for North Carolina rests on the claim that Elizabeth did not go to the Crawford house after the funeral but went instead to the home of her brother-in-law, George McKemey, who lived on the North Carolina side of the Waxhaws. Jackson, himself, always believed he was born in Crawford's house, which was about a mile from the "Carolina road of the Waxhaw Creek." This would place his birth in South Carolina, and this is what most historians accept.

For the first ten or twelve years of his life, Andrew was raised in the Crawford home. He attended several schools in the Waxhaws settlement. . . . His mother, a pious Irish lady, always hoped he would someday become a clergyman of the Presbyterian Church, and she was buttressed in her hope by the fact that her young son was extremely bright and could read at a very early age. But young Andrew gave few indications that he was headed for the ministry—quite the opposite. . . .

At Humphries' school, Andrew learned to read, write, and cast accounts. He later told a biographer that he also studied "the dead languages," by which he presumably meant Latin and Greek. Not that acquaintance with the classical languages ever particularly evinced itself in his correspondence or writings except for some legal phrases which any lawyer would know. Since he was not especially given to books he was a badly-informed man all of his life. His spelling was grotesque and his use of the English language demonstrated considerable contempt for its rules. Still, he was frequently eloquent and persuasive both in speech and writing. Indeed, when left to his own syntax, he was often powerfully expressive. . . .

The fighting and misery of the Revolutionary conflict came to the Waxhaws late in the spring of 1780 when British commander Lieutenant-Colonel Banastre Tarleton with a force of three hundred horsemen surprised a detachment of patriot soldiers, killing 113 and wounding 150. Because many bodies were found broken and mangled, with a dozen or more wounds inflicted on some of them, the engagement was called a massacre, and Tarleton a butcher. Survivors were taken to the Waxhaws meeting house, which had been converted into a hospital, and were tended by Mrs. Jackson and her two sons.

All that summer there were alarms of troop movements of the "murderous tories." Andrew and his brother, Robert, accompanied the patriots on several expeditions, and were present at the attack on the British post of Hanging Rock, where the Americans would surely have gained a victory if they had not paused to drink captured rum. On this expedition the Jackson boys rode with Colonel Davie. Andrew was thirteen, and while it is unlikely he did more than just attend the troops and carry messages, he may have watched and studied Davie as the commander conducted the campaign. Like the future General Jackson, Davie was bold in planning his moves, yet cautious in their execution. . . .

On the sixteenth of August, 1780, American patriots in the South sustained a crushing defeat at Camden by General Charles Cornwallis. Following the victory, Cornwallis turned his army toward the Waxhaws. For the next year, the Carolina countryside was one vast charnel house of butchered Tories and patriots. It was no longer a revolution, but a civil war, with brother fighting brother, father against son, and neighbor killing neighbor. . . .

Following one minor engagement, in which British dragoons sent Americans scurrying, Andrew and his brother took refuge in the house of Thomas Crawford. A Tory neighbor informed the British of their whereabouts. The house was soon surrounded, and the boys were taken prisoner. The soldiers began to pillage the house, smashing furniture, breaking glasses, and tearing clothes into rags. While this was in progress the officer in command of the party ordered Andrew to clean his jackboots which were encrusted with mud. Andrew refused. According to one biographer, his refusal was flung out with the words, "Sir, I am a prisoner of war, and claim to be treated as such." Whereupon the officer lifted his sword and aimed it straight at Andrew's head. Instinctively, the young man ducked and raised his left hand in time to break the full force of the blow. He received a deep gash on his head, however, and another on his hand—two souvenirs of British sentiment he took with him through life. . . .

The two brothers, along with twenty other prisoners, were later taken on horseback to Camden, a distance of forty miles. It was a long and painful journey for the wounded boys, made worse by the lack of food and water. . . . Thirteen British soldiers were eventually surrendered in return for the Jackson boys and five of their neighbors. Mrs. Jackson procured two horses, placing the dying Robert on one, and riding on the other herself. Poor Andrew had to walk the forty miles back home. Wearily, "he dragged his weak . . . limbs, bare-headed, barefooted, without a jacket; his only two garments torn and dirty." On the final leg of the journey, a cold, drenching rain lashed the trio. When they arrived home, the boys were put to bed. "In two days Robert Jackson was a corpse, and his brother Andrew a raving maniac."

His mother's nursing skill and the attention of a Dr. Tongue brought about Andrew's recovery, but it took several weeks of tireless care and devotion. Many months followed before he could be left to himself. With her son out of danger, this incredible woman set off with two other ladies from the Waxhaws to travel the 160 miles to Charleston, there to nurse the prisoners of war held in prison ships, some of whom were Mrs. Jackson's kinsmen. . . . A short time later, while visiting a relative, William Barton, who lived near Charleston, Elizabeth Jackson was taken ill with the cholera, or "ship fever" as it was called, and died after a short illness. She was buried in an unmarked grave. . . .

So, at the age of fourteen, Andrew was orphaned by the war. . . . In 1781, the same year Mrs. Jackson died, Cornwallis surrendered at Yorktown. Although Charleston continued to be occupied by the British for another fourteen months, the war was all but officially over. Several of Charleston's more socially prominent families waited for the British evacuation from the safe distance of the Waxhaws settlement, and while they waited Andrew took up with their sons and for a time led a wild and merry life: gambling, drinking, cockfighting and horse racing—mostly horse racing, a sport he could never resist and on which he lost more money than he could afford. . . .

In a moment of excessive repentance he determined to become a schoolteacher! His own education needed attention, but that did not trouble him. Once he made up his mind there was no stopping him. So for a year, possibly two, Andrew taught school in the Waxhaws country, and he diligently absorbed great chunks of knowledge the day before he passed them along to his students. However, for a fun-loving seventeen-year-old youngster, schoolteaching could not hold his attention for long. . . . For a "young man on the make" the legal profession held much promise, and Andrew was both young and "on the make."

In December, 1784, Andrew gathered his money and belongings and rode north to Salisbury, North Carolina, a distance of seventy-five miles from the Waxhaws, where he entered the law office of Spruce McCay to learn what he had decided would be his new profession. Salisbury was the seat of Rowan County and was situated in the midst of the red clay section of North Carolina. At the town's modest tavern, called the Rowan House, Andrew found quarters and the kind of company that cheered his exuberant spirits, especially after a long day of reading law at McCay's office. For the next two years, he diligently copied papers, ran errands, cleaned the rooms, and did all the other necessary things that supposedly prepared him for admission to the bar. Then, when the business of the day ended, Andrew took off with several other students, one of whom was John McNairy, and together they "burned up" the town. He was really good at this, achieving the rare distinction of being named the leader of all the rowdies and misfits in the community. Said one: "Andrew Jackson was the most roaring, rollicking, game-cocking, horse-racing, card-playing, mischievous fellow, that ever lived in Salisbury." Said another: "He did not trouble with the law-books much; he was more in the stable than in the office." . . .

Early in 1787, Andrew moved from Salisbury. Considering his prodigality, it is quite possible the people of the town made life so uncomfortable for him that he had to leave. Whatever the reason, he left McCay's establishment and spent six months at the office of Colonel John Stokes, one of the most brilliant men of the North Carolina bar. Stokes had lost a hand at Buford's Defeat. In its place, he wore a silver knob that he often banged down hard on a table to emphasize a point. Under the tutelage of this learned and slightly eccentric man, Jackson completed his legal training, and on September 26, 1787 appeared for examination before Judges Samuel Ashe and John F. Williams. Since they found him a man of "unblemished" moral character and one competent in the law they declared that he was authorized to practice as an attorney in the county courts of pleas and quarter sessions within the state of North Carolina.

But, as Jackson soon discovered, there was little law business for a young man of twenty, who was just beginning his profession. For the next year, he poked around Martinsville in Guilford County, North Carolina, staying with two friends who kept a store. He helped out in the establishment and in that way learned still another trade. He was good for business because people liked him and felt comfortable with him. Most agreed that he possessed that indefinable quality called presence. . . . His very appearance commanded attention. Straight and tall, he stood six feet one inch in his stockings. His face was long and thin, and his hair, reddish in color, was quite abundant and fell over his forehead, hiding in part the scar awarded him in the Revolution. The most striking characteristic of his face was his deep blue eyes—eyes that could blaze with such passion when he was aroused as to paralyze with fright those who were the objects of his wrath. . . .

These, then, are some of the bits and pieces that went into fashioning Jackson as a man and politician. And in 1788, politics was not very far from his thoughts. He had learned that his old friend, gaming companion, and fellow student of his Salisbury days, John McNairy, had been elected by the North Carolina legislature to be the Superior Court judge for the western district of the state, which stretched westward to the Mississippi River and had little colonies of settlers huddled along its several rivers. As judge, McNairy had authority to appoint the public prosecutor for the district, and Jackson now decided he wanted this job and prevailed on McNairy to give it to him. Another friend, Thomas Searcy, solicited the office of clerk of the court, and three or four other comrades, all lawyers, took it into their heads to go along too, thus rounding out a small band of young, energetic men who saw, or thought they saw, their future and fortune in the West. . . .

It was at this juncture in the history of North Carolina that Jackson, McNairy, and their friends were about to cross the mountains and head for Nashville. Early in the spring of 1788 they rendezvoused at Morganton, North Carolina. Each man was equipped with a horse, a few belongings, a gun, and a wallet containing letters from distinguished citizens of the old community to the settlers of the new. And off they went along the mountain trace, this unlikely crew of judge, prosecuting attorney, clerk, and lawyers. If nothing else, they would bring a massive dose of law to the West.

➣ Rejecting a Pernicious Custom

Michael G. Martin, Jr.

Boston's Sons of Liberty were not the only American patriots to protest the British tax on tea. News of the Boston Tea Party prompted a group of women from the area around the Albemarle Sound in northeastern North

Carolina to gather at Edenton for a tea party of their own. They pledged to stop drinking British tea and wearing clothes imported from England. It was among the earliest known instances of organized political activity by American women. For Penelope Barker, an organizer of the women's boy-cott—and a woman who had already known plenty of tragedy—the pro-test brought on added risks, as this profile by Michael G. Martin, Jr., in the *Dictionary of North Carolina Biography* makes clear.

 Penelope Barker, revolutionary patriot, was born in Edenton, Chowan County. Her parents were Samuel Padgett, physician and planter, and Elizabeth Blount, daughter of the prominent Chowan planter and political leader James Blount. Penelope had two sisters: Elizabeth, who married John Hodgson, a noted Edenton attorney; and Sarah, who married Joseph Eelbeck, a physician. While still in her teens, Penelope was shaken by a series of tragic blows. Within a year, death claimed her father and her sister Elizabeth. She quickly learned the meaning of responsibility, for the Hodgson household and Elizabeth's children, Isabella, John, and Robert, were placed in her care. In 1745, John Hodgson and Penelope Padgett were married. Two sons, Samuel (1746–55) and Thomas (1747–72), were born of this union. The marriage was a short one, however, for in 1747, Hodgson died.

Again Penelope was forced to assume heavy burdens: the care of five children and the management of the Hodgson plantations. A most eligible widow at nineteen, she soon attracted the attention of James Craven, local planter and political leader, and they were married in 1751. While no children were born of this union, the marriage did result in a sizeable increase in Penelope's wealth. When Craven died in 1755, his extensive estate passed entirely into her hands.

Penelope was only twenty-seven when James Craven died, and her beauty, coupled with her great wealth, attracted many suitors. One of the most prominent of these was widower Thomas Barker (1713–89), Eden-ton attorney and member of the assembly, who married Penelope in 1757. Three children were born to the Barkers, none of whom lived to reach the age of one year: little Penelope survived less than two months, Thomas less than nine, and Nathaniel less than ten. In 1761, Penelope was left to manage the household and plantations alone, for in that year Thomas Barker sailed for London to serve as agent for the North Carolina colony. As a result of the American Revolution and the British blockade of Ameri-can ports, he was forced to remain in England until early September 1778.

In contrast to most colonial wives, Penelope Barker was well accustomed to single-handedly managing her household and lands. Her character had been tempered by tragedy. She had borne five children and mothered her husbands' four others by previous marriages. By 1761 seven of these children had died, and in 1772 her son Thomas Hodgson died at the early age of twenty-five. The lone surviving child, Betsy Barker, also left Penelope's care through marriage to Colonel William Tunstall, a prominent planter of Pittsylvania County, Va.

As the colonial independence movement grew in intensity, with an increase in riots and other extralegal activities in opposition to British taxation, Penelope, because of her husband's position, probably realized as much as any other person in North Carolina the potential costs of such actions. Thus, her leadership of fifty-one Edenton women, on 25 Oct. 1774, in open opposition to Parliament's Tea Act of 1773 must have been well considered. The choice of a tea party as the form for such an action is not surprising. The tea party was in the colonies, as in Britain, the most socially acceptable of gatherings, often including both men and women. Meeting at the home of Elizabeth King, wife of an Edenton merchant, with Penelope Barker presiding, the ladies signed the following resolve: "We the Ladyes of Edenton, do hereby solemnly engage not to conform to ye pernicious Custom of Drinking Tea, or that we, the aforesaid Ladyes, will not promote ye wear of any manufacture from England, until such time that all Acts which tend to enslave this our Native Country shall be repealed." This episode might well have passed unnoticed by history if a caricature depicting the "Edenton Tea Party" had not appeared in the *Morning Chronicle and London Advertiser* on 16 Jan. 1775.

Following the Revolution, Penelope led a more subdued life in Edenton, finally welcoming the return of her husband in 1778 and mourning his passing in 1789. She outlived Barker another seven years and in 1796 was buried beside him in the Johnston family graveyard at Hayes Plantation, near Edenton. The only known portrait of Penelope Barker hangs in the Cupola House, Edenton.

✏ The Best, Wisest, and Purest

R. D. W. Connor

In its first sixty years of statehood, North Carolina was one of the most conservative—and least-developed—American states, largely because of the influence and political philosophy of Nathaniel Macon, whom Thomas Jefferson called "the last of the Romans." Macon was a strict Jeffersonian Democrat who believed the less government, the better. Though North Carolina needed ports, roads, bridges, and other internal improvements to promote commerce and economic development, Macon opposed public expenditures for those purposes, believing they would change southern society for the worse (and hasten the ultimate abolition of slavery). His considerable influence can be attributed to his simple honesty, personal integrity, and unwavering principles.

This profile of his life was excerpted from *Makers of North Carolina History*, by R. D. W. Connor of Wilson, who was himself a highly influential North Carolinian as a teacher, historian, and the first Archivist of the United States.

ᕙ In 1764 the General Assembly cut off the northeast corner of Granville county and formed a new county, called Bute. It was named in honor of an English nobleman, the Earl of Bute, who was a close friend of the King. When the Revolution broke out, Lord Bute was, of course, hostile to the Americans. So, in 1779, the Legislature changed the name of the county to Warren, in honor of the American patriot, General Joseph Warren, who was killed at the battle of Bunker Hill.

It was in this part of old Granville that Nathaniel Macon was born, December 17, 1758, . . . the youngest of eight children. When he was five years old, his father died, leaving his widow with a large family and very little property.

Nathaniel was such a bright, thoughtful boy that all the family agreed that he ought to be given a good education. His first teacher was Charles Pettigrew who taught an "old-field" school in the neighborhood. When Macon was fifteen he entered Princeton College, in New Jersey. The breaking out of the Revolution interrupted his studies there, and in 1776 he returned to North Carolina. For a little while he studied law, but did not like it and never received his license to practise. . . .

The war then seemed to be going against the patriots in the South. Macon thought it his duty to defend his country, so he enlisted in the army as a private. His comrades elected him as their captain, but he declined. During the years 1779 and 1780 he saw much hard fighting. He was at the fall of Fort Moultrie, the surrender of Charleston, the defeat at Camden, and with Greene during his terrible retreat across North Carolina in 1780.

While he was in the army, Macon was elected a member of the State Senate from Warren county. The first he heard of his election was a message from the Governor summoning him to attend the Legislature. Most men would have welcomed such a good excuse for leaving the army. But Macon was not like other men. He refused to leave. . . .

General Greene was much pleased at this spirited reply. But he told Macon that he could do the American cause more good as a member of the Legislature than as a soldier. In the army he was but one man; in the Legislature he might persuade the members to send hundreds of men to the army. And he could also tell the Legislature from his own experience how badly the army needed supplies and equipment. . . .

Macon's services in the Legislature were very useful in obtaining men and supplies for the army. He himself never entered the army again. He refused to accept any pay for his services as a soldier, for he declared that it was the patriot's duty to serve his country without being paid for it.

After the war Macon returned to his farm in Warren county. He called his plantation "Buck Spring," on account of a fine spring where the deer, which roamed his woods in great numbers, were accustomed to drink. In the midst of a splendid grove of oaks Macon built a small, simple house. Grouped around the house were several smaller buildings, called "offices," which were really rooms for his guests. On one side was the kitchen with its great fireplace tall enough for a man to stand erect in. The cooking was done in huge pots hung from hooks over the fire. In the distance were the cabins for the slaves, called the "quarters," and near them were the barns and stables.

Macon loved the country. He used to say that he did not want to live near enough to any man to see the smoke from his chimney or to hear his dog bark. His nearest neighbor lived five miles away. . . .

In his habits he was one of the simplest of men. He never changed his style of dressing. His clothes were made of plain, blue cloth in the style worn during the Revolution. He wore the best linen, a fine cambric stock, a fur hat with a brim, and top-boots into which he tucked his trousers. He was always neat in his person. . . .

One of his most frequent visitors was the famous John Randolph, of Virginia, who was Macon's life-long friend and companion. In 1819, when President Monroe made a tour of the Southern States, he made a special visit to Buck Spring to take part in one of Macon's famous fox chases. Macon was fond of company. He kept open house at Buck Spring and many guests came to share in his well-known hospitality.

Macon's public career began when he was elected to the State Senate in 1781; it lasted forty-two years. He was five times elected to the Legislature, twelve times to Congress, three times to the United States Senate, and once a delegate to the Convention to amend the State constitution. In Congress he was elected speaker of the House of Representatives three times and president of the Senate three times. He was also elected president of the North Carolina Constitutional Convention of 1835. . . .

In public office, though he held high and important places, Macon was as simple and plain as in his own home. He was a real democrat. Whenever the people understand any public question, he declared, they will decide it right. He would accept no offices except those to which he was elected by the people or by their representatives. Thomas Jefferson twice offered him a place in the President's cabinet, but both times he refused because it was not an office on which the people could vote. . . .

He was too honest to take credit for any act which was due to some one else. Once he presented a very able report to the United States Senate. Another senator, thinking that Macon wrote it, praised it very highly. "Yes," said Macon, "it is a good report; Senator Tazewell wrote it." Though he was as true as steel to his friends, he would not violate his public duty to please them. When he was speaker of the House of Representatives, he removed his dearest friend, John Randolph, from an important position because he thought another man could perform its duties better. Nor would he ever appoint any of his own relatives to public office.

Macon was not an orator. Indeed, he had but little patience with speech-making. A few plain, simple words, to explain any subject, were all he cared to hear. His own speeches were short and plain-spoken. The famous Thomas H. Benton, of Missouri, said that Macon "spoke more good sense while he was getting up out of his chair, and getting back into it, than many others did in long speeches."

While in Congress, Macon . . . opposed the famous Alien and Sedition laws, because they were against the liberty of the people and the freedom of the press. Aided by Randolph, he persuaded Congress to vote the money that enabled President Jefferson to purchase the Louisiana territory. He always voted against measures for internal improvements because, he said, the Constitution gave Congress no power to pass such measures. For the same reason he spoke and voted against a protective tariff. . . .

While Thomas Jefferson was President, some of the judges of the Supreme Court severely criticized him and his party. Jefferson and his friends were very angry. They planned to impeach one of the judges, remove him from office, and put one of the President's friends in his place. But they could not carry out this plan without Macon's help. He belonged to the same political party as the President, so the President's friends thought of course Macon would help them.

But Macon thought that it was a wicked scheme and he would have nothing to do with it. "Suppose," he said, "the judges had flattered the President. Would he then threaten them with punishment? Certainly not. And yet flattery is worse than abuse, and is more dangerous. If you would not punish them for the greater offense, why for the lesser?" . . . As nothing could be done without Macon's aid, the plan to impeach the judges failed.

Macon was a close reader of the Bible. In the Bible he read: "The days of our years are three score years and ten; and if by reason of strength they be four score years, yet is their strength labor and sorrow; for it is soon cut off, and we fly away." He resolved that, when he became three score and ten years of age, he would retire from public office and spend the remaining years of his life quietly at home.

When his seventieth birthday came he was a member of the United States Senate, and had two more years to serve before his term would come to its close. His friends urged him to remain in the Senate at least those two years. "Your health," they said, "is still good and your mind is as strong and clear as ever." "Yes," he replied, "my mind is clear enough for me to know that I ought to quit office before my mind quits me." So he wrote to the Legislature and resigned his office as senator, thanking the Legislature for its long confidence in him. At the same time he resigned as justice of the peace and as trustee of the University.

But Macon's services were needed in one more important event in North Carolina. The time had come when some changes were needed in the State constitution. It was decided, therefore, to hold a convention at Raleigh, in 1835, to consider what changes should be made. Many distinguished men were elected members of this convention. But when the convention met, all eyes turned at once to Nathaniel Macon for president, and he was unanimously elected.

Several important changes were made in the constitution. The people of Western North Carolina had long complained that the eastern part of the State had more than its share of members in the Legislature. Each county had two members without regard to its population. The West wished that the number of members for each county should depend upon its population. . . . Since 1776 the Legislature had met once every year; the convention changed the time of its meeting to once every two years. The right to vote was taken away from free negroes. In the future the governor was not to be elected by the Legislature, but by the people, and his term of office was changed from one to two years. . . .

More than once it looked as if the convention would break up in a quarrel. Then the aged Macon would rise from his seat, and with a few calm, patriotic words quiet the raging storm.

Macon died June 29, 1837, at Buck Spring. He himself selected the place for his grave. It was a barren ridge near the center of his plantation, and he selected it because he said it was too poor for any other use. He wished his grave to be marked by a pile of rough stones, which, he said, were good for nothing else. He himself directed the carpenter how to make his coffin, and paid him for it, because he wished to leave no debts to be paid after his death. The last few hours of his life were spent in conversation with his friends and relatives.

Many tributes have been paid to Macon's memory. President John Tyler said of him: "Nothing sordid ever entered into his imagination. He was a devoted patriot whose whole heart—and every corner of it—was filled with love of country." John Randolph said, in his will, Nathaniel Macon was "the best, wisest, and purest man I ever knew."

✑ A Prophet without Honor

Noel Yancey

Nathaniel Macon's opposite in political philosophy was Archibald Murphey, a staunch advocate of internal improvements that would help lift North Carolinians out of poverty. He was a reformer who campaigned for better transportation, schools, and prisons. He also sought legislative reapportionment to break the east's grip on public affairs by increasing representation from the Piedmont and west, where internal improvements were most needed. This account of Murphey's life was written by Noel Yancey, a veteran Associated Press correspondent assigned to Raleigh. It appeared in the September 1988 issue of the *Spectator*, a North Carolina magazine.

✑ "Visionary"—that's the word used most often in describing Archibald De Bow Murphey, one of North Carolina's greatest men. And like so many visionaries, he died in poverty and was buried in an unmarked grave.

Murphey has often been described as the "father of education and internal improvements" in North Carolina, and as a "prophet of a new era" who lived before his time.

Murphey was born around 1777 near the village of Milton in Caswell County. He was the son of Archibald Murphey, an influential local squire who bred fine horses and served as a colonel in the local militia and as a soldier in the Revolution.

The Murpheys provided their son with the best education available in North Carolina toward the end of the 18th century. After learning "the three R's" at home, he studied at Dr. David Caldwell's famed "log cabin college" in Guilford County before enrolling in the second class at the University of North Carolina, where he graduated with high distinction in 1799.

He remained at Chapel Hill as a tutor and instructor until 1801. Meanwhile, he began to study law and was admitted to the bar in 1802. He soon was regarded as an outstanding lawyer at a time when North Carolina had what is still regarded as a host of brilliant attorneys.

A man of slight stature and regular features, Murphey's face was brightened by a pair of strikingly handsome gray-blue eyes. He had a melodious voice and great personal charm, which prompted a fellow attorney to recall, "His handshake, even as a boy, left a pleasant memory."

Murphey's success as an attorney is demonstrated by the fact that by 1812 he had amassed enough of an estate to be considered a wealthy man. His plantation, the Hermitage, on the Haw River three miles south of Graham, had spread over 2000 acres. Its facilities included a grist mill, a distillery, cabins for some 50 slaves and a rambling plantation house that boasted a library containing more than 2000 volumes.

When Murphey went to the state Senate in 1812, he was obsessed with statistics which showed that North Carolina was among the poorest of the states, so poor in fact that many of its most enterprising citizens were leaving to seek their fortunes elsewhere. By 1815, Murphey said the number of emigrants had reached 200,000, including three future presidents of the United States: Andrew Jackson, James K. Polk and Andrew Johnson.

Between 1815 and 1823, Murphey laid down a five-part internal improvement program that called for opening up the state's major rivers—the Roanoke, Tar, Neuse, Yadkin, Catawba and Cape Fear—to navigation by dredging channels, clearing obstructions and digging canals. Murphey told the Senate his plan would end the state's commercial dependence on Virginia and South Carolina and would halt emigration by providing North Carolina farmers with a market for their products.

Even more ambitious was Murphey's plan for developing an educational system in the state. It called for the establishment of two or more primary schools in each county where children would learn the "three R's." The state would pay one-third of the cost of the school buildings and would pay the salaries of the teachers. For further education, he proposed the creation of 10 academies and the expansion of the University to continue the education of the brightest children. Families who could afford it would pay tuition for their children; for the poor, tuition would be free.

Murphey's other reform programs called for holding a convention to revamp the state's antiquated constitution to allow democratic government and to assure the state's western counties of equitable representation in the General Assembly, which was dominated by Easterners. He also proposed rewriting the state's brutal penal code, which allowed mutilation, branding, whipping and confinement in the stocks for minor offenses. In addition, he proposed the creation of state institutions for the insane and the deaf, and construction of a state penitentiary.

Most of the reforms Murphey advocated have since been adopted, but few of them came about during his lifetime. However, the General Assembly did pass in 1817 a bill creating a Board of Internal Improvement with Murphey as chairman, and later enacted a plan to finance the program. The board hired Hamilton Fulton, a capable English engineer, and agreed to pay him $6000 a year—twice what the governor received—to administer it.

After the internal improvements program got off to an auspicious start, the Panic of 1819 did it in. Hard hit by this depression, the people turned against any spending programs, and Fulton, who had once called Murphey's plan feasible, quit. He had become weary of being criticized because of his salary and because he was a foreigner, and he was tired of trying to carry out such an ambitious program with so little funding.

This panic also ruined Murphey financially. Murphey, who believed quite honestly that the internal improvements he proposed would revolutionize North Carolina's economy, invested heavily in stock of the Cape Fear, Haw, Deep and Yadkin River Navigation companies. He also bought large tracts of land along these rivers, confident that the value of his holdings would skyrocket.

Instead, the value of his holdings plummeted so precipitately that Murphey was left bankrupt. In fact, he was arrested and jailed for his debts, which the law then allowed. However, James A. Doakes, the sheriff of Guilford County where Murphey was arrested, refused to lock the door to Murphey's cell until the jailed attorney reminded the considerate lawman that a sheriff could wind up in jail if a prisoner escaped under such circumstances.

When Murphey died in 1832, his dreams for improving North Carolina appeared to be a lost cause. However, younger men such as Governor William Graham and Governor John Motley Morehead wouldn't let those dreams die. In 1838, an Internal Improvements Convention was held in Raleigh. Out of this meeting came the impetus to build plank roads. Then came the dream of a railroad across the state from Beaufort westward over the mountains to the markets of the Midwest, which was stymied by the outbreak of the Civil War.

There is a tombstone at Murphey's grave now; but the state has done little to honor the memory of Archibald De Bow Murphey. It would seem that he would rate at least a statue or other memorial on Capitol Square. The one honor that was bestowed on him was botched. The town of Murphy, the county seat of Cherokee County, was named in his honor, but his name was misspelled.

ॐ *Poetry Buys a Slave His Freedom*

Martha McMakin

The story of George Horton helps to document the aspirations of thousands of North Carolina blacks who were trapped in slavery before the Civil War. Most of them were condemned to lives of illiteracy, and the few who learned to read and write usually found it prudent to keep those skills hidden. George Horton was one of the luckier ones. His ability to read and write enabled him to win his freedom, first from demeaning work, later from bondage. After he was freed by the Michigan Cavalry in Chapel Hill, he went north to Philadelphia where he found a few patrons and eked out a living writing short stories based on Bible narratives. He died there in 1883.

This account of his life in North Carolina was written by Martha McMakin and appeared in the *Goldsboro News-Argus* of April 24, 1966.

ॐ The most popular figure on the University of North Carolina campus in the days before the Civil War was a slave who composed verses for lovelorn students to send to their sweethearts back home.

George Moses Horton, the Black Bard, was the first North Carolinian able to support himself with money earned from his writings.

The state's first Negro poet also has the distinction of being the first southern Negro to publish a book and the second Negro ever to publish in the United States.

The "Illiterate Genius," as he was called, was born in Northampton County about 1798, the property of William Horton who also owned George's mother and her nine other children.

At the age of six, the boy moved with his owner to a plantation in Chatham County, about ten miles from Chapel Hill.

Young George was put to work in the fields as a "cow-boy," work he found very disagreeable and which was no doubt boring to a young man with a quick mind and an ear for verse.

As he worked, he often paced his movements to the tunes of hymns he had learned in church and soon was putting new words to the old melodies.

Young Horton soon developed a passion to learn to read, and although state law forbade the education of slaves, he managed to scrape together a Methodist hymnal, a Bible and a Blue Back Speller and began his self-education.

With the help of white children who were sent to school, George mastered his letters, but the process was long and painful, especially since he was able to study only at night and on Sunday afternoons.

In his autobiography, Horton tells how he looked forward from one week to the next to Sundays when he could bring out all the scraps of paper he had found the week before and study the writing on them.

Although he learned to read without too much difficulty, writing came hard to the young man, so he recited his verses each night to someone in the "big house" who recorded them for him.

In 1815, William Horton decided to divide his slaves among his children. Lots were drawn and son James Horton fell heir to George. One of George's new duties as James' slave was to carry fruit to market in Chapel Hill. The students there became fond of the fun-loving Negro and encouraged him in his poetry writing.

Legend has it that James K. Polk, class of 1818, was one of the first to recognize Horton's talents.

Although his new owner was unaware of his accomplishments, George continued to compose and preserve his copies of his verses for several years. A few of these early poems were published in the old *Raleigh Register* and brought the poet considerable prestige in the county, but little money.

By 1829, at the age of 31, George had written enough poems to fill a small book. *The Hope of Liberty*, a collection of his works, was published that year by Joseph Gales and Sons of Raleigh.

Horton hoped to use the proceeds from the sale of the book to buy his freedom and to sail with other free Negroes to Africa and settle in Liberia. Unfortunately, the book was not a financial success, and its author was forced to return to the fields for three years.

In 1832, James Horton died, leaving his property, including his slaves, to his son, Hall Horton. Possessed of a keen eye for the dollar, Hall thought that writing poetry had ruined George as a field hand and referred to him as that "worthless nigger." George, taking advantage of his earlier experience at Chapel Hill, offered to pay his master 50 cents a day for his freedom if Hall would allow him to move to the university. Since Hall could hire two field hands for 50 cents per day, he gladly consented to George's plan.

Soon after arriving at the University, George became friends with President Joseph Caldwell who provided him with food and shelter. A Mrs. Caroline Lee Hentz, wife of a faculty member and poetess in her own right, helped Horton in his studies and the students in general adopted him as the campus legend.

As soon as his talents were discovered, George was commissioned to write love poems on behalf of the students who then sent them to their sweethearts in their own names.

In his *History of the University of North Carolina*, Dr. Kemp P. Battle writes that "When his employer was willing to pay 50 cents, the poem was generously gushing. Twenty-five cents procured one more lukewarm in passion." Many a young girl's heart beat faster at the sight of one of the poems composed by the Black Bard.

One of his poems, "Poet's Petition" was brought to the attention of Horace Greeley by a school teacher in Warrenton, a Miss Cheney, who had become interested in Horton's work and used her influence with her fiance, Greeley, to have the poems published in the *New York Tribune*. This poem, like so many by Horton, is a plea for freedom.

Bewailing mid the ruthless wave
I lift my feeble hand to thee
  Let me no longer be a slave,
But drop the fetters and be free.

Why will regardless Fortune sleep
Deaf to my penitential prayer
  Or leave the struggling bard to weep,
Alas, and languish in despair?

> He is an eagle void of wings,
> Aspiring to the mountain's height,
>   Yet in the vale aloud he sings
> For pity's aid to give him flight.
>
> Then listen all who never felt
> For fettered genius heretofore,
>   Let hearts of petrifaction melt,
> And bid the gifted Negro soar.

In a letter to Horace Greeley written from Chapel Hill on September 11, 1853, Horton petitioned the editor to free him from the "loathesome fetters", by purchasing Horton's freedom for $175. In return for his kindness, Horton promised to "endeavor to reward your generosity with my productions as soon as possible." Mr. Greeley did not respond.

Before long, George was making several dollars a day and was also flooded with gifts by admiring students. He is said to have been as well dressed as any student on campus as the result of having been given cast-off suits. Books were also acceptable gifts and the Bard's library came to include works by Milton, Virgil, and Shakespeare as well as Johnson, Walker and Sheridan's dictionaries.

Among the other gifts, the students also gave Horton such a love for drink that aside from the 50 cents each day for his master, almost all his money went for whiskey. George once said the students "fattened me into the belief that it would hang me on wings of new inspiration, which would waft me into regions of poetical perfection."

According to one of Horton's critics, the admiration of the UNC students and faculty caused Horton to become "intoxicated with his own cleverness which he tried to impress upon others." It is interesting to note that on more than one occasion Horton tried to prove his own genius.

On September 3, 1844, he wrote to the editor of a Boston paper asking that he "be allowed to submit some poetry (in order to) gratify your curiosity in resolving the problem whether a Negro has any genius or not." As testimony he offered this statement, that he "never had one day's schooling in all the course of my life. . . . I was early fond of hearing people read and by that means learned them in this book." The letter is signed: "George Horton, of colour."

Early in 1865, Michigan Cavalry Volunteers invaded Chapel Hill and quartered on the university campus. Horton welcomed the troops as his liberators and wrote for the soldiers as he had for the Carolina students. One of the officers, Captain Will H. S. Banks, took an interest in the poet and offered to take him north when the troops pulled out. In May the troops left Chapel Hill and were encamped around Lexington until July when Capt. Banks fulfilled his promise and took George with him to Philadelphia.

In the city, Horton published the last collection of his poetry with the help of Banks. The preface included the author's statement that "this work will be offered to the public as one of the many proofs that God in his infinite wisdom and mercy created the black man for a higher purpose than to toil his life away under the galling yoke of slavery."

With the publication of the book, George Moses Horton became a celebrity and for a few years basked in the admiration of critics who celebrated his works as being comparable to those of Phillis Wheatley, the famous Negro poetess. On August 31, 1866, a special meeting of the Banneker Institute of Pennsylvania was held, "the subject being to receive Mr. George Horton of North Carolina, a poet of considerable genius."

Unfortunately for the poet, as the furor over abolition died, so did interest in his poems and he was forced to work at odd jobs to support himself and his family.

He died in 1883.

⟡ The Inseparable Twins

Darryl Traywick

Among the most famous North Carolinians were Eng and Chang Bunker, the original Siamese twins, who were perfectly normal except for being joined at the chests by a narrow band of flesh. After appearing as circus freaks before audiences around the world, the brothers retired to North Carolina, where they married and fathered twenty-two children. This account of their lives is taken from Darryl Traywick's profile of them in the *Dictionary of North Carolina Biography*.

⟡ Eng and Chang Bunker, the first Siamese twins to receive world-wide attention, were born in the fishing village of Meklong, Siam, of obscure parentage. Their nationality became the name for the birth defect in which two persons are physically joined together. Eng and Chang, unlike some grotesquely deformed Siamese twins, were completely normal except for a thick but pliable band of flesh connecting them at the chest. During their childhood the band became stretched enough to allow them to stand side by side with relative freedom of movement. The condition initially caused alarm and consternation among the villagers, some of whom feared the extraordinary birth as a harbinger of doom. Because of a determined mother and their own adaptability, the two boys grew up as normally as possible, even raising ducks to help support their family, and were gradually accepted by the community.

The twins would probably have lived out their lives in obscurity had it not been for a Scottish trader, Robert Hunter, and a New England sea captain, Abel Coffin, who in April 1829 persuaded the twins to go abroad with them. They arrived in Boston in August of that year, having acquired a working knowledge of English on the voyage. During the following eight years, they toured the United States and Europe, first under the auspices of Hunter and Coffin and later with P. T. Barnum. They drew large crowds wherever they went, performing feats of strength and dexterity. They also caused considerable stir among the medical profession, whose members never tired of conducting tests on them and speculating on the cause of and solution to their malady.

Eng and Chang, in their mid-twenties, gave up their original plans of returning to Siam. They decided to become naturalized American citizens, to break with Barnum, and to conduct their own shows. Upon learning that a surname was one of the requirements for naturalization, they accepted the suggestion of a bystander, Fred Bunker, that they use his name.

Touring on their own, the twins acquired considerable wealth but grew weary of life on the road. At the suggestion of Dr. James C. Calloway of Wilkesboro, who met Eng and Chang in New York, they included Wilkesboro in their itinerary. They arrived there on 7 June 1837 and found the quiet little community and surrounding countryside much to their liking. Within two years they stopped touring and opened a general store in Traphill, a nearby community. They also bought some land and began raising corn and hogs.

Shortly after settling in Traphill, Eng and Chang struck up a friendship with two sisters, Adelaide and Sarah Yates. When it became apparent that a romantic relationship was developing among them, the community was outraged. Nevertheless, they were married 13 Apr. 1843, Eng to Sarah and Chang to Adelaide. The former couple eventually had ten children, the latter twelve. All were normal, with the exception of a boy and girl of Chang's, who were deaf mutes.

As their families grew, the twins found it necessary to establish separate residences. In 1846 they moved to nearby Surry County, where they built two houses about a mile apart on the same tract of land. The families of each of the twins stayed at their respective houses, while Eng and Chang took turns visiting every three days. They followed this pattern for the rest of their lives.

The prosperity they achieved as farmers was devastated by the Civil War. To recoup their fortune, they reluctantly decided to rejoin Barnum and tour once again. No longer having the exuberance of youth, they bolstered their spirits with the hope that while touring in Europe they could find a doctor who would separate them. Chang had become dissipated from drinking too much, and was losing his health; consequently, they were becoming irritable toward each other. Unfortunately, no doctor would touch them. They returned home in 1871, having accumulated money but having lost the last hope of separation, which had become the most important thing in their lives.

On the voyage across the Atlantic, Chang suffered a stroke and partial paralysis. He recovered partially, but from that time his health began to decline inexorably. It is remarkable that their families managed to endure the strain as well as they apparently did, considering the increasing severity and frequency of the twins' fights. On 12 Jan. 1874, Chang was stricken with severe bronchitis, accompanied by chest pains. The condition grew worse, and he died in his sleep in the early morning of 17 Jan. Although there was nothing organically wrong with Eng, he was horrified upon waking to find his twin dead, thinking that he would soon follow: they had always regarded themselves as one, signing their names "Chang Eng," rather than "Chang and Eng." A doctor was summoned to try to perform a desperate operation, but Eng died before he arrived. An autopsy conducted in Philadelphia led doctors to conclude that while Chang had died of a cerebral clot brought on by the previous stroke, complicated by pneumonia, Eng had actually died of fright. A partial examination of the connecting band, limited by the family's wish that it not be cut from the front, revealed that their lives were connected by a "quite distinct extra hepatic tract" and that an artery and some nerve connections ran between them; thus, Eng may have suffered from loss of blood from Chang's dying body.

They were buried in a common grave in the White Plains Baptist Church cemetery in Surry County. They were survived by their wives and all but one of their children.

ᢙ Vance Fought Yankees, Confederates

Richard Walser

It has been said that around the turn of the century more North Carolina sons, dogs, horses, and mules were named Zeb than any other name, largely in affectionate tribute to Zebulon Baird Vance, the most beloved man ever elected to public office in the state. This portrait of Vance was written for the *Greensboro Daily News* by Richard Walser, a professor of English at North Carolina State University, in reviewing *Zeb Vance: Champion of Personal Freedom*, a 1966 biography of Vance by Glenn Tucker.

ᢙ The ablest governor of the Confederacy was, according to his latest biographer, the governor of North Carolina. In civil affairs, no one in the South could match his "driving energy and dominating ability."

Because tobacco-chewing Zeb Vance could lead and persuade, because he had an overwhelming affection for his people and they for him, because he believed that personal liberties could be preserved in time of peril—well, there had never been before, nor has there ever been since, any governor of North Carolina quite like him.

In 1862, after serving as a popular officer in action at New Bern and Malvern Hill, he became governor at the age of 32. Vance had been against secession; but then, before Lincoln called for two regiments from North Carolina to go against her sister states, most of the citizens of the state, including her most distinguished, had been pro-Union. After Lincoln's call, Vance said, "I died last night a Union man. I am resurrected today a secession man."

His administration was a matter of "fight the Yankees and fuss with the Confederacy." He firmly believed that the civil leaders of the South were men of small minds. Especially was this true of Jefferson Davis, who slighted former Unionists and gave preferment to less capable secessionists.

Davis was, thought Vance, indifferent to North Carolina and her problems and seemed not to care that her coastline and ports, all except Wilmington, were occupied by the federals. Nor did he have any understanding of the indispensability of blockade-running, which Vance was well aware, kept the Confederacy alive, even as Davis sat in Richmond thinking how to advance his friends and actually impeding the continued success of operation.

When Vance became governor, North Carolina was, among the eleven Confederate states, 5th in total population, 3rd in white population,

7th in wealth, 4th in value of agricultural products, and 3rd in general manufacturing, though without heavy industries.

At once Vance set about to correct this situation. Soon, rifles were being manufactured in the state. The production of salt from sea water was one of his most ardent endeavors, but again Richmond interfered whenever it chose.

Never did Vance relinquish to Richmond the responsibility of providing for and clothing North Carolina soldiers, and soon the Tar Heels were the best equipped men in the army. When he heard of the carnage of North Carolina troops at Antietam, he grabbed his surgeon general and rushed off with ample medical supplies to see his wounded men in person. No wonder the soldiers loved this handsome young Buncombe County mountaineer who took care of their desperate needs.

Vance had no intention but to give vigorous support to the war and, at the same time, see to the welfare of his constituents. Alone among governors, both North and South, he never suspended the writ of habeas corpus, regardless of pressures from Richmond.

His relationship with the state of Virginia was not always cordial. In spite of the fact that by 1864 Lee's whole army was composed of somewhat less than half of North Carolinians and was fed almost entirely from North Carolina, Vance's state got little credit for any successes on the battlefield.

Though Vance requested one, North Carolina was denied a war correspondent. Meanwhile the Virginia newspapers played up the home soldiers and, in times of disaster, blamed the Tar Heels. At such moments Vance was capable of fury.

Repeatedly he complained that Virginia officers were put in command of North Carolina troops. And the fact remains to this day that, while North Carolina gave more privates to the Confederate army than any other state, only 25 of 480 Confederate brigadier generals came from North Carolina. Again, it seems that Jefferson Davis was at fault; the old secessionist was simply unwilling to reward a former Unionist's or Whig's heroism and ability on the battlefield.

Vance wrote Davis some angry letters. If gradually Davis began to dislike Vance, it may have been due to his slow recognition that the North Carolinian was so "everlastingly right." When Vance organized the first governor's conference on record, Davis remained aloof.

All of Vance's wartime agonies never dimmed his sense of humor. He told jokes at which ladies blushed (this biography records them time and time again), and he could laugh at himself—a saving grace in the human condition. If audiences hung on his every word, it was that Vance's nature was one of "sunny gaiety" and a love for life and people.

At war's end, with Vance fighting the conservative peace-forces led by W. W. Holden, he declared with sincerity that the "great popular heart is not now, and never has been in this war." Though always aware that the Southern commoner had been torn to shreds by the factional extremes, Vance nevertheless sought military victory with more practical energy than the slogan-shouting dogmatists, to say nothing of theoretical slow-movers like Davis.

On May 13, 1865, on his thirty-fifth birthday, Vance was arrested at his home in Statesville, then taken to Washington where he remained in the Old Capitol Prison for less than two months. No precise charges were ever made against him. Returning to North Carolina, he became a lawyer in Charlotte. From there he once rushed to the defense of a penniless Confederate soldier named Tom Dula, accused of murder in Wilkes County and years afterwards acclaimed in a famous folk ballad.

He served again as governor, and as United States senator for several terms. At the age of 63, he was dead.

How is a North Carolinian different from a man of another state? In reading this book, one is presented with the glimpse of an answer to this, of course, impossible and presumably unanswerable question. Is integrity the word? Lack of pretense? Love of people, whatever or whoever they are? We cannot say, but Vance is somehow a symbol of North Carolina.

Underneath the vast research of this excellent book, the man is there—this man most beloved by his fellow Tar Heels—a term, by the way, to which he gave dignity and permanence.

If 65 per cent of Mr. Tucker's book is devoted to the four years of the war and we learn little of such matters as Vance's second marriage and of his political career in the Senate, we must forgive Mr. Tucker, one of the Yankees (God bless them!) who have come to our state to settle among us. Arriving in the mountains in 1948, Glenn Tucker wanted to do some writing. Not many years passed before he became so much one of us that he took our great Zeb Vance for his theme.

One wonders if, even with its imbalance, this book is not the finest biography ever written about a native of North Carolina. In anticipation of its appearance in Tarheelia, the publishers have issued a special edition to be sold only in this state.

❧ At the Center of Turmoil

William C. Harris

If Zeb Vance was the most beloved man ever elected to public office in North Carolina, William Woods Holden, a brilliant newspaper editor who became the state's Reconstruction governor, was the most vilified. He managed to be, at one time or another, on all sides of the complex political alignments before, during, and after the Civil War. As a result, he lost his credibility among the people and suffered the ignominy of impeachment.

This account of his career was taken from William C. Harris's 1987 biography, *William Woods Holden: Firebrand of North Carolina Politics.*

❧ William Woods Holden stood at the center of the political turmoil in Civil War and Reconstruction North Carolina. As editor of the Raleigh *North Carolina Standard* during the late 1840s and the 1850s, he revitalized the Democratic party in North Carolina and provided the leadership for its political control of the state before secession and war brought down the curtain on an era. In 1858 he sought his party's gubernatorial nomination but was denied it after a bitter struggle in the state convention. Holden was also the leading North Carolina defender of southern rights during the antebellum period, and though his critics, including later historians, dubbed him "the father of secession" in North Carolina, it was not until the Civil War began that he actually called for the state to leave the Union. Indeed, till then he repeatedly proclaimed his support for the Union. In order to save it, he paradoxically advocated southern rights under the protective umbrella of the national Democratic party. Then, after Lincoln's election, he led the unionist forces that checked the fever of secession in the state. But when Lincoln called for troops to suppress the rebellion after Confederates had fired on Fort Sumter, he reversed his position, and as a delegate to the state convention of May, 1861, he voted to take North Carolina out of the Union.

Although he supported the southern war effort, Holden soon became disillusioned with the state and Confederate administrations. In 1862 he almost single-handedly organized the state's Conservative party, which, with young Zebulon B. Vance as its candidate for governor, won control of North Carolina. After the battle of Gettysburg in July, 1863, Holden organized a peace movement in the state while continuing to proclaim his loyalty to the Confederacy. When Vance refused to support the call for a state convention to protect North Carolina from Confederate oppression and to initiate peace negotiations, Holden in 1864 ran against him for governor. He suffered a humiliating defeat.

After Appomattox, President Andrew Johnson appointed him provisional governor of North Carolina. Holden's main duty was the implementation of the president's mild plan of reconstruction. In the fall, 1865, election he suffered another bitter setback when his Union party, with himself as its candidate for governor, was soundly defeated. Because of the return of his old enemies to power and the failure of the southern states to be restored to the Union under Johnson's program, Holden repudiated the president's leadership and endorsed the congressional or Republican settlement for the South. The congressional plan included the southern ratification of the Fourteenth Amendment and the adoption of black political equality, a radical and potentially revolutionary step. In 1867 he organized the North Carolina Republican party, consisting of much-maligned southern whites called "scalawags," transplanted northerners known as "carpetbaggers," and blacks. In 1868 members of this party drew up a new constitution for the state and subsequently won control of North Carolina. Holden was elected governor, and for almost three years he worked to establish a permanent foundation for the new political order. In the end he failed. When the Ku Klux Klan threatened the Republican ascendancy in 1870, Holden dispatched state military forces into two Piedmont counties to suppress the terrorists and restore the rule of law. The so-called Kirk-Holden War that followed further aroused militant opposition against him and contributed to the Republican defeat in the legislative elections of August, 1870. When the Conservative (or Democratic) General Assembly convened in late 1870, it moved quickly to impeach and remove him from office. In March, 1871, Holden became the first governor in American history to suffer the indignity of expulsion.

Most contemporaries characterized Holden as a bitter, unscrupulous, and arrogant demagogue who frequently changed his political stripes to advance his own political ambitions. Writing in 1883, North Carolina editor Josephus Daniels remarked that Holden had made "bitterer enemies than any other man in our history." Daniels admitted, however, that the former *Standard* editor and scalawag governor was "one of the foremost men in intellectual power and daring that was ever born here." He also predicted, "Whatever people in the future may think of him, one thing is certain—they will think of him."

◀ A New South Pioneer

Brent D. Glass

When Reconstruction ended in 1877, federal troops were withdrawn from the South, and the region was left to rebuild. The Civil War had destroyed the plantation system and convinced many southerners that to prosper they had to industrialize. One of the pioneers in building southern industry was James W. Cannon of Concord, a merchant-turned-manufacturer who made Cannon towels famous around the world and made Kannapolis the world's largest company town. This account of his rise to prominence in the New South was written by Brent D. Glass for the *Dictionary of North Carolina Biography*.

◀ James William Cannon, textile manufacturer, was born near Sugaw Creek Church in Mecklenburg County on April 25, 1852. His father was Joseph Allison Cannon and his mother, Eliza Long. As a boy he worked on his father's farm and attended private school in the session house of the Sugaw Creek Presbyterian Church. At the age of thirteen he went to Charlotte and worked in a general store, where he was paid at first only room and board and later four dollars a month. In 1868 he moved to Concord and was employed as a clerk in the general store of Cannon, Fetzer, and Wadsworth, in which his brother, David Franklin, was a partner. Within three years he was able to purchase an interest in the store, and he became active head of the business. During the next fifteen years, he developed this mercantile operation into one of Concord's leading firms. He became a leader of the community and took an interest in its business and social life.

Cannon's career as an industrialist was exemplary of the economic movement in the late nineteenth century that became known as the New South. As chief cotton purchaser for his store, he noted the weak economic structure in the Piedmont of North Carolina, whereby farmers sold cheap raw materials to northern manufacturers and in turn bought expensive finished goods. Like some of his more ambitious contemporaries, he set out to develop the local industrial potential of his community as a means of escaping this ruinous business cycle. In 1887 he founded Cannon Manufacturing Company. In this venture he himself was dependent upon outside capital to supplement his own investment. He borrowed seventy-five thousand dollars from northern banks and enlisted the technical assistance of the McGill and Wood Manufacturing Company of Philadelphia. Cannon's experience was in trading cotton, not processing it, and in this respect he was typical of many textile pioneers in the South. The testimony of a former employee, who went to work at the first Cannon plant in Concord at age eleven, recalled that Cannon was acutely aware of his lack of technical knowledge. "He would often come up to the mill and look me up, a small boy, and ask me to show him how to operate the machinery. I remember very distinctly teaching him how to put up ends on the spinning frames and to dolph and many other things. At one time when we were cleaning and overhauling the spinning frames, Mr. Cannon donned blue overalls and came into the mill and worked by my side helping in this that he might get this experience. He asked many questions about the work and I tried in my boyish way to answer them."

The first mill, which operated at the site of the present Plant Number 2 in Concord, was completed in 1888. John M. Odell, then Concord's most prominent manufacturer, served as president of the company, and Cannon was secretary-treasurer as well as general manager and superintendent. The plant was small, only four thousand spindles and a few looms, but Cannon cloth rapidly achieved widespread popularity in the South, and by 1900 the company had expanded to Salisbury, Albemarle, Mt. Pleasant, and China Grove. Cannon's success was due in great measure to his marketing skill and his ability to develop a sophisticated sales organization. It was his marketing sense that led to the change in 1898 from Cannon cloth to Cannon towels, the first ever produced in the South. Cannon recognized that the era of home sewing was passing and that the cloth market was becoming more competitive. He also realized that middle- and lower-class southerners could not purchase towels cheaply.

Ultimately Cannon decided to manufacture towels exclusively, a decision that led to the establishment of Kannapolis in 1906. This mill village was originally founded upon a six-hundred-acre tract of land seven miles from Concord on the border of Rowan and Cabarrus counties. As the Cannon empire grew—eventually plants were established in South Carolina, Georgia, and Alabama—Kannapolis became its capital, one of the world's largest unincorporated towns. Designed by E. S. Draper and Company, Kannapolis provided its inhabitants with religious, educational, and recreational facilities. Schools, parks, churches, dormitories, and the South's largest YMCA were built, owned, and operated by the company. Cannon Manufacturing Company, which became the largest producer of towels in the world, and Kannapolis, sometimes known as the City of Towels, stood as the capstones to Cannon's career. [He died in December 1921.]

She'll Serve Humanity

James D. Pendleton

At the turn of the century, Charlotteans knew her as "Dr. Annie," a slim, demure, maiden lady who traveled the city's dusty streets in a black horse and buggy. But in the annals of medicine she is recognized as the first woman licensed to practice medicine in the South, in a day when respectable women simply didn't do such things.

This account of her career was written by James D. Pendleton in the July–August 1974 issue of *Charlotte Magazine*.

Her destiny was decided one night in the spring of 1878 when she was fourteen years old. Waking from sleep in the bedroom of the home in which she had been born in Lemley Township north of Charlotte, she overheard her father as he entered the house and spoke to her mother in the parlor. One of his patients had died. It was not the shock of death alone that disturbed him; he had served as a surgeon in the Confederate Army, and he had seen many men die.

But this was the death of a young woman who had refused to seek medical aid until too late for treatment to help her.

"And do you know why she refused help?" he asked and then answered his own question. "Because she was too embarrassed at the thought of being examined by a *man!*" And then, after a pause he said, "One of our daughters—Annie—must be a doctor and help these people."

"But think of the expense," her mother said. "And then she'll marry and that will be the end of it."

Her father's answer was clinical and direct, "She must never marry. She'll serve humanity."

There is no record that Annie Lowrie Alexander ever questioned her father's plan for her life. Immediate preparations were made; a tutor was hired, and between the tutor and her father, Dr. John Brevard Alexander, she was prepared to enter the Women's Medical College in Philadelphia. She was seventeen, and she had golden curly hair and her eyes were as blue as marbles. Her skin was very fair, and there was a light sprinkling of freckles across her cheeks.

In spite of the real trials and horrors of the Civil War, the attitudes of the late nineteenth century were shot through with a corrupt romantic idealism. Perhaps it was an extension of the puritanical belief that the body was inherently evil. Or perhaps it was a reaction against the theory of evolution that Charles Darwin had presented to the world twenty years earlier by illustrating a troubling kinship between human anatomy and the anatomy of the lower animals. But whatever the cause, in 1880 one did not speak of parts of the human body or of bodily functions in mixed company; the proper place for a young lady of the 1880's was on a pedestal, not in an anatomy lab. Women were the embodiments of beauty and spirituality who should be protected from the harsh physical world, and any woman who would intentionally study physical process was an affront to both her sex and to her society. Annie Alexander found that the male students from nearby Jefferson Medical College in Philadelphia were notorious in their contempt for female students. They shouted insults to the women students they passed in the street. And Annie Alexander would recall vividly that shortly before she was to be graduated in 1884, she encountered three of her future colleagues near the entrance of the medical school. The young men saw her, paused, then ceremoniously crossed to the opposite side of the street. The last one turned at the curb to spit venomously in her direction. It was perhaps her second coming of age. Her father and her professors and her own academic success had taught her that a talented woman could do almost anything she chose to do. The rest of the world would learn more slowly. She was twenty. In one month she would be a medical doctor.

From Philadelphia she went to Baltimore for an internship at the Baltimore Children's Hospital and the teaching of anatomy at the Women's College of Baltimore. But in her second year there, while performing her duties in the hospital during a severe winter epidemic of pneumonia, she herself contracted the disease and after a lingering illness discovered that pneumonia was the least of her problems; she had contracted tuberculosis. It was the end of active practice for a year while she went to her uncle Henry Lowrie's home in Florida where she could be out of doors and in the sunlight. But she was strong, and by 1887, the disease was arrested, and she was able to return to North Carolina to stand the licencing examination before the North Carolina Board of Examiners. Dr. Charles M. Strong, in his *History of Mecklenburg County Medicine*, records that she made the highest score ever made on those examinations. When the examinations were over and the candidates were assembled with their families to be awarded their licenses, the chairman addressed the group and said, "Will all men who wish to join the Medical Society come forward and sign the book." She was the only woman present, but her father who was sitting beside her took her arm and propelled her forward. Her forty years as a physician in North Carolina had begun, but it would be one full year later before she would receive the first income, in the form of two silver dollars, from her practice.

For a time she lived with Mrs. Harvey Wilson in Charlotte, but in 1889, with a ten dollar down payment and a lot of faith in her own future, she bought a house at 410 North Tryon Street. It was a one-story frame house with a stable behind it for the horse, Conrad, that would be her partner on many a long drive to visit patients in both town and country.

Saint Peter's Hospital was the only hospital in Charlotte at that time, and by 1900, Dr. Annie had remodeled her home and added several rooms so that patients could stay overnight there when necessary. She also brought her mother and father to live at her house, and it was there that Dr. J. B. Alexander completed writing his *History of Mecklenburg County*.

It is interesting to note that though she was independent in every way, Dr. Annie continued to be strongly influenced by her father until his death. He was a fairly modern man in his attitude toward women, but he was a reactionary conservative in his attitude toward the automobile, and he opposed his daughter's buying one. It was not until after his death, in 1911, that she sold her horse and buggy and purchased a car of her own. The car provided both new freedom and new problems because it had to be started by hand crank, and she discovered that the strain of cranking irritated the old tubercular scars on her lungs. She hired a teenage black boy to accompany her on her rounds and do the cranking, and he was with her in 1914 in her first and only accident when she was struck by a streetcar. The collision came with such force that the body of the car was knocked completely off its chassis. She was not injured beyond a few strains and bruises, but her young companion was badly cut by flying glass. Her first concern was for him. She took him into a nearby house and went to work on his cuts. She had his wounds sewn up and bandaged before the ambulance arrived. Then, while her car was being hauled away, she walked down the block to call on the patient she had started out to see.

It was through such acts of self control and competence that Dr. Alexander gradually overcame local prejudice against women doctors. In 1909, she was elected for her first of several terms as president of the Mecklenburg County Medical Society. She was elected to the boards of St. Peter's Hospital and of the new Presbyterian Hospital where she also taught courses to student nurses. She was especially interested in organizations that would serve the needs and contribute to the development of young women, and she worked for the establishment of the Charlotte Y.W.C.A. and served on its board. She was on the board of the Florence Crittenton Maternity Home, and she served without fee as school physician for Queens College when it was still the Presbyterian College for Women. Though she herself adhered to her father's early directive against marriage, she took as her own responsibility the education of the seven children of her deceased brother, Robert. She provided complete college educations for two of her nieces, and through her affiliation with the First Presbyterian Church, she provided support for a Chinese woman to complete medical school and begin practice in China. During World War I, she was commissioned a first lieutenant in the army and worked in North Carolina with the U.S. Health Service. By the end of the war, there was little doubt that both she and her professional status had been fully accepted by the community.

Dr. Alexander's life of service came to a close in October, 1929. She had been working long hours and talking at length with a pneumonia patient who was worried about her soul, and in mid-afternoon of October 10th, after the patient had begun to respond to treatment, Dr. Annie promised to call her minister, Albert Sydney Johnson of the First Presbyterian Church, and left the hospital. When she arrived home, she was coughing. She took her own temperature and then told her housekeeper to call her niece, Lottie.

The housekeeper objected, "Miss Lottie's visiting in South Carolina. You don't want to bother her."

"Ona," Dr. Annie said, "I once had tuberculosis. If I have pneumonia now, I won't live through the week. Do as I say." It was a response typical of the first woman to practice medicine in the South: direct, firm, and totally without sentimentality or self deception. Her final diagnosis of her own pneumonia was correct, and three days after the beginning of the illness, she slipped into a coma from which she never recovered. She died at 6:35 on the morning of October 15th, barely two weeks before the stock market crash that would plunge the nation into the depression of the thirties. The Charlotte *Observer* commented editorially that "She came nearer filling the position of the community friend than any other personality in Charlotte." And the editor of the *Charlotte News* summed up her accomplishment in this paragraph: "For more than 40 years she has practised her profession in the homes of the people here, moving among them with a majestic dignity and a proficient touch which enthroned her not only as a medical expert of superb order, but as a woman doing a great work in a womanly way—with tenderness, with soulfulness and with love for her work no more dominant than love for those she served."

❦ *Charles Aycock's Soaring Quality*

Edwin Alderman

Following the death of Zeb Vance, North Carolina's popular affection passed to a new leader, tall, slim, eloquent Charles Brantley Aycock, governor from 1901 to 1905, during a time when North Carolina made great strides in public education. This posthumous tribute to him was condensed from a speech given at the unveiling of his statue on Raleigh's Capitol Square in 1924. The speech was made by Dr. Edwin Alderman, himself a hero of state educational progress as a teacher, a teacher of teachers, a historian, and finally president of the University of North Carolina at Chapel Hill. He was later president of Tulane University and, at the time he made this speech, president of the University of Virginia.

❦ The people of North Carolina have chosen to put aside their cares and businesses this day for a simple and noble process of thought—the enshrining in their hearts and memories of a man whom they grew to love; a fellow citizen who incited them to lofty action; and of a public servant who modestly, but radiantly, served the interests of his people and mankind. . . .

We are giving thought today not to the death of Charles Brantley Aycock, for such as he can never quite be imprisoned with the dead, but to his steadfast and romantic life which shall endlessly endure, inspire, and teach. . . . It is not my part or purpose . . . to present to you today a formal memorial address, but rather to speak as one who knew Charles Aycock when both of us had youth and walked together in the early morning of life; to seek to re-create his gallant figure in some faint measure for the eyes of those who did not know him; and to pick out for contemplation some of the saliences of his character, which thus move a great people to set him up so grandly at the center of their life.

I had sight of Charles Aycock for the first time in the fall of 1878, . . . at the University of North Carolina, in the little academic village of Chapel Hill, which both of us then were learning to love. . . . He was a Senior and I a Freshman. . . . He was plainly rural to the ordinary eye, but only a dullard could fail to perceive a certain distinction in his presence, a certain authority in his manner, and a certain significance in the very cadences of his voice. Through the mists of memory, I see him standing clear against the stark simplicity of that environment—a figure of vividness and strength, the bony structure of his great projecting forehead, blue eyes that had in their depths speculation and aspiration, and, now and then, a flash such as warriors have in the hour of battle; a mouth scornful of weakness and set in grim lines of pride and purpose—about the whole personality a soaring quality, a lift of the head, a lilt of the voice as of one not bound to earth and the things of the earth, but aware and wistful of better things that are not seen and fiercely bent upon their attainment. . . .

We were all of us poor. We knew each other and called each other by names. Student ambitions tended almost entirely toward law, politics, or scholarship. The tocsin soon to sound the birth of the great industrial awakening, which was to transform our civilization from an agricultural into an industrial democracy, had not quite sounded. Our standards demanded character not possessions. . . . The one thing we learned more valuable, perhaps, than all the learning of the meagre and struggling University, and which the bronze figure of Charles Aycock will proclaim to generations of youth, was the beauty that lies in annexing oneself in youth to some large truth and some just cause with the knowledge that though we fail, the cause will not fail but goes marching on, and our souls march on with it, because we believed in it and gave it service.

It was my good fortune, as soon as I entered as a worker into the world of men, to find myself a fellow citizen with Charles Aycock in a small, sincere, dignified, progressive community, not given to over-praise or over-blame, but level-headed, equable, just, and wonderfully kind. Goldsboro was almost as well adapted to train the young citizen as Chapel Hill had been to train the young scholar. Aycock was busy building a home and laying, by honest labor, the foundations of his great professional reputation. I was learning, to my astonishment, the fateful significance of education in a scheme of self government. We sometimes walked and talked together about all the framework of the land and the things that seem significant when life lies before. These contacts revealed to me that Aycock, like Lincoln, was not primarily a logician or a polemic but a poet and a man of letters. I do not mean that he actually wrote verse, but I do mean that his mind worked best through images created by his imagination. . . .

We talked of education now and then. My own mind at that time was just possessing itself of the profound and exciting conviction which has been the moulding force in my life, . . . that every human being has the same right to be educated that he has to be free. One of the cherished hopes of my heart . . . is that I may have dropped some thought into the soil of his creative mind . . . about the free education of all the people as the foundation of a democracy and the highest function of an enlightened Commonwealth, . . . the vision which, in later years, he carried in such knightly fashion to the citizenry of North Carolina. . . .

The story of the way in which Charles Aycock, self-forgetful and thrilling with purpose and energy, went to a tax-hating people and convinced them that ignorance was no remedy for anything; that taxation, though it may be a curse, when used wisely and sanely, is the greatest beneficent contrivance of civilization to achieve high public ends; and that faith in trained men and women was the supreme tenet of American democracy, has become a political legend. . . .

There was a pleasing versatility about Charles Aycock. He had interest in many things. He loved nature and he loved books. There was joy to him in the procession of the seasons, . . . and there was delight to him in the companionship of the great masters of thought and phrase potent in his age like Tennyson, and Carlyle and Macaulay. But he most loved men and men loved him. . . .

Aycock not only loved masses of men philosophically, but the individual man was near to his curiosity and his interest. Many great liberal souls like Thomas Jefferson and Woodrow Wilson have loved mankind and would have been willing to go to the stake to protect all men against tyranny and oppression, but they were not particularly interested in any individual, ordinary Tom Jones whom they met along the roadside. Aycock loved Tom Jones on the roadside, especially if it was a North Carolina roadside and a Tar Heel Tom Jones. . . .

Aycock was an ambitious man, but he did not lend his voice to the mob or find contentment with tawdry public acclaim or give ear to popular frenzy. He was the very antithesis of the demagogue. He went out among the people in an interesting moment of social assertion, and there came to him a mounting enthusiasm that so expressed itself in tone, gesture, manner, and substance, as to move strongly any body of men. Like Gladstone, what he received from his hearers as vapor, he returned to them as rain. . . .

States like individuals have moods of mind. It was Aycock's good fate to find his birthplace in the mood of greatness on the eve of "burgeoning," to use his own word, into its intensest expression of power, and hospitable to every intimation of liberalism and progress. I venture to assert that the period stretching between 1890 and the present constitutes North Carolina's true golden age, for it has been the age when her old men beaten in war, used patience and magnanimity, when her young sons, disciplined in self-denial and nurtured on lofty pride, developed a passion for constructiveness, a genius for sympathy, and a method of education. It has been the age when all the people, young and old and high and low have discovered in unity and community effort the secret of social growth and by wise and steady use of the new instrument have placed North Carolina in the front rank of American states in industrial vigor, in educational advancement, in idealistic fervor.

In his crusading form, North Carolina beheld herself pleading with herself to lay aside provincialism and narrowness of view, to think continentally, not parochially, and to clothe herself in the beautiful raiment of a modern state. To the people who heard him, he was an incarnation and an allegory of themselves lifted up into great powers by the might of genius and the strength of ten. What Aycock desired and pleaded for, and what others before and after him pleaded for in that great historic moment in North Carolina has now in amazing measure come to pass. The "epic of democracy" which he chanted so eloquently and personified so vividly, seems to be at hand. . . .

I had sight of my old friend, then Governor of North Carolina, for the last time in Athens, Georgia, in the year 1902. He was closing an address to a great educational conference in these words, still speaking in pictures—"God give us patience and strength that we may work to build up schools that shall be as lights shining throughout the land—ten, fifty, a thousand candle-power. Behind this movement for the education of the children of our land there stands the One who said 'Let there be light.'" I still remember the pride I had in the reflection that Charles Brantley Aycock had traveled a long distance from the cotton fields of Wayne to that hour. Authority and high station sat upon him becomingly and in his mien dwelt the repose and dignity of a leader and ruler of men.

❧ A Pioneer in Educating Blacks

A. M. Burns III

In 1987 North Carolina dedicated its first state historic site honoring a woman and a black. It was the Palmer Memorial Institute, from 1902 to 1971 a pioneer preparatory school that annually enrolled about 200 to 300 black high school students.

Established at Sedalia, near Greensboro, the school was patterned after eastern preparatory schools for whites and drew students from the country's leading black families. Its many distinguished alumni included jazz singer Marie Cole, wife of Nat "King" Cole; Metropolitan Opera contralto Carol Brice; and North Carolina Representative H. M. "Mickey" Michaux, Jr., of Durham.

The school reflected the grit, values, and personal style of its prim but strong-willed founder, Charlotte Hawkins Brown, a Vance County native who was educated in Massachusetts. In addition to music, tennis, French, and traditional academics, the school emphasized religion, good manners, good grooming, and clear speech. Its female students wore uniforms and its males wore blazers; once a week they donned evening clothes to attend a formal tea or dinner. To instill pride, the school was one of the first to require a course in black history.

When school desegregation began in the mid-1950s, Palmer Institute found it increasingly difficult to attract students and closed in 1971. It is now a state historic site.

The following profile of its founder was written for the *Dictionary of North Carolina Biography* by A. M. Burns III.

☙ Charlotte Hawkins Brown, a pioneer in education and race relations, was born on a farm near Henderson, the granddaughter of a slave. Her mother, Caroline Frances Hawkins, moved to Cambridge, Mass., when Charlotte was a small child; there she married Edmund Hawkins, a brick mason.

A precocious child, Charlotte Hawkins distinguished herself as a superior student and a gifted musician in the Cambridge public schools. She attended Allston Grammar School and the Cambridge English High School. As a high school senior she met a woman who was to have a profound influence on her life, and the chance meeting was a story she never tired of telling. Employed as a babysitter for a Cambridge family, she was one day rolling a baby carriage down the street with one hand while carrying a copy of Virgil in the other. The juxtaposition attracted the attention of a passerby—Alice Freeman Palmer, second president of Wellesley College—who took an immediate interest in young Charlotte Hawkins. On learning that the girl planned to enter the State Normal School at Salem, Mass., following high school graduation, Mrs. Palmer insisted on assuming responsibility for her expenses.

A second chance meeting, in 1901, with the field secretary of the Women's Division of the American Missionary Association, led Miss Hawkins to her life's work. She was persuaded by the field secretary to return to her native North Carolina to serve the American Missionary Association in its effort to bring education to southern Negroes. After receiving permission to leave Salem Normal School prior to the graduation of her class, she returned south on 10 Oct. 1901, bound for what she thought was a well-established mission school at McLeansville, a whistle-stop eight miles east of Greensboro. Four and a half miles from McLeansville, at what would later be called Sedalia, Miss Hawkins found the school, a crude building that served as a combination church and school, peopled with fifty barefoot children.

From these meager beginnings made even more desperate by the American Missionary Association's decision to close the school in 1902, Charlotte Hawkins worked to establish a new kind of school in rural North Carolina. Remembering her own experiences in the Cambridge public schools, she endeavored to create at Sedalia a school that would emulate the New England ideal in combination with the best of industrial education. Drawing on her friendship with Alice Freeman Palmer, Harvard's Charles W. Eliot, and Charles D. McIver, she returned to Massachusetts to solicit funds for her school, raising just enough to give the school life for one more year. She then reorganized the school and named it Palmer Memorial Institute, in honor of Alice Freeman Palmer, who had died in 1902. The first class met in a remodeled blacksmith's shed, and with the strong support of the people in the community the school survived. Her persistence on the school's behalf gradually found for her the support of Boston philanthropists, and she was also successful in enlisting the assistance of influential southern whites in nearby Greensboro. By 1910 property valuation amounted to $10,000, and the school's growth was just beginning. Support continued to develop, both in Greensboro and in Boston, highlighted by the interest of Mr. and Mrs. Galen Stone of Boston, who gave the school funds well in excess of $100,000 during the 1920s. Such generosity, coupled with the founder's skill and perseverance in procuring funds—she raised $350,000 in 1925 alone—made possible an impressive expansion and modernization of the school's facilities, despite disastrous fires in 1917 and 1922. The period of the depression, however, was a trying time for the school, although by 1946 the school's physical plant was valued at more than $500,000.

As her school grew in size and reputation, Charlotte Hawkins achieved state and national recognition. She spent the academic year 1927–28 studying at Wellesley, and she lectured frequently at Smith, Wellesley, Mt. Holyoke, and Radcliffe colleges, and at Howard University, Hampton Institute, and Tuskegee Institute. She received six honorary degrees, among them honorary doctorates from Lincoln University, Pa., in 1937, Wilberforce University in 1939, and Howard University in 1944.

She was also actively involved in efforts to improve race relations in the South. She was a charter member of the Southern Commission for Interracial Cooperation, a charter member of the Southern Regional Council, a member of the executive board of the Southern Region of the Urban League, a member of the Negro Business League, and a member of the home nursing council of the American Red Cross. In 1940, Governor

Clyde R. Hoey of North Carolina appointed her to the state Council of Defense, thereby breaking a southern precedent by naming a black to that prestigious committee. In 1945 she received the second annual Racial Understanding Award of the Council for Fair Play, a group of northern and southern people interested in promoting racial harmony. She was also the first black woman to be elected to the National Board of the YWCA and was elected to that post by white women in the South through membership in the South Atlantic Field Committee. As president of the Federation of Colored Women's Clubs in North Carolina, she led a successful drive for the establishment of a state-funded home for delinquent black girls.

Charlotte Hawkins married Edward S. Brown on 12 June 1911. She was a Congregationalist and, although a lifelong Republican, a strong supporter of the New Deal, largely through her association with Eleanor Roosevelt.

She resigned the presidency of Palmer Memorial Institute in 1952, to be succeeded by her associate and former student Wilhelmina M. Crosson; she continued to serve as director of finance until 1955. Poor health sharply curtailed her activities in her later years, although she retained her strong interest in the school she had founded until her death in 1961 at L. Richardson Memorial Hospital in Greensboro.

ᑫ Buck Duke: Philanthropist or Robber Baron?

Jonathan Daniels

No other North Carolina family has achieved the wealth or excited the public interest (some positive, some negative) as have the Dukes of Durham, especially James Buchanan Duke, whose genius created the American Tobacco Company, Duke Power Company, and the Duke Endowment. This essay reflects the mixed feelings that North Carolinians still have for the Duke family and its most famous son, "Buck."

The profile was condensed from *Tar Heels*, a 1941 collection of essays by Raleigh editor-author Jonathan Daniels, who as a public figure was himself the object of mixed feelings.

ᑫ Not all the old folks in Durham liked the Dukes. I remember the old politician, sweating in his little office in the summer. He was fat and scornful. His lips drew up off his teeth toward his fleshy nose.

"They were common people," he said. "The Dukes weren't just plain. They were common."

He moved his head on his wrinkled neck like an old turtle.

"I knew Buck Duke. He didn't have any more sentiment than a snake. As soon as his father died he tore down his house and built a factory on the place. He sold the home place to one of the meanest men in the county. He never loved any land. This man he sold the place to was so mean that his neighbors burned down his barn. He got his mules out but they were burned bad. Their backs were raw. But he worked them till they died."

"He wasn't a Duke," I said.

"No," he admitted regretfully. "He wasn't a Duke. But they were common people just the same."

I am not convinced. It is a strange but maybe natural phenomenon in the South, where all the people were deeply poor, that those who escaped to riches are almost always described as common. Sometimes they are. But it has not seemed quite genteel to have millions of dollars. Where the Old South persists, which is generally where poverty has persisted also, it still seems to. . . .

James Buchanan Duke has been lost for some years now between the equally false legends of pirate and philanthropist. He was both and neither. But the Dukes, almost more than any other family in North Carolina, are its people and its story. A dirt road turns off the highway to the old Duke place. A mile away, another turns off to Fairntosh Plantation where the rich Camerons lived among their slaves when the Dukes were poor. If the aristocratic Camerons marked the State, it was with a silk scarf. The Dukes flailed it with the same country strength they applied to pulverizing the leaf in their first long factory. Maybe they robbed it. Perhaps they enriched it. The certain thing is that they changed it more than any other people ever did before—or since.

More than any other, I think their city of Durham (Durms, the Negroes call it), may be the State now. Durham is the New South because there was no Old South there for it to be. When the Civil War ended four miles up the road, when Johnston surrendered to Sherman seventeen days after Lee had given up to Grant, Durham was three stores, two barrooms, a post office and a carpenter shop. What has happened there since is not only its history but North Carolina's. Back to the east from the wasteland of Caswell, the agriculture of tobacco, full of quarrel and complaint and hard work, runs almost to the sea. Buck Duke himself carried a wagon-load of tobacco east to the sounds once to swap for mullets. He said, the old folks report, that he never would build a factory in the easy-going east. To the west plenty of factories spread and some tobacco, also. The Dukes, who made money in tobacco, put money into textiles before they put money, also, into utilities to run all the mills. In Durham itself, Duke University rises as the chief tobacco blossom on the land and, also, perhaps as the pushed flowering of the pathetic, hard, Methodist ignorance from which the Dukes emerged. Also, from Durham, maybe, grew the modern politics of power and textiles and tobacco corporations.

The Duke University man and I turned off the highway on the side road which leads to the Duke Homestead. . . . It is a good old house. The Dukes were not poor whites. Washington Duke, the founder of the fortune, was at one time a tenant farmer in the day when poor black men were slaves. Later, he owned a slave himself, a girl named Caroline, who helped care for the house and the children after their mother was dead. Wash's father was a deputy sheriff and captain of a militia company, and the house which Wash earned and built was the sort of country house most North Carolina farmers lived in. They live in similar houses still, but without box bushes in front of them. . . .

Washington Duke came back from the war with two blind mules and fifty cents. He had been no war man, but the same war which dragged him off brought the Rebel soldiers of Johnston and the Yankees of Sherman together at the village where Durham was to be. Both sides stole tobacco and both liked it. When they went home they wrote back, willing to pay cash for some more tobacco like that which they stole. What looked like theft had turned out to be a beginning in the tremendous advertising which has attended tobacco since. Wash Duke was forty-six when he came home. His boy Brodie had been old enough to go to war and after the war to shift, and successfully, for himself. Wash's younger boys were Ben, twelve, and Buck, ten. Before a dozen years had passed they already were, by North Carolina standards, getting rich. So were other men in Durham. When Anne Thackeray called on Lord Tennyson she found him smoking "Bull Durham" tobacco. But the Duke brand was Pro Bono Publico. It was not as popular, and that was at least one of the reasons the Dukes turned to cigarettes.

There were only four Dukes in the drama of the State, Washington or Wash, as the State called him, and three sons. That was all. They emerged from the obscurity of poverty, and the blood is already back again in the obscurity of riches. Nobody named Duke is now important in the life of the State. . . .

Old man Wash had less than six months in school, but he was a converted Methodist at ten. They tell funny stories about him still. When his greatest boy, Buck, was moving to the conquest of the tobacco world, he said that there were three things he never could understand, "Ee-lectricity, the Holy Ghost and my son Buck." I doubt that he was the only one who had such difficulty. I think he must have been a grand old man, and I base that faith not only upon the memories of the Methodists as to his devoutness, but also upon the stories about his affection, even as an old man, for ladies who sang very sweetly for him. His oldest boy, Brodie, who shared the family's ability though he was Wash's first wife's son, made his wild doings news for the land. He had a weakness—or a strength—for the ladies and the bottle and often both together, but, still, had a hard business head on his shoulders.

Benjamin was the second son and, like Buck, son of pretty Artelia (Telia) Roney, Wash's second wife. He was both delicate and devout all his life. Happily married he eschewed Brodie's vices and he lacked Buck's power. But he paid a closer, gentler attention to North Carolina details than Buck did. He probably helped keep Buck closer to the State.

But Buck (James Buchanan) was the core of the legend, its strength. Indeed, I think because of his vices as well as his virtues he is the almost perfect folk hero of the North Carolinians. Yet, they never loved him, scarcely knew him, and think of him still as more of a financial abstraction able to get and give money than as a flesh and blood man. They think of him as tobacco and water power, philanthropy and piracy. . . .

He was born on the ground floor—the dirt floor—in tobacco. He had the money to get in on the ground floor in electric power. Hardly anybody even remembers James Bonsack, the Lynchburg boy, who invented the machine which in a real sense made both machine-made cigarettes and Buck Duke. This is no reflection on Buck Duke. All great men are the products not only of themselves but of their times. . . . He was a child worker in his father's factory. But the important dates are that he went to New York to open a small factory there when he was twenty-seven. He got the cheapest room he could get—in Harlem, to which so many other Southern boys of a different color have gone since. When he was thirty-three, triumphant over the older cigarette makers, he was president of the $25,000,000 American Tobacco Company. The finances of those years are remembered in detail, but I think the young man has been forgotten. . . .

What needs to be remembered is the boy. He was, by North Carolina standards, which I think are pretty high, almost a beautiful boy. The country boy who went to New York in 1884 was six feet two, broad shouldered, red-headed. He had clear eyes, a strong nose and a firm mouth. I am sure there was never anything bigger than the determination on riches in his heart. Obviously he worked hard. In the evenings he hung around tobacco shops, not in idleness but in observation. . . .

I refuse, however, to believe that Duke was nothing but a dollar mark in those years. It is in the record that, when he was thirty-three and more than a millionaire, he had a team of high-stepping horses, at least three good-looking vehicles for the horses to pull and a big Negro to sit on the box wearing a high hat with a cockade on the side and a moonstone pin in his tie as big as a small toadstool. I do not believe a young North Carolinian, as rich and good-looking as Buck Duke was then, always rode alone. Also, when he was thirty-six he began to buy his great New Jersey estate. There must have been parties and people, maybe ladies. He was Brodie's brother, if he was also Ben's. . . .

Certainly, when he married the first time, the lady did not turn out to be quite the lady she should have been. Duke named a mineral water salesman as corespondent and a year after the marriage he was free again. He passed fifty free. The slim young Southerner was thicker about the middle then. It is possible that, even as rich as he was then (his company had assets of nearly $300,000,000), he was lonely. He saw a widow. In her middle thirties she was beautiful.

Mrs. Duke was a Southern Cinderella who found the glass slipper twice. Well-born in Macon, Georgia, as Nanaline Holt, she was the daughter of a widow who kept a house in Macon where not boarders but "paying guests" were gladly received. Nanaline was a pretty girl and she gave her friends the impression that she did not like genteel poverty. When she married William Inman (they called him Will), who was one of the catches of Georgia, her friends were both elated and surprised.

"Nannie," they said, "has sat down in the honey tub."

Mr. Inman was dead and she was beautiful in black when Duke first saw her, so they say in Georgia.

"Who is she in mourning for?" Duke asked.

"Her husband."

"That's good," he said.

He knew what he wanted. They were married on July 23, 1907, exactly twelve days after the Department of Justice moved against the American Tobacco Company as a combination in restraint of trade. Nannie sat down then in such a honey tub as Georgia did not dream existed. . . .

The Duke story as the North Carolina story did not end with the dissolution of the tobacco trust. . . . As early as 1904, six years before the Supreme Court cracked his company up, he began to make investments in hydroelectric plants in the Carolinas. Even then, I think, he began to come home. He did not build the Carolina Piedmont, though he had investments in it long before he began to create the electric power to turn its spindles. The main line of the Southern Railroad which runs in at Danville and out of North Carolina beyond Gastonia, had been making a good deal of sense around its slogan, "A mill a mile," while Duke was preoccupied with tobacco. (Along that road now runs Route 29 which is the Gold Avenue of the industrial South.)

But Duke came home in person to take a house at Charlotte, central city on that golden road of railroad and highway, power line and line of brick mills, in the last years of his life. . . . He was a big man who came back. His private car rolled not only into sidings near the legislators, but also, and earlier, into little drab towns near potential power sites. Duke, who by that time looked in both clothes and girth almost like the conventional portrait of millionaire, got off with his engineers and secretaries and assistants and contemplated the poor country about the streams which were to make the State—or some people in it—rich. . . .

In North Carolina then, he was just a rich man and a tough fighter getting old. He had the praises of the rich and the anticipatory Methodists. He was still well hated by the tobacco growers who blamed him for their poverty which did not disappear as he got rich. Even the Methodists had long been split around the Duke benefactions which began with Wash and continued with Ben and Buck. People talked about both tainted money and the evils of tobacco. . . .

On December 8, 1924, when he was sixty-eight years old, Duke made an announcement which some of the cynical declared was the beginning of his campaign to become a saint. . . . He made drama, nevertheless, when he announced from Charlotte the creation of the biggest gift to education and charity and health in the Carolinas which had ever been made. . . . Six months later he began to die of pernicious anemia. Nobody then could cure that. Ten months and fifteen days after the announcement of his first great gift, North Carolina read his will. There were other big gifts in it to people and for purposes. But the provision which was most sensational in the State was in that first announcement which provided that if Trinity College should change its name to Duke University there were big millions for its building and support. By gift and will together he presented $80,000,000. North Carolina was impressed but not suppressed.

"All Buck Duke asked," the wags said, "was to substitute Duke for Father, Son and that Holy Ghost which Wash never could understand."

It was a magnificent gift. It has been magnificently used. Not only has it built a great university. It has also helped other colleges, built country churches, supported old preachers, fed orphans and helped build hospitals which receive a dollar a day from Duke for every charity patient in their wards and rooms. Nobody can laugh it off. . . .

It was a lot of money. It is a lot of money still. But it came just before the millions began to come from Washington from a New Deal which would have killed Buck Duke of apoplexy if he had not already been safely dead of pernicious anemia. It has not seemed so much beside those millions. It may seem less as spending goes on—if it does. But it was a tremendous gesture which erected the faith of North Carolina in its powers as it served its weaknesses. Nobody else ever made so much money in North Carolina. Only a very few ever made such a splash in the outside world as Duke did. Certainly none ever left such tangible evidence of it. . . .

⨠ The Mother of Good Roads

Jeffrey J. Crow

She was everything the traditional, tough-talking, cigar-smoking male road-builder and highway advocate was not. She was small and thin, had a piercing, high-pitched voice, and, like all other women, couldn't even vote. Yet from 1915 to 1921 she was the driving force behind North Carolina's bold program to lace the state with public highways. When newly elected Governor Cameron Morrison suggested that the state under-take a less ambitious program, she threatened to take her protest to the people, and the governor backed down.

On the wall in the lobby of the North Carolina Highway Building is a plaque designating Harriet Morehead Berry the "Mother of Good Roads." The following brief account of her career, written for the American Public Works Association by Jeffrey J. Crow, publications chief for the North Carolina Division of Archives and History, explains why.

⨠ When the North Carolina General Assembly of 1921 authorized the issuance of $50 million in bonds to establish a state highway system, the *Raleigh Times* described it as "primarily the work of Miss Hattie Berry of Chapel Hill, secretary of the State Good Roads Association." Miss Hattie had always proved "willing and able to furnish actual, usable information on anything connected with the roads of the State, [and] to her more than to any one person or groups of persons is due the thanks of those who desire to bring North Carolina out of the mud." Echoing similar senti-ments, the Raleigh *News and Observer* credited Berry with "one of the most stupendous pieces of legislation in the history of the state. . . . It was her bill in the beginning, and it was her indefatigable work that held the General Assembly in line until it had voted."

At a time when many observers still considered woman suffrage a radical idea, Harriet Morehead Berry took the lead in enacting what some critics viewed as the "most drastic piece of legislation . . . ever . . . attempted," a program "too idealistic for North Carolina." Berry's opponents, however, had consistently underestimated her. Her triumph appeared to come quickly, but it was in fact the culmination of years of diligence, persistence, and more than a little pluck.

Harriet Morehead Berry was born in Hillsborough, North Carolina, in 1877. She enrolled in the State Normal and Industrial College (now the University of North Carolina at Greensboro) in 1893, graduating four years later with a brilliant record. After teaching for a few years, Berry joined the staff of the North Carolina State Geological and Economic Survey in 1901. Originally serving as a stenographer and statistician, she was appointed secretary of the survey in 1904. Through the efforts of Joseph Hyde Pratt, state geologist, and Hattie Berry the state's geological survey became the cutting edge of the good roads movement in North Carolina.

Until the first decade of the twentieth century, the good roads movement was primarily localized. Often led by engineers, county organizations seeking short-distance, reliable roads to interlock with the nation's railroads managed to build a few miles of macadam or soft-surfaced roads, but these quickly deteriorated with the introduction of the automobile and without proper maintenance. By 1910 proponents of good roads were thinking in terms of long distances, more tourism, and booming business opportunities.

The North Carolina Good Roads Association was formed in 1902. From its inception until 1919 the association had a small membership, few funds, and only Pratt and Berry to plead its cause through such publications as the *Southern Good Roads* magazine, the association's official organ. The work of the state geological survey and the Good Roads Association often became indistinguishable in these years. Under the auspices of the University of North Carolina at Chapel Hill the survey held road institutes attended by county commissioners, road engineers, and public-spirited citizens who recognized the advantages likely to result from a state highway system.

In 1915 Berry helped to draft the law establishing the North Carolina State Highway Commission. This statute left road building in the hands of each county but authorized Pratt and his fellow engineers to begin laying out a state system of roads connecting county seats and main cities. The good roads movement received an additional boost in 1916 with the passage of the first federal highway act, which provided funds for road building in all the states. In 1917 the Tar Heel legislature authorized the state highway commission to accept federal aid, but the individual counties seeking those monies had to provide the matching funds. By 1920, 87 of North Carolina's 100 counties had sought and received federal funding for roads.

When the United States entered World War I in 1917, Pratt entered the army and Berry became the acting head of the geological survey and the Good Roads Association. In Berry's words, she "had a free hand for the first time" to carry out some of her ideas. She called a meeting in Raleigh in December 1918 to discuss means of pushing the assembly to enact the necessary legislation for a state highway system. Berry drafted a bill that became the cause célèbre of the 1919 legislative session. Behind the scenes Berry almost singlehandedly led the fight. With no stenographer, she had to do much of the work herself, burning "the midnight oil practically the whole time," she later recalled. Debate centered on the virtues of soft-surfaced roads versus hard-surfaced. The former were cheaper but inadequate to the demands of modern transportation. The good roads advocates chided supporters of soft surface as "dirt-daubers." But many businessmen and politicians opposed the idea of the state going into the road building business and especially disliked the long-term indebtedness associated with a large bond issuance. North Carolina had been dragged into the U.S. Supreme Court in 1904 by South Dakota and, in a precedent-making decision, was forced to pay in full certain railroad bonds it had scaled down drastically in 1879.

The Good Roads Association's bill failed to pass in 1919, but Berry had learned a lesson. She immediately set about organizing a statewide campaign to pressure the next legislature, sitting in 1921, to establish a comprehensive state highway system. During the next two years Berry spoke in 89 counties and traveled some of North Carolina's worst roads by wagons, buses, and automobiles. Women became key field workers for the association, recruiting new members, speaking in favor of good roads, and distributing propaganda.

Though frail in appearance, Miss Hattie possessed a strong voice and radiated a great self-confidence. She relished a good fight but never forgot an insult or slight. One newspaper called her simply "the best woman politician in the state."

She had to be, for by 1920 the campaign for good roads brought her increasingly under attack. A rival good roads organization, based in Charlotte, favored a trunk highway system connecting larger cities only. Berry, on the other hand, insisted that the state highway system connect every county seat and principal town. . . . These opposing views led to a rift in the good roads movement, and in November 1920, shortly before the General Assembly convened, some members of the executive committee of the Good Roads Association suggested that a man administer the campaign for good roads during the coming legislative session since it might be too much for a woman. To that notion Miss Hattie icily replied, "the weak shoulders of a woman have for the past fifteen years carried this proposition, and I propose that the weak shoulders of a woman should continue to carry it."

She won her point, but the fight wasn't over. The new governor, Cameron Morrison of Charlotte, recommended in his inaugural address that the counties pay for half the cost of building and maintaining roads. The Good Roads Association was stunned. Poorer counties could not possibly raise enough tax revenues for a massive road building program. At a dramatic conference with Governor Morrison, good roads backers urged a 5,500-mile highway system funded by the state. Miss Hattie pointedly reminded the governor that a plank in the state Democratic platform of 1920 (which she had drafted) called for the state, not the counties, to build roads. After the meeting Morrison told a reporter that, "If it hadn't been for that waspish woman I could have had my way."

The success of Berry's campaign to organize grass-roots support for a state highway system can be measured by the fact that the Good Roads Association grew from 272 active members in 1919 to 3,741 in 1920 and 5,500 in 1921. Over 25,000 names had been collected on petitions for good roads and over 195 circular letters had been mailed out in less than two years. By the time the legislature met in 1921 the passage of a state highway system act was a foregone conclusion. During the debate in the assembly Berry was given a desk next to the speaker's where she answered innumerable notes from assemblymen on the floor. The 1921 law embodied the principal features of Berry's program. It provided that the state "lay out, take over, establish and construct, and assume control of approximately 5,500 miles of hard-surfaced and other dependable highways running to all county seats, and to all principal towns, State parks, and principal State Institutions, and linking up with State Highways of adjoining States and with National Highways. . . ." Moreover, the expense of construction and repair was to be borne by the state, relieving "the counties and cities and towns . . . of this burden."

The good roads movement in North Carolina, coming as it did near the climax of the Progressive era, dramatized the shift from local funding and control to state financing and responsibility for roads and road building. It also represented government's growing professionalism and expertise in dealing with social and economic problems too large and too complicated for the local community or governmental unit to cope with effectively. But in the end it took the determination and dedication of one woman to galvanize the campaign for good roads. Berry's successful fight probably cost her her job, for she lost her post with the state Geological and Economic Survey in 1921. Later she returned to public service to help organize credit unions and savings and loan associations throughout the state before her retirement in 1937. When she died in 1940, few questioned her accolade as North Carolina's "Mother of Good Roads."

ᕕ Brother Exum Takes Her Seat

In May 1920, when Lillian Exum Clement of Asheville won the Democratic primary that made her the first woman to sit in the North Carolina legislature, only men could vote. Women's suffrage was such a divisive issue that the North Carolina legislature, meeting in special session, refused to ratify the proposed Nineteenth Amendment. It wasn't until August of 1920, when Tennessee's assent added the amendment to the Constitution, that women were granted the right to vote. But by then Miss Clement didn't need it. Her nomination was tantamount to election.

This résumé of her brief legislative career appeared in the *Asheville Citizen-Times* of May 8, 1960.

ᕕ At the turn of this century it was a long way from the hills of Buncombe County to the State Capitol in Raleigh.

A long way for a man to go. Longer for a woman.

Lillian Exum Clement made the journey in 27 years, and this is her story.

She was born on the North Fork in the Black Mountains, near Black Mountain, the sixth child of George W. and Sarah Elizabeth Burnette Clement. Her father was the son of a planter whose plantation near Hillsboro had been destroyed in the War Between the States.

Young George had come to the mountains to build a new life. Exum's mother was a daughter of the Burnette family of Charleston who had settled the North Fork when it was still Indian Country.

Little Exum attended a one-room school in Black Mountain until her early teens when her father moved the family to Biltmore, where he was helping to build the Biltmore House. In Biltmore, she attended the All Souls Parish School and later the Normal and Collegiate Institute and Asheville Business College.

Exum Clement was already ambitious. She wanted a career. Her first job was at the sheriff's office. Whether her experiences in this contact with legal procedure or some earlier experiences were the deciding factors that were to shape her course is not known; but at this time she remarked to her brother: "Mankind has written millions of laws for thousands of years to enforce only eight fundamental ones. I am going to study law."

For eight years she remained office deputy, serving under Sheriffs Hunter, Williams and Mitchell. During this time she also studied law, first with J. J. Britt, then Robert C. Goldstein.

On Feb. 7, 1916, Miss Clement passed her bar examination—and received one of the prizes which were offered for the highest grades.

In speaking of Miss Exum and her work, Mr. Goldstein said: "She has an unusual legal mind, being very capable, thorough and systematic in all the courses and has never missed a class or varied in her time of reporting for work one minute during the time she was a member of my class. She is not only familiar with the principles of law, but with its history and philosophy as well.

"She studied under exceedingly difficult conditions, working during the day and attending classes at night."

The law courses taught by Mr. Goldstein were similar to the ones taught at the University of North Carolina. Exum took her examination with 68 men. Some, as had she, had read law under practicing attorneys, but the majority of the hopefuls were graduates of colleges and universities.

Amidst a scene most unusual for the staid and dignified Superior Courtroom, Miss Clement, Buncombe County's first woman lawyer, took her oath before Judge W. F. Harding and assumed her place as a member of the Asheville Bar.

Judge Thomas A. Jones presented her with a bouquet of carnations and welcomed her into the fold of Buncombe's practitioners. He was the first to call her "Brother Exum."

On Feb. 2, 1917, in room 15 in the Law Building near the old County Courthouse, L. Exum Clement hung out her shingle, thus becoming the first woman in North Carolina to begin the practice of law unsupported by affiliation with attorneys of the opposite sex.

Her friends surprised her with a handsome office desk, and the local attorneys gave her a fine, matching chair.

Within a fortnight she had won her first case, and she spent the next four years earning a reputation as a shrewd and able criminal lawyer. Though she was quite taxed to keep her busy schedule she still found time to serve as chief clerk of the draft exemption board.

The lady lawyer found she had a man-sized job. In spite of her well wishers and enthusiastic friends, she realized she was working against a "show me" attitude.

In 1920 the nation was aflame with controversy. There were riots, parades and much speech-making. The national ratification of the 19th Amendment was the topic of the day. The cry of Woman's Suffrage was loud in our land.

At this difficult time, "Brother Exum" was approached by the leaders of the Democratic Party to run for representative from Buncombe County to the State Legislature. She surprised everyone by consenting, for she was not a Suffragette. Perhaps she was, in turn, surprised when the Democrats backed her 100 per cent.

What faith these men displayed in Exum Clement's ability, how revolutionary the choice of a woman candidate in those troubled times, what a shock to the nation when a Southern Gentlewoman was elected over her male opponent—by a landslide victory of 10,368 votes to 41, the largest majority ever polled in the state up to that time, and—most remarkable of all—elected in an entirely male ballot!

Headlines screamed: "Western North Carolina Takes The Lead, Miss Clement, First Woman Legislator In The South."

The staid *New York Times* expressed its admiration for the men of western North Carolina for daring to set a precedent.

The first day in the House of Representatives she occupied seat 59, the chair held previously by Brownlowe Jackson of Hendersonville.

"It is the best seat in the House," said Mr. Jackson when he came up to congratulate Miss Clement.

"I hope it will be a lucky one," said the member from Buncombe.

Before the opening of the session, many friendly representatives came to her to extend their congratulations and give her a cordial welcome, to which she responded pleasantly and graciously.

To the visitors in the gallery she was obviously the feature of the occasion. Some came to the door of the House in order, they said, "to get a peep at the lady."

She did not look like a lady politician of the day. She was slender, feminine and comely, with a soft musical voice and large, dark eyes which inspired confidence.

That day, in a statement to a reporter from the Raleigh *News and Observer*, she said:

"I was afraid at first that the men would oppose me because I am a woman, but I don't feel that way now. I have always worked with men, and I know them as they are. I have no false illusions or fears of them. You may quote me as saying, 'I am definitely for them.'

"I am, by nature, very conservative, but I am firm in my convictions. I want to blaze a trail for other women. I know that years from now there will be many other women in politics, but you have to start a thing," she said with a smile.

If the friends and enemies of the "Hon. Exum" thought she would be merely ornamental in the House they were soon to learn otherwise.

She introduced what became known as the Clement Bill—a measure calling for private voting booths and a secret ballot. She believed this was the only democratic way.

Her own party, with the exception of a few, deserted her. They expressed their belief that politicians would lose direct contact with their voters under the method Rep. Clement proposed.

Dr. Clarence Poe contended that the Clement Bill contemplated nothing revolutionary, that it was in harmony with considerations of elemental righteousness.

Editorials in the *Asheville Times* pointed out that a man could not buy votes if he could not see to their delivery.

There was pandemonium that day in the House and the bill was crushed. Exum Clement knew the bitter taste of defeat, but she had a word for it for the gentlemen of the press: "I have had a new sensation today; I have felt the steam roller go over me."

She, however, was not beaten. She presented the Clement Bill again, but at a tactful time, and it was approved.

As a special honor, Speaker of the House Grier asked her to preside over the Assembly for the debate over the controversial bill to authorize the state to spend $50,000,000 on a road building program.

The Raleigh *News and Observer* referred to "The little woman with the grand old man Rafe Doughton and nice young man John McBee and their 10-day battle." The issue passed by a vote of 102 to 11.

The bill she presented for unification of a state and county for forest conservation purposes was enacted by a unanimous vote.

Her bill which became known as the Pure Milk Bill, calling for tuberculin testing of dairy herds and sanitary dairy barns, was called by state physicians and health authorities as "the best step ever."

The lady from Asheville was certainly making her presence known.

Reporter W. T. Bost of the *Greensboro Daily News* wrote: "Miss Exum Clement, glued to the wall on the east side of the Capitol, today sent through the reverend and grave Senate her divorce bill reducing from 10 to five the years of abandonment necessary to a decree for divorce.

"Which is just another way of saying that both House and Senate thought so well of this timid and unobtrusive little feminine Episcopalian as to put through her measure, against which there has been more theological fulmination than almost anything since Adam and Eve.

"She didn't beg anybody, she never does, didn't leave her post. She is as true to her job as the needle to the pole and just as constant. When this bill went to the House it was so impressively backed by this slip of a legislatress that it created not a ripple. In the Senate it aroused debate, but it impelled men little given to oratory to speak for it."

The successful divorce law behind her, with adjournment of the Assembly, Exum returned to her native Buncombe to ask for confidence in her favorite project. She hoped to secure the approval of her voters for a bill she planned to introduce.

It had long been her dream to see the Lindley Training School become a state-controlled institution. This was a home for unwed mothers and delinquent girls who had taken the first step on the wrong road.

She expected some opposition because of the subject matter, but was totally unprepared for the shocked denunciations or cruel evasiveness she encountered, with accusations of upholding the waywardness of questionable young women and rewarding wrong-doing.

At a rally where she pleaded for a sensible approach to this undeniable problem, she was greeted not with flowers but with overripe eggs and vegetables.

Brushing her clothes, she stood quietly waiting for the obvious curiosity of most of the crowd to silence the cat-calls. How could this lady legislator possibly address a mixed crowd on the daring subject of "the fallen woman"?

When finally allowed to speak, she said simply:

"Tonight I am reminded of a time long ago by a city gate, when the weapons of the people, who had passed judgment on a woman, were not eggs but hard stones. It is not for you nor me to condemn nor to cast the first stone.

"Rather to render aid to the unfortunate so they may also go their way and sin no more."

In her spattered dress, she made an appealing figure; true, some turned away in self-righteous disdain; but many remained.

It was a long meeting.

The Lindley Home exists today under another name.

Exum Clement became Mrs. E. E. Stafford during the third month of her term in the Assembly. It was necessary for the General Assembly to enact a special law to change her name for the Assembly Roll Call, the state's founding fathers, never dreaming this situation would ever arise, made no provision for it.

At St. James Episcopal Church in Hendersonville, Exum married her fiance of two years, Eller Stafford, a staff writer and telegraph editor of the *Asheville Citizen*. It was a very quiet wedding.

She did not run for public office again; however, she was appointed by Gov. Morrison as a director of the State Hospital at Morganton. She also served as registrar of the Fannie Patton chapter of the United Daughters of the Confederacy and was one of the founders of the Asheville Business and Professional Women's Club, which she also served as secretary.

Exum Stafford was called back to Raleigh for a special session of the House and again presided from the speaker's chair.

In 1925, after only four years of marriage, "Brother Exum" lost her most important fight.

Both the House and the Senate passed resolutions of regret upon being informed of her death of pneumonia.

A daughter of her time, she held to the best of the old days while adopting the best of the new. She demonstrated that the modern woman can be the affectionate wife and loving mother, and also crusade for the causes in which she believes.

Her death was received as a distinct shock throughout North Carolina. From all over the United States, people telegraphed their sorrow and regret.

She was laid to rest before hundreds of her friends, and her pallbearers were her fellow attorneys and Mayor John H. Cathey.

L. Exum Clement Stafford lies in the Clement family plot in Riverside Cemetery in Asheville, a simple headstone bearing only her name marking her grave.

But her real monuments are the 17 bills she introduced in the General Assembly, 16 of which are now laws which in one way or another benefit the lives of us who live in her state.

And this could be her epitaph:

"A law is initiated as the need occurs. Some people are able to recognize the necessity sooner than others. Those that see and are willing to fight for what they see are the great ones."

It was written centuries before she was born and half a world away, by a man named Plutarch.

But it could have been written for L. Exum Clement.

❧ Breaching the Savage Ideal

W. J. Cash

Beginning in 1900 the Progressive Era stirred winds of change across the nation and brought to the fore a new generation of southern intellectuals, men and women emboldened to write and speak for social reform. In North Carolina they were led by Dr. William Louis Poteat, a biologist at Wake Forest College, and by Drs. Howard Odum and Rupert Vance, sociologists at the University of North Carolina at Chapel Hill.

The impact of their criticism and analysis is reflected in this brief essay condensed from Wilbur J. Cash's 1941 masterpiece, *The Mind of the South*.

❧ In the early 1900's, William Louis Poteat, returning from study at Wood's Hole and the great biological laboratory of the University of Berlin to his alma mater, the Baptist Wake Forest College in North Carolina, had begun to teach biology without equivocation, to set forth the theory of evolution frankly and fully, as having, as he said, more evidence behind it than the Copernican theory—certainly the first wholly honest and competent instruction of the sort in a Southern evangelical school, and the first in Southern schools of any sort save such exceptional ones as I have before noted.

What is more wonderful, he survived, though a storm swirled about his head all the years of his life, and though he needed all his quite unusual gifts as a diplomat and an orator to accomplish it—and not only survived but in a few years was made president of his college.

Seeing that, others plucked up heart; from this beginning such instruction spread slowly over Dixie until by 1920, though there were plenty of schools left in which the old attitude still lingered, it was no longer true of any of the more important ones. . . .

In the social sciences, the strait-jacket had been stretching and rending also. Powerfully held in the traditional feeling that their proper role was to propagate the old sentimental-romantic legend, to defend the South and brace its self-esteem, the professors of history progressed toward a more rational method slowly enough. . . .

In economics the advance was even slower. Adam Smith still was generally presented as having the same absolute validity as Isaac Newton. And the teaching of the branch was mainly in the hands of dull men who carefully avoided examining the current scene in the South itself.

But in sociology a very notable beginning had been made. For as early as 1911 Howard W. Odum had come back from Columbia, where he had written his notable monograph on the social and mental traits of the Negro, to begin to teach in his native Georgia. And a few years later he removed to the University of North Carolina, to enter upon the work there which has made him famous.

But the mention of Odum suggests something else which ought to be made explicitly clear here. If I say that the economics faculty, for instance, avoided the current Southern scene, it must not be thought that such was the invariable rule for all the faculties. On the contrary, there was in evidence, from the late 1890's on, a growing tendency on the part of a growing handful of men to turn directly to examining and criticizing the South. And still further, there was also a growing tendency for the majority of the faculty in many schools to back them up in it, or at least to maintain their right to their heresies.

In 1902, for instance, Dr. Andrew Sledd, a professor at Emory College in Georgia, published an article in the *Atlantic Monthly* in which he not only scourged lynching but also attacked Jim Crow laws as incompatible with fundamental human rights. For that Emory immediately dismissed him, and his colleagues on the faculty, perhaps intimidated by the uproar of the press against him as a "Boston equality citizen" (he was, in fact, a Virginian), silently acquiesced. . . . Shortly after that, however, Emory was removed from its village of the same name to Atlanta and reorganized as Emory University; and Sledd was invited to return to its faculty, where he remained until his death.

Again, the very next year after Sledd's article, John Spencer Bassett, then serving as professor of history in Trinity College, a Methodist institution at Durham, North Carolina, which has since become Duke University, published an article in the *South Atlantic Quarterly*, issuing from Trinity and edited by himself, wherein he carried iconoclasm to the point of asserting that, after General Lee, Booker T. Washington, the Negro, was the greatest man born in the South in a century. The demand for his dismissal was so great and strident that even Josephus Daniels, in general one of the most liberal and intelligent editors the South has had, was swept into the current and regularly printed the professor's name as "bASSett." But the president of the college told the trustees that he would resign if Bassett were sacrificed, and the whole faculty secretly went on record to the same effect. Faced with that ultimatum, the trustees, after a stormy debate, voted to retain him. . . . It is perhaps not without significance that Bassett, though a native North Carolinian, did not tarry long before retiring to the North. . . .

With the coming of the 1920's, however, what had gone on growing desultorily through the years was to receive enormous new impetus, to take on form and cohesion and direction. One important factor for this result was Progress itself, for along with the feverish rise in the urge to build and speculate in industry and commerce went a surge in the passion for Education—taking the characteristic form of pouring out money more and more lavishly on it. The great part of these new funds went to the public school systems, with the result that the old-fashioned country schoolhouse almost disappeared from most sections of the Southern landscape, to give place to the consolidated rural school, with large buildings and many teachers. But the colleges and universities, public and private, almost universally came in for greatly expanded income also. . . . There was a veritable influx of men from the North, both native Southerners and Yankees, in the years between 1920 and 1927.

The old-fashioned type of history professor was still plentifully in evidence, but in the better schools the younger men were all likely now to smile when a chauvinistic student protested a plain statement of facts. In the economics department the young men were beginning to tweak Adam Smith's nose, and occasionally one of them would even be quoting Karl Marx under the rose. Freud, Adler, Jung, Watson, Dewey, Veblen, Nietzsche, Spengler, names like these were the stock-in-trade in increasingly large numbers of classrooms. Already when Mr. Mencken's celebrated essay "The Sahara of the Bozart" appeared, there were a few men in Southern English departments to suggest that while it all might be very wicked, it still had an uncomfortable lot of truth in it. . . .

At the University of North Carolina, Odum and his associates, such as Rupert Vance, were carrying out, with the aid of Rockefeller funds, the monumental series of studies which was to culminate in the publication of *Southern Regions in the United States* in 1936. The cases of the Negro, his psychology as well as his sociology; of the cotton-mill worker; of the tenant and sharecropper, of the cotton farmer in general; of cotton altogether; of the wasted resources of the South—all these and many more were coming in for the most exhaustive investigation and analysis. . . .

And out of Chapel Hill and all the lesser centers which followed Odum's lead, numbers of young men and women were going out through the schools of the South to hand on and expand the new attitude in ever widening circles. By the end of the decade even the high schools were beginning remotely to feel the influence, both of the new knowledge and of the new inquiry. . . .

I cannot do proper justice to all the men and institutions who played their part here. There are literally a hundred names—like that of E. C. Branson, whose work in rural socio-economics at the University of North Carolina was second only to Odum's. . . .

On the other hand, it is not to be assumed that I imply any universal renaissance in the Southern schools in the period. As a matter of fact, a great many of them remained little affected by the new forces. . . . So late as 1931 Dr. Carl Taylor was dismissed from his post as dean at the North Carolina State College of Agriculture and Engineering mainly because his activities in behalf of free speech and civil liberty had antagonized the cotton-mill magnates who dominated it. And three years later still, poor Clarence Cason, who taught journalism at Alabama, felt compelled to commit suicide, in part at least because of his fear of the fiercely hostile attitude which he knew that both the school authorities and his fellow faculty members would take toward his criticisms of the South in his *90° in the Shade*, published by the University of North Carolina Press a few days after his death.

None the less, what I have said sufficiently indicates, I trust, the important thing for our purposes: that a decisive breach had been made in the savage ideal, in the historical solidity and rigidly exacted uniformity of the South—that the modern mind had been established within the gates, and that here at long last there was springing up in the South a growing body of men—small enough when set against the mass of the South but vastly large when set against anything of the kind which had ever existed in Dixie before—who had broken fully or largely out of that pattern described by Henry Adams in the case of Rooney Lee and fixed by Recon-struction; men who deliberately chose to know and think rather than merely to *feel* in terms fixed finally by Southern patriotism and the preju-dices associated with it; men capable of detachment and actively engaged in analysis and criticism of the South itself.

ᘓ Waynesville Wonder Makes All-American

When Coach Wallace Wade moved from Alabama to Duke University in 1931, a new emphasis was put on college football in North Carolina. Not only was the recruiting of skilled players intensified but so was the outpouring of publicity designed to promote them as stars and candidates for All-American honors. Many football players in the state have since won that distinction, but the first to do so was tall, rawboned mountaineer Fred Crawford who played tackle at Duke.

This brief account of his All-American selection appeared in the *State* magazine of December 9, 1933.

ᘓ The development of Fred Crawford, Duke football star chosen by four press associations this year as an All-American tackle, is one of the outstanding achievements of Wallace Wade, known for years as a peer among coaches of the country.

Crawford, a native of Waynesville, picturesque North Carolina mountain city, was selected by the Associated Press, United Press, Newspaper Enterprise Association and Central Press for the coveted honor of being a member of the mythical All-American eleven.

Crawford's consistently brilliant performances on football fields have been praised by sports writers, coaches, officials and scouts wherever he has been seen in action. He is Wade's first real star since that brilliant coach transferred from Alabama to Duke.

A terror on defense, Crawford was equally as powerful on offense. Coach Wade, declaring Crawford to be the fastest man getting under punts he has ever seen, used the Waynesville player frequently for that purpose.

Crawford, a son of the late Congressman W. T. Crawford, began his football career in Waynesville, where he played end on the high school squad. He was used at end during his sophomore year at Duke, but was sent back to a tackle berth this year, a position he best loved to play.

Crawford loves the game of football, and is said by his teammates to consider playing the game his whole existence. He is a fighter, coming from a family of fighters who settled in the western Carolina mountains, where they became a leading family of the state.

Crawford has brought much honor and glory, not only to Duke, but to the entire state. He plans to become an aviator after his graduation next year.

An indication of Crawford's character is contained in a statement he made after a disputed referee's decision in the Georgia Tech game. Asked if he was offside, as officials asserted, Crawford declared that he had been. The play which was recalled would have given Duke at least a tie with the Georgians, and possibly victory.

For those interested in statistics Crawford is 22 years of age; weighs 190 pounds, and his height is six feet, two inches.

ᴥ Senator Sam Tells Stories

Sam J. Ervin, Jr.

After Zeb Vance and Charles Aycock, North Carolina's next most beloved elected official was probably Sam J. Ervin, Jr., a Morganton judge who was appointed to the U.S. Senate and rarely opposed for reelection. "Senator Sam" arrived in Washington in the mid-1950s, just in time to serve on the Senate committee that censured Senator Joe McCarthy, and retired in the mid-1970s, after heading the Watergate investigation that forced the resignation of President Nixon. In the meantime he gained a reputation as a defender of the Constitution and a teller of funny stories.

Here are several of his tales, taken from his 1983 book, *The Humor of a Country Lawyer*.

ᴥ Zeb Vance, the state's most beloved son, was also one of the nation's most gifted raconteurs. When Vance was chosen senator, Yankee General Kilpatrick, of Pennsylvania, stated in a letter to the *New York World* that at the end of the Civil War he had captured Vance and made him ride two hundred miles on the bare back of a mule.

Vance sent a letter to the *World* in which he stated that Kilpatrick had knowingly lied. He had surrendered on May 2, 1865, to General Scholfield, who had kindly permitted him to await further events at his home in Statesville; he was re-arrested at Statesville on May 13, 1865, by Major Porter, who extended to him nothing but courtesy, and conveyed him by buggy and train to General Kilpatrick's headquarters; and he never saw a mule during the entire trip, but on his arrival at General Kilpatrick's headquarters "thought he saw an ass." Vance closed his letter by affirming that subsequent events had confirmed that opinion.

Judge Walter D. Siler of Chatham County authored many witticisms. One of them had as its target the understandable habit of Josephus Daniels, the famous publisher of the Raleigh *News and Observer*, to mention with frequency his fine services as secretary of the navy under President Woodrow Wilson.

A member of the North Carolina Legislature whose pride in the state knew no bounds undertook to end any doubt in respect to the authenticity of the Mecklenburg Declaration of Independence. To this end, he introduced a resolution affirming that the patriots of Mecklenburg County really did meet in convention at Charlotte on May 20, 1775, and declare themselves to be independent of tyrannical King George III.

The resolution inspired Judge Siler to comment: "If this Legislature is going to determine historical truth by legislative fiat rather than by research, I'm going to insist that it pass a law declaring that Josephus Daniels was in fact Secretary of the Navy during Woodrow Wilson's administration. Josephus has told that so often, nobody believes it anymore."

When I enrolled as a freshman at the University of North Carolina in September, 1913, I was assigned to an 8:30 A.M. class in American history, which met in a lecture room on the second floor of the Old West Building and was taught by Professor Daniel Huger Bacot, a descendant of the French Huguenots of Charleston, South Carolina. Professor Bacot had a dour countenance, and no one suspected he possessed a sense of humor.

On Halloween some mischievous students, who were bent on embarrassing the supposedly humorless professor, managed to lead a cow up the steps to the lecture room and tie her to the corner of Professor Bacot's desk.

News of this spread abroad, and all of the members of the class were in their seats before the time scheduled for its opening the following morning. Professor Bacot entered the classroom and cast a fleeting glance at the cow, which stood beside his desk quietly chewing her cud. After so doing, the professor said, "Young gentlemen, I'm delighted to observe that the intellectual strength of my audience has increased so much since my last lecture." He then lectured on American history for an hour without paying any more heed to the cow.

Farmer Bob Doughton told me a story which congressmen who are accustomed to polling their constituents to ascertain how they should vote ought to heed. When he first went to the House, Farmer Bob wrote letters to constituents whose views he respected, asking them how they thought he ought to vote on crucial issues. He desisted from his practice, however, on receiving the following reply from an Ashe County farmer.

"Bob Doughton, I've got my spring plowing to do, and I can't spend my time telling you how to vote. We elected you to Congress at a big salary to study these questions and vote on them in the way you think best for us. If you're too dumb or too lazy to do that, come home and we'll send somebody else to Congress in your place."

Zeb Vance became a candidate for Buncombe County's seat in the North Carolina House of Representatives at an early age. His adversary was an elderly gentleman. They met in debate at the courthouse in Asheville. Vance's adversary spoke first. He assured the audience that his young opponent's character was good, and that he would say nothing derogatory about it. He strenuously insisted, however, that the voters should cast their ballots for him because Vance was too young and inexperienced to represent Buncombe County at Raleigh.

In replying, Vance said, "It would not be fair for you to hold me responsible for my youth. Except for those unhappy people who commit suicide, nobody has anything to do with the time of his entrance into the world or his exit from it. The campaign's on, and the time for candidates to make political promises is here. I'm going to make you a political promise, which, unlike many political promises, will be kept. If you will overlook my youth and inexperience this time and send me to the legislature, I'll never be so young and inexperienced again as long as I live."

Vance was elected.

Robert Gregg Cherry, who was known as Gregg, and I served in the North Carolina House of Representatives in 1931. Afterwards he tried numerous cases before me when I presided in the superior court of his home county of Gaston.

In late January, 1948, Governor Gregg Cherry called me, told me that North Carolina Supreme Court Justice Michael Schenck had retired a few minutes before because of ill health, and offered me an immediate appointment to the Supreme Court as his successor. Inasmuch as this was a bolt out of the blue to me, I asked the governor to let me consider the matter until the next day, and he acceded to my request.

I lay awake all night, torn between my ambition to serve on the Supreme Court and my realizations that I still owed debts incurred during the Great Depression, that I had three children to educate, and that my income as a practicing lawyer was about three times the emoluments of a state Supreme Court justice.

On the following morning I informed Governor Cherry I had decided to decline the high honor he had tendered me.

Soon thereafter, Fred S. Hutchins, a longtime friend in Winston-Salem, called me and told me that the Forsyth County bar had endorsed me that morning for the vacancy caused by Justice Schenck's retirement. As its representative, he had advised Governor Cherry that I was its choice for the vacancy and had learned that I was also the governor's choice but that I had declined the post. The governor had told Fred that he would be pleased if Fred could persuade me to change my mind.

Fred did, and on February 3, 1948, I became a member of the court. I served until June 11, 1954, when I resigned and qualified as a member of the United States Senate. Meanwhile, I had been nominated without opposition and elected without difficulty to the remainder of Justice Schenck's term and a regular term of eight years.

After I took my oath of office as a Supreme Court justice, I was seated on the bench in the extreme left seat assigned to the junior member, and my right-hand colleague, Justice Seawell, whispered to me, "You've got the best seat on the court. You can look out the window and watch the squirrels running up and down the trees on the capitol grounds and ignore the nuts who argue cases before us."

ᕦ *One of Smithfield's Favorites*

Karl Kohrs

Of the many North Carolinians who have achieved distinction in Hollywood—including Cecil B. de Mille of Washington, Anne Jeffries of Goldsboro, Sidney Blackmer of Salisbury, and Randolph Scott of Charlotte—none excited imaginations in the way that Ava Gardner of Smithfield did. A stunning beauty, she became a goddess on the screen, the embodiment of the smoky, mysterious, husky-voiced siren.

But her personal life never matched her screen image. Marriages to band leader Artie Shaw, actor Mickey Rooney, and, at the height of her stardom, to singer Frank Sinatra brought only fleeting happiness. In 1953, when her marriage to Sinatra was going sour, syndicated columnist Robert Ruark, a fellow North Carolinian from Wilmington and Southport, wrote a sassy commentary on her career. *Parade* magazine sent a reporter to Smithfield to sample opinion among Ava's home folks. The reporter filed the following story.

🐌 "Ava? Why, I've known Ava Gardner since she was knee-high to a duck," said genial N. L. Perkins, veteran Smithfield tobacco auctioneer.

"Remember going out to her Dad's farm one day and there was Ava, barefoot, sweepin' up acorns. She was about seven or so.

"I said to her Daddy: 'Brother Jonas, is this your baby?' 'Yes, she is,' he says. 'Well,' says I, 'if she was my child, I'd get right on a train and take her out to Hollywood.' "

Folks like Mr. Perkins here in Smithfield (Pop. 6,500) like to talk about Ava Gardner. She's one of their favorite citizens.

They remember her as that cute little daughter of J. B. Gardner, who had a tobacco farm at nearby Brogden.

Brogden is—literally—a wide place in the road. It has a consolidated school (where Ava was a pupil), a "teacherage" (where the teachers board, and where Ava's mother once was matron) and a general store, run by Mrs. D. L. Creech, Ava's oldest sister.

Ava is the youngest of the six Gardner children—five girls and one boy. Her brother, Jack, and another sister, Mrs. John A. Grimes, live in Smithfield.

"Ava was a Christmas baby," said Mrs. Grimes. "She was born December 24. We were all grown up when Ava came along.

"She was a lively kid, real cute. She was a healthy child, but something was always happening to her. When she was about a year old, she got hold of a can of lye. Mother caught up with Ava just as she was putting some of the lye into her mouth."

Acting quickly, Mrs. Gardner swabbed Ava's mouth with vinegar, then made her swallow the white of an egg. That saved her life. As the doctor said, five minutes more and Ava might have died.

When Ava was about six, one of her sisters accidentally struck her under the right eye with a hoe. A tiny scar still shows.

At school, Ava took her lessons seriously—and that involved her in another mishap. Halfway home from school one day, she realized she had forgotten her books, and ran back to get them. The doors were locked.

But one side door, Ava found, had a broken pane. She squeezed through the small open square. A splinter of glass in the frame cut a deep gash in Ava's leg—but she got her books and limped home.

Mishaps or not, Ava liked adventure. She was acrobatic and had a great flair for hanging by her heels.

Ava was a great favorite with the boys, but had few "steadies." Said her sister: "Sometimes when boy friends came to call, Ava would beg us to go to the door and tell them to go home."

About her first "big" high school date—a football star—Ava once said: "I couldn't think of a thing to say—so we just sat."

At school, Ava was the "lone wolf" type—didn't belong to school clubs, wasn't interested in sports. Once she was "drafted" as substitute on the high school girls' basketball team. She shot one basket after another, until the coach took her out of the game—fast. Ava was lobbing the ball into the wrong basket.

Smithfield regards Ava as a home town girl who made good, and everybody's for her. Ava and Frankie? That's water under the bridge, most of her friends say.

Mayor Rayford Oliver sums it up: "I'm right proud Ava's from Smithfield."

❧ Dr. Frank's Radiant Spirit

Tom Wicker

When Dr. Frank Porter Graham died in February 1972, friends from around the world rushed to Chapel Hill to attend his funeral. Among them was *New York Times* associate editor Tom Wicker, a Hamlet native who was a student at the University of North Carolina during Dr. Graham's presidency and as a young reporter had covered the 1950 Willis Smith–Frank Graham campaign for the U.S. Senate. The following is the tribute Wicker wrote to Dr. Graham in the February 20, 1972, issue of the *Times*.

❧ The last time I talked with Dr. Frank P. Graham, it was in the company of his old friend and a former teacher of mine, Phillips Russell, a man of strong opinions. Mr. Russell took to denouncing President Nixon with the considerable spirit that has always animated him.

Dr. Graham, then a frail old man in fading health, grieving the death of Mrs. Graham, touched Mr. Russell's knee. "Now, now, Phillips," he said, "I've seen Mr. Nixon with his family. He must be a very moral man."

Just this week, a few days before his death at 85, Dr. Frank—as he was familiarly known to thousands of sons and daughters of the great university he did so much to build—was talking with his minister about the possibility of life on other planets. As the Rev. Vance Barron recalled it at the funeral service in the University Presbyterian Church this morning, Dr. Frank said that, whatever other forms of life there might be, "they cannot know anything higher about God than we know, because God has revealed his love to us, and there cannot be anything higher than 'God is love.'"

It was that gentle heart, that loving spirit, far more than his great achievements, that made Frank Graham's life so radiant. In good times and bad, in theory and fact, in word and deed, he loved his fellow man and in that way best loved his God.

As a history teacher the memory of whose lectures still delights an older generation of students; as the president who made the University of North Carolina into the light of the South in the hard days of the nineteen-thirties and forties; as a U.S. Senator ultimately defeated in a racist campaign so bitter that twenty years later it still marks the politics of this state; as one of those who began the modern civil rights movement under President Truman; and in his last active years as a tireless international servant of the United Nations—in all these different and usually thankless tasks, his gentleness never deserted him, the love in his heart never withered. He was, Wayne Morse once said, "the most Christlike man I've ever known."

He was nevertheless a hard fighter.

When one of his faculty was accused of the heinous crime of lunching with a black man, Dr. Frank calmly told the trustees, "If Professor Erickson has to go on a charge of eating with another human being, then I will have to go first." As a magazine writer commented at about that time, Frank Graham had planted "one foot firmly on the Sermon on the Mount and the other on the Bill of Rights."

In its obituary, the *Chapel Hill Weekly* told how even the formidable John L. Lewis discovered that Dr. Frank's gentle spirit was not mere softness. In a 12-hour session, Mr. Lewis had been brought to an agreement to end a wartime strike by Dr. Graham, then an N.L.R.B. negotiator. "Who locked me in with that sweet little S.O.B.?" Mr. Lewis later complained.

Still, it was not his deeds nor his strength that most distinguished Dr. Frank. He could salve a student's troubled spirit with a smile and lift men's hearts by example. In the meanest trial of his life, his spirit held him steady and a whole generation of North Carolinians could learn from him what was meant by courage under fire and charity of the soul.

That was in 1950, when he ran for the Senate seat to which he had been appointed by Gov. Kerr Scott, father of North Carolina's present Governor. In the Democratic primary, despite repeated charges that he was somehow pro-Communist and unpatriotic, Dr. Frank got more votes than anyone up to then had received for any state office—but with three candidates in the race, he just failed to win a majority. In the runoff, the attack shifted to the worst kind of racist charges, and he was defeated. On the race question as on the human question, Frank Graham was ahead of his time.

Yet, he never struck back with lies and innuendo of his own, nor later denounced the men who had slandered him. Dr. Frank did not make the common, fatal error of public men—he never believed his cause was so precious, his victory so necessary, that they could justify any tactic or any means.

So he could stand in the Senate as he was about to leave it and deliver a farewell address unmarked by bitterness, infused with a vision of America and of humankind unaltered by his ordeal:

"In this America of our struggles and our hopes," he said, "the least of these our brethren has the freedom to struggle for freedom; where the answer to error is not terror, the respect for the past is not reaction and the hope of the future is not revolution; where the integrity of simple people is beyond price and the daily toil of millions is above pomp and power; where the majority is without tyranny, and the minority without fear, and all people have hope."

The hard men, the practical men, the so-called realists will never share or know that vision. But then they will never even know that, whatever the momentary situation, they can win nothing that matters; or that in the everlasting verities of the heart, Frank Graham never lost.

❧ Ed Murrow's Inquiring Mind

Charles Kuralt

Edward R. Murrow was another North Carolina Quaker who, like Daniel Boone and Dolley Madison, went on to achieve fame somewhere else. This tribute to him was condensed from a 1971 address to the North Carolina Literary and Historical Association by Charles Kuralt of Wilmington and Charlotte, another North Carolinian who achieved distinction as a writer and broadcaster for CBS. The full address appeared in the April 1971 issue of the *North Carolina Historical Review*.

❧ I speak here of a man who, it seemed to me at the time I knew him, was the best man I had ever known. Nothing has happened since then to make me alter that judgment. Others, who knew him far better than I, shared that feeling. He was not the most courageous man I've ever known, nor the most honest, I suppose, nor the best writer—not by far—nor the best thinker . . . though courage and honor he had in full measure, and he was a fine thinker and writer. What lifted him above his fellows, I believe, was the one principle that seemed to light his life: the search for truth, his belief that freedom *depended* on people willing to search for truth, his single-mindedness about that. That is the thing that elevated him and all who knew him. On his death, the unemotional Eric Severeid spoke on the air that shattering, emotional farewell of Shakespeare's:

> . . . Good night, sweet prince,
> And flights of angels sing thee to thy rest!

And those who knew Edward R. Murrow felt that benediction appropriate.

You will pardon me if I speak personally at first. I was nine or ten, and I remember my parents listening to the radio, waiting for his broadcasts from London during the war. "This is London. Early this morning, we heard the bombers going out. It was the sound of a giant factory in the sky. . . . It seemed to shake the old gray stone buildings in this bruised and battered city beside the Thames. . . ." The radio was on all the time, but when Edward R. Murrow reported from London, the kids at our house didn't talk, even if we didn't always listen.

And then I was fourteen and the winner of a schoolboy speaking and writing contest, and with my mother in a hotel room in Washington, where I had gone to receive my prize. Somebody called to say, "Be sure to listen to Murrow tonight." We did, and at the end of his broadcast there was that same voice, quoting a few lines from my speech. I met the president of the United States that same day, but when I woke up the next morning, the thing I remembered was Edward R. Murrow saying my words.

And then I was fifteen, and Ed Murrow was to make a speech in Chapel Hill. A friend called me in Charlotte to ask if I would like to come up to hear him. I sat in the audience at the Carolina Inn and I remember thinking, "Look how close I am to him, right here in the same room with him," the kind of thing star-struck fifteen-year-olds think. He spoke about the job ahead for television news, to develop the same kind of tradition of courage that the best newspapers had long enjoyed. Afterward my friend said, "We're taking him to the airport in the morning, would you like to come along?" So I skipped another day of high school to ride to the airport with Edward R. Murrow. I wanted to know about London and New York and the world, but he would not speak, except to ask questions of the university student driver and—horror of horrors—of *me*. He questioned us in turn. So I worked on the high school newspaper, did I? What was its name? I wanted to say the *Times* or the *Herald* or the *World*, but I was forced to listen to my own voice saying, "The *Rambler*, that's its name, the *Rambler*." Do not ask any more questions about Central High School, I remember thinking, tell us about the blitz, tell us about CBS, and Ned Calmer, and Robert Trout. But he went on, looking out the window at the cotton fields that used to line the back road to the Raleigh-Durham Airport, remarking that it was pretty poor-looking cotton. I thought, hysterically, "Please do not spend this whole trip this way. Nobody cares about the *Rambler*, or the opinions of that kid who's driving, or the damned cotton." But that was how he spent the whole trip. I am sure he enjoyed that drive, in a passive way. But I *actively* hated it, was actually relieved to see him climb the steps of the plane, so as not to have to suffer any more of his questions. The student driver, by the way, who waved Mr. Murrow into his plane was Bob Evans, who was also to become a CBS News correspondent. I went back to the car, miserable, embarrassed, wishing I had never come along, too young and inexperienced to realize that I had spent an hour with a consummate reporter, who, facing an hour with nothing more to dig into than the opinions of a couple of kids and nothing more to study than the state of the cotton crop, dug into, studied, what there was at hand.

And then I was twenty-two and walking into the CBS newsroom in New York, on invitation, to talk about a job. It was just a little room, I was surprised by it, a few people working at typewriters, a bank of wire machines against the far wall. And then I saw him, from the back, in shirtsleeves, his galluses about to slip off his oddly small shoulders, his head bent over the AP machine, unmistakably, there he was. And for me that little room became a great hall. A few minutes later an executive was offering me $135 a week to work in that room as a writer, from midnight 'til 8:00 A.M. Yes, yes, I said. I would have said yes if I had had to pay *them* to work there.

It was hero worship, but what a hero he was! It dawned on me in the months that followed that it was not only the young, impressionable beginners who felt this way about Ed Murrow. It was everybody who knew him. "Well," he would say sometimes at the end of the day, "we have done as much damage as we can do. How about a drink?" The invitation was for everybody within the sound of his voice. And we would all go down to Colbee's on the ground floor of the CBS building, and pass an hour, the well-known correspondents and the seasoned editors and the young kids, all together, all *drawn* together, by Murrow. It was very nearly the best camaraderie I have ever felt, and it helped me survive in New York on $135 a week. He always bought the drinks.

There came a day when I wrote for him—an appalling idea, but that was the way radio worked. I actually wrote the news portion of his radio broadcast a few times, while he worked on the commentary. He would toss what he had written across to me to read over, while he timed and edited what I had written. Once, I found that he had written the expression "including you and I." I debated with myself before pointing out that it should be "you and me," wondering what he would say. What he said was "Good catch." It was such a little thing, all these are such little things, but it is a measure of what we all thought about Murrow that I remember to this day Murrow saying to me, "Good catch."

Well, he said other things. He wrote me notes, complimenting me on something I had done, or quarreling with something I had said on the air, or with the way I had said it. He did the same for many others at CBS News, especially the young correspondents, and he did it even after he had left the network. He was, until the end of his life, gracious and generous beyond all hope of explanation. . . .

It gave me pride in those days, and it gives me pride now, to think of Ed Murrow as a North Carolinian. It gave *him* pride. He always considered himself a Tar Heel from Guilford County, though as his recent biographer, Alex Kendrick, points out, his family moved to the state of Washington before he was six and at that time he was "obviously too young to be whistling Dixie."

No matter, he loved to refer to his upbringing on Polecat Creek, and more than once, I heard him explain that Guilford County was where Andrew Jackson "came from." On such occasions, I was a silent Mecklenburger, having ridden my bicycle past the nearby monument which marks the spot where Andrew Jackson came from in Union County—and past the other monument a few miles away in South Carolina marking the spot where Andrew Jackson came from.

Where Ed Murrow came from, there is no such doubt. It was the Center Community of Friends, Guilford County, North Carolina. He was born there, April 25, 1908, the youngest of the three sons of Roscoe and Ethel Murrow, and he was christened Egbert Roscoe Murrow, which seems to me to have been two strikes against him. (It must have seemed so to him, too. He had changed his name by his senior year in college. His mother wrote, "I think Egbert is not happy with his name. If I had known how it looked when written out, I wouldn't have given it to him. It didn't look pretty.")

Ed Murrow's roots in Guilford County went back more than a hundred years. He came, on his father's side, from a line of Whigs, antisecessionists, Quakers. His grandfather, Joshua Stanley Murrow, had a 750-acre farm, served as a Republican state senator, and helped establish what is now A & T University. His maternal grandfather, George Van Buren Lamb, on the other hand, fought in the Civil War with the Twenty-second North Carolina regiment, meaning he fought at Manassas, Seven Pines, Harper's Ferry, Gettysburg, and so on and on to Appomattox.

The son of Joshua Stanley Murrow and the daughter of George Van Buren Lamb, Roscoe and Ethel, were neighbors and were married, and Ed Murrow's first memories were of a comfortable house made of poplar and walnut, with a wide porch and a great fireplace. From his father, Ed Murrow inherited the habit of long silences, practiced before that fireplace. From his mother, he learned a striking manner of speech, a kind of old-fashioned precision with inverted phrases like "this I believe" and verb forms like "it pleasures me" which, as Alex Kendrick points out, Ed Murrow used, on and off the air, all his life.

It was a strict household. Ed Murrow's mother forbade smoking, drinking, cardplaying, and work, or play, on Sunday. A chapter of the Bible was read in the house each evening and several chapters on the Sabbath. Ed Murrow grew up to be a smoker, a drinker, an enthusiastic poker player, and not much of a Bible reader. But some of Ethel Lamb Murrow's other precepts took better hold of his life. She taught her sons to be responsible, to be in control of their lives, to respect other people, including the opinions of other people, to love the land, and to keep the peace.

His family moved to the Puget Sound in 1913, lived in a tent before they found a house, and Ed Murrow grew up in the Northwest, working in logging camps, playing on the school baseball team. He became a debater and president of the student body. He went to Washington State University, where he was fortunate enough to have a great teacher, Ida Lou Anderson. It was she who taught him to love words and thoughts. . . .

After graduation, Ed Murrow went to New York as president of the student federation and spent his early twenties immersed in international student affairs. He worked his way to Europe more than once, married his Janet Brewster, and in 1935 accepted a job as CBS "director of talks," which meant that he was in charge of rounding up speakers for the network, in America and in Europe. Then, less than three years later, in 1938, he got a chance to speak for himself. In the previous year he had been made CBS European director, and he had gone to Vienna to arrange for a program of Christmas music. He was still there when Austria fell into Hitler's embrace in March. By intricately arranged broadcast lines to the United States, he reported: "Hello, America. . . . Herr Hitler is now at the

Imperial Hotel. Tomorrow, there is to be a big parade. . . . Please don't think that everyone in Vienna was out to greet Herr Hitler today. There is tragedy as well as rejoicing in this city tonight. . . ."

His broadcasts from Vienna that month were his first. He had no formal news background or training. Those broadcasts were models of careful, accurate journalism. When people say that Ed Murrow was born to do what he did in life, that first month in Vienna may be taken in evidence.

And so that was how it all began. By some miracle, it seems to me, the time and the place and the man came together. The birth of serious broadcast journalism can be said to be Ed Murrow's radio reports from Vienna in 1938. It was a long way from Polecat Creek, by way of Puget Sound logging camps and international student meetings—but he got there in time.

Many people in this room remember what followed. Night after night, "This is London." Thirty years ago this month:

> Christmas Day began nearly an hour ago. The church bells did not ring at midnight. When they ring again, it will be to announce invasion. . . . This is not a merry Christmas in London. This afternoon . . . one heard such phrases as, "So long, Mamie," and "Goodnight, Jack," but never, "A merry Christmas." It can't be a merry Christmas, for those people who spend tonight and tomorrow by their firesides in their own homes realize that they have bought this Christmas with their nerve, their bodies and their old buildings. . . . I should like to add my small voice to give my own Christmas greeting to friends and colleagues at home. Merry Christmas is somehow ill-timed and out of place, so I shall just use the current London phrase, goodnight, and good luck.

And that was how the phrase originated, the one with which he was to close his broadcasts after the war.

It was after the war that he made his greatest contributions to broadcasting, in my opinion, and to his country. . . . Ed Murrow's inquiring mind led him to do his great documentary, "Harvest of Shame," years before the national conscience was aroused to any kind of war on poverty. . . . He was the first on network television to report on cigarettes and lung cancer, years before the surgeon general's first report on that subject. And after the national political campaign we have all just lived through, it may cleanse your soul to hear the words he spoke on March 9, 1954, the night of his "See It Now" broadcast devoted to Senator Joseph McCarthy. He might have been moved to say them again in 1970:

> We will not walk in fear, one of another. We will not be driven by fear into an age of unreason if we dig deep in our history and our doctrine and remember that we are not descended from fearful men, not from men who feared to write, to speak, to associate and to defend causes which were for the moment unpopular. . . . The actions of the junior senator from Wisconsin have caused alarm and dismay. . . . And whose fault is that? Not really his; he didn't create this situation of fear; he merely exploited it, and rather successfully. Cassius was right. "The fault, dear Brutus, is not in our stars but in ourselves."

He died in the spring, five years ago, before his time. His ashes were scattered at his farm in Pawling, New York. But to me, he will always belong to Guilford County. I am southerner enough to believe that there really is something born into a man that helps determine what he will become, and if that is so, then there was a century of good earth and hard work and woods and creeks and wild flowers born into Edward R. Murrow. And a Scotch-Irish and English Quaker dignity and decency and respect for the truth.

At his death, he had been director of the United States Information Agency and an adviser to presidents and prime ministers. He was holder of fourteen honorary degrees and all the prizes of his profession, honorary Knight Commander of the Order of the British Empire, Chevalier of the Legion of Honor, an officer of the Order of Leopold.

But we don't remember him for his honors. We remember him, finally, for his deep and abiding belief that we could take it; that there was never any excuse for insulating the people from reality; that escapism was the eighth, and deadliest sin; that the American people were wise beyond the comprehension of those who would trick us or delude us or tell us lies; that we were decent and responsible and mature and could be counted on every time if only we could be supplied our fair measure of the straight facts.

We don't remember him for his honors. We remember him for how he honored us.

✧ Andy Griffith Makes People Laugh

Lillian Ross and Helen Ross

One of the best advertisements for life in North Carolina's small towns has been television's "Andy Griffith Show," set in mythical Mayberry, North Carolina, which looks and sounds suspiciously like Mount Airy, where Andy Griffith grew up.

Acting and entertaining did not come easily for Griffith, who had to learn how to appeal to and hold an audience, as he reveals in this first-person account in *The Player*, a collection of show-business profiles by Lillian and Helen Ross. (The errors in geography—Goldsboro is in eastern, not western, North Carolina—obviously result from interviewer misunderstanding.)

✧ I was born on June 1, 1926, in Mount Airy, North Carolina—an only child. My parents, Carl and Geneva Griffith, still live there. My daddy worked in a furniture factory. . . . I was a little old white-headed boy, and the other kids made fun of my blond hair. And they teased me about a birthmark on the back of my head. My mother told me she had seen a strawberry patch just before I was born, and she always called the mark my strawberry patch. We lived in a little old wooden house. We had an old Majestic radio, which provided our only entertainment, and which gave us much joy. We heard good country music over the radio. I was raised a Baptist, and most of my early social life revolved around the church. Later on, I joined the Baptist Young People's Union and did my early courting there. I started entertaining when I was in the third grade at the Rockford Street Grammar School, in Mount Airy. I sang two choruses of "Put On Your Old Gray Bonnet." The other kids laughed at the way I sang it and called me "Pandy Andy" and "Andy Gump," from the funnies. . . .

The first show I ever saw was when I was five and my daddy and mother took me to Winston-Salem, about thirty-five miles away, to see a road-company production of "Carmen." All that clapping and clanging and carrying on! I sure did enjoy it. At the age of eleven, I played a farmer in a Christmas play about religion put on at the Second Baptist Church in Mount Airy. When I was fourteen or fifteen, I got attracted to swing music, and about that time I went to see a movie called "Birth of the Blues," with Bing Crosby and Mary Martin. In it, there was a man playing a trombone. I had been asking for a musical instrument of some kind, but my daddy couldn't afford it. He fed me and clothed me, but he couldn't stretch his pay far enough to buy me a musical instrument. . . .

I was in the Mount Airy High School by then, and I got myself a job with the N.Y.A. sweeping out the school after classes. I started making monthly payments of six dollars on a thirty-three-dollar trombone I had seen advertised in the Spiegel mail-order catalogue. It took me five and a half months, but then I got this trombone, and I was the happiest boy in all North Carolina. It was a tenor trombone—silver-plated. Then I started looking around for someone to teach me how to play it. Just about that time, a new minister, a man named Ed Mickey, came to our town for the Moravian Church, which had a band made up entirely of brass instruments. . . . So I took my trombone to him, and he said he would teach me how to play it. For three years, he gave me a free lesson once a week. Ed Mickey taught me to sing and to read music and to play every brass instrument there was in the band, and the guitar and the banjo besides. I was best at playing the E-flat alto horn.

When I was sixteen, I joined the church, together with my mother and daddy. We had been Baptists, but it was all Protestant anyhow, so it didn't make any difference. I was very happy with the Moravians. All the other band members accepted me. They didn't ever make fun of me. When Ed Mickey had a call to serve another Moravian church, somewhere else in the state, I became the leader of the band until the church could bring in a new preacher. A lot of the people used to point to me and say, "There's our next preacher." I was beginning to get that idea myself. The preacher was the cultural leader of the whole town. . . .

In the summer of 1944, I entered the University of North Carolina, in Chapel Hill. I started out studying for the ministry. I took courses in sociology, and I hated them. I took Latin and Greek, too, and I found the classes long and dull. I missed my music. So I went to Bishop Pfhol, who was the Bishop of the Southern Province of the Moravian Church, and told him how I felt. I asked him if I could get permission to specialize in music, which he granted. I started playing the E-flat bass sousaphone in the college band and singing in the glee club, and I got to fooling around in the Drama Department. They had a group called the Carolina Playmakers, which put on an operetta once a year—usually Gilbert and Sullivan. I auditioned just to get into the chorus, if I could, and was lucky enough to get the role of Don Alhambra del Bolero, the Grand Inquisitor, in "The Gondoliers." When the review of the show came out in the school paper, my performance was referred to as the best. From that point on, I was in every musical show they produced. I began to think I might be an opera singer, and decided to drop studying for the ministry.

I met my wife, Barbara Edwards, in the Carolina Playmakers. She was a music major, and was an accomplished singer and actress. We graduated together in June, 1949, and that August we were married. . . . While I was in college, I didn't have any notion of how I was going to become a professional entertainer. All I knew was that I wanted to get up there and perform. I spent my summer vacations working at the furniture factory in Mount Airy. It's always been typical of the Southern states to stage historical pageants. I made my stage début in one—"The Lost Colony," by Paul Green. It's still put on every year on Roanoke Island, in a place called the Lost Colony, which is the site of the first English settlement in North America. The pageant is based on the story of Sir Walter Raleigh. For three seasons, I played Sir Walter Raleigh at night, after work in the factory. . . .

Then, when I wanted to get married, I realized I had no visible means of support, so I took a job as the music teacher at the Goldsboro High School, in the western part of North Carolina. I taught for three years, through the spring of 1952. I wasn't talented at teaching. I couldn't handle the kids. I wasn't a good teacher. It wasn't that I didn't want to be a good teacher, it was that I couldn't do it. I didn't enjoy it. . . . I'm not in the entertainment business to make money. I've never particularly cared one way or the other about that. I came from a poor background. I was happy as a child. I was happy as a teen-ager. I was happy as a young adult. I never had capital, but I was never unhappy because of that. When I discovered I could entertain, I worked hard at it. It's the only thing I do well. I can't be a company director, I can't be an accountant, I can't make furniture, but I *can* entertain.

While I was teaching high school, my wife was the musical director at the Methodist and Episcopal churches in Goldsboro. In the spring of 1952, we were both studying singing with a teacher named Katherine Warren, in Goldsboro, when a publicity man who was a friend of hers stopped to see her on his way to New York. He offered us a ride to New York in his car and suggested that he set up an audition for us at the Paper Mill Playhouse, in Millburn, New Jersey. We jumped at the chance. That was our first visit to New York. We stayed at the Statler Hotel for a week, and went around to night clubs to watch other performers, and got scared to death by the city—a large, overpowering, frightening thing. At the audition, we lined up with over two hundred other people. Barbara sang "In the Still of the Night," and I sang "Dancing in the Dark." We were turned down. Someone standing around there told me my voice was overly brilliant—almost unpleasantly so. I didn't mind so much. In my own heart, I believed it. So I decided to quit singing and start telling jokes. . . .

That fall I took out three hundred dollars in teachers' retirement pay that I had accumulated, and we borrowed a thousand dollars, and we bought a used station wagon. We rented a house in Chapel Hill, seventy-five miles from Goldsboro, and then wrote a brochure about ourselves, describing a song-and-comedy act, and got it printed up. We got lists from civic organizations of every convention or dinner that was planned in the State of North Carolina for the next six months. We figured that at least one out of every hundred would have need of entertainment. Pretty soon, job offers began to trickle in. We got into our station wagon and travelled to each and every job. Our usual fee for our act was sixty dollars. Barbara sang Puccini arias and popular standards. I played the guitar while she did interpretive dances. And I delivered a monologue I'd made up, called "What It Was—Was Football." It went over in a big way. There were some civic clubs, and so on, that asked us back for a second appearance. At one luncheon show, after I had done "What It Was—Was Football," a representative of Capitol Records came up to me and said he wanted me to record the monologue for his record company, which I did. We had been paying eighty-five dollars a month in rent for our house, which we hadn't been able to furnish very lavishly, and we had a student boarder who paid us twenty-five dollars a month. Our record started selling all over North Carolina, and then all over the United States, and we began to make enough money to furnish our house and pay off our debts.

We moved to New York four days before New Year's of 1954, with the intention of trying to get work to do in night clubs. . . . My first big, important professional appearance was on Ed Sullivan's "Toast of the Town" in 1954. I felt numb and was scared to death. I was too frightened to do my football monologue the way I was supposed to do it. I was too nervous. It came out amateurish. I couldn't time it out properly. To this day, I can't actually remember doing it at all. But I knew it was a failure. My second professional job was at the Blue Angel. I felt like a failure there, too. In a night club, people are eating and talking and moving around. To control them and command them to pay attention to you and enjoy it is the hardest job in the world. I did "What It Was—Was Football" and other monologues that I wrote, including "Conversation with a Mule" and a couple on "Hamlet" and "Carmen." The night after I closed, Burl Ives opened there. I went to the opening. What I saw was a master at work. Your eyes reflect what you feel. My eyes had reflected fear. The eyes of Burl Ives reflected what he was doing and singing. He sang some of the songs that were my own favorites. He even had a community sing in that supper club—everybody singing "Goin' down the Road Feelin' Bad." I learned a very important lesson from that experience, and that was how to draw and hold your audience, and that a person with something to say has to get the attention to be heard saying what he has to say. After that, I continued with my own monologues and put songs back into my act and went out on the road for two years, working night clubs in the South and Southwest. I learned how to entertain. . . .

In 1955, I was cast in the leading role, Will Stockdale, in the dramatization of "No Time for Sergeants," by Ira Levin, on Broadway. That was my first big chance. I had read the book *No Time for Sergeants*, because I'd met the author, Mac Hyman, while I was travelling in the South. . . . After I had appeared in "No Time for Sergeants" for almost the entire run of three hundred and forty-five performances, Elia Kazan put me in the movie "A Face in the Crowd." When I showed up to work on that movie, it was the first time in my life that I had seen a motion-picture camera. . . . I worked with some pretty outstanding people in that movie—some pretty fine men and women. Two of them were Patricia Neal and Walter Matthau, who were the first professional actors I ever got to know well. Making that movie was three months out of my life I wouldn't swap for anything. That was the first time I was called upon to play a serious dramatic part. It was the part of a guitar player, a down-and-outer who achieves fame and sudden acclaim. The reviews of that movie in New York were five good and two bad. I learned all I know about acting in making that one movie with Kazan. . . .

He taught me how to relate anything I had ever heard or ever read to what I was doing at the moment for the movie. I'd go over and tell him, "I had an experience once." And he'd say, "Yeah, tell me." Then he'd listen, and say, "Yeah, that's right, that's right." And I'd transfer that thought to what I was then doing. Since my experience in that movie, I've tried to do everything I could to make myself feel any part that I was playing. . . .

I'm limited as an actor. There are things other actors can do that I can't do. Other actors can act in a lot of fine things. I know I can't do the conventional serious dramatic acting. I'm not cut out to be a dramatic actor. I tried it. I played in "The Male Animal" on "Playhouse 90" in 1958, and I just couldn't do it. There's no point in doing what you don't enjoy, and if you don't do something well you can't enjoy it. I have an excellent time now doing my television show, called "The Andy Griffith Show." It's a weekly filmed situation comedy in which I star as Andy Taylor, the sheriff in a small Southern town. Making the television series takes a great deal of concentration, and you have to know what you're doing. But I enjoy doing the same character every week, and I don't have any difficulty in getting into that character at all. When I'm supposed to feel happy or angry or humorous, I'm able to make myself feel those things. I wouldn't mind playing the same kind of man for the rest of my life. I would like to continue to give people some small thing to make them laugh. What I would like to do, whenever I act or entertain, is to say some small truth. No preaching—just to have some small thing to say that is true.

ᕫᐞ *A Power in the East*

Rob Christensen

For nearly a century, the University of North Carolina at Chapel Hill was the only public institution of higher learning with a claim on the affection and resources of the people of the state. But on the eve of the twentieth century, North Carolina began chartering other institutions: to educate blacks, to train teachers, and to meet the demand for technicians and engineers in agriculture and industry. Soon those institutions were competing for state dollars.

No education leader better personifies that competition than Dr. Leo Jenkins. As chief administrative officer at East Carolina College at Greenville from 1960 to 1978, he transformed a small, teacher-training institution into a burgeoning university with its own medical school. His success raised hopes and instilled pride in eastern North Carolina, revived sectionalism in state politics, and ultimately forced the reorganization of all the state's higher education institutions under one governing board.

This profile by Rob Christensen appeared in the Raleigh *News and Observer* on June 25, 1978, as Jenkins was about to retire as chancellor of East Carolina University. Jenkins died in January 1989.

ᕫᐞ The high and mighty of North Carolina politics gathered on a platform in Ficklen Stadium in Greenville one day last May. There were Governor James B. Hunt Jr., and former Governors Robert W. Scott and Terry Sanford, Senators Jesse Helms and Robert Morgan, and Lieutenant Governor James C. Green.

It was commencement day at East Carolina University, but the political heavyweights had not come to watch the 2,828 students receive their diplomas. They were there because Leo W. Jenkins was making his last commencement address before retiring as ECU chancellor.

These men had all been to Greenville before. They had dined in the chancellor's yellow brick house and had posed to have their picture taken with their arms around Leo. The pictures now hung in a passageway in the chancellor's home which Jenkins jokingly refers to as his "Rogues Gallery."

For seventeen years Jenkins had held a center-stage position in North Carolina politics. He had been the driving force behind the transformation of once lightly regarded "Eee Cee Tee Cee" [a sing-song abbreviation for East Carolina Teachers College] into one of the major universities in the state—complete with its own medical school and big-time college athletics. In the words of one long-time political observer, Jenkins had crafted "a star in the crown of an impoverished region."

He accomplished it by becoming a skilled politician and using regional pride to build a formidable political base. And he had emerged as one of the leading spokesmen for the east. Jenkins was probably one of the few college presidents who could stop at a gas station or a country store and be greeted: "Give 'em hell, Leo."

"I want to admit—number one—that I am a politician and I'm going to die a politician," Jenkins said in a recent interview. But Jenkins, a gutsy political street fighter, had also made countless enemies along the way. He battled the state's educational establishment, which believed that the state could not afford another major university. And he was accused of building an empire for his own self-gratification.

"I took the opposite view from the Grantland Rice philosophy," he said. "I don't believe this business of it's not important if you win or lose, but how you play the game. I believe it's mighty important that you win."

Not surprisingly there are two different views of Jenkins as he steps down as chancellor.

"I think unquestionably it will be said, 'Here was a leader and a fighter for eastern North Carolina, a man who could get things accomplished,' " said R. W. Howard, a Greenville bank executive and long-time friend of Jenkins.

Said H. Dail Holderness of Tarboro, retired chairman of Carolina Telephone and Telegraph Company: "I can't think of anyone who has done more for eastern North Carolina than Leo Jenkins."

But there are those who are more skeptical and who believe Jenkins exploited regional prejudices, using tactics which splintered the state's educational leadership. Said one educator: "He unified the east around an idea—almost to the extent of developing a paranoia—that everyone was against us."

But on that May commencement day, Leo Jenkins didn't have to rely on the opinions of others to evaluate his work. He could almost reach out and touch his accomplishments. There were, first of all, the 40,000-seat Ficklen Stadium and the nearby Minges Coliseum. Across Charles Street was the home of the School of Allied Health and Social Professions and the Developmental Evaluation Clinic.

Over on Tenth Street there was the A. J. Fletcher Music Center and on College Hill Drive there were the high rise dormitories. Elsewhere were the Leo Jenkins Fine Arts Center, the nursing school building, and the Brewster liberal arts classroom building, the new biology building, the new student center, and more. And, of course, there was the medical school.

Leo Jenkins would seem an unlikely political hero for a rural area like eastern North Carolina. He was born in 1913 in Succassuna, New Jersey, the son of an oil refinery worker. He has never lost his harsh, fast-clipped northern New Jersey accent or his aggressive, blunt, Yankee demeanor.

Jenkins arrived in Greenville in 1947, a short time after his release from the Marine Corps. He had excelled in the Marines, entering as a buck private at the beginning of World War II and leaving as a major. He won the Bronze Star when he was the only officer to survive the first wave landing at Red Beach One on the South Pacific island of Guadalcanal.

He came to ECU after a brief stint as assistant to the New Jersey commissioner of education. Then ECU President John Messick, a former colleague at Montclair State Teachers College in New Jersey, had invited him down to become dean of instruction.

Leo Jenkins likes to talk. Ask him a question and he will talk 20 minutes non-stop, switching subjects several times, and throwing in a humorous anecdote or two, free of charge. When Messick was unable to make a speaking engagement, he would send his garrulous young dean.

"I tried to think," Jenkins recalled, "what could help them, what would they want to hear. So I started trying out for size some of those dreams."

By the time he was named president in 1960, he had developed "The Speech." It went something like this: Eastern North Carolina was "one of the last places that typify the good America." It was a land of clear skies, clean water, pristine beaches and a place where there existed a "people who hadn't been spoiled—still courteous, still polite." But the east was "a sleeping giant," a "neglected agrarian region" that lagged behind the rest of the state. There needed to be a renaissance, and the center for that renaissance would be ECU.

In a 1964 article written for the *News and Observer*, Jenkins outlined his dream: "There is a need in eastern North Carolina for a focal point and an articulate spokesman to spark a new era of progress for the region. This center, like the settlement houses of the social reformers in the blighted areas of cities, can be a place where ideas flow freely. . . . It could be the clearing house, meeting place and workshop for all the people and agencies striving to use the total area approach for betterment of the economic, political, social and cultural life of the region."

The message from the unabashed, chauvinistic speech was clear. The future of the small teachers college in Greenville and the future of eastern North Carolina were inextricably intertwined. The speech was delivered to Moose lodges, PTAs, Sunday school classes, political rallies, high school football banquets, book clubs and Jaycees. Rarely would Jenkins turn down an invitation, speaking four or five nights per week, year after year. He gave 250 high school commencement addresses, including the graduation speech heard by Governor James B. Hunt Jr., [when he was a student] at Rock Ridge High School in Wilson County.

Jenkins was building a political base. He had plunged into North Carolina politics shortly after he arrived here. He was active, for example, in promoting Governor Kerr Scott's [1949] road bond issue. As Jenkins went along, he began to forge ties with legislators that he would call on when he came to Raleigh with an armful of ambitious plans.

"We had to do it (build ECU) through the legislature and the only way we could do that was to go to the various pig pickings, fish frys and rat killings," Jenkins said. "I attended literally hundreds of these. You get a legislator aside and talk to him and then you get another legislator aside and talk to him. That's where most of the lobbying is done."

And he entertained people in his home. One year he estimated that 4,500 people ate in his house. Many of them had never before been invited to have dinner with a college president.

And he did the necessary political chores. "In order to stay in good with the political establishment we had to do favors," Jenkins recalled. "If a legislator would write me on behalf of some student and the student was not eligible at all (for admission), rather than flatly turning him down it was much easier to get the legislator on the phone and let him be the first to know what you were going to do. . . .

"And we would stay with this youngster until we could get him in some place. There is always some place in America that wants a body. . . . So we'd say, 'Look, we'll get your youngster in college X. If he makes good at college X, he can transfer after the first year, or after the second year.' The recipient would be happy, the legislator would be happy, and we'd have a friend."

Soon after becoming president, Jenkins started going to the legislature with his proposals to develop a major university. There were the creation of a nursing school, the start of a business school, a new emphasis on the arts, including drama, music and painting. There were big-time athletics and there was the medical school.

Rarely did Jenkins miss an opportunity to make a pitch. When Senator John F. Kennedy visited Greenville while campaigning for president in 1960, Jenkins talked him into publicly urging that ECU be admitted into the Southern Conference.

His best weapons, Jenkins said, were the facts. And the facts were, Jenkins told legislators, that eastern North Carolina did not have a major university, did not have enough roads, did not have enough doctors, was poor and lacked cultural life.

"The time was appropriate for doing things in eastern North Carolina," said former Governor Terry Sanford. "Those of us who live in the eastern section feel we have been generally neglected," Sanford said. "That may not be so, but we felt that way."

Friends say Jenkins also saw it as a personal challenge. His singleness of purpose is illustrated by the story he tells of how ECU and several other colleges were promoted to university status during the 1967 General Assembly session.

"When they (his opponents) knew we would probably get university status, some legislators said the best way to beat those fellows is to give university status to all of them (state financed colleges). Some of the rednecks down there [in Raleigh] won't like that at all. They'll be very angry because some of the black schools will get university status," said Jenkins, mimicking his opponents.

"So we met with four or five of our senators, including Bobby Morgan. . . . We talked 'til about three o'clock in the morning in the Velvet Cloak. We finally decided—look—if they are going to play that game, let's play the game right back again. We don't care if they make Podunk High School a university. . . . All we are interested in is East Carolina College."

As Jenkins' plans became increasingly ambitious, the opposition from the education establishment—the state Board of Higher Education and the University of North Carolina—became louder. Some of the most vocal opposition came from North Carolina's major newspapers, which argued that Jenkins was an educational Babbitt, pouring the state's modest treasury into his own empire in Greenville. Jenkins said he was the subject of about 90 editorial cartoons over the years, most of which are hanging in his house. Only two, he said, are favorable.

Jenkins said he believes the newspapers attacked him because they were allied with the major Piedmont universities. "They (the newspapers) were very close to the main universities," he said. "They thought they were helping home base—they would be more popular in their circles."

Some feel Jenkins was able to use the press opposition to his own advantage. "The newspapers made him an anti-hero," said one Jenkins critic. "They tried to expose him and in the process they made him a hero." Jenkins acknowledges that his image as the little college president fighting all the big city types helped him. "People are fascinated by the underdog who is struggling," Jenkins said.

Rhetorical overkill and bombast were part of the Jenkins style. For example, in an April 1973 speech, Jenkins said, "Some of the people opposing the medical school at East Carolina University would make the Godfather look like a Rover Boy." One Jenkins critic observed that "maybe like the blacks and like the women, he had to overstate his case (to get his point across)."

When the chairman of North Carolina National Bank criticized plans for the medical school in 1975, Jenkins threatened to pull the college's money out of the NCNB Greenville branch, according to newspaper reports. Jenkins subsequently denied he made such a threat.

Jenkins also had ways of pressuring unfriendly legislators. "We'd have to let our alumni know, our friends know, that we don't have a friend in Representative X or we don't have a friend in Senator Y," Jenkins said. "I think in some cases it taught some people a lesson.

"We realized we would have to get some of our people in there (the legislature) and we most certainly have," Jenkins said. Among his closest political allies were Senator Robert Morgan (a former student), Representative Horton Rountree, Governor Hunt and Jesse Helms, then a Raleigh television editorialist.

Jenkins lists as among his toughest opponents Fourth District Congressman Ike F. Andrews (formerly a state representative), former state Senator Lindsay C. Warren Jr., and former state Senator L. P. McLendon Jr. By 1971, Jenkins' drive to make ECU a major university had helped set off bitter in-fighting among North Carolina's education leaders. In a remarkable speech delivered in Wrightsville Beach in 1971, Governor [Robert] Scott lambasted the education leaders. "It's comical," Scott said. "It's vicious. They've got an intelligence system that's unbelievable. Bill Friday, Leo Jenkins, Cam West. . . . They're like kids. It's sickening."

Friday was president of the University of North Carolina, and West, at the time, was director of the state Board of Higher Education. Partly as a result of that fighting, the General Assembly in 1971 voted to reorganize higher education, creating the UNC Board of Governors to oversee the 16-campus system of state-supported colleges. No longer would Jenkins have quite the same freedom to sell his programs to the legislature. But by that time Jenkins had gotten nearly everything he wanted.

Since 1947 the campus had grown from 18 buildings on 140 acres to 74 buildings on 411 acres. During that period, the school grew from 1,605 students to 12,000 and the payroll increased from 180 employees to 1,614.

Jenkins argues with those who feel his ambitions for ECU hurt North Carolina's education system. "I think competition is the life-blood of America," Jenkins said. "The more competition we have among colleges and universities, the better off we will be. I think we ought to make them run for their money," he added.

While he was making the other campuses run for their money, Jenkins was leaving most of the administration of ECU to his subordinates. Jenkins' management style was to surround himself with talented people and let them run the university. Even his critics acknowledged that ECU was a well-run school.

But the critics have often questioned the academic rigor of the campus, saying Jenkins emphasized quantity over quality. "People can't document that," said Jenkins. He ticked off a list of education benchmarks: all of ECU's nursing graduates passed the state certification exam last year; ECU teaching graduates performed better than those of most other schools on the state certification exam; in the last three years, the O. Max Gardner Award, given to one outstanding professor in the 16-campus UNC system, has twice gone to an ECU professor.

Jenkins will leave all this behind Friday. He says he doesn't want to stick around Greenville, looking over the shoulder of Thomas B. Brewer, the new chancellor. Jenkins has been hired as a part-time twelve-thousand-dollar-a-year economic development consultant to Governor Hunt. Jenkins also hopes to continue to make speeches and possibly be host on a radio or television talk show somewhere in North Carolina.

In all, he hopes to make about fifty thousand dollars per year in retirement, slightly more than he made as chancellor. As a retirement gift he was given fifty thousand dollars and a new car by his supporters. He plans to divide his time between a Raleigh apartment and a condominium at Pine Knoll Shores at Atlantic Beach. He says he will devote more time to his hobbies—painting land- and seascapes and fishing for blues, spot and croaker. . . .

Jenkins has never been shy about how he thinks history should judge him. As his official biography, put out by the ECU news bureau, says of his retirement, "And Leo Jenkins would step, not only into the annals of education, but also into the history of leadership in North Carolina."

When asked how history will ultimately judge Jenkins, one educator paused and said: "It depends on who writes it."

❧ The Mellowing of Billy Graham

Frye Gaillard

After holding crusades in every corner of the world, evangelist Billy Graham of Charlotte and Montreat may be America's best-known preacher. But, as this essay makes clear, he has not been universally admired. Like many other evangelists in the southern Bible Belt, he rose to prominence by espousing the gospel—and the social agenda of the ruling class.

In the wake of recent criticism, however, his tone and message have changed, as author-reporter Frye Gaillard makes clear in this essay, condensed from his book *Race, Rock and Religion: Profiles from a Southern Journalist*, published in 1982.

❧ The stadium suddenly filled with the sound of his voice, rich and honey-toned and gently pleading, the words familiar after so many years, falling on the crowd of 32,000. His thoughts and phrases were mostly unremarkable, streams of certainty about the power of the faith, the disaster that looms at the end of other paths.

"You come forward now, men and women, black or white; you come, hundreds of you. It'll only take a moment to come. Mothers, fathers, young people too. The ushers will show you. You may be an elder or a deacon in the church, but you come. . . ."

And they did come, moving forward silently in numbers that were startling—some weeping softly, others holding hands and popping Juicy Fruit gum, but coming, streaming down the aisles from throughout the arena, the choir as always singing, "Just As I Am." And above it all the same hypnotic voice.

"You come now. . . . It's important that you come. There's something about coming forward and standing here that helps settle it in your mind. . . ."

When you see Billy Graham in that kind of setting—when he stands before the crowd with his sun-tanned face and his pale blue stare, with the odd, lingering innocence of some aging surfer—it's a little hard to fathom what it all really means. There is an air about him of absolute sincerity. But what about the substance? What are crowds left with when the service is over? What vision, what understanding of the depths of Christianity?

His critics have answered such questions harshly, contending over the years that there's a clunking banality at the heart of Graham's message, a sanitized, Americanized understanding of Jesus that renders him irrelevant to 20th-century turmoil.

Reinhold Niebuhr was one of the first to make the charge. In the tumultuous summer of 1956—a time when Martin Luther King and his followers were boycotting buses in pursuit of integration—Niebuhr wrote an article for the *Christian Century*. He quoted the epistle of First John ("If a man sayeth he loves God and hateth his brother, he is a liar") and urged Graham to speak out about racial upheavals.

Other critics emerged in the '60s and '70s, culminating in 1979, when journalist Marshall Frady produced a biography of Graham—an eloquent critique that drew wide acclaim. Frady concluded that Graham, the farmboy evangelist from the outskirts of Charlotte, was so affected by the wooings of the powerful that he could no longer distinguish between Richard Nixon's America and the Kingdom of God. . . .

But two years later, the criticism is fading. There is a widespread feeling that Graham has mellowed, almost suddenly and strangely, and that his thinking has taken on at least a faint prophetic tinge. He speaks out now on a host of social issues, from hunger to nuclear weapons, declaring during a recent crusade in Baltimore:

"We are staring at the possibility of war in the Middle East, or an invasion of Poland. We are spending a million dollars a minute on armaments all over the world, little nations working on the atomic bomb. . . . People are hungry and starving in Somalia and other places. . . . Have we gone mad? . . . Are we seeking the genocide of the whole human race?" . . .

The first time I met him, I did not expect to like him.

It was a misty June Sunday in 1979, a couple of months after the appearance of Frady's book. Graham meandered into the living room of his spacious log home, hidden away on a mountain in the town of Montreat. He moved with a slouching, good-natured gait, his arms dangling loosely at his side, and he seemed very different from his TV persona—vastly more vulnerable and even a little shy.

My awareness of him had crystalized during bursts of public certitude, in the heat of the '60s, amid all the national agony over Vietnam. He would pound at the pulpits on television crusades, inveighing against the storms of youthful rebellion. "There is just too much negativism," he would say in those days. "There are too many people knocking our institutions. . . ." And he would call to the podium assorted young Marines, clean-cut and earnest, to explain how God had helped them kill Communists.

On domestic moral issues, he was equally as shrill. In 1971, for example, in his hometown of Charlotte, all the city's powerful gathered in his honor—on an unseasonably hot October afternoon, with a private reception featuring Danish lobster tails and cross-shaped sandwiches and a 30-pound cake in the shape of a Bible. There was also a public ceremony with 12,000 people, during which he offered inflated recollections of his boyhood hardships.

"We also wrestled with poverty, if you go by today's standards, except we did not know we were poor. We did not have sociologists, educators and newscasters constantly reminding us of how poor we were." Then he added to the applause of the crowd: "We also had the problem of rats. The only difference between then and now is we didn't call upon the federal government to kill them. . . ."

But eight years later in the summer of '79—in the reassuring privacy of a drizzly afternoon—his tone sounded different. He sank back leisurely on a padded couch and discussed the social implications of the Christian Gospel. As the conversation bounced from topic to topic—from nuclear war and hunger to capital punishment—he revealed some instincts that hadn't been apparent.

He was troubled, he said, by the resumption of capital punishment, the taint it could inflict on American justice.

"I just don't know," he explained. "We live in a time of horrible and hideous crimes. But one of the hesitations I've always had is that so many more blacks are executed. The system has always been too one-sided, and many of the people on death row are poor people who couldn't afford good lawyers.

"There is no perfect system of justice on this earth. God will have it at the judgment. But this is a very imperfect system. And execution makes the imperfection final."

But then he added in an odd little demurral: "Of course, I have never taken a stand on capital punishment. . . . I have to be careful what I say about a great many things."

Such hedgings have always been characteristic of Graham. Even in the cloister of his Montreat home, with its flock of friendly dogs and expansive hearth of old-fashioned brick, he seems inescapably aware that he is an institution. His identity is tied to his sense of mission, and he will let nothing—absolutely nothing—jeopardize his calling.

"My main focus is the Gospel," he explains with some urgency, as if it matters a great deal that his visitor understand. "I'm concerned about what it can do for you, for a person's life. There may be issues distantly related to the Gospel, or perhaps they are deeply related. But the gift of an evangelist is a very narrow gift."

His awareness of that gift has defined his life—ever since his six-teenth year, when, as a handsome, thoroughly ordinary teenager, given to mischievous transgressions regarding girls and fast cars, he and a buddy decided to take in a revival in Charlotte.

They winced at the ferocity of the presiding evangelist—an itinerant, florid-faced anti-Semite named Mordecai Ham—but they moved forward tremulously at the altar-call. Graham says today that he almost didn't go. But at the last possible moment, with an ill-defined guilt surging violently inside him, he walked hesitantly up the aisle and asked Jesus to forgive him.

The experience left him with an exalted sense of propriety, a tendency to scold his friends for the most minor misbehavior—and before long you could find him on Charlotte street-corners, stalking and raging and preaching to pedestrians, charging them to repent before it was too late.

A year and a half later, in 1936, he and a friend, Grady Wilson, graduated from high school and set off to South Carolina for a summer of traveling, selling Fuller brushes and witnessing for Jesus when the opportunity arose. Then he went away to college—first to the hard-bitten, ultra-fundamentalist Bob Jones University, where he was miserable, then on to the more warm-hearted Florida Bible Institute.

There, in the suburbs of Tampa, his thinking and style took on the first hints of polish. His faith seemed to deepen. His fire and brimstone understanding of sin became at least a little tempered by his sunny disposition, his gathering optimism about the effectiveness of faith.

And after graduation, as his evangelizing gained momentum in the 1940s, the crowds were caught up in his natural, vibrant decency. He still lunged about the pulpit and lashed at the air with his pointed forefinger—still warned them urgently of the ravages of hell. But there was an undeniable compassion about him, then as now, when he stood before the people at the altar invitation, and told them softly:

"I have no power to save anybody, to forgive anybody, to heal anybody. . . . I'm praying right now while I'm talking to you. I'm praying, 'Lord, help me say the right thing to that person before me. . . .'"

But there was another major component to Graham's appeal—one that caught the attention of some powerful people and thrust him suddenly into superstardom. Not only did he embody all the traditional American virtues, . . . he also saw America as God's great hope, a righteous instrument to evangelize the world.

During a Los Angeles crusade in 1949, he proclaimed that the planet "is divided into two camps. On the one side we see Communism. On the other, we see so-called Western culture, with its fruit and its foundation in the Bible, the Word of God, and in the revivals of the seventeenth and eighteenth centuries. Communism, on the other hand, has declared war against God, against Christ, against the Bible. . . ."

Such words fell pleasantly on the ears of William Randolph Hearst, the irascible West Coast newspaper magnate. "And that was when," explains Grady Wilson, Graham's associate evangelist for more than 30 years, "Mr. Hearst gave the order to 'puff Graham.' "

What Mr. Hearst ordered his reporters quickly did, and suddenly Graham's picture was splattered across the pages of the nation's biggest papers—prompting soon afterwards Time-Life's Henry Luce to get into the act. And as Wilson remembers it, "Mr. Luce ran a three-page color spread and story. . . ."

Graham was stunned, perhaps even frightened, by the sudden and unrelenting gales of attention. He remembers that he telephoned a colleague in Chicago and told him: "You better get out here. Something's happening, and I don't know what it is. It's way beyond me."

Such feelings of inadequacy are not at all surprising. Graham has about him a genuine, deep-rooted, almost awesome humility—a rigorous understanding of his own ordinariness—that's still intact after 30 years of accolades. It is, perhaps, his most touching trait. But it has a peculiar flip side—a lingering need to justify himself, which has left him, unfortunately, susceptible to flattery.

And the flattery has come from the highest of places—beginning with Hearst and Luce and spreading quickly into the realm of politics. After the Los Angeles crusade, Graham and his team moved on to Boston—"the closest thing to a real revival we've experienced," says Grady Wilson. There, amid the emotion of overflow crowds, they attracted the attention of House Speaker John McCormack—a Massachusetts Catholic, who was impressed by the effectiveness of Graham's appeal.

"He decided that Billy should meet President Truman," says Wilson. So the visit was arranged—Graham, Wilson and a couple of other team members talking stiffly with Truman, then suddenly and exuberantly suggesting a prayer. Truman seemed somewhat embarrassed by it all, but such misgivings faded in the minds of his successors.

Eisenhower, Johnson, and Richard Nixon—even the urbane John Kennedy—recognized the benefits of cordiality with Graham. They praised him publicly and courted him privately—Eisenhower calling him "the greatest ambassador that America has"—and Graham, for his part, returned the admiration.

"Nobody," says former Johnson aide and protege Bill Moyers, "could make Johnson feel he was right quite like Billy Graham could." And

Johnson, of course, was in need of that, for like Nixon after him, he was presiding over a war and a national dissolution—the ungluing, as Moyers noted, of the veneer of consensus that held the country together.

It became clear in those bitter days—despite careful hedgings and disingenuous denials—that Graham had planted his feet on a particular side of the chasm. While insisting that he was neutral on the war, he poured forth an uncountable number of statements like these: U.S. troops "know why they are fighting in Vietnam, and they believe what they are doing is right. . . . We either face an all-out war with Red China or a retreat that will cause us to lose face throughout Asia. . . ." And when Martin Luther King denounced the war, Graham called it "an affront to the thousands of loyal Negro troops who are in Vietnam."

His critics became numerous in the wake of such pronouncements. Protestors began showing up at his speeches, armed with placards denouncing his stands. Even other ministers began to criticize him harshly—and not just the Ivy League liberals, who believed that Jesus was a social reformer, but also a growing number of evangelicals.

Chief among the latter were a pair of clerics, Jim Holloway and Will Campbell, who headed a loosely-knit Christian confederation called the Committee of Southern Churchmen. Holloway was a teacher at Berea College in Kentucky, Campbell a Southern Baptist expatriate from Mississippi, a renegade preacher who had been deeply involved in the civil rights movement.

In 1971, during the peak years of friendship between Graham and Richard Nixon, Campbell and Holloway wrote an open letter, published in a religious journal called *Katallagete*. They urged Graham to take a cue from the Old Testament prophets and to use his influence to lobby for peace: ". . . Why do we address ourselves to you, Dr. Graham? . . . We believe the only way you, or any of us, can *minister* to the White House or the Pentagon is to *prophesy* to the White House and the Pentagon in the tradition of Micaiah, son of Imlah. And you, our brother, have been and will be the prophet summoned to those halls. We shall not."

Graham generally responded to the criticism pleasantly. "I want you to know," he wrote Campbell and Holloway, "that I do not take it personally and am not the slightest bit offended. Sometime we might be able to sit down privately and discuss the points you have raised. . . ." But that was it. The meeting didn't happen, for Graham simply resubmerged—with a kind of gee-whiz overflow of modesty and gratitude—into the stream of acclamation that came his way.

"All this for a preacher—and an evangelist at that," he beamed in

1971, when 12,000 people, including Richard Nixon, turned out in Charlotte for a day in his honor. "I'm sure," he added graciously, when asked about the crowds, "they're coming to see the President, not me. . . ."

But then suddenly, it was gone. Nixon resigned in the throes of scandal, and Graham—who had supported him with more ardor and affection than he had ever felt for a political figure—found his own reputation in a severe state of taint. He was bewildered. He listened to the tapes, with all the vulgarities and sinister plottings, and two years later, he told Marshall Frady:

"I just couldn't understand it. I still can't. I thought he was a man of integrity, I looked upon him as the possibility of leading this country to its greatest and best days. And all those people around him, they seemed so clean, family men, so clean-living. Sometimes, when I look back on it all now, it has the aspects of a nightmare. . . ."

In the wake of that experience that brought him up short, confronting him starkly with the complexities of human nature, the evil that can lurk beneath benign exteriors, Graham has emerged as a more reflective person. He has absorbed a variety of thought-provoking experiences, and his relationship to American politics and culture—his understanding of America's mission in the world—is not what it was. . . .

"I'm concerned," he will tell you, "about the terrifying weapons that are being developed at the moment, on all sides, the proliferation of nuclear arms. . . . Countries, especially in the Middle East, are working feverishly on the atomic bomb, and one of them could easily push a button and unleash an atomic war in the Middle East which could draw the whole world into it. . . .

"I feel that the Scriptures teach that not only are we to be peacemakers—the Scriptures say that we are to work hard at peace and live peaceably with all men. . . . I am not for unilateral disarmament. I think we have a right to defend ourselves . . . but I do feel that as human beings on a planet that can self-destruct we ought to sit down and say, 'Here, we must negotiate this.' . . ."

He continues to talk, acknowledging freely the things he doesn't know, the mistakes he has made, the regrets about his past and his lapses of wisdom.

"There are issues," he admits, "that I don't know the answer to. I don't know the answer to when a fetus becomes a person. . . . I don't think any of us really knows. There are people that think they do, but I don't. There are areas like this on which I'm not qualified to speak. . . . So I would say that in that sense there has been a pilgrimage in my thinking over a period of years that has accelerated maybe in the last five years. . . .

"My gospel hasn't changed, but the application of the gospel in social and political areas has changed. . . . I might have been influenced by my trips to Eastern Europe where I saw vast groups of people who are praying and hoping for peace. In Poland, Hungary and other parts of the world, where everytime there is a war in Europe they seemed to be trampled on by either side.

"You know, Eisenhower once said publicly that I was the greatest ambassador that America had. . . . Of course at that moment when he said it in the 1950s, I was pleased. Now I would not be pleased because I feel that my ministry today is a world ministry. I think now when I say something, 'How is this going to sound in India? How is it going to sound to my friends in Hungary or Poland?'

"I don't ever want to dodge the truth, and I don't ever want to back down on what my convictions are. But I'm beginning to see that there are more sides to some of these questions than I once thought. I am not as dogmatic."

◁ A Buttoned-Down Boat-Rocker

Luisita Lopez

No other lawyer has done as much to break down racial barriers for blacks in North Carolina as Julius L. Chambers of Mount Gilead and Charlotte. At one point in the 1960s, he had school desegregation lawsuits pending in more than fifty of the state's school districts, including *Swann v. Mecklenburg*, which became the national test case for busing to achieve desegregation. This profile, written by Luisita Lopez and published in the *Charlotte Observer* of December 10, 1972, looks beyond the lawsuits to reveal the man behind them. Since this profile was written, Chambers has moved to New York City to become executive director of the NAACP Legal Defense Fund, directing legal efforts on behalf of blacks all over the country.

◁ You could see the black boy, a nervous child smaller than his 13 years, running across the fields, or hitting balls out back or climbing trees— Lord, his father remembers with a smile, you could hardly get him down from those trees.

But on this late afternoon in the spring of 1949, the boy was sitting quietly in the living room of his four-room house in Mount Gilead, N.C., listening somberly to his father. He watched the lanky man hold back tears, the lines on his 43-year-old face deepening. His mother, a sturdy woman whose stern discipline matched her firm belief in the Bible, sat by in silence, her eyes downcast.

Slumped on a chair, Bill Chambers slowly explained to his family that he had lost the $2,000 a white fellow who operated a trucking outfit in town had owed him. Chambers had maintained and repaired the man's rig, buying parts for it out of his own pocket, over a period of months. That morning the man had refused to pay the bill, jeering at Chambers and driving off with the rig. The few white lawyers downtown, where Chambers had spent the afternoon knocking on doors asking for help, had turned him away, one by one.

The elder Chambers—"Shine" to many of his customers who had known him since the days he washed model-T Fords for a living—and his wife, Mathilda, had put 20 years into building their business, a combination garage-general-store on the outskirts of Mount Gilead, a farming community of 1,200 people south of Albemarle, 40 miles northeast of Charlotte.

They had been doing well enough to save a little money, secure bank loans and send their two older children, a boy and a girl, to Laurinburg Institute, a private all-black boarding school about 100 miles away in Laurinburg.

The family had big plans for that $2,000. Their third child, 13-year-old Julius, was about to enter high school and they had hoped to enroll him, too, at Laurinburg Institute. Julius had dreamed of that, following his big brother's footsteps. Now, his eyes glued to his father's face that spring day in 1949, the boy absorbed the hurt. Disappointment and anger filled his mind. He would help his father. He would become a lawyer.

That, at least, is the way Julius LeVonne Chambers—now 36, prominent and well-off—remembers the boyhood incident that he says propelled him to law school and to his crucial role in the tumultuous desegregation of the Charlotte-Mecklenburg schools, and the extensive busing that enraged vast numbers of white parents.

His broad face immobile, Chambers coolly insists that he has no sympathy for the thousands of white parents who see busing as an outrageous infringement of their own rights and those of their children. Yet, when pressed, he concedes having felt some fleeting concern when his 6-year-old son, Derrick, who last year attended the private and integrated Myers Park Baptist Church kindergarten, got on a school bus for the first time this fall to attend the first grade at Oakdale Elementary School, three miles away from home, a 20-minute ride beyond the city limits on the northwest side of town.

And Chambers admits that his own parents, ironically, sent three of their four children to private school partly because they didn't want them "waiting out there in the cold" for the bus.

"My parents' case was different," he contends. "The buses were ancient and the school in Troy was terrible. Their situation isn't comparable to that of parents today. . . ."

He explains that at the public high school in Troy, to which he traveled 12 miles each way on an old bus, a castoff from a white school, learning took a back seat. Students were made to kill and cut up hogs on the principal's farm; and English class consisted of doing errands. "When I entered college, I didn't know how to write an essay and could hardly spell."

He also cites as a reason for his disdain of white busing opponents the long-time busing of other black children miles from their homes past white schools they were forbidden by law to attend. . . .

Chambers insists that race—not busing itself—is the real issue behind the white community's opposition. But he stops short of saying that antibusing whites are racists. "Let's say," he shrugs, "they have a lot of hang-ups."

Chambers reclines his compact 5-foot-7½ frame against the back of his swivel chair, his hands pulling on a rubber band. "There are a lot of misguided whites, . . . but there are some blacks, too, who are misguided. Blacks and whites are not all that different." . . .

Julius Chambers, for all his inclinations as a community boat-rocker, wears the trappings of the establishment. He is immaculately conservative in neatly cut suits, vests, close-cropped hair. He fits the mold of the corporate businessman, the hard-driving executive of 36. No fiery rabble-rouser, no strident militant raising a clenched fist, Chambers sits well in board rooms, among long-socked men with their briefcases and distinguished credentials. He has accepted testimonials from the best law schools in the nation; he has taught seminars at Ivy League universities; he has gained membership in exclusive societies like UNC's Order of the Golden Fleece, and in reputable, liberal organizations like the Southern Regional Council.

Until just a few years ago, Chambers was a largely unknown young lawyer who had 10 years ago attracted a flurry of headlines upon becoming the first black to edit the University of North Carolina's Law Review. Then, in the late 1960s, he captured wide attention—which he claims to dislike—with his handling of the school case, *Swann v. Charlotte-Mecklenburg Board of Education.* . . .

Chambers studied law at UNC and at Columbia University, where he took a master's degree while working as a law clerk for the Legal Defense Fund's headquarters in New York City. By the time he opened his office in Charlotte, in July, 1964 he had acquired a handful of diplomas—a B.A. from N.C. Central University in Durham, a master's degree from the University of Michigan and his two law degrees.

He started general practice—with the help of an undisclosed sum of money advanced by the Legal Defense Fund—in what his partner Adam Stein describes as a "cold-water flat" above a finance company at Brevard and East Trade streets. Stein, a white Princeton, N.J., native, who had interned one summer with Chambers, joined him a year later and together they formed one of the few biracial law firms in the South, the first in Charlotte.

In eight years the firm—Chambers, Stein, Ferguson & Lanning—has mushroomed. Stein now heads a branch in Chapel Hill and there are 11 members—including five whites—in the firm, currently handling some 1,200 cases, 40 per cent of which involve civil rights (among them, about 30 school desegregation lawsuits in North Carolina.) The firm's lawyers represent a diverse number of individuals and groups—the cafeteria workers at Duke University, the predominantly white firefighters' union in Charlotte and other Carolinas cities. But their clientele consists primarily of poor blacks who often cannot afford to pay.

The firm, whose income Chambers declines to discuss, makes its money off the more lucrative cases: tort claims, real estate and property litigation, contracts.

Their temporary offices, drab, dimly lit, are on a wing of the third floor of the White House Inn on West Trade Street. On a recent Monday afternoon, two disheveled, weary-looking women sat on cheap vinyl sofas in the reception room, thumbing through law magazines and copies of the *Wall Street Journal*, the only reading available. Chambers' office, large and cluttered with metal bookcases heaving with briefs and magazines shows no signs of affluence.

But within months, the offices will be moved to a yellow brick-and-glass seven-story building that Chambers, his brother, Kenneth, an obstetrician, and other black professionals are building—and hoping to fill with white and black tenants—on East Independence Boulevard and McDowell Street at a cost of $3.2 million.

His investment in the building, Chambers says, is proof of his faith in Charlotte, a city he has adopted as his home. His attachment to Charlotte is not unlike that of many people who come here for good jobs, because the city is growing yet livable, a good place to raise children, accessible and convenient. He says he wants to help shape the city to fit his concept of the ideal community—where parks are within walking distance of all children, where government services are extended to blacks and whites alike, where a black family can buy a home in any neighborhood without fearing for their safety or for the value of their property. He wants integration at every level and says he will push for it, using the prime weapons at his command—the law and the courts.

Chambers's courtroom style and his intimate knowledge of the law have gained him substantial praise, which he insists embarrasses him. The compliments come mainly from legal experts and people outside Charlotte. Jack Greenberg, for instance, the director of the Legal Defense Fund, describes Chambers as "among the great civil rights attorneys in the nation." And when a group of people in North Carolina called former Attorney General Ramsey Clark in Washington asking him to recommend an attorney, the name of Julius Chambers quickly came to mind.

Chambers's meticulous preparation, his understatement, the crisp, impersonal tone are cited by those who have observed him in court.

Among them is Judge James B. McMillan, who shared center stage with him during the school case. McMillan regards him as a "first-class lawyer, a man of great courage and capacity" and is particularly impressed, he says, by Chambers's pursuit of change through "orthodox legal methods." The 55-year-old judge cites Chambers's fact-packed arguments, saying that when the case started "I frankly thought it was a lot of foolishness (on the part of blacks), but as it developed and the facts were brought out, I was persuaded." . . .

Julius Chambers lives comfortably in a three-bedroom brick house on a quiet, grassy subdivision off Beatties Ford Road, the west side's business and traffic artery. The house is typically suburban with a trimmed lawn (he hires a black yardman at $1.60 an hour) and a driveway big enough to accommodate his Lincoln Continental and his wife's new Mercedes-Benz sedan. The furnishings are French provincial, glass and leather. Modern paintings hang in the living room and den. A Fisher-Garrard Stereo system is tucked in a corner alongside racks of record albums—the Supremes, Gloria Lynne, other black entertainers.

Evenings at home with his family are unusual for him. Frequently he's traveling to meetings in Atlanta or Durham or Washington or he's out of town working on a case. Even when he's in town, the calendar is jammed—a movie, a concert, a party (he is said to be a fair dancer and a mean poker player).

But when he's home, he shares the "insanities of the day" with Vivian, his wife of 12 years, a small and vivacious woman from Kannapolis with a master's degree in education, and plays with their two adopted children, Derrick, and two-year-old Judy.

On slow Sundays, when they often skip church although he is a trustee of Friendship Baptist, he lets off steam on the golf course, where he is reputed to be a tough man to beat.

Flung in the barrel-shaped chair at the round table in the den, his Scotch and water within reach, booted feet propped up, Chambers discusses his comfortable way of life—his cars, his yardman, his parties.

"I'm setting an example for blacks so they can see what can be achieved through education and hard work. I remember when I was a kid seeing blacks taking a lot of stuff to make $5 a week and wondering, how in hell can people survive? You know, blacks want the same thing as whites . . . a nice house, a good job, money in the bank."

He is impatient with babble, disdains his critics, . . . says he feels at ease among people of prominence and affluence, but maintains that the people he really admires are simple and ordinary.

He mentions some of the people he listens to every day at the office— the tearful woman whose house has burned down and has nowhere to go, the man whose young son was put in jail, the family cheated out of the downpayment on a house. And he says he keeps in touch with the "black folk," traveling to remote towns all over the state to attend mass meetings.

". . . There's a beautiful lady in Greene County. She writes badly but she filed a lawsuit to desegregate the schools there. And there's a fellow in Reidsville who calls me up once, twice a week, always at 6 in the morning or very late at night wanting advice. He's out there working. And the man from Roanoke Rapids, and people in Jacksonville, in Murphy, all over the state, people you'll never hear about. . . ."

He ticks off the names, the places, in his dull, dry monotone, his perfect graduate-school diction, keeping whatever emotion he might feel well out of sight. His fingers crushing the cellophane cigarette wrapper, dropping it in the ashtray.

Julius Chambers, after all, is a man who prides himself on his "reflective, sober thinking," a man whose emotions seem remarkably impervious to the tumult that has surrounded his adult life.

He is so unshakeable that on that icy February night, almost two years ago, when his wife telephoned him in Raleigh to say that his office was burning down, he reflected on the frozen condition of the roads, fixed himself a drink, and went to sleep.

Generals William T. Sherman and Joseph E. Johnston meet at the Bennett Place for discussions leading to the close of the Civil War, Frank Leslie's *The American Soldier in the Civil War: A Pictorial History* (New York: Bryan, Taylor and Company, 1895). Courtesy North Carolina Division of Archives and History, Raleigh.

❧ George Washington Visits Salem

Adelaide Fries

In 1791, President Washington made a tour of the southern states. He spent thirteen days in April traveling by horse and carriage across North Carolina's Coastal Plain from Halifax to Wilmington through what he called "some of the most barren country I ever beheld." He went on to Charleston and Savannah and returned in May to spend nine days crossing North Carolina from Charlotte to Danville, Virginia. In the Piedmont he noted the lands were "of a fine red cast and well timbered."

This account, from *The Records of the Moravians*, edited by Adelaide Fries, describes his welcome to Salem.

❧ *May 31.* At the end of this month the congregation in Salem had the pleasure of welcoming the President of the United States, George Washington, who was returning from his tour of the Southern States. We had previously been informed that he would pass through our town on his way to Virginia. Today we received word that he had left Salisbury, thirty-five miles from here, this morning, so the Brn. Marshall, Köhler, and Benzien rode out to meet him. As he approached the town several tunes were played, partly by trumpets and French horns, partly by the trombones. In his company were only his secretary, Major Jackson, and the necessary servants. As he descended from his coach he greeted those who stood around in a friendly manner, showing his good will especially to the children who were there. Then he talked on various matters with several Brethren who had accompanied him to the room which had been prepared for him. At first he said that he was leaving in the morning, but when he heard that the Governor of this State had expressed a wish to wait upon him the next day he decided to rest here over one day. He sent word to our musicians that he would like some music during his evening meal, and it was furnished to him.

On the following day, that is on *June 1st*, the President and Major Jackson, guided by several Brethren, visited the workshops, the Choir houses, and other places in our town, and he expressed his approval of them, especially of the waterworks and the service they gave. An address had been prepared, in the name of the Brethren in Wachovia, expressing our dutiful sentiments toward the government of these States, and the President set a time at which he would receive it. In accordance therewith, at two o'clock it was presented to him by several Brethren, and after Br. Marshall had read it, as is customary, and presented it to him, the President in the same manner gave his answer, couched in favorable terms, and both papers are appended to this diary. Six Brethren were invited to dine with him, and during the meal music was again furnished.

Many came from the neighborhood, and from our other congregations, to the President, the most notable man in this country; and the President gladly gave them opportunity to gratify their wish.

Toward evening the Governor of this State, Mr. Alexander Martin, arrived from his estate, which is on Dan River only about forty miles from here. He, with the President and Major Jackson, attended a singstunde in the evening, the singing being interspersed with instrumental selections, and they expressed their pleasure in it. In the evening the wind instruments were heard again, playing sweetly near the tavern. Secretary Jackson inquired concerning our foundation principles, and was much pleased when we presented him with copies of the *History of the Unity* and the *Idea Fidei Fratrum*.

At four o'clock in the morning of *June 2nd* the entire company left, and the Brn. Marshall and Benzien accompanied them to the boundaries of Wachovia.

≈ *A Vote to Unite the State*

Burke Davis

In 1849, North Carolina began to address its need for improved transportation. The legislature entertained two proposals for building railroads. One called for the state to help finance an east-west line from Goldsboro to Raleigh to Greensboro and south to Charlotte, linking the Coastal Plain to the Piedmont. The line would be the centerpiece of a "North Carolina Plan" for public improvements. The other called for private investors to build a north-south route from Charlotte to Danville, linking the South Carolina railroad to another in Virginia. The second option was called "the Danville Steal."

The following account shows how those options created a personal and political dilemma for Senator Calvin Graves of Caswell County, through which the proposed Charlotte-to-Danville line would run, bringing the promise of prosperity. The account was excerpted from *The Southern Railway, Road of the Innovators*, by Burke Davis, a Durham native who was raised in Greensboro, edited newspapers in Charlotte and Greensboro, and later wrote fifty books, many of them on events in North Carolina history.

❧ North Carolina was probably the first southern state to hear the call of the railroad age—and one of the last to heed it. As early as 1822 the prophetic Dr. Joseph Caldwell, president of the University of North Carolina, proclaimed the benefits to be had from a rail line linking the port of Beaufort with Asheville in the mountains.

With the aid of Judge Archibald DeBow Murphey, a leading Tar Heel historian, Dr. Caldwell campaigned for a system of canals and improved waterways to reach every part of the state, to be supplemented by railroad lines. Before his death in 1832, Judge Murphey had passed his enthusiasm to a young law student in his office—John Motley Morehead. For the rest of his active life Morehead was to campaign for railroads as a means of overcoming North Carolina's isolation. Soon after he became governor of the state in 1841, Morehead urged the legislature to approve a large network of railroads, canals, and turnpikes, and took up the railroad cause when he left office in 1845.

While he and his colleagues were stumping the state to fan public interest in their railroad projects and other public improvements of "The North Carolina Plan," two distinguished Americans visited the state and helped to shock lethargic legislators into action. Senator Stephen A. Douglas of Illinois, one of the most celebrated orators of the day, came on a romantic mission, to court a young woman who lived in Rockingham County. And Dorothea Dix, a well-known reformer, came to promote the establishment of hospitals for the mentally ill. These two visitors found travel over North Carolina roads so trying that they appeared voluntarily before the legislature to brand "the worst-roads state" as a trial to all travelers. Both Douglas and Dix urged building of railroads as an antidote to the isolation and backwardness that gripped the state in that era. By 1849 these combined efforts yielded results. A bill creating the North Carolina Railroad, to run for 223 miles from Goldsboro in the east to Raleigh, Greensboro, and Charlotte, came before the Assembly, where it was hotly debated.

The climax of Morehead's campaign came in January 1849, when the railroad bill, having passed the House by a narrow margin, came before the Senate for its final reading. Presiding over the Senate was a tall, bony Jacksonian Democrat from Caswell County—Calvin Graves, "The Baptist Enigma," whose party stoutly opposed Morehead's program of public works. The bill came to a final vote before a packed chamber.

Graves called for the question, a clerk called the roll, and a tally clerk announced: "The vote is twenty-two ayes and twenty-two nays, a tie." Graves rose slowly to cast his own vote, the fate of the railroad in his hands. Though his Democratic party had consistently stood against railroads, his constituency favored them. Graves had been given an agonizing choice.

Graves pounded his gavel and called in a clear voice, "The vote on the bill being equal, twenty-two ayes and twenty-two nays, the Chair votes 'Yea.' " The chamber erupted in bedlam. By voting against his party, Graves had committed political suicide. He was never again to hold public office. But his vote in the interest of what he felt was best for his state became a landmark in North Carolina history. A new pattern of development grew in the wake of his courageous stand.

Morehead staged meetings in every county and conventions in several county seats along the proposed route. He made short work of raising the necessary capital. A rousing rally in Greensboro raised $190,000, another in Raleigh, $40,000, and during a convention in Hillsboro in 1850, with only $100,000 to go, Morehead announced that he would join with any nine other men to take $10,000 each in stock. Within a few moments the $1 million goal had been reached. Morehead was named president of the road and Major Walter Gwynne, former president and engineer of the Portsmouth & Roanoke Railroad, became chief engineer. Ground was broken in Greensboro in 1851, and Senator Calvin Graves turned the first spadeful of earth.

Construction moved rapidly, thanks to Morehead's shrewd management. He contracted with stockholders who lived along the route to clear and grade the right of way and build bridges, or to furnish timber and crossties. These men were paid in both stock and cash. With hundreds of stockholders on the line at work with their slaves, the work force in July 1852 was 1,828 men and boys, 785 horses and mules, and 44 oxen. By September 1854 the road was open from Charlotte to Concord, a twenty-one-mile stretch; the entire eastern end between Goldsboro and Raleigh opened a month later. Rails reached Salisbury and Durham in January 1855, and the road was completed a year later at a point near Greensboro.

Celebration of the event was postponed until 4 July, when an excursion train ran the length of the road, past local parades, barbecues, band concerts, and balloon ascensions. It was more than seven years since Calvin Graves had cast his costly vote for progress, and now all Tar Heels, Democrat and Whig, could take pride in the accomplishment.

ᴄᴇᴠ *War Ends at Bennett Place*

Burke Davis

The Civil War began in South Carolina but ended in North Carolina—at a farmhouse called the Bennett Place, west of Durham, where General Joseph Johnston of the Confederacy surrendered to the rumpled, red-haired, cigar-chewing General William Sherman.

This narrative, condensed from *Sherman's March*, a 1980 book by Burke Davis, reflects the anxiety, confusion, and distrust of those final, tumultuous days.

ᴄᴇᴠ On April 12 in the city of Raleigh, North Carolina's perplexed leaders debated how—and whether—they should surrender to the approaching Sherman. At three in the morning Governor Zebulon Vance was at his desk in the otherwise deserted capitol, dashing off dispatches. For a week or more Vance had been harrying his staff as it directed rail shipment of supplies to westward stations beyond Sherman's reach, mountains of food and clothing that Vance had withheld from the stricken Confederacy despite the pleas of Jefferson Davis; the governor placed the needs of his state above the cause itself.

Dim lamps on the desk revealed a coarsely handsome, barrel-chested, six-foot mountaineer with a leonine head, flowing locks and intense blue eyes. He had been a remarkable war governor. Even now it was a point of pride with Vance that he had been a Union man until the moment that war became inevitable. . . .

Vance had openly scorned "the little men" who directed the Confederacy, but under his leadership North Carolina had fought the war with a fierce and uniquely independent spirit, as if she were fighting alone. Vance had raised almost 200,000 troops, more than any other rebel governor— and 41,000 of these had been killed. Vance had resourcefully clothed his troops from state-owned textile mills and armed them with British weapons smuggled in by the state's own blockade-runners. But now, as panic spread among Raleigh's civilians and there were frequent reports of Sherman's steady approach to the city, the governor realized that the end was at hand. . . .

It was three days since Lee had surrendered to Grant at Appomattox, but the news had not reached Raleigh—the rudimentary telegraph system had been disrupted, and ranking Confederates who had learned of the event kept the secret; . . . Vance knew nothing of this as he worked before

dawn of April 12; he imagined that it was he who must conduct unprece-
dented high-level negotiations with the enemy.

The governor was interrupted by a delegation of two former governors, both also staunch Union men of prewar days—William A. Graham,
who had also been a senator, secretary of the Navy, and candidate for Vice-
President; and David L. Swain, who was now serving as president of the
University of North Carolina. The old men urged Vance to call the legislature into emergency session so that North Carolina could sue for peace
and invite other rebel states to join her. . . . Vance agreed to their proposal
for a truce—but only after he had talked with General Joseph Johnston,
who had arrived in the city. The general advised Vance to remain in Raleigh
and to attempt to negotiate, provided Sherman treated him "with respect."

Vance, Graham and Swain composed a letter to Sherman, which
Vance signed, a request for a personal interview to discuss "a suspension of
hostilities" and "the final termination of the war." Vance appointed Graham
and Swain commissioners to deliver his message to Sherman, and then
sought a safe-conduct pass for them from Johnston. There was a delay.
Johnston had been summoned west to the town of Greensboro, where
President Davis, paused in flight, was trying to deal with the collapse of
his government. General Hardee finally issued the pass, and the old men
set forth to find Sherman, who was advancing along the railroad from
Smithfield to Raleigh.

The aging peacemakers, apparitions from the past in old-fashioned
long-tailed coats and beaver hats, drew attention as they strode through
Raleigh streets with three state officials at their heels. Word of their mission had leaked out in some way, for several Confederate officers growled
after them as they passed that "such cowardly traitors ought to be hanged."
The procession reached the railroad station about ten-thirty that morning
and boarded its "train"—a rickety car drawn by a wood-burning locomotive of uncertain age—which was in charge of Conductor Dallas Ward, a
nineteen-year-old lately promoted from the rank of newsboy. The purpose
of the excursion was a mystery to Ward until he was ordered to fly a scrap
of dirty white cloth atop his engine, when he realized that surrender was at
hand.

Ward was apprehensive, and the peace party did little to allay his
fears: "Only a few words were spoken, and they were almost in whispers."
The engine heaved asthmatically and the train moved out of Raleigh, past
groups of staring Confederate soldiers; Ward expected them to open fire
on the car at any moment.

The peacemakers were buffeted by a series of unanticipated adventures. First, the imperious General Wade Hampton halted the train, exam-

ined their papers and denounced the mission, but ended by rushing a courier ahead to Sherman, asking him to receive Graham and Swain. The train crept forward once more, but was halted within less than two miles by a rider from Hampton: Hardee had withdrawn his safe-conduct pass, and the train must return to Raleigh. Graham and Swain protested that Hampton must deliver this order in person, and within a few moments the cavalryman rode up to explain that he had already notified Sherman that the conference had been cancelled—and that he had also arranged safe passage for them back to Raleigh by writing to General Kilpatrick, whose troops had by this time seized the railroad near the city.

The engineer reversed the train and backed it in the direction of Raleigh, but as they passed through a cut, Federal soldiers boarded the car. "They piled down on us like wild Indians," Ward remembered. Graham and Swain were ordered out and led to Kilpatrick's quarters, and most of the other men of the party were systematically robbed by the Federals, who took $2,200 in Confederate currency and a watch from Ward's pockets.

Little Kil greeted Graham and Swain in an ebullient mood. He read to them a dispatch—their first news of Lee's surrender—and lectured them while the old men stared in shocked silence, stunned by the almost incredible report. "The war is virtually over now," Kilpatrick said, "and any man who sheds blood will be a murderer." He had a band play "Dixie" for the old men, then sent them toward Sherman once more, a few miles to the southeast at Gulley's Station.

The train now moved even more sedately, for thirty or forty Federal soldiers rode atop the coach. Along the route, other bluecoats were cheering—for Lee's surrender or for the train itself, which they supposed had come to offer the surrender of Johnston's army.

Sherman greeted the old men at the track, and assured them that he would do all in his power to arrange peace terms with North Carolina. He echoed Kilpatrick's sentiments: The fighting was over, so far as he was concerned.

It was now late afternoon, and Sherman invited the peace party to stay overnight—though Vance had expected their return no later than four o'clock. The general talked with Graham and Swain for hours during and after supper, his speech as rapid, darting, disconnected and vivid as ever. He said he wanted to make "an amicable and generous" settlement with North Carolina, and that he hoped Vance and other officials would remain in Raleigh and keep the government in operation. He wrote a response to Vance's letter, enclosing a copy of an order he issued to Federal troops, who were to "respect and protect" Vance and other officials of the state and city. The rather perfunctory letter ended: "I doubt if hostilities can be suspended between the army of the Confederate Government and the one I command, but I will aid you all in my power to contribute to the end you aim to reach, the termination of the existing war."

Sherman's manner became abrupt when someone mentioned the burning of Columbia. The subject had obviously become a tender one: "I've been grossly misrepresented in regard to Columbia," he said. "I changed my headquarters eight times during that night, and with every general officer under my command, strained every nerve to stop the fire. I declare in the presence of my God that Hampton burned Columbia, and that he alone is responsible for it."

Later in the evening Sherman reminisced about his career as an educator, and told Swain that he had captured several of his former students from Chapel Hill during the war, soldiers so young that they should not have left the campus. The conversation prompted a reunion between Swain and the Missourian general, Frank Blair, commander of Sherman's XVII Corps, who had attended the University of North Carolina almost twenty years earlier.

Graham slept in Sherman's tent with the general, and staff officers shared quarters with others of the party. Henry Hitchcock, whose mother had been one of Swain's schoolmates, gave up his tent for the old man.

During the afternoon of April 12, Governor Vance had waited anxiously in Raleigh, since he and other state officials were in danger of capture in the absence of word from Sherman. Late in the day he had a report from General Wheeler that the commissioners had been captured, and Vance then decided to flee. He first wrote Sherman, saying that Raleigh's mayor, William H. Harrison, was authorized to surrender the city; he asked that Sherman spare public buildings, including the capitol and the state museum. Late in the night, accompanied by two volunteer aides, Vance rode westward on horseback to a Confederate camp eight miles outside the city. . . .

In Sherman's camp, the peace commissioners rose before dawn and were escorted to their train by the general, who sent them off with hearty handshakes. "I wish you a safe trip back to Raleigh," Sherman said. "I'll be there in a few hours." . . .

Sherman entered Raleigh at seven-thirty and took over the governor's mansion as headquarters. He telegraphed Grant of his arrival and then issued his troops orders against pillage in unusually stern terms. He also urged them to show kindness to North Carolinians, especially to the poor. . . .

Some seventy-five miles to the west of Raleigh, in the overgrown village of Greensboro, the remnants of the Confederate government had halted in their flight southward. On April 11 a decrepit train came down from Virginia bearing President Davis and five members of his cabinet, the last load of fleeing rebel officialdom, part of a striking wave that had rolled from Richmond ahead of Grant's advancing troops. . . .

The Confederate president and his party found Greensboro, a small town of 2,000 and a rural county seat, now overrun by soldiers of Johnston's army. The town saw in the great men of the Confederacy travel-worn figures in top hats and Prince Alberts: Secretary of State Judah P. Benjamin; Stephen Mallory of the Navy; Postmaster General John Reagan; Attorney General George Davis; Secretary of Treasury George Trenholm. . . .

Jefferson Davis had summoned Joseph Johnston to Greensboro on April 12. . . . It was a conference chilled by the war-long hostility between Johnston and the president. . . .

John C. Breckinridge, the new secretary of war, reached Greensboro with official word of Lee's surrender at Appomattox, and the next day met with Davis and several cabinet members, a "funereal session," as John Reagan recalled it. Davis doggedly repeated his theory of eventual victory: "Our last disasters are terrible, but I do not think we should regard them as fatal. I think we can whip the enemy yet, if our people will turn out."

The president then asked Johnston's opinion, and the general advised Davis to sue for peace, since the Confederacy lacked money, credit, troops and ammunition. "It would be the greatest of human crimes" to continue the war, he said. The president could not conceal his irritation. He nervously folded and unfolded a newspaper until the general had finished speaking.

In the end, after a long, aimless discussion, Johnston said, "It is traditional for field commanders to open negotiations. Why not let me approach Sherman?" Davis acquiesced and dictated a brief message, which he ordered Johnston to forward to Sherman. The president then prepared to continue his flight to the south.

Johnston's message reached Sherman late on April 14, asking for a truce "to permit the civil authorities to enter into the needful arrangements to terminate the existing war."

Sherman replied immediately, saying that he could offer the terms of Appomattox. Pending a settlement, the armies should hold their positions. . . .

By the morning of April 16, when Johnston received Sherman's reply, Jefferson Davis had fled southward. The rebel general, left on his own, proposed to Sherman a meeting between the lines for the next day. The delighted Sherman telegraphed Stanton that he thought the rebels would surrender, and sent copies of the correspondence with Johnston. He added, "I will accept the same terms as General Grant gave General Lee, and be careful not to complicate any points of civil policy."

On April 17, as Sherman and other officers boarded a train for the front, a telegrapher brought a freshly decoded message from Stanton, which Sherman read with a sense of shock: "President Lincoln was murdered about 10 o'clock last night in his private box at Ford's Theatre in this city, by an assassin who shot him through the head with a pistol ball . . .".

Sherman thrust the paper into his pocket and turned to the telegrapher: "Has anybody else seen this?"

"No."

"Then don't tell anyone—by word or look, until I return. I'll be back this afternoon."

The little train puffed toward Durham's Station, some twenty-five miles away, while staff officers chattered about the coming truce and the solemn commander sat, alone with his secret.

Kilpatrick and a cavalry escort met the general at Durham's Station and rode with him toward Hillsboro. Within four to five miles they met a group of Confederate officers, and Sherman greeted Johnston, whom he had never met in all their years of army service. In contrast to the disheveled Sherman, the Southerner was immaculate in a handsome gray uniform, his silver beard and mustache neatly groomed, a frail and soldierly little man with a prominent forehead, a Roman nose and wide mouth—a gamecock who looked as if he would peck, one soldier thought. . . .

Johnston's staff officers guided the party to a tiny farmhouse nearby, the home of Daniel Bennett. Mrs. Bennett met the generals at the door, agreed to give them use of her house, and took her four children to an adjoining cabin. Sherman and Johnston entered a room about eighteen feet square, simply furnished but clean, its pine floor scrubbed as white as a bone.

Sherman handed Johnston Stanton's telegram announcing the death of Lincoln. Sweat beaded the Confederate's face as he read. "It's a disgrace to the age," he said. "The greatest possible calamity to the south. I hope you don't charge this to the Confederate government."

"I know that you or General Lee would have no part in it—but I can't say as much for Jeff Davis . . . and men of that stripe." Sherman then said his own troops knew nothing of the murder and that he feared they might react violently to the news. "I'm afraid some foolish man or woman in

Raleigh might say or do something to madden our men and that the town would fare worse than Columbia did."

The generals agreed that continuing the war would be "murder" and began a general discussion of peace terms. Sherman said he wanted to spare the Southern people further suffering, and offered the terms Grant had given Lee. Johnston reminded him that his message of April 14 had merely requested a truce so that civilian authorities could negotiate.

Sherman shook his head. "The United States does not recognize the Confederate States, and I can't submit an agreement from civil authorities."

Johnston retorted quickly: "My situation is not at all what Lee's was," he said. "I'm four miles in advance of you, and I'm not surrounded." The Confederate then proposed that they overlook minor differences and make a permanent peace—he would surrender all remaining Confederate armies in the territory south to the Rio Grande. Though Sherman questioned Johnston's authority to make such a sweeping settlement, he was excited by the prospect. He seemed to forget his instructions. His eyes sparkled; Johnston noted his "heightened color" as he spoke of restoring peace and unity to the country. Lincoln and Congress had agreed that restoring the Union was the object of the war, Sherman said—his recent conference with Lincoln had convinced him of that.

The generals seemed to be near an understanding until Johnston asked amnesty for Jefferson Davis, his cabinet and ranking officers. The two were still haggling over this question when Johnston left the cabin briefly to send a message to Confederate Secretary of War John Breckinridge, asking him to join the negotiations the next day. . . .

Sherman returned to Raleigh in the early morning, strengthened his provost guard, cleared the streets, and herded troops into their camps. Only then was the news of Lincoln's death announced to the army. Most soldiers took the news calmly. . . .

Sherman and Johnston resumed their conference at the Bennett cabin the next day. The Confederate began by assuring Sherman that he had authority to surrender all Southern armies, but asked that in return Sherman grant "political rights" to rebel soldiers.

Sherman replied that Lincoln had long since offered to restore rights of citizenship to surrendering Confederates below the rank of colonel. "And Grant at Appomattox extended this to all officers, including General Lee." . . .

Sherman sat at one of Bennett's crude tables and wrote rapidly, composing, as he later explained, "some general propositions, meaning much or meaning little, according to the construction of the parties—what

I would call 'glittering generalities'—and sent them to Washington . . . That would enable the new President to give me a clew to his policy . . . and to define to me what I might promise, simply to cover the pride of the Southern men . . .".

The armies were to remain in position under a truce that could be suspended after a forty-eight-hour notice. Meanwhile, President Johnson and his Cabinet would consider the terms Sherman had offered: The rebel armies would disband and deposit their arms in state arsenals; the troops would agree to keep the peace and obey Federal laws, but some of them were to keep their arms for use against guerrillas.

Upon taking oaths, state officers would be recognized and local governments would continue to function. Federal courts would be reestablished.

Southerners were guaranteed "their political rights and franchises, as well as their rights of person and property."

Once Confederate armies disbanded, there would be a general amnesty.

Sherman handed his draft across the table. "That's the best I can do," he said. . . .

✎ The Hanging of Tom Dula

Manly Wade Wellman

In the folk-singing days of the late 1950s, the Kingston Trio scored a national hit with the song "Hang Down Your Head, Tom Dooley," based on a real-life hanging in North Carolina a century earlier. The 1868 case gained national attention through the pages of the *New York Herald*, which had a reporter on the scene.

This account of the hanging was taken from *Dead and Gone: Classic Crimes of North Carolina*, a 1954 book by Manly Wade Wellman.

✎ The Civil War was over, in Wilkes County as in a lot of other places, and some of those who had marched away marched back again. Among these lucky ones was handsome young Tom Dula, who lived in Happy Valley and, you may be sure, had every reason to be happy.

He had served with the 26th North Carolina Regiment, and few indeed had returned from the decimated ranks of that repeatedly battered unit. The 26th had been raked with fire at New Bern, hideously punished at Malvern Hill. It had almost been wiped out at Gettysburg, where of all the regiments in Pickett's bloody charge it suffered worst. . . .

Courage is a relative characteristic, and to say that Tom Dula won a reputation for soldierly daring among those of the 26th who lived to tell of it is to say at once that he was a hero. He fought hard and frequently and well, and he was never even wounded. If General Bryan Grimes had scowled death away, Tom Dula had smiled death away; it was like the old tale hunters told, about how Davy Crockett grinned the raccoon out of the tree.

Home he came, with his parole in his pocket, to the slopes above the Yadkin. Happy Valley had its contrasts, cultural and ethical as well as scenic. Vividly, even luridly, these contrasts were set forth by a contemporary journalist:

"The community . . . is divided into two entirely separate and distinct classes. The one occupying the fertile lands adjacent to the Yadkin River and its tributaries is educated and intelligent, and the other, living on the spurs and ridges of the mountains, is ignorant, poor and depraved. A state of immorality unexampled in the history of any country exists among these people, and such a general system of free-lovism prevails, that it is 'a wise child that knows its father.' "

One must take note that these words were written by a northern correspondent for the New York *Herald* and remember the tendency of outsiders, already here recognized, to misjudge North Carolina's mountain folk. Not all the cove-dwellers above Happy Valley were unlettered, for one Bob Cummings was a school teacher among them. Poverty they may have known, for the land was poor and sometimes almost perpendicular, but they worked that land and from it gained their living. That many of the community were personable and bold will shortly be demonstrated. As to what the *Herald's* representative referred to as "free-lovism"—well, Tom Dula was back home, and he liked the girls and the girls liked him.

He was a good-looking man in his early twenties. Nearly six feet tall, with dark eyes and dark curly hair, he moved gracefully, paid smiling compliments, and he was a fiddle-scraping, banjo-picking caution. These were gifts of appearance and talent well calculated to stimulate feminine interest. Tom Dula began his conquests on a sensibly modest scale, with Laura Foster, the pretty but more than formally hospitable daughter of Wilson Foster.

Laura Foster was blue-eyed and chestnut-haired and hot-blooded. She had met other men of Happy Valley half-way, or perhaps closer than that. Indeed, it was considered something of a phenomenon that School-master Bob Cummings had admired her to no avail whatever. He was small and lean, and had been a conspicuous rule-proving exception to the way Laura lavished her favors on suitors.

Tom Dula was back from the war late in April or early in May of 1865, and probably he won Laura Foster's heart that same sweet summer—"courtin' summer," mountain folk sometimes say as young couples stroll along a trail, hand in hand. Like many another flighty damsel, Laura settled down solidly to a singleness of affection. Other young men who came calling found themself no more warmly welcome than Bob Cummings. Laura wanted Tom Dula, and nobody else.

That Lothario of the laurel thickets proved to be by no means so single of heart. Laura Foster he continued to meet, flatter, and fondle, but his great natural talents for romantic adventure found outlet in several other directions. One of those who melted before his smile was Pauline Foster, Laura's cousin. Possibly it was through Laura that Tom met Pauline; quite probably it was through Pauline that Tom met Ann Melton.

Here, certainly, was a woman who at first sight would make a man's mouth go dry to its roof and his eyes protrude like door knobs. . . . This paragon, who . . . would have been the reigning belle of a far larger and more sophisticated population, was the more remarkable for her elegance in that she was totally illiterate. It becomes increasingly evident that she had a fine natural mind, and the characteristic presence and pride of a surpassing mountain beauty. She was married, but her husband, James Melton, is only a name in the record. . . .

In addition to beauty and poise, Mrs. Melton possessed land and money. She employed Pauline Foster as a servant in 1865 and early in 1866, and Tom Dula, visiting the maid, must have dallied with the mistress. He had no great wealth; for, like some other soldiers, he returned from fighting with no great appetite for working. But by early spring of 1866 he was solidly established in the affections of lovely Ann Melton. . . .

May came to the mountains, bright with flowers and balmy with warmth. On the 25th of that month, Wilson Foster wakened to call his daughter, and she was not in her bed. Absent, too, was a brown mare named Betty, which had been tethered in the yard.

A search of Laura's room showed that she had packed her clothes. An elopement? Wilson Foster and his sons suspected that. Or Laura may have gone visiting relatives in Watauga County, though why so secretively nobody could suggest. But days went by, and no news came of what had befallen her. . . .

It was three weeks later, on June 10, that someone led a gaunt brown mare to the Cowles store at Elkville.

"Found her tied to a tree, up at the Bates place," said the man. "She'd gnawed off the bark. Was tied up a right smart of time."

The Bates place was no residence, but a thickly wooded section, popular as a lovers' rendezvous. And somebody identified the mare as Foster's Betty.

Word flew over the ridges and down the coves. Men dropped tools or fishing rods or moonshine jugs and formed up into search parties. Everywhere they scoured, up slope and down hollow, staring into 'brown pools, peering behind logs, prying up rocks.

Near the spot where Betty had been tied, the brush showed a trampled disorder, as by a violent struggle. In widening circles around that point rode a party of searchers. A mile and a half away, a horse shied and snorted. Dismounting, the men prodded here and there until they found a grave hidden in a thick tangle of laurels.

They fetched spades and picks, and dug. Among them was Bob Cummings, the teacher who had courted Laura with so little encouragement. Soon enough earth had been scooped away to reveal a rotting body. . . .

Several recognized the dress.

"Laura had a gold tooth on the left upper side of her mouth."

The diggers opened the grave the rest of the way. Laura Foster lay doubled and twisted. Both her legs had been broken, as though to make them fit into the short hole hastily dug to hide her. A deep stab had pierced Laura's once delectable bosom, penetrating to the heart. Under her lay a parcel of clothes, the baggage she had flung over Betty's saddle.

The body was carried to Elkville, and there Coroner G. A. Carter held inquest and performed an autopsy. Cummings was a witness at that hearing and was listened to with attention that varied from the admiring to the suspicious. . . .

Tom Dula had been at Cowles' store when Laura's body was carried in, and his handsome face had scowled fearsomely.

"I will have vengeance on whoever killed her," he announced sternly. Next day he was gone from Happy Valley.

But another former suitor of Laura, Jack Keaton, had likewise fled. When it came to that, Bob Cummings, so glibly the amateur detective at grave and inquest, had vanished. So had Jack Adkins, and so, too, had Ben Ferguson. You could take your choice about who was guilty, and why. . . .

In mid-July, the loafers who whittled and spat in front of the Cowles store saw a cavalcade of five horsemen amble into Elkville. At the head of the party rode little Bob Cummings, grim, tense, and triumphant. Jack

Adkins and Ben Ferguson carried rifles and guarded the other two riders, each tied to his saddle. The prisoners were Tom Dula, smiling as usual, and Jack Keaton.

"I will charge these men with murdering Laura Foster," announced Cummings, almost stuffily triumphant, "and I also ask the arrest of Mrs. James Melton."

It turned out that Cummings and his two friends had traced Dula and Keaton to a hiding place in Tennessee. Cummings had written an adequate simulation of a writ of extradition, and they had handed it to Tennessee officers, who arrested the pair and turned them over to the North Carolinians. . . . A day later, Ann Melton was also locked up.

Keaton, more doleful about his arrest than Dula, proved more fortunate as well. He was able to prove an alibi and was set free, while Ann Melton and Tom Dula were bound over to the fall term of court on a murder charge. Into Wilkesboro then rode a striking figure, burning-eyed and fierce-moustached, who was immediately recognized and loudly cheered from both sides of the street.

Zebulon Baird Vance, thirty-six years old in 1866, was one of North Carolina's heroes. He had organized the 26th North Carolina Regiment in 1861 and had served as its first colonel while Tom Dula was a rookie private. Vance resigned his colonelcy in 1862 to become governor, but he had never lost his love and concern for the brave, bullet-torn 26th. Arrested by the victorious Federals at the close of the war, he had been released on parole and had been practicing law in Charlotte. When word came of Dula's arrest, Vance had packed his saddle bags. Hang one of the 26th? Not if Zeb Vance could prevent it. He announced himself as counsel for Dula and asked that his client be tried separately from Ann Melton, whose presence in a courtroom Vance judged to be a potential danger to any defendant except herself. He succeeded in gaining a change of venue to Statesville in Iredell County. Solicitor Walt Caldwell, who was preparing the case for the state, seemed in danger of being devoured alive by the fiery and picturesque Vance.

But the solicitor was talking quietly to Cummings, who explained, step by step, his case against Dula.

Cummings had coaxed a confidence with Mrs. Betsy Scott, a laundress, who had seen Laura an hour or so after she had ridden from home early on the morning of May 25. Laura had sat brown Betty without a saddle, holding a sack of clothing in front of her. She had told Mrs. Scott that she was heading for the Bates place, and that she intended to meet Tom Dula there and go with him to be married. Hearing this story, Cummings had paid Mrs. Scott to keep it a secret until he called for it to be told.

Meanwhile, would Mrs. Scott spy on Ann Melton, while doing laundry at her home? Mrs. Scott would, and did, and it was through her that Cummings heard of Dula's hiding place in Tennessee. As to Cummings' reason for all this relentless trailing—"I loved her," he said of Laura Foster.

Dula went to trial before Judge Ralph Buxton, at the fall term of court. Vance had procured as associate counsel Judge R. F. Armstrong and R. P. Allison, and these did their best to shake the circumstantial evidence brought against Dula. Cummings was excoriated for his highly irregular methods in making the arrest. The testimony of Betsy Scott was challenged and attacked.

One telling piece of information established a motive for Dula. He had suffered from venereal disease, and blamed this upon Laura Foster. He had declared, in the hearing of several, that he would "put through whoever gave it to me." . . .

Vance objected to much of the testimony as merely hearsay. Finally, standing before the jury, he pleaded in heart-stirring periods for his client's life.

"I have known Tom Dula during years of strain and stress, when a man's soul was tried," he vowed at the top of his resonant and expressive voice, "and I tell you in all sincerity that never did a better soldier live, and never did one action of his ever lead me to believe him capable of murder."

There were ex-Confederates on the jury, and chiefly to them did Vance address himself when he recalled the desperate days of war.

"Is there a man among you," he wound up, "with a spark of love for the Lost Cause but can see that even if Tom Dula killed this lewd woman, Laura Foster—this minion of the devil—that the life of this man, who fought for what he thought best for your family and mine, is worth a hundred lives of such women as that dead viper."

Apparently twelve men disagreed with Vance as to the logic of this suggestion. Tom Dula was found guilty of murder in the first degree and was sentenced to hang.

Vance appealed to the State Supreme Court, urging in particular that a great deal of Mrs. Scott's evidence was only hearsay and therefore incompetent. . . . A new trial was ordered, and in January, 1868, Dula faced another jury.

Again the charges, again Vance's earnest defense, and this time more evidence, damning both to Dula and to Ann Melton. There were those who told that Dula and Ann had conferred earnestly on the day before Laura Foster's disappearance, and that Ann had given her lover a canteen full of whiskey—to heighten his courage, it was implied. And on the day when Laura was seen riding toward the Bates place, Ann was reported to have been absent from home for hours, returning with wet dress and shoes, to lie on her bed as though exhausted.

As before, the verdict was guilty. Vance's new appeal to the Supreme Court was unsuccessful. The hanging was set for May 1, 1868.

Meanwhile, Ann Melton's trial still remained to be held, after several delays. Zebulon Vance declared his earnest belief that she, and she alone, was guilty of the murder, and that his client and friend was sacrificing his life for her. On April 30, when Tom Dula had but a few hours of life left to him, his mother sent a letter begging him to make full confession. Dula seemed unmoved. He declined the spiritual comfort offered by a Methodist preacher but asked for pencil and paper. Awkwardly he scrawled a few lines:

"Statement of Thomas C. Dula: I declare that I am the only person that had a hand in the murder of Laura Foster." . . .

May Day had dawned, bright and beautiful. Dula declared himself ready to receive baptism, and the minister whose company he had previously rejected came to perform the rite. Sheriff Wasson led Dula from his cell just before noon. Crowds had gathered, including large numbers of young women. The solemnity of the occasion was recognized by a special police order closing all saloons and bars. . . .

A wagon waited, with a coffin upon it. Into the wagon climbed Dula, and upon the coffin he sat. With him rode the sheriff, the minister, and his sister and brother-in-law. One account says that he tuned and played his fiddle. . . . He rode, rather like a hero, between thronged curbs until he reached the depot. In front of that structure Sheriff Wasson had caused to be erected a scaffold of mountain pine, two stout uprights with a crossbar.

Thousands pressed close, men and boys climbing trees for a better view. A hollow square of armed deputies surrounded the scaffold as the wagon halted beneath it. Now Sheriff Wasson told Dula that he might speak to the crowd if he so desired.

To that invitation Tom Dula responded with hearty relish. He addressed the waiting citizenry in a voice that rang among the trees and echoed from the buildings. One may mourn that his remarks have survived only by indirect quotation in the columns of the *Herald*:

"He spoke of his early childhood, his parents, and his subsequent career in the army, referred to the dissolution of the Union, made blasphemous allusions to the Diety, invoking that name to prove assertions that he knew were, some of them at least, false. The politics of the country he discussed freely, and upon being informed, in reply to a question of his, that Holden was elected Governor of North Carolina, he branded that person as a secessionist and a man that could not be trusted. His only reference to the murder was a half explanation of the country and the different roads and paths leading to the scene of the murder, in which his only anxiety was to show that some two or three of the witnesses swore falsely against him. He mentioned particularly one, James Isbell, who he alleged had perjured himself in the case, and concluded by saying that had there been no lies sworn against him he would not have been there."

This address, which lasted nearly an hour, must have rambled extensively but was heard with the utmost attention. When Dula had finished, the time was past two o'clock. He took an affectionate farewell of his sister. Sheriff Wasson lowered the noose over his curly head, and he made a last joke.

"You have such a nice clean rope," he observed, "I ought to have washed my neck."

The noose drawn tight, the horses were whipped up and the wagon was yanked from under Tom Dula's feet. He dropped only a short distance, and his neck was not broken. He did not struggle as he dangled and strangled to death. Dr. Campbell pronounced him dead about 2:30, and his body was cut down and given to his relatives.

Meanwhile, mountain fashion, folks started to sing about him, in terms affecting enough:

> Oh, bow your head, Tom Dula,
> Oh, bow your head and cry;
> You've killed poor Laura Foster
> And you know you're bound to die.
>
> I take my banjo this evening,
> I pick it on my knee;
> This time tomorrow evening
> 'Twill be no use to me.
>
> I had my trial at Wilkesboro,
> Oh, what do you reckon they done?
> They bound me over to Statesville
> And there's where I'll be hung.

∿ *A Visit from General Lee*

Charles Bracelen Flood

In March 1870, after five years as president of Washington College at Lexington, Virginia (later renamed Washington and Lee), General Robert E. Lee began to feel his vitality ebb. He suffered chest pains and a shortness of breath. At the insistence of his concerned faculty, he went south for a two-month vacation that turned out to be more strenuous than staying at home.

This account of his journey through North Carolina was excerpted from *Lee: The Last Years*, by Charles Bracelen Flood, published in 1981. The trip did not offer the rest Lee sought. After returning home, he suffered a stroke and died the following October.

∿ On the evening of March 28, Lee and Agnes crossed into North Carolina on a train. They were going through little-populated areas, and their presence was known only to a startled few individuals who boarded their coach.

The state that they were entering had been a tower of strength during the war. With less than 10 percent of the Confederacy's population, North Carolina sent forward 20 percent of the South's soldiers; one quarter of the Confederates killed in action were from North Carolina. Lee had seen them storm the slopes at Gettysburg; the Twenty-sixth North Carolina started the battle with eight hundred and eighty men and ended it with a hundred and seventy-two. Sick, hungry, sleepless, North Carolinians had been among the very last of the immortal scarecrows who marched up to stack their arms at Appomattox.

At ten o'clock that night the Lees stepped down onto the station platform that served the quiet little town of Warrenton. No one knew that they were coming; Lee assumed that they could find a hotel.

A local merchant named Will White, who was a Confederate veteran, was at the station, meeting his sister on the incoming train. He blinked. It seemed impossible, but that was General Robert E. Lee standing at the depot in the middle of the night, accompanied by a very pretty black-haired young woman, both of them apparently lost. Soon the commander of the Army of Northern Virginia and his daughter were asleep under the roof of this veteran's surprised and delighted parents.

The next morning, when the Lees' impromptu hosts discovered that they had come to visit the grave of their daughter and sister, they tactfully sent them off in a carriage by themselves. As Lee picked up the reins, their hostess handed Agnes an armful of white hyacinths.

Lee was silent as he turned the carriage off the main road and headed through a forest of cedars to the rural cemetery. Annie Lee haunted the family's memories; with all that they had endured, with all that Lee and Custis and Rooney and Rob had risked and survived, it seemed unthinkable that of the seven children the only wartime death was that of Annie, stricken by typhoid at a place far from the fighting and dead at twenty-three. Lee called her "the purest and best" of his children. Because of a childhood eye injury that marred her looks, no picture was ever made of Annie. In a letter he wrote her from San Antonio, Texas, in 1860, Lee spoke openly of family friction in a way that he did with none of his other six children. Back on the frontier after nearly two years spent principally on leave at home at Arlington in his effort to save the family farms, Lee said to Annie, "It is better too I hope for all that I am here. You know I was much in the way of everybody, and my tastes and pursuits did not coincide with the rest of the household. Now I hope everybody is happier." No letter to or from Lee added to this clue that life at Arlington was not always the idyll that the family, including Lee himself, remembered it as being. He was at that time a worried man—worried about his army career, which was at the mercy of a system of promotion by seniority; worried about the outcome of the struggle to put the neglected Custis farms on a paying basis; troubled about the stark vision of God and humanity that came to a colonel who had to read the burial service under a summer Texas sun for "as handsome a little boy as I ever saw—the son of one of the sergeants, about a year old; I was admiring his appearance the day before he was taken ill. Last Thursday his little waxen form was committed to the earth." Most of all he had been worried about the growing rift between North and South. When it came, Annie Lee wrote a friend in Georgia that she had received a letter from an equally dear Northern friend: "She asks me if we intend to make Virginia a graveyard, and I have replied 'not for us, but for you.' "

Arlington was a Northern graveyard now; Lee and Agnes were approaching the cemetery in a North Carolina cedar forest where Annie lay. The news of Annie's death had come in a letter delivered to Lee at his headquarters near Winchester. He read it and with astonishing self-control went over some military correspondence brought to his desk just then by his gallant young aide Walter H. Taylor, who had no idea that anything was wrong. Taylor left the tent with this sheaf of papers; when he returned unexpectedly a few minutes later he found Lee with the letter in his hand, crying.

Here was the cemetery in the woods. Lee and Agnes got out of the carriage in the silence, Agnes with the white flowers in her arms. They had no trouble locating the grave. These far from rich country people had taken up a collection among themselves to erect a granite column twelve feet high for the daughter of Robert E. Lee.

That evening, the Lees boarded the train that was to take them all the way to Augusta, Georgia. It was the first night that either had spent in that recent invention, the Pullman sleeping car.

As Lee and Agnes retired for the night in their curtained berths along the aisle, they were unaware that the nature of their trip was about to change dramatically. At midnight the train would stop to take on passengers at Raleigh, the capital of North Carolina. The telegraph operator at the Warren Plains station had wired ahead four words: GENERAL LEE IS ABOARD. Even at this hour, the news went through Raleigh like a flame; people poured down streets to the station. Long before the train pulled in, the crowd was waiting.

A startled Agnes awoke to hear a roar of "Lee! Lee!" coming from the platform outside the curtained window next to where she was lying in her Pullman berth. She did not raise the curtain, and her father, also blasted from sleep by this cheering, did not look out his window either. "We were locked up and 'mum,'" Agnes wrote her mother of this first mass encounter with her father's admirers.

By sunrise, the telegraph lines of the South were humming. At little depots where the train did not even slow down Lee's veterans were out, many holding on their shoulders children born since the war, hundreds of them named after him. The Lees had their curtains up now; for them, shortly after dawn, the South was passing by as a succession of babies being held up to the train at red-clay crossroads, women waving handkerchiefs from buckboard wagons, and dignified-looking men suddenly thrusting their hats into the air and howling the Rebel Yell.

It was before the day of dining cars; at meal times, the train stopped and the passengers went into a nearby restaurant, sometimes located in the station itself. Lee saw that even in a small place he would be mobbed, and he and Agnes decided to stay on the train and forgo breakfast. In a few minutes a procession crossed the platform and entered the car; it was the proprietor of the restaurant and his staff, carrying an enormous breakfast on trays. After the train pulled out, the porter appeared with a basket of fruit. There were some Federal soldiers on the train, enlisted men of the

Regular Army, and they had chipped in and bought this fruit for General Lee while the train was stopped.

Now came the larger towns. Salisbury, North Carolina, had its entire population there, and a band thundering out the Confederate battle songs. On to Charlotte, North Carolina, and a larger crowd and a bigger band. Out of the throng came Colonel James L. Corley, Lee's self-appointed guide through what lay ahead, reporting for duty just as he had promised back in Richmond, shouldering his way through just the sort of tumult he had expected.

The train soon crossed into South Carolina. Here was the state that had been wildest for secession; a colonel who watched a South Carolina brigade withstand three hours of Federal assaults at Second Manassas wryly called it "the consummation of the grand debate between Massachusetts and South Carolina." In those terms, there had been much more to come; after his "march to the sea" reached Savannah, Georgia, Sherman turned and marched north through South Carolina, leaving an avenue of wreckage forty miles wide. The correspondent for the *New York Herald* who was with Sherman for the entire campaign wrote, "As for wholesale burnings, pillage and devastation committed in South Carolina, magnify all I have said of Georgia some fifty-fold." Half the state's property values were lost during the war. South Carolina's Reconstruction government was one of the South's worst: two hundred trial judges were said to be unable to read, and an historian wrote of the notorious general assembly that "legislation was by bribery."

It was pouring rain when the train reached Columbia, the state's capital. Two thirds of the city was burned at the war's end. For Lee's arrival a holiday had been declared. Stores and offices were closed. There was a parade to the station; to the sounds of trumpets and drums, a long grey column of Confederate veterans marched in step through the rain, followed by more bands and many civic groups. The organizer of the welcome was Colonel Alexander Haskell, commander of the Seventh South Carolina Cavalry and a man who repeatedly had been invaluable to Lee's army in crucial combat situations. His was a fighting spirit that enabled him to say that when he and his men withdrew from Richmond a week before Appomattox, "the idea of subjugation never dawned upon us."

Columbia, too, was only a fifteen-minute stop on the train's route south, but when Lee looked out the window he knew that this time he would have to emerge. On the platform in the rain stood a long rank of his former officers. The first to catch his eye was Brigadier General E. Porter Alexander, who had been the young commander of Longstreet's artillery. It was Alexander who suggested on the last morning of fighting at Appomattox that Lee turn his army into small guerrilla bands that should slip through the Federal lines and organize further fighting throughout the South. Had Lee acted on the suggestion instead of quickly rejecting it, the cost to the South in additional lost lives and property and prolonged suffering might have been incalculable. So many had died as it was, but at least these men on the platform were alive; Alexander was standing with his little daughter beside him, her hand in his.

Lee put on his hat and coat and stepped into the cold rain, his eyes looking from under the dripping brim at men who had saluted him in a hundred rainstorms, on battlefields and on the march. The band struck up; little girls came forward and handed him bouquets as the crowd cheered itself hoarse. Everyone wanted a speech, but Lee simply lifted his hat in the rain and bowed. The band thundered on again. General Alexander came forward with his little daughter; Lee swept the child up in his arms and smiled at her reassuringly amidst the drums beating, the trumpets, and the sound of his veterans giving voice to the Rebel Yell.

After traveling for twenty-four hours on the train, they reached Augusta; there they were, as Agnes put it, "whirled" off to the Planter's Hotel to spend the night. Lee had hoped for a day and a night of complete rest before going on to Savannah, but even Colonel Corley was unable to save him from a morning-long reception at the hotel. "Crowds came," Agnes wrote home to Lexington, describing a line that passed through for hours—veterans on crutches, farmers and laborers and their wives, and "the sweetest little children—dressed to their eyes." Those who were too young to introduce themselves had "tiny cards in their fat little hands—with their names." In the case of the boys, often the first part of the name was Robert E. Lee.

A boy of thirteen came to the hotel that morning on his own. He wiggled his way through the crowd until he got right next to Lee and then stood silently and unabashedly admiring him. The boy's name was Woodrow Wilson.

ᔰ Ringing in a New World

Phillips Russell

The University of North Carolina survived the Civil War but not Reconstruction. Its endowment squandered in Confederate bonds, the institution lacked students, faculty, and public confidence and was closed from
1870 to 1875—until a constitutional amendment again insulated its trustees and faculty from legislative politics.

One of the strongest advocates of that amendment was Cornelia
Phillips Spencer, a schoolteacher and education advocate who peppered
North Carolina newspapers with letters to the editor about the deplorable
conditions in Chapel Hill.

This account of the university's reopening was condensed from *The
Woman Who Rang the Bell: The Story of Cornelia Phillips Spencer*, a 1949
book by her nephew Phillips Russell, a UNC professor of journalism and
creative writing.

ᔰ The year 1873 saw the village and Cornelia's spirits sink even lower
than during the darkest days of the war. Then, an atom of hope might have
been seen; now there was none. Poverty, weeds, sickness, and empty days
sat at every street corner. Silence draped itself on every college wall. Not
anywhere in town or on campus was there life or motion.

Late in the year Miss Nancy Hilliard, once so generous with food and
good humor, died, destitute, in her little tavern room. "No minister in
town, and no religious service or observances, unless you call such the
tolling of our church bell," wrote Cornelia to her brother Charles. "Just as
it began, and the little procession moved from the door, the *University-bell*
joined in. . . . It was pitiful to see [deaf-mute] Lem Yancey following Miss
Nancy to her grave with his head bent down." To keep up her spirits and to
occupy a mind that might have become morbid had it been idle for a day,
Cornelia resorted to her old love of teaching. She taught both a white
Sunday School class and a Negro one, and organized sewing circles of little
girls.

And then on a sleety day early in 1874 her brother Charles wrote her
from Davidson College that he had heard there was hope the University
might soon be reorganized. He had no details to give, but the mere hint
was so enlivening that Cornelia was happy and uplifted even while the
sleet of a January ice storm tinkled against her windows; and when her
brother Charles sent some money to her for "old Couch," the village
hermit, she was able to joke with Couch, saying if he didn't wash his face

and make himself look like a white man, no woman would marry him. "You ought to have seen his old bleared eyes," she wrote. Later when Couch lay dying she went to his wretched shack, taking with her her little niece, Lucy Plummer Phillips, and herself washed his face. In a moment she exclaimed: "Why, Lucy, he's got blue eyes!"

Going on such errands was characteristic of Cornelia; she knew not fear and loved every soul that could claim Chapel Hill as home. She was capable of stopping any citizen to give either praise or reproof, and she could be emphatic with both. She once walked up to a leader in the Negro community and said without preliminaries: "No race can rise that does not value the chastity of its women—remember that." And walked on. . . .

All during these years of the seventies Cornelia's notes, letters, and newspaper correspondence that had so long pleaded for the reopening of the University were like seed sprouting in the slow soil of winter; outwardly there was no sign of germination, yet below the surface there was a slight but perceptible stir of life. Men had by now tired of hatreds and repression; they longed for days of peace and upbuilding work.

In the spring of 1875 word came to Cornelia that the University trustees had found a way to raise some money and the courts were being liberal. In early March she was able to write June [her daughter] about the exciting outlook. On March 20 a telegram from Kemp P. Battle at Raleigh brought the sudden and tonic news that the legislature had passed a bill permitting the reorganization of the University and even guaranteeing it a measure of support.

This day was her fiftieth birthday; but about that she cared nothing. She ran to her mother with the news. She ran to her neighbors with the same joyful story. She came back home to walk the floor and wait for the demonstration she was sure would come. Surely the happy villagers would turn out with fife and drum, parade the streets with torches and red fire. An hour, two hours, she waited, watching the streets. At last, no longer able to contain herself, she called to her daughter June, who happened to be at home. She and June collected two children of a neighbor, Susan and Jenny Thompson, and together they started for the campus. On the way they gathered the faithful villager, once the postmaster and University bursar, Andrew G. Mickle. Cornelia marched them all through the Episcopal churchyard and over the broad campus path to the South Building in which hung the college bell and rope. And finding all these silent, she climbed to the belfry and seized the rope. And then she rang and rang and rang. . . . She did more than ring a bell; she rang out an old world of defeat and inertia and rang in a new world of hope and belief. It was an incident that Frank P. Graham, in his speeches as president of the University in the depressed 1930's, used to dwell upon. His report to the trustees in December, 1930, ended with this paragraph:

"In the tragic era, Mrs. Cornelia Phillips Spencer, staunch champion of the public schools and University, received March 20, 1875, a message from the committee in Raleigh that the University was to be opened again. For five years the bell had not rung in Chapel Hill. For five years she had worked and prayed for that day. She climbed the stairs to the belfry and with her own hands rang the bell which has never ceased to ring to this day. The people of North Carolina were on the march again. Under God, we will not turn back now!"

๛ Walter Hines Page Attacks the Mummies

Walter Hines Page

In 1886, as the North Carolina legislature again rejected proposals for establishing a state agricultural and mechanical college, young Walter Hines Page, a Cary native then living in New York, wrote a sarcastic letter to the *State Chronicle*, a Raleigh newspaper he once edited, comparing North Carolina's leadership to Egyptian mummies. The letter aroused a storm of angry protests—and a year later led to the founding of what is now North Carolina State University.

Walter Hines Page went on to edit several national magazines, including *Harper's*, and even as an expatriate continued to exert great influence on his native state. He concluded his career as U.S. ambassador to Great Britain during World War I.

๛ It is an awfully discouraging business to undertake to prove to a mummy that it is a mummy. You go up to it and say, "Old fellow, the Egyptian dynasties crumbled several thousand years ago: you are a fish out of water. You have by accident or the Providence of God got a long way out of your time. This is America. The old Kings are forgotten, and this is the year 1886 in the calendar of a Christ whose people had not even gone to Egypt when you died." The old thing grins that grin which death set on its solemn features when the world was young; and your task is so pitiful that even the humor of it is gone.

Give it up. It can't be done. We all think when we are young that we can do something with the mummies. But the mummy is a solemn fact, and it differs from all other things (except stones) in this—it lasts forever. They don't want an Industrial School. That means a new idea, and a new idea is death to the supremacy of the mummies. Let 'em alone. The world must have some corner in it where men sleep and sleep and dream and dream, and North Carolina is as good a spot for that as any. There is not a man whose residence is in the State who is recognized by the world as an authority on anything. Since time began no man nor woman who lived there has ever written a book that has taken a place in the permanent literature of the country. Not a man has ever lived and worked there who fills twenty-five pages in any history of the United States. Not a scientific discovery has been made and worked out and kept its home in North Carolina that ever became famous for the good it did the world. It is the laughing stock among the States. . . .

The cause—the prime cause that is at the bottom of all this, is the organization of society, of the trades, the professions—of everything—against improvement. It is not simply because we are poor. They were poor in Georgia and Tennessee and Virginia twenty years ago, as poor as we are. Yet they are a long way ahead of us in giving every man a chance and in making intellectual and social progress. . . .

It isn't the people that are wrong.

Who is it, then?

It is the mummies. And the mummies have the directing of things. Do you want examples? If you know anything, you can name examples yourself. Count on your fingers the five men who fill the highest places or have the greatest influence on educational work in North Carolina. Not one of them is a scholar! Count the five most influential editors in the State. Not one of them could in the great centres of journalism earn $10 a week as a reporter. Go around all the leading sources of power in the same way, and you will see what is the matter. Yet when a man tells the plain truth because he loves North Carolina, the same fellows howl, 'Traitor!' . . . Men in North Carolina do not speak out what they think, but submit (as no other people ever submitted) to the guidance of the dead. I hold this to be cowardly. I think the time is come—you have made a good occasion by your recent work in the *State Chronicle*—for a getting at the truth, for independent action, for a declaration of independence from the tyranny of hindering traditions. In God's name, with such a State, filled with such people, with such opportunities, are we to sit down quietly forever and allow every enterprise that means growth, every idea that means intellectual freedom to perish, and the State to lag behind always, because a few amiable mummies will be offended? It would be cheaper to pension them all, than longer listen to them.

The utmost reverence for all men that are honest and energetic, the profoundest faith in the capabilities of our people and the sincerest affection for the old home have dictated what I have written, and I have written with soberness and with truth and for intellectual and social freedom.

༒ A Voice in the State Capital

Josephus Daniels

For nearly a century, the Raleigh *News and Observer* has exerted a powerful influence over the public affairs of North Carolina. Whether friends or foes, most political leaders have had to reckon with its vigilant reporting and its forceful editorials. This narrative reveals how the *News and Observer* came to be a spokesperson for the North Carolina Democratic party.

The account was condensed from *Editor in Politics*, one of a series of autobiographies by Josephus Daniels, who purchased the *News and Observer* in 1894 and whose heirs still control it.

༒ In June, 1894, Secretary Hoke Smith delivered the commencement address at the University of North Carolina. As his father had been a professor there before 1860, Hoke had fond memories of the place. He invited me to accompany him. On that visit I had a talk with General Julian S. Carr, of Durham which had far-reaching influence on my life. He informed me that *The News and Observer* was in a bad financial condition. . . . He asked me if I was still of the opinion that I would like to edit *The News and Observer*, and recalled that a few years before I had talked with him about the matter and he had told me that if I could buy the paper he would give me financial backing. I now answered that I was very anxious to get the paper and would do anything to secure it. . . .

General Carr had sold me *The State Chronicle* in 1885 and had permitted me to fix the price and terms. His friendship was manifested in affection and financial support. We were both staunch University men and active members of the Methodist Church, never missing a commencement or a conference. He was a native of Chapel Hill and left the University before he was of age to enter the Confederate Army. Returning, he became a partner of Colonel W. T. Blackwell and James R. Day, later buying them out and becoming head of Blackwell's Durham Bull Tobacco Company. He had advertising genius and was a pioneer in testimony advertising, printing pictures of Gladstone, Tennyson, and other distinguished men smoking Durham Bull tobacco. It was said that his next advertising feat would be to paint the Durham Bull on the pyramids. He made Durham Bull the biggest and widest-known smoking tobacco in the world and was reputed in the eighties to be the richest man in the State. . . .

Returning to my conversation at Chapel Hill, General Carr suggested that R. T. Gray, Esq., prominent lawyer, be retained to buy the paper when it was put up for sale at auction. I told him it would be essential, if I were to secure it, that my name should not be mentioned in connection with it at all. I knew Colonel A. B. Andrews, of the Southern Railroad, would not wish me to have the paper, and if he thought as earnest an advocate of railroad regulation as I had been would be in charge, he would either buy it or help somebody else to do so. I told General Carr I was quite sure that if the Duke interests had any intimation that I was to edit the paper, they would not be agreeable because my paper had been severe on the methods of the Tobacco Trust. . . . General Carr agreed and said he would ask Mr. Gray to retain a lawyer to make the purchase who was not closely enough associated with either one of us to arouse suspicion. I went back to Washington in great suspense and anxiety. I did not dare go to Raleigh or to Durham until the matter was worked out. . . .

On July 17 *The News and Observer* announced that "*The News and Observer* was yesterday sold to J. N. Holding for $6,810.00 and until the sale is confirmed by the court, the paper will be carried on as usual." The bidders were R. T. Gray, J. N. Holding, and S. W. Holman. Holman bid up to $6,700 and that evidently was his limit. It was then knocked down at $6,810 to Mr. Holding and it was reported generally in Raleigh that he was representing Edwards and Broughton. He denied it and said that it was the intention of the buyers to make the paper the best in the state and it went without saying, he added, that it would be true as steel to the Democratic Party.

I then went to Raleigh from Washington, and in company with Mr. R. T. Gray, who had received the transfer from Mr. J. N. Holding, I asked Mr. Holding to become a stockholder in the paper and a director. He said, "What have you got to do with it?" "Well," I said, "you bought it for me." He answered, "The dickens I did. I had no idea you were in any way connected with it. I thought you were too happy in Washington to think about coming back to Raleigh to run a newspaper." . . .

Upon the organization of the new company, *The News and Observer* was valued at ten thousand dollars. As a matter of fact, with the lawyer's fees and the money General Carr had put into the purchase of it and the paying of its debts, it had cost him that much. . . . I travelled from Washington to Occoneechee, General Carr's farm, to discuss with him a plan that I had worked out to secure liquid capital and to buy some new printing machinery, by trying to get one hundred men in North Carolina each to take a share of one hundred dollars. I told him the paper was bound to lose money for a time and I could not call upon him to put it up and I didn't have it. He agreed to the plan. I sent a letter to a hundred picked men in North Carolina, stating that I had bought the paper, outlining what I hoped to do with it, and asking each one to send $100 for one share of stock, saying it would be in the nature of preferred stock and whether the paper paid or not each stockholder would secure the daily edition free ($7.00) each year in lieu of dividend. . . .

The responses to that letter were better than I expected. Out of the hundred letters sent, over seventy drew favorable responses immediately, and others later—and this in a period when money was so tight that $100 was as big as $1,000 is now. Most of those responding wrote letters which gave me much encouragement. Some offered to take additional stock.

On August 8, the sale having been confirmed, *The News and Observer* announced that from what it had heard Josephus Daniels had obtained control of *The News and Observer*. . . .

When I purchased *The News and Observer* and consolidated it with my weekly *North Carolinian* it was my heart's desire to call the combined papers *The North Carolinian*. My interest then in the outside world was secondary. My horizon, except for quadrennial interest in national politics, was centered in my native State. I returned home to serve in its educational, political, industrial, and religious progress. Therefore, the name *North Carolinian* fixed both the home of its publication and its spirit. Moreover there had gone into the consolidated papers the hopes, labors, and disappointments of a score of high-minded writers and patriots who had spent themselves in the endeavor to build up a prosperous and useful journal. Before my purchase *The News and Observer* had become the residuary of the unsuccessful *Sentinel, News, State Chronicle, Observer*, and *Intelligencer*, and maybe other paper ghosts. My paper really represented the forward looking spirit of the *State Chronicle* and the *Farmer and Mechanic*. It seemed to me there was no name so suitable for the paper I hoped to make as the name of my State. I argued with friends that *The News and Observer* had no significance as to its habitat—that it might as well be printed in Maine as in North Carolina, whereas the name *The North Carolinian* had tar on its heels and would represent and speak for the State whose name it bore and no other name was so fitting for a paper at North

Carolina's capital. My friends and family, advertising agents, subscribers, directors, all opposed my suggestion. They said the old name had history and prestige, that to change the name would be like starting a new paper. "The people are accustomed to call their morning Raleigh paper *The News and Observer* if they like it, and 'The Nuisance Disturber' if they don't like it, and if you change the name now in the transition of editors, advertisers will think it is a new paper and advertisers steer clear of new papers." . . . I had to yield to superior numbers, though if the paper had been paying well I would have taken the chance. But as I was buying a paper showing a monthly deficit I did not dare to make the venture, much as I wished to do so. . . .

ᕽ *The Illegal Play That Saved Football*

Jack Claiborne

In 1888, when college football made its debut in the Carolinas, baseball was the dominant spectator sport. But in the century since then, football has overtaken its slower, more subtle outdoor rival. One of the reasons is the forward pass, which has made football more open, faster, and often more thrilling.

The following story helps explain how the pass became a staple of football strategy. An earlier version of this story by Jack Claiborne appeared in the *Charlotte Observer* of September 10, 1988.

ᕽ In the fall of 1888, teams from Wake Forest, Trinity College (now Duke University), and the University of North Carolina introduced college football to the Carolinas. In the century since then, teams from those schools and others have fought many stirring battles, but none that was more influential in shaping the game of football than the conflict between UNC and the University of Georgia on October 26, 1895, in Atlanta.

All the great quarterbacks of modern times—from Sammy Baugh to John Unitas to Joe Montana—owe their careers to one spectacular play occurring in that game. It was the play in which North Carolina introduced the forward pass.

It was not just the pass, then an illegal maneuver, that made the contest memorable, but also one man who was present to witness it and recognize its potential for transforming the game. Without that innovation, football might have been outlawed for its violence and brutality, as college boxing has been.

At the time, football was under widespread attack. So savage were its collisions of muscle and bone and so heavy its toll in gouged eyes, fractured skulls and broken necks that critics were calling for its abandonment. Injuries in the 1889 season were so severe that the UNC faculty and trustees had cancelled the Tar Heels' 1890 schedule.

The forward pass helped to relieve public concern by converting football from a struggle of raw nerve and brute strength into a contest of speed, skill and deception. The threat of a pass dispersed the players massed at the line of scrimmage by forcing them to defend a much wider territory.

The very setting for that 1895 game gave the encounter a special significance. It was played in Atlanta as a part of the Cotton States and International Exposition, a trade fair that brought visitors from around the world to witness the rise of an industrial New South.

It was at that exposition that black educator Booker T. Washington proposed "the Atlanta Compromise," by encouraging blacks to accept segregation and social inequality in exchange for education and wider economic opportunities. In the preceding week, President Grover Cleveland had visited the exposition but had left before the football game.

On that chill, gray Saturday afternoon, 1,500 spectators gathered at Atlanta's Jackson Park, most of them wearing the crimson and black of Georgia. The crowd arrived in horse-drawn carts, buggies, and four-in-hand coaches called tallyhos. The Duryea brothers of Massachusetts had incorporated the first American company to manufacture gasoline-powered automobiles earlier that year.

Included among spectators were William Atkinson, the governor of Georgia, and Hoke Smith, a Newton, N.C., native who was editor of the *Atlanta Journal* and also U.S. secretary of the interior.

Also present was Dr. Edwin Alderman, a pioneer in teacher education in North Carolina and later president of the University of North Carolina. He was in Atlanta to deliver the keynote address to the Southern Education Association, which timed its annual convention to coincide with the Exposition.

But for the history of football the most important spectator was John A. Heisman, the innovator for whom college football's coveted Heisman Trophy is named. Then coaching at Auburn, he was in town to scout Georgia, Auburn's next opponent, and he followed the game from the sidelines along with a knot of others.

No doubt there were illegal forward passes in many other football games, but it was John Heisman's account of the North Carolina pass that gave the play its historic significance. Writing years later in *Collier's* magazine, Heisman recalled that the pass occurred when UNC fullback Joel Whitaker Jr. of Warrenton dropped back to punt.

Cries of "Block it! Block it!" rang from the Georgia stands. At the snap of the ball, Georgia linemen brushed past UNC blockers to prevent Whitaker's kick. The harried punter saw teammate George Stephens alone in the right flat and heaved the ball toward him. Stephens caught it and fled 70 yards for the game's only touchdown.

"Georgia was stunned," Heisman wrote. Glenn "Pop" Warner, the Georgia coach, knew the pass was illegal and howled in protest. But the referee, who had apparently not seen the play clearly, allowed the touchdown to stand.

"I had seen the first forward pass in football," Heisman recalled and added that he immediately sensed its potential. At the time, "football was in danger," he wrote. "Too many boys were being carried to hospitals. . . . Some had died and others were doomed to lives of paralysis. The mass plays and the crushers . . . were killing the game as well as the players.

"Remembering the desperate fling of that tired boy from North Carolina, I wrote to Walter Camp, chairman of the rules committee. Here was a way to open up the game we loved. . . . The forward pass would scatter the mob. With the forward pass, speed would supplant brute strength. Lighter, faster men would succeed the beefy giants whose crushing weight maimed or killed their opponents."

But Walter Camp, then coaching at Yale, did not respond. Mass plays continued, casualty lists grew and so did public alarm. Even the introduction of padded helmets in 1896 did not improve the game's image. By the turn of the century, many colleges had abandoned the sport, and influential newspapers were calling for its ban. Among the critics was Theodore Roosevelt, the sportsman who in 1901 had become president of the United States.

In 1905, at the insistence of Heisman and others, including Lt. Paul Dashiell of the Naval Academy, Dr. Harry Williams of Minnesota, and John C. Bell of Pennsylvania, Walter Camp amended the rules to make passing legal in 1906.

Even then the weapon's potential was not immediately appreciated except among a few schools in the Midwest. The big Eastern and Ivy League powers that then dominated football relied on brute strength and the rushing game.

The first breakthrough for the pass came in 1913, when a team from little-known Notre Dame, led by quarterback Gus Dorias and a rough-hewn end named Knute Rockne, came to the Plains at West Point and shocked heavily favored Army, 35–13, with a deadly demonstration of passing. It was Notre Dame's first flash of football greatness.

After that, the pass gained wider acceptance. But it was not until the 1930s that a tall, slim cowboy, "Slinging Sammy" Baugh of Texas Christian, gave passing its modern status. Later, as a Washington Redskin, Baugh made the pass a staple of professional football.

Contemporary accounts of the 1895 UNC-Georgia game differ slightly from John Heisman's recollection. They report that UNC's Stephens did indeed sprint 70 yards for a touchdown, but make no reference to a forward pass. The *Atlanta Journal* story said the score came on "a fumble play." The same account later referred to the aerial as "a bad pass." It also deplored an altercation that interrupted play and was quelled only after Atlanta police were summoned. That might have been "Pop" Warner's protest.

Though the UNC forward pass was not mentioned in contemporary accounts, it has been cited by football's most respected historians, including Princeton's Dr. H. L. Baker, author of *Football Facts and Figures*, and former *New York Times* football writer Allison Danzig, who wrote the authoritative *History of American College Football*.

John Heisman was not the only witness of that 1895 game to go on to success. The man who threw the pass, Joel Whitaker, finished UNC, earned degrees in both medicine and dentistry and taught at Indiana University.

The man who caught the pass, George Stephens, a native of Summerfield in Guilford County, earned a degree at Chapel Hill, entered the insurance and real estate business in Charlotte, founded the American Trust Co. (a forerunner of NCNB), and later developed Myers Park, an exclusive Charlotte neighborhood that became a national model for suburban development. Stephens also invested in newspapers and for a brief period was publisher of *The Charlotte Observer* and later of *The Asheville Citizen*.

Even the referee who failed to notice that the UNC pass was forward went on to fame, but not in football. He was Robert Worth Bingham, an Orange County native and UNC alumnus who entered the practice of law, married Mary Lily Kenan Flagler, and with her wealth purchased the *Louisville Courier-Journal*, through which he became a power in Kentucky politics. In 1933, President Franklin Roosevelt named him U.S. ambassador to the Court of St. James.

As if to prove that they didn't have to rely on referee Bingham's selective vision, the 1895 Tar Heels returned to Atlanta five days after their victory over Georgia and defeated the Bulldogs again, 10–6, this time without benefit of an illegal pass.

∾ *George White's Farewell to Congress*

George H. White

Conforming to a pattern set elsewhere in the South, North Carolina amended its constitution in 1900 to deny voting rights to most of the state's blacks. Among the victims of that denial was Representative George H. White, the last black then serving in the U.S. Congress and the last to represent North Carolina in the twentieth century.

Then forty-nine years old, the graying, courtly White was a contradiction to all the caricatures of black legislators as ignorant buffoons. A native of Bladen County, educated at Howard University, he practiced law at New Bern; headed the State Normal School (now Fayetteville State University) for blacks; was elected to the North Carolina House in 1880, and to the North Carolina Senate in 1884; and served as a state district attorney eight years before winning two terms in Congress.

This moving speech, delivered January 29, 1901, as the House was debating a farm bill, was his farewell to national politics. The Mr. Kitchin he refers to was Representative William W. Kitchin of Halifax County, then completing his second term. Kitchin remained in Congress until 1909, then resigned to become governor of North Carolina. Kitchin's brother, also referred to by Congressman White, was Claude Kitchin of Scotland Neck, who succeeded White and served twenty-two years in the House, the last four as Democratic majority leader. Representative White's speech was excerpted from the *Congressional Record*.

∾ I want to enter a plea for the colored man, the colored woman, the colored boy, and the colored girl of this country. I would not thus digress from the question at issue . . . but for the constant and the persistent efforts of certain gentlemen upon this floor to mold and rivet public sentiment against us as a people and to lose no opportunity to hold up the unfortunate few who commit crimes and depredations and lead lives of infamy and shame, as . . . representatives of the entire colored race. And at no time, perhaps, during the Fifty-sixth Congress were these charges and countercharges, containing as they do, slanderous statements, more persistently magnified and pressed upon the attention of the nation than during the consideration of the recent reapportionment bill, which is now a law. . . .

In the catalogue of members of Congress in this House perhaps none has been more persistent in their determination to bring the black man into disrepute and, with a labored effort, to show that he was unworthy of the right of citizenship than my colleague from North Carolina, Mr. Kitchin. During the first session of this Congress, while the Constitutional amendment was pending in North Carolina, he labored long and hard to show that the white race was at all times and under all circumstances superior to the negro by inheritance if not otherwise, and the excuse for his party supporting that amendment, which has since been adopted, was that an illiterate negro was unfit to participate in making the laws of a sovereign State and the administration and execution of them; but an illiterate white man living by his side, with no more or perhaps not as much property, with no more exalted character, no higher thoughts of civilization, no more knowledge of the handicraft of government, had by birth, because he was white, inherited some peculiar qualifications . . . that entitled him to vote, though he knew nothing whatever of letters. . . .

I might state as a further general fact that the Democrats of North Carolina got possession of the State and local government since my last election in 1898, and that I bid adieu to these historic walls on the 4th day of next March, and that the brother of Mr. Kitchin will succeed me. Comment is unnecessary. In the town where this young gentleman was born, at the general election last August for the adoption of the constitutional amendment, . . . Scotland Neck had a registered white vote of 395, most of whom of course were Democrats, and a registered colored vote of 534, virtually if not all of whom were Republicans, and so voted. When the count was announced, however, there were 831 Democrats to 75 Republicans; but in the town of Halifax, same county, the result was much more pronounced.

In that town the registered Republican vote was 345, and the total registered vote of the township was 539, but when the count was announced it stood 990 Democrats to 41 Republicans, or 492 more Democratic votes counted than were registered votes in the township. Comment here is unnecessary, nor do I think it necessary for anyone to wonder at the peculiar notion my colleague has with reference to the manner of voting and the method of counting those votes, nor is it to be a wonder that he is a member of this Congress, having been brought up and educated in such wonderful notions of dealing out fair-handed justice to his fellow man.

It would be unfair, however, for me to leave the inference upon the minds of those who hear me that all of the white people of the State of North Carolina hold views with Mr. Kitchin and think as he does. Thank God there are many noble exceptions to the example he sets, . . . men who have never been afraid that one uneducated, poor, depressed negro could put to flight and chase into degradation two educated, wealthy, thrifty white men. . . .

I would like to advance the statement that the musty records of 1868, filed away in the archives of Southern capitols, as to what the negro was thirty-two years ago, is not a proper standard by which the negro living on the threshold of the twentieth century should be measured. Since that time we have reduced the illiteracy of the race at least 45 percent. We have written and published near 500 books. We have nearly 300 newspapers, 3 of which are dailies. We have now in practice over 2,000 lawyers and a corresponding number of doctors. We have accumulated over $12,000,000 worth of school property and about $40,000,000 worth of church property. We have about 140,000 farms and homes, valued at in the neighborhood of $750,000,000 and personal property valued at about $170,000,000. We have raised about $11,000,000 for educational purposes, and the property per capita for every colored man, woman, and child in the United States is estimated at $75.

We are operating successfully several banks, commercial enterprises among our people in the Southland, including 1 silk mill and 1 cotton factory. We have 32,000 teachers in the schools of the country; we have built, with the aid of our friends, about 20,000 churches and support 7 colleges, 17 academies, 50 high schools, 5 law schools, 5 medical schools, and 25 theological seminaries. We have over 600,000 acres of land in the South alone. The cotton produced, mainly by black labor, has increased from 4,669,770 bales in 1860 to 11,235,000 in 1899. All this we have done under the most adverse circumstances. We have done it in the face of lynching, burning at the stake, with the humiliation of "Jim Crow" cars, the disfranchisement of our male citizens, slander and degradation of our women, with the factories closed against us, no negro permitted to be conductor on the railway cars, . . . no negro permitted to run as engineer on a locomotive, most of the mines closed against us. Labor unions—carpenters, painters, brick masons, machinists, hackmen, and those supplying nearly every conceivable avocation for livelihood have banded themselves together to better their condition, but, with few exceptions, the black face has been left out. . . .

With all these odds against us, we are forging our way ahead, slowly, perhaps, but surely. You may tie us and then taunt us for a lack of bravery, but one day we will break the bonds. You may use our labor for two and a half centuries and then taunt us for our poverty, but let me remind you we will not always remain poor. You may withhold even the knowledge of how to read God's word and learn the way from earth to glory and then taunt us for our ignorance, but we would remind you that there is plenty of room at the top, and we are climbing. . . .

Now, Mr. Chairman, before concluding my remarks I want to submit a brief recipe for the solution of the so-called American negro problem. He asks no special favors, but simply demands that he be given the same chance for existence, for earning a livelihood, for raising himself in the scales of manhood and womanhood that are accorded to kindred nationalities. Treat him as a man: go into his home and learn of his social conditions; learn of his cares, his troubles, and his hopes for the future; gain his confidence; open the doors of industry to him; let the word "negro," "colored," and "black" be stricken from all the organizations enumerated in the federation of labor.

Help him to overcome his weaknesses, punish the crime-committing class by the courts of the land, measure the standard of his race by its best material, cease to mold prejudicial and unjust public sentiment against him, and my word for it, he will learn to support, hold up the hands of, and join in with that political party, that institution, whether secular or religious, in every community where he lives, which is destined to do the greatest good for the greatest number. Obliterate race hatred, party prejudice, and help us to achieve nobler ends, greater results, and become more satisfactory citizens to our brother in white.

This, Mr. Chairman, is perhaps the negro's temporary farewell to the American Congress; but let me say, Phoenix-like, he will rise up some day and come again. These parting words are in behalf of an outraged, heartbroken, bruised, and bleeding, but God-fearing people, faithful, industrious, loyal people—rising people, full of potential force.

Mr. Chairman, in the trial of Lord Bacon, when the court disturbed the counsel for the defendant, Sir Walter Raleigh raised himself up to his full height and, addressing the court, said:

"Sir, I am pleading for the life of a human being."

The only apology that I have to make for the earnestness with which I have spoken is that I am pleading for the life, the liberty, the future happiness, and manhood suffrage for one-eighth of the entire population of the United States. [Loud applause].

ᴄᴧ. *The Wright Brothers Learn to Fly*

Harry Combs and Martin Caidin

For five years in their Dayton, Ohio, bicycle shop they had read and studied flying. For four summers they had launched gliders off Kill Devil Hill on North Carolina's Outer Banks, where winds were usually favorable. They had been there four months in December 1903, waiting for a chance to test their new, two-wing airplane powered by a homemade gasoline engine.

This dramatic story of those tests was condensed from *Kill Devil Hill: Discovering the Secret of the Wright Brothers*, a 1979 book by Harry Combs and Martin Caidin.

ᴄᴧ. At half past one on the afternoon of Monday, December 14, the brothers extended a flag from the side of the workshed, which could be seen from the Kill Devil Hill Life Saving Station just over a mile distant. This was the prearranged signal that a powered flight would be attempted, for the brothers wanted every opportunity to have witnesses present if they were successful in sustaining their aircraft for any distance.

Soon after the flag went up, John T. Daniels, Robert Wescott, Thomas Beacham, W. S. Dough, and "Uncle Benney" O'Neal came to the shed and the waiting airplane. They pitched in to move it a quarter mile to the intended launch site. To make it easier to move the 600-pound airplane that distance, the brothers had the men roll it on its 60-foot track (which Wilbur had named the "Junction Railroad") to the end; then they would pick up the rear sections of track and move them forward to become the front section. It took about 40 minutes to get the machine into position.

The airplane's skids rested on the launching dolly—a six-foot plank that itself rested on a smaller wooden section attached to two small wheels in tandem. The wheels were modified from bicycle hubs, with ball bearings to reduce friction, and ran along the metal top of a two-by-four-inch monorail.

By now, two small boys and a dog had come along to watch the strange behavior of these stranger adults. They stayed only long enough for the engine to start, with its popping clatter, whereupon they took off in full flight for the nearest hill, scurrying beyond the crest to safety.

The rail rested along the gentle slope of the hill, and the machine was secured on its launching dolly by wire to keep it from moving until the operator signaled for the craft to be released. The brothers moved the coil box into position, connected the wires to start the engine, and moments later heard staccato thunder and saw their propellers whirling. They removed the wires and the coil box, inspected everything carefully. Just after three o'clock, Wilbur tossed the coin. He waited as Orville called out his choice—Wilbur won. The older brother slid onto the wing, snugged himself into the hip cradle, looked to his right to see Orville nod. Another man was at the left wingtip. Wilbur judged everything about him. The machine rested on a downslope because the wind was but five miles an hour. He might fly, and he might not. The wind made it all marginal. Wilbur readied himself. . . .

A hand lever operated the elevators, which extended well ahead of the wings, moving it up or down as the pilot intended. . . . To coordinate controls, the pilot in the hip cradle worked the rudders and wing warp by wires attached to his hip cradle. If he wanted to turn to the left, he moved his body in that direction, and the cradle moved to the left. This warped the right rear wingtips to the down position, and the left rear wingtips to the up position, and at the same time, automatically, the rudders moved to compensate for yawing effects in the turn. . . .

The engine rumbled, the propellers whirled, and Wilbur shouted that he was ready to fly. He reached down before him and grasped the restraining wire to release its grip. . . .

> . . . Before I myself was ready [Orville related], Will started machine. I grabbed the upright the best I could and off we went. By the time we had reached the last quarter of the third rail (about 35 to 40 feet) the speed was so great I could stay with it no longer. I snapped watch as machine passed end of track. (It had raised from track six or eight feet from end.) The machine turned up in front and rose to a height of about 15 feet from ground at a point somewhere in neighborhood of 60 feet from end of track. After thus losing most of its headway it gradually sank to ground turned up at angle of probably 20° incidence. The left wing was lower than the right so that in landing it struck first. The machine swung around and scraped the front skids (bows running out to front rudder) so deep in sand that one was broken, and twisted around until the main strut and brace were also broken, besides the rear spar to lower surface of front rudder. Will forgot to shut off engine for some time, so the record of screw turns was mostly taken while the machine was on the ground. The engine made 602 rev. in 35½ s. Time of flight from end of track was 3½ sec. for a distance of 105 ft. Angle of descent for the 105 feet was 4° 55'. Speed of wind was between 4 and 8 miles.

The details notwithstanding, neither of the brothers thought Wilbur had achieved a successful flight—only its promise. The machine had left the ground higher than its landing and in an unsustained flight, and obviously had touched down out of control. Thus, it failed to meet the hard definitions of sustained and controlled flight. . . .

They could hardly wait to make another flight the next day. The *Flyer* was repaired, and they chafed to get into the air. But the winds hardly stirred. When they awoke Thursday, they couldn't believe their ears. A subdued roar came to them, a rumble that rose and fell in the distance. They looked toward the ocean and saw the surf boiling before a bitter, howling wind of nearly 30 miles an hour.

They went outside and stared. Finally, there was nothing to do but return to their shed to be out of the numbing wind. They sat about, depressed, listening to the wind shrieking through loose boards, blowing jets of sand around them. . . . As they waited out the gusty winds on the morning of December 17, while sand whistled along the floor, they knew that getting into the air would be flirting with death itself. But there came a time when you simply threw the dice and had it; you took your whack at what you wanted so desperately to do, and that was it. . . .

Although the brothers had been practicing with gliders, their total experience with a power machine was the three and a half *seconds* of Wilbur's attempt three days before. Their tank contained enough fuel to fly the machine about eight miles in calm air; although the brothers did not seriously set their aim on such a distance, they had discussed the possibility of remaining low over the sands and flying off the four miles to the village of Kitty Hawk. Ideal conditions could make it possible, they mused. . . . But conditions were far from ideal; the winds blew at 24 to 30 miles an hour.

At ten in the morning they marched into the teeth of the wind and raised their signal flag for their witnesses and helpers to join them. In the meantime they began laying their launching track, less than 200 feet west of their large work hangar and pointing straight north. It was so cold that the brothers often had to return to their shed so that they could cup their hands over their stove to get feeling back into their fingers. However, they were perfectly dressed, as was their custom, for the occasion, in full suits, right on down to starched white collar and tie.

Finally, four men from the life saving station appeared, hands in pockets, jacket collars pulled up high, to watch the proceedings and, if needed, to help. Daniels and Dough had been there on the 14th, and with them were infrequent visitors from former times, W. C. Brinkley and A. D. Etheridge. A fifth spectator was a teenager from Nags Head, Johnny

Moore, who happened to be at the station on a visit and had joined the others on the trek to the Wright camp.

Orville set his tripod and camera in place, aiming carefully so that when the release was pressed the airplane would be shown just as it left the track; he assigned this task to John Daniels. . . .

Orville slipped aboard the bottom wing, grasped the controls, and secured himself within the hip cradle. . . . Wilbur took his position at the right wingtip and then motioned to the five onlookers, urging them, as Daniels related, "not to look sad, but to laugh and hollo and clap our hands and try to cheer Orville up when he started." Wilbur turned back to his position as the five whooped and shouted and clapped hands. Above all this noise, the sputtering engine and its staccato barking, the whirl of the propellers and muted thunder of wind and shouting of onlookers, there came Orville's cry that he was ready; and his hand moved; and an instant later the restraining wire released the machine.

> On slipping the rope [he recorded in his diary], the machine
> started off increasing in speed to probably 7 or 8 miles [an
> hour]. The machine lifted from the track just as it was entering
> on the fourth rail. Mr. Daniels took a picture just as it left the
> tracks. I found the control of the front rudder quite difficult on
> account of its being balanced too near the center and thus had a
> tendency to turn itself when started so that the rudder was
> turned too far on one side and then too far on the other. As a
> result the machine would rise suddenly to about 10 ft. and then
> as suddenly, on turning the rudder, dart for the ground.

The *Flyer* dashed out about 100 feet from the end of the tracks and in a final lunge for the ground that covered an additional 20 feet, it whacked solidly against the sand, skidding along and cracking one skid as it slid straight ahead and came to a halt. Orville's hand reached out at once to shut off the fuel supply petcock. The props whispered as they wound down, blurred, showed their blades instead of a blur, and clacked to a halt.

In light of the conditions and circumstances, the results were greatly impressive. Orville had flown into the teeth of a gale of 27 miles an hour and had managed to cover a distance of some 120 feet. He had been in the air for 12 seconds. . . .

After Orville's first trial . . . the brothers discussed the excessive sensitivity of the front elevator. If they had made glider tests, as was their original plan, they would have taken a few days to reduce the size of the elevator or in some way modify the system to reduce the sensitivity. But time had become so bitter an enemy, as strong as the cold itself, that structural changes were out of the question. Now that they understood the problem, they would attempt further flights using extreme care in controlling the amount of elevator travel.

Orville recorded that

> at 20 min. after 11 o'clock Will made the second trial. The course was about like mine, up and down but a little longer over the ground though about the same in time. . . . At about 20 minutes till 12 o'clock I made the third trial. When out about the same distance as Will's, I met with a strong gust from the left which raised the left wing and sidled the machine off to the right in a lively manner. I immediately turned the rudder to bring the machine down and then worked the end control. Much to our surprise, on reaching the ground the left wing struck first, showing the lateral control of this machine much more effective than any of our former ones. At the time of the sidling it had raised to a height of probably 12 to 14 feet. . . .

It was approaching midday, and Wilbur prepared for the fourth flight. It began exactly at twelve o'clock. . . .

Wilbur took his position on the flying machine, the engine sputtering and clattering in its strange thunder. His peaked cap was pulled snug across his head, and the wind blowing across the flats reached him with a sandpapery touch. As he had felt it do before, the machine trembled in the gusts, rocking from side to side on the 60-foot launching track. He settled himself in the hip cradle, feet snug behind him, hands on the controls, studying the three instrument gauges. He looked to each side to be certain no one was near the wings. There were no assistants to hold the wings as they had done with the gliders, for Wilbur believed that unless a man was skilled in what he was doing he ought not to touch anything, and he had insisted on a free launch, for he knew the craft would require only 40 feet in the stiff wind to lift itself into the air.

Wilbur shifted his head to study the beach area. Today was different. The wintry gale had greatly reduced the bird population, as far as he could see. It had been that way since they awoke. Very few of the familiar seagulls were about beneath the leaden skies.

Wilbur turned to each side again, looked at his brother, and nodded. Everything was set, and Wilbur reached to the restraining control and pulled the wire free. Instantly, the machine rushed forward and, as he expected, was 40 feet down the track when he eased into the air. He had prepared himself for almost every act of the wind, but the gusts were too strong, and he was constantly correcting and overcorrecting. The 100-foot mark fell behind as the aircraft lunged up and down like a winged bull. Then he was 200 feet from the start of his run, and the pitch motions were even more violent. The aircraft seemed to stagger as it struck a sudden down-draft and darted toward the sands. Only a foot above the ground Wilbur regained control, and eased it back up.

Three hundred feet—and the bucking motions were easing off.

And then the five witnesses and Orville were shouting and gesturing wildly, for it was clear that Wilbur had passed some invisible wall in the sky and had regained control. Four hundred feet out, he was still holding the safety altitude of about 15 feet above the ground, and the airplane was flying smoother now, no longer darting and lunging about, just easing with the gusts between an estimated 8 and 15 feet.

The seconds ticked away and it was a quarter of a minute since Wilbur had started, and there was no question, now: the machine was under control and was sustaining itself by its own power.

It was flying.

The moment had come. It was here, now.

Five hundred feet.

Six hundred.

Seven hundred!

My God, he's trying to reach Kitty Hawk itself, nearly four miles away!

And, indeed, this is just what Wilbur was trying to do, for he kept heading toward the houses and trees still well before him.

Eight hundred feet . . .

Still going; still flying. Ahead of him, a rise in the ground, a sprawling hump, a hummock of sand. Wilbur brought the elevator into position to raise the nose, to gain altitude to clear the hummock; for beyond this point lay clear sailing, good flying, and he was lifting, the machine rising slowly. But hummocks do strange things to winds blowing at such high speeds. The wind soared up from the sands, rolling and tumbling, and reached out invisibly to push the flying machine downward. The nose dropped too sharply; Wilbur brought it up; and instantly the oscillations began again, a rapid jerking up and down of the nose. The winds were simply too much, the ground-induced roll too severe, and the *Flyer* "suddenly darted into the ground," as Orville later described it.

They knew as they ran that the impact was greater than that of an intentional landing. The skids dug in, and all the weight of the aircraft struck hard, and above the wind they heard the wood splinter and crack. The aircraft bounced once, borne as much by the wind as by its own momentum, and settled back to the sands, the forward elevator braces askew, broken so that the surfaces hung at an angle. Unhurt, aware that he had been flying a marvelously long time, mildly disappointed at not having continued his flight, stuck in the sand with the wind blowing into his face and the engine grinding out its now familiar clattering, banging roar, Wilbur reached out to shut off power. The propellers whistled and whirred as they slowed, the sounds of the chains came to him more clearly, and then only the wind could be heard. The wind, the sand hissing against fabric and his own clothes and across the ground, and perhaps a gull or two, and certainly the beating of his own heart.

It had happened.

He had flown for 59 seconds.

The distance across the surface from his start to his finish was 852 feet.

The air distance, computing airspeed and wind and all the other factors—more than half a mile.

He—they—had done it.

The Camels Are Coming

Nannie M. Tilley

One result of the U.S. Supreme Court's 1912 breakup of the American Tobacco Trust was the modern cigarette business. Under the trust, the four major tobacco companies—American, Liggett and Myers, P. Lorillard, and R. J. Reynolds—specialized in different products to avoid direct competition. After the breakup, R. J. Reynolds, whose specialty had been flat-plug chewing tobacco and Prince Albert pipe tobacco, introduced a new cigarette that, on the eve of World War I, revolutionized the industry.

The following account, taken from Nannie M. Tilley's 1985 history, *The R. J. Reynolds Tobacco Company*, describes the impact that Camel cigarettes and the dramatic "The Camels are coming" advertising campaign had on Reynolds's competitors and cigarette consumption.

Perhaps no one has described the impact of this revolutionary new cigarette, the first truly American cigarette, better than the American Tobacco Company's George Washington Hill in his frank answer given when asked what important event in the cigarette business occurred in 1913. . . .

Reynolds introduced Camels. I recall the first newspaper campaign was a teaser. I thought it was a joke; I thought they were wasting their money. "The Camels are coming," was their caption. It was not any joke. In town after town, when they introduced Camels, other cigarette brands were swept to one side. As I told you, the Fatima brand was the one great outstanding brand, and it capitalized on the Turkish taste in those days, the trend towards Turkish cigarettes, and, as I described, they had on the Fatima package "Turkish Cigarettes" large, and the word "blend" small. They [Liggett and Myers] were not particularly fond of the word "blend"; they wanted to show "Turkish."

Camel went them one better. It showed on its package "Turkish and Domestic Blend," and the domestic part our people analyzed as largely burley. This brand was put on and swept other brands to one side. I worked the road in those days, and it was very discouraging. Territory after territory swung over into the Camel column. Our brands could not stand up against it. Our salesmen were down because everybody was talking about this new taste in cigarettes. The public wanted the new taste. The public commented on the new taste, and that is what we in the Sales Department got—"Well, yes, you make good cigarettes, but they don't taste like Camels," and that was what we were up against.

And Camels introduced price competition, too, because Camels were put up to sell at 10 cents a pack—in the oval package of 20s, against the Fatima, the Zubelda, the Omar brand of the American, the Zubelda of Lorillard, the Fatima of Liggett & Myers, Turkish blends at 15 cents, and Camel was 10 cents.

Well, I went back home after my road work and I went to Mr. P. S. Hill, and I told him that if things went on like they were, we would not be in the cigarette business very long, so, "Well," he said, "what are we going to do?" . . .

So, my father and I talked it over a great deal, and finally I said to him, "Well, we will have to go to Charley Penn." Charley Penn was our vice president in charge of manufacturing plug tobacco and up until that time had had nothing to do with the manufacture of cigarettes at all. "Charley Penn knows how to handle burley tobacco and dip it. We will have to try and have Charley Penn blend us a cigarette that is better than Camels." So we experimented and we got Mr. Penn into the picture. . . .

Meanwhile, my father told me to get up a name, and I went through the old brands of the American Tobacco Company and I found a brand that was put out in smoking tobacco called Lucky Strike, and I thought that was a good name, but I did not like the package, because the package was kind of Elizabethan—had a lot of curlicues and scrolls on it, so I got an artist to work on the package, simplified it, and made the nice circle without any curlicues, and wrote the first things we put on the package and got the package all right, at least, I thought it was all right.

In the meanwhile, Penn had experimented in connection with blends, and he had a blend which our people thought was really [a] good burley blend, made under the processing that we had previously only used in connection with plug and smoking tobaccos, but never in connection with cigarettes. This tobacco had to be wrung out on a wringer. It was dipped into this mixture and wrung out on a wringer, and our first machines were used on the Mayo branch in Richmond, Virginia, and we shipped this burley tobacco wrung out on a wringer up to the 22nd Street factory [in New York City]. . . .

Now, we had to put out Lucky Strike. The competition of Camel forced us to put out Lucky Strike. . . .

But, Fatimas was a 15-cent pack; Turkish blend cigarettes 15 cents a pack. Camels had capitalized on the Turkish atmosphere by the minarets and mosques on the Camel package.

I won't tell you what they said about Camels, the mosques and the minarets, but Camels came out at 5 cents less; at 5 cents less, and, Mr. Reynolds put on the back of his Camels, and it is there to this day, "Do not look for premiums or coupons as the cost of the tobaccos blended in Camel Cigarettes prohibits the use of them." . . .

I have forgotten what Camels were doing, but they were doing plenty. And, Liggett & Myers had come in. Now I don't know what the other fellows' blends are, but my report is from my men that the Chesterfield cigarette definitely changed its blend. It was a Virginia [flue-cured] cigarette originally. At any rate, they made a cigarette which has had a great popular appeal. They came into the picture.

Lorillard was still sticking by the old things, and if my recollection serves me, I don't think Lorillard got into the burley type of cigarette until Old Gold came out in 1926.

So the Camel became the agent for producing the modern cigarette industry. It should be noted that George Washington Hill credited Reynolds not only with a revolutionary brand, but also with a revolutionary change in prices and advertising as well as with the elimination of premiums. By late December 1913, the editor of *Tobacco* declared that the Camel had "already been accepted as a standard brand wherever it has been offered to the public." He noted that the blend of "Turkish and domestic tobaccos had received instant recognition as well as much sincere praise." Walter Reynolds wrote on 14 December 1914 that the "rush for Camels is now on, and we are running all the packers to full capacity. It looks as though we will have to run over time this month, to supply the demand." The first carton of Camels had been established in interstate commerce about fourteen months earlier, on 3 October 1913, by a sale to Charles E. Hughes and Company of Danville, Virginia, by Rice Gwynn.

☙ The Babe's First Homer

Elizabeth Simpson Smith

The City of Fayetteville enjoys many distinctions. It was named for Marquis de Lafayette, French hero of the American Revolution. It was once North Carolina's capital, and the place where the state ratified the U.S. Constitution and approved the charter for the state university. It was also a center of slave trade, and from 1917 to the present the home of Fort Bragg, the nation's largest military base.

But little in Fayetteville's past inspires as much pleasure as its association with Babe Ruth, America's greatest sports hero. This account of the Babe's memorable visit to Fayetteville, written by Elizabeth Simpson Smith, was taken from the March–April 1979 issue of *Tar Heel: The Magazine of North Carolina*.

☙ Picture this: March, 1914, Fayetteville, N.C.; a balmy day in a ballpark, with only a whisper of a kite-flying wind. The Baltimore Orioles, in the throes of spring training, are playing their first intrasquad baseball game, the Buzzards vs. the Sparrows.

A moon-faced, six-foot-two-inch rookie stalks to bat for the Buzzards, takes a practice swing, belts a ball across the right field fence and into a corn field. The batter slings his cap to the ground, circles the bases with a whoop and a holler, zooms into home plate.

Babe Ruth, age eighteen, has just hit the first home run of his professional career.

How did he do it? Like he hit all the subsequent homers, the Babe said later. He took a good gander at the pitch, twisted his body into a backswing, lit into the ball as hard as he could. A monument now marks the spot where the ball fell, 350 feet from home plate. Not bad for a raw rookie before the days of the lively ball.

Fayetteville was full of firsts for George Herman Ruth: the first time he left his home town of Baltimore; the destination of his first train ride; the spot where he acquired his nickname Babe. But most of all the trip to North Carolina represented freedom from St. Mary's Industrial School, to which his parents had assigned him as an "incorrigible," off and on, since age seven. At five he hung around his father's bar, at seven he chewed tobacco, at ten he drank whiskey. Under the shadow of St. Mary's high walls and patrolling guards, Babe played sandlot baseball with such style that the Orioles heard of him and hustled out to sign him up just as he approached manhood. A few mornings later he arrived in North Carolina, astonished at the mild temperature and the fact that the whole world wasn't exactly like Baltimore.

Fayetteville was such a utopia that young Ruth jumped from bed at five a.m. and trotted to the depot to watch trains before breakfast. During off hours he gawked around the hotel, riding the elevator, watching the operator level it off with the floors. Finally he bribed the operator into letting him handle the contraption. A few minutes later he left a door open on the third floor, stood rubbernecking up and down the corridor while he sent the elevator up another flight. Suddenly a player down the hall screamed at Ruth to pull his head inside. He did, in the nick of time.

Naturally Babe got quite a dressing down from his manager, and the players took up where the manager left off. Finally one of them took pity on Ruth, defended him by saying he was "just a babe in the woods." The name stuck.

Babe Ruth arrived in Fayetteville with a five-dollar advance burning his pocket and nursing a sore arm. On the train trip, his teammates, employing a customary trick used on rookies, had convinced him he should rest his pitching arm all night in the clothes hammock swinging above his berth. Babe complied.

Babe Ruth hit 714 home runs in his career, a world record he held until Hank Aaron hit his 715th in 1974. But Ruth still holds the record of sixty home runs in a 154-game season, most long hits (119), most total bases (457) and most bases on ball (170) in a season. He retired in 1935 with a lifetime slugging percentage of 342.

Babe Ruth never forgot his first spring training and said later in his career that he had been to some bigger places than Fayetteville, but darn few as exciting.

Incidentally, the Buzzards won 15–9.

☙ Defeating the Monkey Law

Willard B. Gatewood, Jr.

At the time that laws laying groundwork for the famous Scopes trial were passed in Tennessee, the North Carolina legislature was turning back efforts to pass a similar law. The proposal was called the Poole bill, after Representative David Scott Poole of Raeford, a spare, tight-lipped country printer, editor, and schoolteacher who introduced the measure, which would have banned the teaching of evolution in any tax-supported institution of the state.

The following account was condensed from *Preachers, Pedagogues, and Politicians: The Evolution Controversy in North Carolina, 1920–1927,* by Willard B. Gatewood, Jr.

☙ The hearings on the Poole bill opened on February 10, 1925. The unusually large crowd in attendance forced the committee to transfer its proceedings from a small room in the Agriculture Building to the Hall of the House of Representatives. With the understanding that each side would have an hour to present its case, the proponents of the measure initiated the proceedings. As manager of the bill, Poole himself began by explaining the gravity of the situation in which nothing less than "the religion of the Lord Jesus is on trial." He utilized the standard argument that since the State was forbidden to teach theology, it naturally had no right to teach that the Bible was a myth and Christianity a mere superstition. He pointed out that such practices were not only unconstitutional but clear violations of the will of a majority of North Carolinians.

The first speaker introduced by Poole was James R. Pentuff, a Baptist minister from Concord, whose elaborate academic pedigree was, according to some observers, as dubious as his recent involvement in a fertilizer manufacturing enterprise. Nevertheless, as the star performer in the anti-evolution cast, he appeared in the role of an expert on biological evolution.

The Darwinian theory was, according to him, a "mere figment of imagination without any basis in fact and hence should not be foisted upon school children as science." He pointed out that Darwin was an agnostic whose infidel theory had long been "exploded," but publishers and teachers continued to spread the heresy because they were unwilling to "dig in and keep up" with the new scientific developments. In conclusion he related what his niece had told him about being forced to study Darwin at the University. The *Raleigh Times* described Pentuff's discourse as a prime demonstration of the "crass ignorance" characteristic of clerical pseudo-scientists who sought "to clear the right of way for the divine plan." The Concord minister retaliated by suing the *Times* for slander.

Following Pentuff's address to the Committee on Education several committee members who favored the Poole Bill assumed the floor. Julia Alexander [of Charlotte, the legislature's only female member] proclaimed her belief in "the Bible from cover to cover" because it was a supernatural book. She explained that if she believed otherwise, she would be "afraid to go back to Mecklenburg." Two other committeemen, Ralph Hunter, a minister of the Associate Reformed Presbyterian Church, and Robert Madison, a professor of languages at the Cullowhee Normal School and a Methodist steward, endorsed the position of Pentuff and expressed their intentions to fight the "insidious doctrine of evolution." . . .

The pause that followed the anti-evolutionists' arguments pointed up the lack of co-ordination in the opposition camp. The momentary silence ended, however, when [Harry Woodburn] Chase rose to address the audience. A thunderous applause greeted the University president, who had chosen to represent his institution rather than send members of the science faculty. His advice to Collier Cobb, a well-known University scientist and outspoken defender of evolution, indicated that Chase had no intention of allowing faculty members to risk their academic reputations in the legislative arena. "I am planning to go down [to Raleigh] myself," Chase said, "and I believe it would be better for me to be the goat . . . than for a man who is known to be teaching evolution to be put in a position where he might have to defend himself."

A hush fell over the applauding crowd as the slight, white-haired Chase began his address. Describing himself as a representative of an institution long respected for its intellectual honesty, he stated that he was "not here to discuss evolution as a biologist but to speak in behalf of human liberty." Both church and state, he continued, were primarily interested in the moral welfare of the individuals entrusted to their care, yet the church was attempting to deny teachers a privilege that its ministers exercised without restraint. The Poole Bill would prohibit the teaching of evolution in the classroom without interfering with the preaching of evolution from the pulpit. Chase further declared that the implications of the Poole Bill were to him the cause of far more concern than the mere matter of teaching evolution, because the measure in effect was an "abridgement of the freedom of speech guaranteed by the Constitution." "Shall we," he asked, "write into that article of the Constitution *except* to school teachers?" He concluded with the declaration: "Mr. Chairman, . . . if it be treason to oppose the bill offered in the name of tyranny over the mind for the purpose of abridging the liberty of one class of our people, I wish to stand here in the name of progress and make my protest." A little later, when Chase was reminded that the University appropriations had not yet cleared the Legislature, he snapped: "If this University doesn't stand for anything but appropriations, I, for one, don't care to be connected with it." Representative Thomas L. Neal of Caswell County, a member of the Education Committee and a Presbyterian elder, accused the University president of trying "to sidetrack the main question by raising the issue of free speech" and promised to send his sons to Davidson College in order to insure their safety from the Darwinian heresy.

Two members of the North Carolina State College science faculty continued the argument against the anti-evolution bill in the absence of President [Eugene C.] Brooks. Bertram W. Wells, a botanist, and Zeno P. Metcalf, an entomologist and an old hand at fighting anti-evolutionists, sought to demonstrate the compatibility of Christianity and the evolution theory. "I am here," Wells declared, "as a living exponent of the Christian religion in all its essentials and also of evolution *as a fact.*" He then offered a brief explanation of the scientific method in an attempt to refute Pentuff's charge that evolution was a mere "figment of the imagination." Representative Neal interrupted to ask when, in the process of evolution, man acquired a soul. The professor, joined by Chase, replied that such a question was "unanswerable" and "quite beside the point" since scientists generally recognized the existence of a soul. Representative Madison then put the question in a slightly modified form: "May I ask the gentlemen from State College at what stage of transformation of man from an amoeba that he parted with his tail and acquired a conscience?" Before anyone else could answer, Chase quipped: "Does the gentleman mean that they occurred at the same time?" Only after vigorous raps of the gavel did the Chairman quiet the roar of laughter provoked by Chase's retort. Madison's query caused William Louis Poteat to stir restlessly in his seat in the crowded gallery. Turning to a friend, the Wake Forest president whispered: "Biologically he [man] has never lost his tail and here is some evidence that he has never acquired a conscience."

During the three hours of committee hearings, various individuals spoke on the issue. . . . Already taut, the atmosphere reached a new level of tension when the committee's vote resulted in a tie and threw the fate of Poole's bill into the lap of Chairman [Henry Groves] Connor. Without the slightest hesitation, Connor announced: "I break the tie by voting for an unfavorable report on the bill." As he had anticipated, however, the proponents of the resolution drew up a minority report which was designated as special order of the House for 8:00 P.M., February 17, 1925.

A feeling of despair had gripped Chase as he emerged from the committee hearings. After a "most careful nose-counting" of the 120 members of the House, he calculated that only 55 votes could be mustered against the Poole Bill. Outside the chamber he met Tom Bost, the correspondent for the *Greensboro Daily News*, who inquired about his despondent attitude. When Chase explained his anxiety about the outcome of the legislation, Bost replied: "But what are you worrying about? If you have 55 men of your own in the House, you are all right, because Poteat has 20 alumni there." Although Chase found it difficult to believe that the Baptists would support his cause, Bost was confident that the Wake Forest–educated legislators would remain loyal to what they had learned at the feet of Dr. William Louis Poteat. Obviously, the traditional Baptist emphasis upon the separation of church and state and Poteat's long-standing defense of intellectual freedom were not lost upon the Wake Forest alumni in the General Assembly when they came to grips with Poole's measure. The final outcome of the legislation, which revealed the essential accuracy of Bost's prediction, was, in effect, a personal triumph for Poteat, whose "boys" furnished a virtual phalanx of opposition.

The week between the committee hearings and the floor debate was a period of frantic activity on the part of the protagonists in the legislative fight. . . .

President Chase, all the while, busied himself with speeches, conferences, and correspondence to galvanize public sentiment against the Poole bill. . . . Chase outlined the specific reasons for the University's determined opposition: (1) the vague and ambiguous nature of the measure placed every teacher of natural science in jeopardy and exposed him to humiliation for any statement that he might make regarding evolution; (2) the measure infringed upon the teacher's freedom of speech and upon the *state* college students' liberty to learn, since it placed restrictions only upon the study of biology in state-supported schools; (3) the bill was designed to silence teachers only, leaving preachers free to expound evolution without restraint; and (4) the free competition of ideas was essential in the search for truth, for which the passage of a law was no substitute. Chase's statement reached a wide audience through the elaborate coverage it received in the press and undoubtedly prodded some of the more timid University alumni to take a definite stand against the legislation. . . .

Chase's activity produced immediate results. Petitions opposing the anti-evolution bill which had been circulated by University alumni appeared on the legislators' desks. Twelve University scientists drew up a statement in which they argued that the theory of evolution was indispensable to the teaching of science and frankly declared that "the evidence in favor of the theory is now overwhelming." This statement was handed to Connor for "use at his discretion." Telegrams to legislators and state government officials came from various parts of North Carolina. Rather typical was the message to the Governor from S. J. Ervin, Sr., of Morganton: "The Poole Resolution threatens incalculable injury to our schools and colleges. Prejudice against our churches on the part of the young people who will attribute this intolerance to the influence of the churches and thereby to the cause of religion. May we beg your influence against it." Although Governor McLean avoided involvement in the controversy, Sam Ervin, Jr., heeded his father's advice by joining the crusade against the measure. . . .

On February 17, 1925, at eight o'clock in the evening, Speaker Pharr brought down the gavel amid a tumultuous confusion in the House. The "surging crowd" that thronged the chamber refused to heed the Speaker, even when he ordered the sergeant-at-arms to clear the aisles "of the jam." The "vast popular showing" moved the *Greensboro Daily News* to remark that "holiness had never hobnobbed in such impressive array." Amid the confusion, Connor pleaded with the crowd to allow the legislators to proceed with their deliberations in an orderly fashion, otherwise police protection would have to be requested from the city of Raleigh. Such pleas were futile, and after a quick conference with Poole, he moved to adjourn the proceedings. The passage of the motion meant the cancellation of "the big show" many had trekked to Raleigh to witness.

The following day, February 18, the House resumed its deliberation of the anti-evolution measure under relatively peaceful circumstances. The next two days brought forth a virtual plethora of parliamentary maneuvers. . . . In the course of the debates most of the ardent anti-evolutionists had an opportunity to speak in behalf of their cause. The author of the controversial measure, Poole, pledged his confidence in the "integrity of our state institutions" and frankly admitted that he had never intended to precipitate a "fuss over the question of separation of church and state." . . .

In their turn, the opponents of the anti-evolution legislation fired a few salvos of their own. Representative Sam Ervin of Burke County, heeding his father's advice, heaped ridicule upon the Poole bill. "Such a resolution . . . ," he observed, "serves no good purpose except to absolve monkeys of their responsibility for the human race." . . .

At a critical moment in the House debates on February 19, 1925, silence fell over the chamber as the weary legislators turned their attention to the large, shambling figure who had gained the floor. Walter Murphy, the Rowan legislator and former University quarterback, had decided to speak his mind on the issues. And his address left no one in doubt regarding his position, for he denounced the Poole Bill and its substitutes as pernicious measures likely to create far more problems than they would ever solve. For Murphy, a man's religion was "strictly a matter between him and his God" which scarcely needed legislative supervision of the sort envisioned by the various bills; actually, he said, a statute attempting to regulate the relationship between theological and scientific beliefs would be the epitome of absurdity. "I am not so much interested," he concluded, "in what I am evolved from as in whither I am going. That which shall come to me in the future as far as good is concerned will come through the atoning blood of Jesus Christ." In short, he counseled the legislators to leave the problem of salvation to some other agency and concentrate upon those problems more likely to achieve solution through legislative action. According to many sources, Murphy's address "clinched" the death of the anti-evolution movement in the General Assembly of 1925. Since Chase was one of those who considered the speech decisive, it was perhaps no coincidence that the University selected the commencement exercises of 1925 as the occasion to bestow an honorary degree upon Walter Murphy.

Following Murphy's address on February 19, 1925, the House refused to consider the Connor substitute by a vote of 70 to 41. Then, turning to the original proposition, it killed the Poole Resolution by a vote of 67 to 46. An analysis of this vote reveals that the majority of the alumni of both the University and Wake Forest College in the House opposed the anti-evolution legislation. Approximately one half of those who endorsed the Poole measure claimed no collegiate training whatsoever, although all four medical doctors in the chamber favored its passage. . . .

❧ *Justifying the Sales Tax*

J. C. B. Ehringhaus

During the Great Depression of the 1930s, North Carolina was the only state in the Union not to suspend support of public education for at least some period of time. One reason it didn't have to was the 3 percent sales tax, levied in 1933 after the state had taken responsibility from distressed counties which were paying schoolteachers in scrip.

The fight over the sales tax was the bitterest in a long series of controversies over depression-induced reforms. In this excerpt from one of his speeches, Governor J. C. B. Ehringhaus explains the need for the "emergency" tax—which remains one of the main supports of the public school system.

❧ I believe in economy—drastic, rigid economy. I have preached it. I have practiced it. I shall continue to advocate it. I shall continue to stand against wastefulness and extravagance in any activity. But there is a point, even in economy, beyond which self-respecting government cannot go. For to do so means not merely an abdication of its functions but social bankruptcy, collapse of morale, and repudiation of our constitutional, social and political obligations. Government must make reasonable provisions for the activities contemplated by its constitution or it surrenders and invites the scorn and contumely of its citizens and the world at large.

We are simply facing a terrific emergency and the manifest necessity for the levy of some new taxes if the schools and the State's credit are to be saved from utter wreckage. A six months term with no chance for extension is a poor educational opportunity at best; inadequately financed, it is a delusion, a snare, and an utterly unjustifiable waste and extravagance.

You will permit me in passing to observe that I am quite sincere in saying that I loathe either form of sales tax, but I love the honor and credit of my State and the maintenance of its self-respect more even than I dislike such impositions. There are some things more odious, more undemocratic, more objectionable even, than this form of taxation. They at least have the virtue of universal application and something of relation to ability to pay, if spending has reasonable relationship to income.

ᴥ *The Indians Scalp the Klan*

Wyn Craig Wade

Like most southern states, North Carolina is plagued periodically by outgrowths of the Ku Klux Klan, which, like bad seed, take root in some dark, fetid, and forgotten corner of the state. But occasionally the revival of Klan activity has an amusing aspect, as in this January 1958 encounter between Klansmen and Lumbee Indians in Robeson County.

The following account is an excerpt from *The Fiery Cross: The Ku Klux Klan in America*, a 1987 book by Wyn Craig Wade.

ᴥ If Carter's Klan [in Alabama] was the most demonic of the late 1950s groups, then the North Carolina Knights of the Ku Klux Klan was the most ludicrous. James "Catfish" Cole was the driving force behind the Carolina Knights, and Cole had been convicted numerous times for reckless driving, drunken driving, and driving without a license. Once a carnival huckster and circus pitchman, Cole now fancied himself a Baptist minister. "I'm a minister of the Gospel," he informed a gathering, "and I'm here to tell you God's side: He never meant for niggers and whites to mix." If Catfish had stuck to such profound sermons, he might have been better off. Instead he decided to launch a crusade against the Lumbee Indians of Robeson County.

The proud and independent Lumbees, who had never had a tribal organization, had lived peaceably and prosperously as farmers in Robeson County for over two hundred years. Members of the county upheld a formal three-way segregation for blacks, whites, and Indians, but Cole charged that "Indian women and white men" were "running around together." His group burned crosses in front of the home of a Lumbee woman who was supposedly guilty of relations with a white man, as well as on the lawns of Lumbees who had moved into a white neighborhood. Catfish decided to hold a mass rally against the Lumbees on January 18, 1958. Although he announced that five hundred Klansmen would turn out for the rally, only forty showed up. When the little group got to the deserted field where the rally was to take place, they found to their horror that the road was lined up and down with nearly a thousand Indians. Reporters and photographers soon arrived. Although the Klansmen refused to have anything to do with the press corps, the Lumbees happily posed for photographers. Some of them laughed, gave whoops, and one performed a war dance in the middle of the road. When Cole realized that no more Klansmen were coming, he tried to begin the evening's festivities. Without warning, the Lumbees began whooping, rushed the Klansmen, smashed their floodlight, and demolished their electrical generator and public address system. After gleefully running off with the large KKK banner, several of them paused to fire shotguns at the dust-churning tires of Klansmen who couldn't escape from the scene fast enough. Journalists had a field day: "Look who's biting the dust! Palefaces!" *Life* magazine concluded that, like Custer, "the Klan had just taken on too many Indians." For his misguided part in the fiasco, Catfish Cole was indicted for inciting a riot and was sentenced to eighteen to twenty-four months in prison.

ᐁ Founding the Research Triangle

Luther H. Hodges

In the second half of the twentieth century, the movement to diversify and expand North Carolina's economy emphasized the Research Triangle as a symbol of the state's rising sophistication in industry, technology, and education. As this narrative explains, the Triangle and its research facilities were the result of a happy combination of personalities and circumstances.

The narrative was taken from *Businessman in the Statehouse*, by Luther H. Hodges, a 1962 memoir of the author's six years as governor of North Carolina.

ᐁ The heart and hope of North Carolina's industrial future is the Research Triangle. While it is actually a good deal more complex, the Research Triangle should be thought of as basically three things. First, it is an actual tract of land—the five-thousand-acre Research Triangle Park spread over the beautiful central Carolina countryside, which a decade ago was empty pineland and where now a half-dozen laboratories and research buildings are a promise of even more to come. Second, the Research Triangle is the larger area surrounding the park, triangular in shape, with corners at Raleigh, Durham, and Chapel Hill—the homes of three of North Carolina's greatest institutions of higher education, North Carolina State College, Duke University, and the University of North Carolina. Finally and most important, the Research Triangle is an idea that has produced a reality—the idea that the scientific brains and research talents of the three institutions, and their life of research in many fields, could provide the background and stimulation of research for the benefit of the state and nation. In a way, the Research Triangle is the marriage of North Carolina's ideals for higher education and its hopes for material progress.

It should be a matter of pride for all North Carolinians that within less than a decade we have conceived the idea and moved quickly and dramatically to make it a reality. In future years—it may well be sooner than most imagine—our Research Triangle will create benefits that will touch every citizen in our state, as well as many throughout the South and the nation. . . .

The idea of a Research Triangle, utilizing the personnel and facilities at institutions of higher learning at Chapel Hill, Durham, and Raleigh, was talked about in several forms during the early 1950's. The late Howard Odum, sociologist at the University of North Carolina, talked of a research institute for the development of southern resources to be operated jointly by the University and North Carolina State College. The triangle idea apparently was voiced publicly first by Romeo Guest of Greensboro, vice president of a construction company. . . . He prepared a brochure that pictured the three universities in a triangle, and emphasized their combined potentiality for research work.

Of course, research was being carried on at all three of the institutions. But to have let the matter rest with no more than an indication of the possibility, . . . and without preparing a much more comprehensive plan, would have let the idea die aborning. Guest was one of the first to realize this. So he talked of the idea of seeking industrial laboratories to locate in the present Research Triangle area with a number of people, including especially Brandon Hodges of Asheville. Hodges saw the Research Triangle as a co-operative venture between industries and the institutions.

The idea was mentioned to me by Brandon Hodges in early 1955 and immediately I saw the potential it held for North Carolina. It was discussed . . . as a means to promote the state and to attract industry. The key to its development was co-operation among the University of North Carolina, Duke University, State College, my office, and the business and industrial leadership of the state. There was a need for organization, and, with North Carolina's future at stake, there was also a need for the maximum amount of action.

A Governor's Research Triangle Committee was formed in the spring of 1955 and the late Robert M. Hanes of Winston-Salem was named chairman. He accepted the responsibility and spent much time, money, and effort to make this dream a reality, which it became just before his death.

One of the first things that we did was to talk with the officials at the three schools to see what resources they could offer. . . . President Gray appointed three persons from the University at Chapel Hill and three from State College in Raleigh, and President Edens appointed three from Duke to a "working committee."

J. Harold Lampe, dean of the School of Engineering at State College, was named chairman of the working committee. This working committee was asked to find out how many people on the faculties of the three great institutions were then engaged in research or scientific work and whether there were other research people and facilities in the Triangle area; to write a statement of policies and purposes consistent with the Research Triangle idea; and to begin looking for a full-time executive officer.

A subcommittee of the working committee found that we had nearly nine hundred people in the Research Triangle area who were doing research or scientific work. In addition, this subcommittee's report listed various research facilities, such as laboratories, special equipment, and libraries, located in the area. This survey proved that there were enough research facilities in the area to continue with the project, as well as an academic atmosphere that should in the long run attract people to the Research Triangle area. . . .

The working committee also . . . recommended that Dr. George L. Simpson, Jr., professor of sociology at the University of North Carolina and an associate of the late Howard W. Odum, be hired as director. He agreed to take a year's leave of absence from the University to map out a workable program and went to work in October, 1956.

Dr. Simpson made his first report to the Research Triangle Committee and the working committee in January, 1957. In it he proposed that efforts be made to make industry and government agencies acquainted with the research resources and environment of the Research Triangle; that a research park be established, if possible, in the center of the Research Triangle; and that a research institute be established to do contract research for industry and government. The Research Triangle Committee adopted the program. . . .

Brochures giving facts of interest on the area's resources in a number of research fields, such as pharmaceutical, electronic, and chemical, were prepared and sent to officials in thousands of companies across the United States. Dr. Simpson traveled as much as possible to urge people to visit and consider the Research Triangle. He was later joined by a number of faculty members from the three institutions, who traveled about the country "selling" the Research Triangle during the summer. Chairman Hanes provided the extra funds needed to support these travels.

By the fall of 1957, a good beginning had been made in acquainting the nation's business and governmental leaders with the Research Triangle. And several companies had expressed considerable interest in the Triangle area as a possible site for new laboratories they were considering.

The idea of the Research Triangle was growing rapidly on paper by early 1957 and with it the need for a research campus such as had been proposed at the January meeting of the Research Triangle Committee. There were many questions and many problems arising from the dream of a Research Triangle Park. For instance, would residents of an area within the Research Triangle be willing to option their land—and what could be used for money to pick up the options? We began looking for an angel.

People in North Carolina were asked first. However, most Tar Heels at the time did not quite grasp the full implication of the Research Park idea or did not have money readily available for such a project. During a discussion of the project with William Saunders, then State Conservation and Development director, he suggested his friend Karl Robbins might be interested in such a project. Mr. Robbins, who then lived in New York, had owned textile mills in North Carolina and was greatly interested in this state. I had known him for about twenty years.

We invited Mr. Robbins down for a breakfast meeting at the Mansion with Saunders, Simpson, and me. Selling him on the Research Park project was surprisingly easy. I had been talking for only about five minutes when he interrupted me. The gist of his remarks were, "You need not say anything more, Luther. I understand. It is a wonderful idea and a money-maker. I'll back you and will put up to a million dollars in the project." This was a great milestone. Mr. Robbins was well acquainted with Romeo Guest of Greensboro and he engaged Mr. Guest to handle the park matters for him. Guest, in turn, named William Maughan of Durham as land buyer. The project developed rapidly.

A special press conference was called September 10, 1957, to announce plans for the multi-million-dollar Research Triangle Park, on a four-thousand-acre tract in the southeastern corner of Durham County and a portion of Wake County. At that time, Mr. Robbins already had committed about $750,000 in options for land and was planning to spend an additional quarter million for utilities for the area. Although he was not present, Mr. Robbins said in a statement, "North Carolina has been good to me and I am proud to play a part in her future growth."

❧ *The Sit-Ins Begin*

William H. Chafe

One phase of the 1960s movement for civil rights for American blacks began innocently in Greensboro. Within a week it had swept the South, ending lunch-counter segregation in many cities and demonstrating the effectiveness of a powerful new tool in opening public accommodations to blacks.

This account of the movement's early drama was condensed from *Civilities and Civil Rights: Greensboro, North Carolina, and the Black Struggle for Freedom*, a 1980 book by Duke University historian William H. Chafe.

❧ On February 1, 1960, four young men from North Carolina Agricultural and Technical College set forth on an historic journey that would ignite a decade of civil rights protest. Walking into downtown Greensboro, they entered the local Woolworth's, purchased toothpaste and other small items, and then sat at the lunch counter and demanded equal service with white persons. "We do not serve Negroes," they were told. But instead of leaving, the students remained. The next day they returned, their ranks reinforced this time by fellow students. Their actions sparked the student phase of the civil rights revolution. Within two months, the sit-in movement had spread to fifty-four cities in nine states. By mid-April, the Student Non-Violent Coordinating Committee (SNCC) had formed in Raleigh, North Carolina, to carry forward the battle. Within a year, more than one hundred cities had engaged in at least some desegregation of public facilities in response to student-led demonstrations. The 1960's stage of the freedom movement had begun.

The Greensboro sit-ins constituted a watershed in the history of America. Although similar demonstrations had occurred before, never in the past had they prompted such a volcanic response. The Greensboro "Coffee Party" of 1960, one observer noted, would rank in history with the Boston Tea Party as a harbinger of revolutionary shifts in the social order. The Southern Regional Council—a voluntary agency supporting interracial progress—agreed. The demonstrations, the council declared, showed "that segregation cannot be maintained in the South short of continuous coercion." Not only was the South in for a time of change; more important, the terms of that change would no longer be dictated by white Southerners. The long road that would lead from Greensboro to Selma to Black Power and beyond had found its starting point.

The sit-ins occurred against a backdrop of continued black frustration with Greensboro's racial policies. No issue provoked greater resentment than the minimal school desegregation that occurred in the years after 1957. Although Greensboro was no Little Rock, word quickly spread that black children and black families suffered greatly during the desegregation experience. An American Friends Service Committee investigation concluded that six out of the seven families that had sought transfer to all-white schools in Greensboro in 1957 had experienced some form of harassment. The father of one student was fired; another family was forced to have its telephone number changed due to threats. As Brenda Florence walked to her first day of school at Gillespie Elementary School, hecklers yelled, "Go home, Nigger." A year later she returned to an all-black school, her family unwilling to have their daughter endure any longer the trauma of white rejection. . . .

The young men who would revolutionize the civil rights movement in 1960 grew up in this environment. Three of the original four sit-in demonstrators had spent their adolescent years in Greensboro. They had attended Dudley High School, where they encountered teachers like Nell Coley, who instilled a sense of pride and provided a model of strength. Ezell Blair, Jr., recalled an eleventh-grade English teacher who had taught him Langston Hughes's verse, "My Soul Runs Deep Like a River." The literature of black protest and history challenged students to carry the fight forward. Joseph McNeil, a Greensboro demonstrator who had been reared in Wilmington, North Carolina, also had encountered teachers who had been "dynamic and straightforward [and] who would tell you what your rights were as citizens, what you should have, what you don't have, how you're going to get them." . . .

By the fall of 1959, all four young men were freshmen at A&T. They became close friends and they spent evenings talking about the condition of blacks in America and the need to take action so that they might have a better life. . . . "We challenged each other, really," David Richmond remarked about the rap sessions. "We constantly heard about all the evils that are occurring and how blacks are mistreated and nobody was doing anything about it. . . . We used to question, 'Why is it that you have to sit in the balcony? Why do you have to ride in the back of the bus?' "

All around were influences that reinforced the instinct toward action. One of the students worked in the college library with Eula Hudgens, an A&T graduate who in 1957 had participated in Freedom Rides to test local compliance with a Supreme Court decision ordering desegregation of the interstate bus system. Hudgens spoke frequently with Joseph McNeil about her own experience, and was not surprised when the young men acted. In that same fall and winter, the students talked with Ralph Johns, a white clothing-store owner who had long supported the NAACP and had been committed to the idea of demonstrating against segregated public facilities. Johns's involvement in the black community, Joseph McNeil noted, "was far greater than [that of] any other merchant." He was one of the few white people to show support for the college as well as for black protest, and he talked frequently about the need to mobilize students into a more active role. . . .

Gradually, the resolve to act crystallized. The immediate catalyst for the sit-ins is unclear. Blair recalled watching a TV documentary on Gandhi that inspired him with its model of "passive insistence" on freedom. For McNeil the role of Johns was crucial. . . . Still others pointed to a December 1959 episode when McNeil returned from a trip to New York and was refused food service at the Greensboro Trailways Bus Terminal. Ultimately, though, the decision to act came when they found each other. "The thing that precipitated the sit-ins," Franklin McCain declared, "was that little bit of incentive and that little bit of courage that each of us instilled within each other."

The four young men gradually drew from their conversations a determination to take a direct step. McNeil initially suggested the sit-in tactic. One night shortly before the sit-ins he told his friends: "It's time we take some action now. We've been . . . people who talk a lot, but [with] . . . very little action." . . . On a Sunday night at the end of January, Ezell Blair, Jr., came home and asked his parents if they would be embarrassed if he got into trouble. "Why?" his parents wondered. "Because," he said, "tomorrow we're going to do something that will shake up this town." Nervous and fearful, afraid that someone might "get chicken," the four friends shored up each other's confidence until the next afternoon. "All of us were afraid," Richmond recalled. "But we went and did it."

The scenario had been well rehearsed. Stopping off at Ralph Johns's store, the students agreed that Johns would call a friendly reporter at the local newspaper at a pre-arranged time to alert her that the sit-ins were occurring. The four freshmen, in the meantime, purchased school supplies and sundry items at Woolworth's, being sure to keep their receipts. They then moved to the lunch counter. When they were refused service, Blair said: "I beg your pardon, but you just served us at [that] counter. Why can't we be served at the [food] counter here?" Customers walked by, noting the quiet demeanor of the students. The manager came and failed to persuade them to leave. Instead, the students stated their intention to return the next day and to stay until they were treated just as white customers at the food counter were. By that time, McCain noted, "We had

the confidence . . . of a Mack truck. . . . I probably felt better that day than
I've ever felt in my life. I felt as though I had gained my manhood . . . and
not only gained it, but . . . developed quite a lot of respect for it." The same
exultation permeated the group. They had done it! "I just felt that I had
powers within me, a superhuman strength that would come forward,"
McNeil remembered. "I don't know how the crusaders felt, but [I got] a
heightened sense of duty . . . once things really started to go." . . .

Almost immediately, the students knew they were not alone in their
struggle. That night the campus buzzed with word of their feat, as well as
with discussion of their determination to return the next day. The sit-in
leaders got in touch with the president of the student body and other
campus leaders, seeking to coordinate transportation and assure discipline
among the demonstrators. On Tuesday morning, twenty-five men and four
women students arrived at Woolworth's. Some of the men wore ROTC
uniforms, the others coats and ties; the women wore dresses. All carried
books and study materials, using the time when they sat at the lunch
counter to prepare their lessons. That evening during its regular monthly
meeting, the local NAACP chapter endorsed the students' actions and
voted to give them legal assistance.

By Wednesday morning, participation in the demonstrations surged
as students occupied sixty-three of the sixty-five seats at the lunch counter.
A Student Executive Committee set strategy, informed students about the
latest developments, and recruited new demonstrators. "We did an hour-
by-hour job," Richmond noted. "We had students to take each other's
places at the counters. We had a carpool to transport everybody. We had a
place where everybody would come and register for the whole week." . . .

The next three days revealed that a spontaneous action by a few had
triggered a massive social movement. On Thursday, for the first time, three
white women from the Women's College campus in Greensboro joined the
demonstration, as did students from some of the other colleges in the area.
With most seats in Woolworth's occupied, many black students began
demonstrating at the S. H. Kress store down the street. Also for the first
time, white teenagers and young men mobbed the aisles in Woolworth's
and heckled the sit-in demonstrators, greeting them with abusive and
threatening language. . . . By Friday, more than three hundred students
were taking part in the protest. Three white men were arrested, one for
setting fire to a Negro man's coat as he sat at the lunch counter.

The demonstrations Saturday brought the wave of protest to a crest.
Hundreds of students, including the A&T football team, descended on the
downtown area to continue the demonstrations. They were met by members of white gangs who waved Confederate flags and heckled blacks

sitting-in at the L-shaped lunch counter. Carrying small American flags purchased in advance by student leaders, the football team then formed a flying wedge that moved through the whites to permit new demonstrators to replace those at the lunch counters. "Who do you think you are?" the whites asked. "We the Union Army," the football players responded. . . . That evening, sixteen hundred students participated in a mass meeting. Convinced by their leaders that a message had been delivered loud and clear, they voted to cease demonstrations in order to provide time for "negotiation and study."

By that time the revolutionary new tactic the students had discovered had already begun to transform student consciousness elsewhere. Even as Greensboro's black students temporarily set aside their protest actions, young people in other cities were taking them up. One week to the day after the demonstrations had started in Greensboro, black students in Winston-Salem and Durham held sit-ins at local lunch counters. The next day demonstrations began in Charlotte, and the day after that in Raleigh. By the end of the week students were sitting-in across the state. Although a national representative of CORE had arrived on the scene, there was no conspiracy or collective planning involved. Rather, each group had acted upon its own impulse, drawing on the example that had been set the week before. As one Charlotte demonstrator explained, the sit-ins were a "means of expressing something that had been in our minds for a long time."

 *Social Fabric*

Women examine goods in a country store, *Harper's Weekly*, 20 April 1872, from a sketch by Mary L. Stone. Courtesy North Carolina Collection, Wilson Library, University of North Carolina at Chapel Hill.

A Bucolic Society

William S. Price, Jr.

At its settlement, North Carolina's population was widely scattered across a vast, forested landscape, a pattern that, though the state is now more thickly populated, persists to this day. In this essay, excerpted from *The North Carolina Experience: An Interpretive and Documentary History*, William S. Price, Jr., explores some of the social and religious implications of that dispersal.

Because of its early isolation from its northern and southern neighbors, North Carolina was frequently characterized as a bucolic society composed primarily of small landowners. Certainly, the colony never produced large numbers of planters equal in wealth to their counterparts in Virginia and South Carolina; but particularly after 1720, North Carolina's economy burgeoned to the extent that a number of sizable fortunes were made. The wealth of a merchant such as Samuel Cornell in New Bern or a planter such as "King" Roger Moore on the Lower Cape Fear rivaled that of merchants and planters elsewhere in the South. . . .

If the average white settler in early North Carolina was an immigrant who had established himself on a small farm, he shared many experiences with other colonists in similar circumstances. He had entered North Carolina either overland or by water. In either case he had traveled a great distance, usually accompanied by his family. Many different factors accounted for settlement in North Carolina. The colony drew large blocs of religious dissenters including Christoph Von Graffenried's New Bern Palatines and the Moravians of Salem and ethnic groups such as the Highland Scots, but the primary attraction was for men drawn by the hope of owning their own land and of making some semblance of a fortune.

The first months of settlement were hard. Farmers had to plant their crops, build or acquire a home, and set up housekeeping. Virtually every newcomer went through a period of sickness shortly after arrival, ranging in degree from a general malaise to death. This period, referred to as "seasoning," resulted from Europeans, Africans, and native Americans coming together in one pool of contagion where each group passed its diseases to the other. Africans brought hookworm and dengue; Europeans, smallpox, typhus, and mumps. Indians were unusually susceptible to these maladies, and epidemics were an important factor in the devastation of the native American population in the eighteenth century.

Even after the "seasoning" period, sickness was a constant companion of life on a frontier. Infant mortality was very high; no statistics were kept, but extant eighteenth-century graveyards attest to the high death rate among the very young. A number of people in early North Carolina practiced medicine, but even when they had undergone training in Europe, their techniques sometimes impeded the natural healing process of the body.

A major facet in the overall health picture of the colony was the quality of the diet. Large quantities of meat were available: beef, poultry, and a variety of game offered a respite from the predominance of pork. Plentiful corn was the basis of most bread as well as being used in general cooking. Orchards and wild berries abounded, and such fruits were ultimately drunk as well as eaten. Carolinians' use of alcoholic beverages was sizable; in addition to making wine, cider, and brandy, colonists imported large quantities of rum and malt liquors. Despite the widespread availability of food, there was little knowledge of or attention to nutrition. As would be expected in a class-stratified society, the diet of the wealthy planter or merchant was a good deal more varied and wholesome than that of those at the lower end of the social ladder.

The houses of typical white settlers were plainly furnished. Feather beds were prized commodities to be passed from one generation to another, as were table furnishings and other articles that modern families take for granted. A farmer with fifty or a hundred acres of land and a few head of cattle accumulated little movable wealth to pass on at his death.

Women, particularly those in frontier areas, often married at an early age. They bore and reared many children (one authority suggests that the average eighteenth-century family in North Carolina contained four children), conducted a variety of income-producing labors, and performed a staggering amount of domestic chores that might range from churning butter to making clothes.

Although there was a school in Pasquotank County as early as 1705, institutionalized education was rarely available to young North Carolinians. The chief educational instrument in the colony remained the family. Children were taught certain skills by their parents, and apprenticeships served to educate many. Even sons of the reasonably well-to-do often read law with a prominent local attorney rather than travel outside the province for more formal training.

Such schools as existed were generally associated with churches. Although the Anglican church had been established with tax support in acts of 1701 and 1703, it never flourished in North Carolina. Resentment over establishment and the absence of a resident bishop were but two factors retarding its growth. Missionaries sent to the colony by the Society for the Propagation of the Gospel were often less than ideal ministers. Dissenting sects proliferated; the first man known to preach in the colony (in 1672) was a Quaker. Lutherans, Presbyterians, Baptists, Methodists, and other sects existed, sometimes in the same community, throughout the province. Yet despite the variety of denominations and the appeal of certain sects, the fact is that most colonists had no religious affiliation.

☙ An Indian Path to Salvation

William Byrd II

English-educated William Byrd II of Westover in Virginia served on the joint commission to survey the boundary between North Carolina and Virginia in 1728. His *History of the Dividing Line* is an American classic.

In this excerpt, Byrd writes of the religious beliefs of a Saponi Indian called Bearskin, who served as a commission guide. Byrd's reaction to Bearskin's theology is typical of what a colonial aristocrat might have thought, but it provides modern readers with an intriguing glimpse of tribal beliefs in early North Carolina. The excerpt is taken from William K. Boyd's edition of the *History*; we have retained the original paragraphing and punctuation but have modernized the more eccentric spellings and regularized the capitalization.

☙ In the evening we examined our friend Bearskin, concerning the religion of his country and he explained it to us, without any of that reserve to which his nation is subject.

He told us he believed there was one supreme God, who had several subaltern deities under him. And that this Master-God made the world a long time ago. That he told the sun, the moon, and stars their business in the beginning, which they, with good looking after, have faithfully performed ever since.

That the same power that made all things at first has taken care to keep them in the same method and motion ever since.

He believed God had formed many worlds before he formed this, that those worlds either grew old and ruinous, or were destroyed for the dishonesty of the inhabitants.

That God is very just and very good—ever well pleased with those men who possess those God-like qualities. That he takes good people into his safe protection, makes them very rich, fills their bellies plentifully, preserves them from sickness, and from being surprised or overcome by their enemies.

But all such as tell lies, and cheat those they have dealings with, he never fails to punish with sickness, poverty and hunger, and, after all that, suffers them to be knocked on the head and scalped by those that fight against them.

He believed that after death both good and bad people are conducted by a strong guard into a great road, in which departed souls travel together for some time, till at a certain distance this road forks into two paths, the one extremely level, and the other stony and mountainous.

Here the good are parted from the bad by a flash of lightning, the first being hurried away to the right, the other to the left. The right-hand road leads to a charming warm country, where the spring is everlasting, and every month is May; and as the year is always in its youth, so are the people, and particularly the women are bright as stars, and never scold.

That in this happy climate there are deer, turkeys, elks, and buffaloes innumerable, perpetually fat and gentle, while the trees are loaded with delicious fruit quite throughout the four seasons. That the soil brings forth corn spontaneously, without the curse of labor, and so very wholesome that none who have the happiness to eat of it are ever sick, grow old, or die.

Near the entrance into this blessed land sits a venerable old man on a mat richly woven, who examines strictly all that are brought before him, and if they have behaved well, the guards are ordered to open the crystal gate and let them enter into the Land of Delights.

The left-hand path is very rugged and uneven, leading to a dark and barren country, where it is always winter. The ground is the whole year round covered with snow, and nothing is to be seen upon the trees but icicles.

All the people are hungry, yet have not a morsel of any thing to eat, except a bitter kind of potato, that gives them dry-gripes, and fills their whole body with loathsome ulcers, that stink, and are insupportably painful.

Here all the women are old and ugly, having claws like a panther, with which they fly upon the men that slight their passion. For it seems these haggard old furies are intolerably fond, and expect a vast deal of cherishing. They talk much and exceedingly shrill, giving exquisite pain to the drum of the ear, which in that place of the torment is so tender that every sharp note wounds it to the quick.

At the end of this path sits a dreadful old woman on a monstrous toad-stool, whose head is covered with rattlesnakes instead of tresses, with glaring white eyes that strike a terror unspeakable into all that behold her.

This hag pronounces sentence of woe upon all the miserable wretches that hold up their hands at her tribunal. After this they are delivered over to huge turkey buzzards, like harpies, that fly away with them to the place above mentioned.

Here, after they have been tormented a certain number of years, according to their several degrees of guilt, they are again driven back into this world, to try if they will mend their manners and merit a place the next time in the regions of bliss.

This was the substance of Bearskin's religion, and was as much to the purpose as could be expected from a mere state of nature, without one glimpse of revelation or philosophy. It contained, however, the three great articles of natural religion: the belief of a God; the moral distinction betwixt good and evil; and the expectation of rewards and punishments in another world.

Indeed, the Indian notion of a future happiness is a little gross and sensual, like Mahomet's Paradise. But how can it be otherwise, in a people that are contented with nature as they find her, and have no other lights but what they receive from purblind tradition?

✒ *Quarrels among the Baptists*

Robert M. Calhoon

Factionalism among North Carolina Baptists has its origin in divisions that arose before the American Revolution. This essay, condensed from Robert M. Calhoon's *Religion and the American Revolution in North Carolina*, helps to explain the cause of those tensions.

✒ The Revolution intruded deeply into the affairs of several denominations. As we have seen, it demoralized the Anglicans, thrust the Presbyterians into a position of political leadership, and jeopardized the security of Quaker and Moravian pacifists. The Revolution had a less clear-cut effect on the two other major denominations of the late-eighteenth century. Nominally part of the Anglican church, the Methodists would not emerge as a separate denomination until after the end of the War for Independence. The Revolution came in the midst of a long upheaval in the life of the North Carolina Baptists. While there is no reason to doubt that Baptists overwhelmingly supported the Revolution, the crisis of authority *within* the Baptist movement during the late-eighteenth century was for many of them a more immediate, intense reality than the larger national rebellion against British authority. The rise in the numbers of Baptist converts in rural North Carolina from the 1750s to the 1780s expressed a hunger for a more emotional, unrestrained culture and a need for charismatic leadership. That style of religious life would not spread beyond scattered groups of Baptists until the Great Revival of 1800, but its roots reached back to the middle of the eighteenth-century.

The crisis of authority among the North Carolina Baptists grew out of the rivalry between the Regular Baptists, who preached a rigorous Calvinist belief in the depravity of man, election by grace, and predestination, and the Separate Baptists, who affirmed Calvinism but subordinated theology to the overriding need for an ecstatic conversion experience. The Reverend Shubal Stearns, a former Connecticut Congregationalist, led a band of fifteen Separate Baptist converts to North Carolina where they established a church and settlement at Sandy Creek in present day Randolph County in 1755. Stearns's revivalist preaching converted hundreds of backcountry people. By 1758 the membership of the Sandy Creek Church grew from sixteen to 606, and by 1772 Stearns's followers had founded forty-two Separate Baptist Churches in Virginia, the Carolinas, and Georgia.

A pioneer Baptist historian, Morgan Edwards, left this vivid description of Stearns and his ministry:

> Mr. Stearns was but a little man, but a man of good natural parts and sound judgment. Of learning he had but a small share, yet was pretty well acquainted with books. His voice was musical and strong, which he managed in such a manner as, one while [meaning simultaneously], to make soft impressions on the heart, and fetch tears from the eyes in a mechanical way; and anon, to shake the very nerves and throw the animal system into tumults and purturbations. All the Separate ministers copy after him in tones of voice and actions of body; and some few exceed him. His character was indisputably good, both as a man, a christian and a preacher. In his eyes was something very penetrating, seemed to have a meaning in every glance, of which I will give òne example; and the rather because it was given me by a man of good sense, I mean Tiden Lane. "When the fame of Mr. Stearn's preaching (said he) had reached the Atkin, where I lived, I felt a curiosity to go and hear him. Upon my arrival I saw a venerable old man sitting under a peach-tree with a book in

his hand and the people gathering about him. He fixed his eyes upon me immediately, which made me feel in such a manners as I never had felt before. I turned to quit the place but could not proceed far. I walked about, sometimes catching his eyes as I walked. My uneasiness increased and became intolerable. I went up to him, thinking that a salutation and shaking hands would relieve me: but it happened otherwise. I began to think that he had an evil eye and ought to be shunned; but shunning him I could no more effect than a bird can shun the Rrattle [sic] snake when it fixes his eyes upon it. When he began to preach my perturbations increased so that nature could no longer support them and I sunk to the ground."

In a further description, Edwards employed the testimony of an early Separate Baptist preacher, Elnathan Davis. A backcountry dandy, Davis went to one of Stearns's baptismal services to mock him only to come away shaken by the power of Stearns's personality and then overwhelmed by a sense of "dread and anxiety, bordering on horror" which did not lift until he acknowledged his "faith in Christ." Edwards's account continues,

Davis . . . had heard that one John Steward was to be baptized, such a day, by Mr. Stearns; now this Steward, being a very big man, and Shubal Stearns of small stature, he concluded there would be some diversion if not drowning: therefore he gathered about 8 or 10 of his companions in wickedness and went to the spot. Shubal Stearns came and began to preach; Elnathan went to hear him while his companions stood at a distance. He was no sooner among the crowd but he perceived some of the people tremble as if in a fit of the ague: he felt and examined them in order to find if it was not a dissimulation: meanwhile one man, leaned on his shoulder, weeping bitterly; Elnathan, perceiving he had wet his white new coat, pushed him off, and ran to his companions who were sitting on a log, at a distance; when he came one said, "Well, Elnathan, what do you think now of these damned people?" He replied, "There is a trembling and crying spirit among them: but whether it be the spirit of God or the devil I don't know; if it be the devil, the devil go with them; for I will never more venture my self among them." He stood a while in that resolution; but the enchantment of Shubal Stearn's voice drew him to the crowd once more. He had not been long there before the trembling seized him also; he attempted to withdraw, but his strength, failing and his understanding confounded he, with many other, sunk to the ground. When he came to himself he found nothing in him but dread & anxiety, bordering on horror. He continued in this situation some days, and then found relief by faith in Christ. Immediately he began to preach conversion work, raw as he was, and scanty as his knowledge must have been.

Every effort by Regular Baptist leaders in North Carolina and Virginia to secure a merger with the Separates during the 1760s and early 1770s failed because of the Separates' insistence that baptism had to follow—rather than precede—a specific conversion experience. Many Regular Baptists had joined churches before the spread of revivalism in the 1750s had made the conversion experience the paramount event in Baptist spiritual life. The Separates demanded, as a condition of merger, the excommunication of persons who had joined the church prior to their conversion or without any distinct conversion experience; as a result of this hard line, attempts at merger collapsed in 1775. Two years later, however, the newly formed Kehukee Association of Regular Baptists—which was the closest to the Separates in belief and practice—persuaded four Separate churches to join them.

The incorporation of likeminded Separate and Regular Baptists into the Kehukee Association and the growth of the new association during the 1780s stabilized relations among North Carolina Baptists, though it could not eliminate the tensions inherent in a highly individualistic and anti-institutional fellowship. The dominant characteristic of the Baptists remained the autonomy of the individual congregation. Baptist vitality continued to spring from the acceptance of emotionalism and the open expression of love and affection which could transform an isolated rural church into "a close supportive, orderly community," as Rhys Isaac has written, "a refuge from the harsh realities of disease, debt, overindulgence and deprivation, violence and sudden death which were the common lot of small farmers." . . .

❧ Engage in Domestic Employments

Thomas Ruffin

In this 1826 letter to his daughter Catherine, Judge Thomas Ruffin of Hillsborough, one of North Carolina's most distinguished antebellum lawyers who was for twenty years chief justice of the state supreme court, offers an example of the instruction that upper-middle-class fathers offered their daughters to prepare them for their role in life.

The letter is excerpted from *The Papers of Thomas Ruffin*, edited by J. G. de Roulhac Hamilton and published by the North Carolina Historical Commission in 1920.

Newbern, March 14th 1826.

My dear Child—

I had heard before receiving your letter of the improvement in Thomas' health, by the way of a friendly note from Mr. McRae. Your kind letters were however not the less acceptable; for one not only likes to know that something favorable has occurred, but to be informed of all particulars, which alone give full assurance of the reality of the happy events. . . .

I am pleased to hear that you have in prospect the leisure that promises a resumption of your history. I must enjoin it on you to *study* it several hours daily. I suppose you are finishing *Hume*. That done, take up Miss Aikens Memoirs of Elizabeth and James I. This course will supply you employment, if properly read, until my return—when I promise myself much pleasure in conversing with you upon the events recorded by those authors. You must allow me to hope that the time is near at hand, when I may do much of my reading *through you*, by the helps of our discussions of your studies. I hope that after the book is out of your hands, the subjects are not cast out of your mind. The true province of reading is not confined to a knowledge of the facts related in history. Reading furnishes food for reflection; and the habit is a valuable one and ought to be early formed of *thinking* and again going over in the mind the passages perused in the day. Such a practice serves the two-fold purpose of impressing the facts on the memory and leading the understanding into a train of exercise necessary to its improvement and strength. It is necessary too that you should engage often in domestic employments, which will set a limit to the hours employed in reading; for that cannot be profitably pursued under frequent and irregular interruptions. But the needle or knitting form no impediments to thought or conversations; and I fear I have observed that *work* wants some charm to keep you engaged long in it. Meditation on points of history and points of character in some of its personages will furnish an employment delightful in itself and divesting labor of all its drudgery. Lively conversations with your young friends and sober and dutiful ones with your Mother would fill up all chasms and give the highest zest to both your litterary and manual pursuits. Besides the solid knowledge to be acquired from history, it is my request that you undertake a course of reading for your evenings tending to enliven your fancy and chasten your imagination and likewise put into a proper train your notions of morals. For the former purpose, I suggest Select Poetry and the Spectator; Scott, Pope, Thompson, and Shakespeare are my favorite Poets. The Bible is the great fountain as well of morals as Religion and is to be best known. That I would follow up with the Spectator *again*. You see, I am a disciple of Addison. He is a young Lady's best instructor: His sentiments are all refined and chaste; his style simple, but it is elegant simplicity; his English, purely idiomatic; his religion, orthodox; his figures, perfect and his Imagination lively. There is nothing *coarse* from beginning to end. The Spectator is a finished model of the epistolary and colloquial style. Your evening's reading, being lighter, may be *aloud*, to the family seated around the Tea Table. I am aware, that I am much wanting in my duty both to your Mother and my children in not affording them, by a large house, more privacy and more facility of study. Neither retirement nor proper domestic order is completely attainable in our present establishment. I hope before long to alter that matter for the better. But in the mean time, I would not have you wholly neglect yourself. True Philosophy teaches us to improve all our present opportunities to the utmost: Make the best of what is in your power; and consume not your time in useless repinings at the absence of some desirable accomodation nor encourage a spirit of discontent by brooding over past ills. Because we might do *more* with other advantages, furnishes no excuse for not doing *much* with our present opportunities.

⌘ Tavern Life among Lawyers

Robert Strange

Robert Strange, author of *Eoneguski, or, the Cherokee Chief*, an early North Carolina novel, was a Virginia native who settled in Fayetteville in 1815 to practice law. As a superior court judge, he traveled western North Carolina from 1827 to 1836 and gathered material from which he wrote this scene from *Eoneguski*, describing the lodgings that circuit-riding lawyers and jurists came to know too well.

⌘ In the ruder stages of society the quantity of food is a matter of much more importance than its quality; and in the more early periods of civilization food can be dispensed with altogether, for a season, if an abundant supply of intoxicating liquors be only substituted. Thus it is the practice to provide at places where men are wont to assemble, rather against the demands of artificial thirst, than hunger or the necessity for sleep.

The tavern which had contributed to give Waynesville the rank of a town, wanted all the substantial utility of such an institution. Drink, truly, such as it was, could be obtained there in great abundance; but eating and sleeping were matters altogether of too trivial concern to merit the provident attention of the landlord. From pure kindness of heart, therefore, and not in compliance with any avaricious yearnings for gain, did Mr. Holland, to supply the defect of accommodation at Waynesville, open his hospitable doors. Thither, amongst others, the gentlemen of the bar resorted for that comfort for which they would have sought in vain any where else in the vicinity of Waynesville. It was, in fact, a great inconvenience, both to him and his worthy spouse, but from the motives before mentioned they submitted to it, and although he could not afford the finding both his guests and their horses altogether gratis, yet the old gentleman took from them barely enough to defray his actual expense, without accepting any thing for trouble. Yet of this he had a large share, and it is to be feared that his courtesy was not very gratefully repaid by those who were its recipients. His piety was notorious, and although he did prevent, by the most positive prohibition, the desecration of his mansion by card playing, yet in that day, when there were no temperance societies to back him in what would have been considered a manifest breach of common civility, as well as a gross encroachment upon personal freedom, he could not withhold from his guests intoxicating drinks of the best quality within his reach, and had thus frequently the mortification, from the abuse of his favors, to perceive himself instrumental in the production of consequences disgraceful to them, distressing to his family, and painfully offensive to his own moral sense. To most outbreaking profanity he was compelled often to submit, though not without some word or look expressive of his disapprobation; and his ears were not spared occasional disdainful hints relative to the graces by which, in spite of them, he scrupulously accompanied every meal.

To Mr. Holland's the gentlemen of the long robe repaired, after the very sudden dissolution of the court, as described in the last chapter, amusing themselves as they went, and even after their arrival, with good humored raillery upon Johns, Rowell, and Smoothly, relative to their respective parts in the closing scene. These gentlemen, like those of the profession in other parts of the State, were exceedingly free and easy in their intercourse with each other out of court, and it would have argued great want of tact in any one seriously to have resented a sally of pleasantry of which he might be the subject. Mr. Holland, although a pious man, was not one of those who imagined religion to consist in a vinegar countenance or starched formality of manner, and enjoyed as much as any of them the humor of the scene, which he succeeded at length in gathering almost entire by putting together the several parts furnished by each contributor. "Why, Smoothly," he said, after laughing until his very sides were sore, "you must have enjoyed the squire's quid, you held on to it so long. I think a'ter awhile you'll make a tolerable tobacco chewer."

"Well, father Holland," said Smoothly, "don't you think a gentleman might be excused for washing down such a joke as that with a good drink?"

"Ah, Smoothly," said Rowell, who was constantly vacillating between good purposes and evil practice, "any thing for an excuse."

"Well boys," said old Johns, "I am like the feller who, hearing one cry out for licker bekase he was cold, and another bekase he was warm, called to the waiter, 'Bring me a glass of brandy and water, bekase I likes it.' So Holland do let me have something to drink, bekase I likes it. I second Smoothly's motion."

❧ Services at a Country Church

George Higby Throop

This description of a country church service in 1849 is from George Higby Throop's novel *Bertie*. A northerner who had taught in eastern North Carolina, Throop brought an observant eye to details that were so familiar to Tar Heels of that day as to be commonplace.

The physical setting of the church, the socialization (even the courtship) among its congregation, the presence of blacks, the fervor of the preacher are all characteristic of antebellum life in the eastern half of the state.

❧ We were not long in reaching the church. It stood in a grove of noble oaks. It was a plain, wooden structure, without spire, or shutters, or paint. As is usual at a country church in the South, there was a well near by, with the necessary sweep, and bucket, and trough. A few had already arrived; and, scattered here and there among the trees, were the horses, hitched to the overhanging branches, while the carriages stood in a motley group by themselves. Handing the ladies to the church door, we joined the little group outside, now constantly increasing, in which my uncle, the squire, and Uncle Baldy were in quiet conversation. The area around the church, from which the underwood had been thoroughly cleared, was speedily thronged with a medley of vehicles, the majority of which were family coaches; while, among them, you might also see lighter carriages, buggies, sulkies, carts and wagons. At intervals, among the trees, were rude deal-tables supported by stakes.

And now came a scene of bustle. Horses and carriages were thronging in from every direction, almost invisible in the clouds of dust. Not a few came on foot; and the larger portion of these last were negroes who had walked, probably from five to fifteen miles, to attend the meeting. Servants were hurrying to and fro. Greetings were exchanged. My uncle had a feeling of pride in being regularly at his post near one of the doors, where he had a hearty word and cheerful smile for everybody. It was his custom, too, to pay particular attention to the ladies of his acquaintance, especially the widows; concerning whom he rather liked to be rallied, though he had not the most distant idea of marrying again. I saw him handing the charming Mrs. Blossom from her carriage, while the professor, who had also arrived, stood at a little distance, evidently at loss to decide how his own civilities might be received. He advanced somewhat awkwardly and paid his respects, and his reception was most gracious. The smile was unmistakeable; and as the professor returned from the church-door, he set the ubiquitous white hat more erect!y upon his head, drew forth his bandana with a grand flourish, and took care to leave one-half thereof, when he returned it to the pocket, hanging conspicuously outside. He then drew himself up, threw back his head, and expanded his broad chest, wearing an air of self-gratulation and consequential dignity that revealed to me a shade of his character that I had not before discovered. The church was soon filled. Its occupants were chiefly ladies, a few gentlemen only being seated inside, the greater part sitting or standing near the doors, where temporary seats had been provided. Some appeared intent upon the services; but by far the greatest number continued to converse in a low tone until near the conclusion of the services.

The preacher was a tall and somewhat stoutly made personage of about fifty. His dress, if not of homespun, was assuredly well nigh as plain. His collar, unstarched but scrupulously white, rolled negligently over; exposing a large and well-formed neck. The prevailing expression of his face, which was one of strongly marked features, was that of simple earnestness and benevolence. His high, but somewhat narrow, forehead overhung grayish and deep-set eyes. The mouth and chin were indicative of much strength and decision of character, and the whole presence of the man reminded me very strongly of the personal appearance of Patrick

Henry. The tones of his voice, as he began reading the well known hymn

> Children of the Heavenly King,
> As we journey let us sing.

were singularly full, and rich, and deep; and I could see that at the outset he was (perhaps unconsciously) creating a feeling of seriousness in his little congregation. The air to which the words were sung, though not then familiar to me, was a simple and heart-stirring melody, in which nearly every one joined; and the roof rung with it. Then came an earnest prayer, and another hymn; and the preacher announced for his subject the Year of Jubilee.

He began by saying that thirty years ago he had stood in the same pulpit. "I had," he continued, "many warm friends here at Lebanon"—(the country churches have usually some such distinguishing name). "There was old Brother G———, who has gone home to his rest. He is in heaven, my brethren. He has heard the welcome words,

> Servant of God, well done!

which you sung at his grave. There was good old Brother H———. He's at home, too; one of the forty-and-four thousand that sing the song of Moses and the Lamb. His frail body is dissolved, and the eyes that wept over him will see him no more forever. Forever? *Here*, on earth, I mean. There was pious Sister B———. Many of you remember her, though, as I look around, I see only here and there a face I know. Yes, here is her son. My brother, are you a soldier of the cross? The spirits of the departed are waiting here to carry home glorious tidings. Come! who'll enlist to-day for the holy war?"

Simple as was the exordium, and imperfectly as I have described it, it brought the tears to many an eye. The talking was hushed outside the church. The aisles and pulpit steps were soon tenanted, and the listeners gathered around the doors and windows. With the same simplicity of which I have spoken, the preacher then gave a brief account of the Year of Jubilee.

He spoke first of the antiquity of the Sabbath; of the necessity of periodical rest; of the duty of observing the Sabbath as a necessity of our animal, moral, and intellectual nature, rather than an arbitrary law; of the results of cheerful acquiescence in the requirement. Then he adverted to the seventh year similarly set apart; and, finally, of "the sabbath of years"— the Jubilee. He spoke of the proclamation of liberty; of the returning of "every man unto his possession" and "every man unto his family"; of the abundance of the previous years whereby all necessity for toil was removed; of the redemption of property; of restoration from servitude. He drew a simple and most affecting picture of the changes that ensued on the advent of that year; of the delirious excitement of the poor debtor as the day drew near, and of the feelings with which he looked down from some neighboring hill, or over the hedge, upon the familiar features of the old homestead. He then pictured to us the nearer approach of the day; of the last few hours; of the expected sentinels, trumpet in hand, awaiting the hour that should usher in the year; and then that shout from all Israel "of thousands as of one," and the trumpet-blast that rung from hill to hill throughout the land!

"Sinner!" said he, at length, in a low, pleading, earnest tone, "you are toil-worn, you are bankrupt, you are the slave of sin; you are helpless, hopeless. I proclaim to you good tidings. The Year of Jubilee is come. Come *home!* You shall *rest!*

> You that have sold for naught
>   Your heritage above,
> Shall have it back unbought;

You shall be free. You shall have hope and joy in the dark valley. You shall live and reign forever. Will no one come?"

A low voice now struck the air of

> Blow ye the trumpet, blow,
>   The gladly solemn sound.

The effect was startling. Scarcely a voice among the hundreds that was not swelling the mighty chorus. A young girl, perhaps some sixteen or seventeen years of age, now rose, delirious with excitement, shouting, sobbing, laughing, and exclaiming "O! I am *so* happy!" and threw herself into the arms of a lady near her. Another, a beautiful girl, crossed to the side of the church opposite to that on which she had been seated, knelt before a schoolmate and begged her to go to the altar. In spite of every effort, I felt the tears streaming from my eyes; and, on looking round, I found that there were few who were not similarly affected. The professor had withstood it all until the young girl of whom I have spoken rose from her seat and knelt, when he buried his face in his hands and sobbed aloud. Ladies went to their acquaintances, parents to children, children to parents, brothers to sisters, and sisters to brothers. The preacher descended to the altar. One by one came a score of his congregation around him. Amid sobs, and groans, and shrieks, the rich tones of the preacher were heard in prayer. A hymn followed, the benediction was pronounced, and the congregation was dismissed.

The deal benches were now removed from the church by the negroes and placed near the table. It is the custom for planters to carry a quantity of bread, fowls, barbecue (roast shoat), bacon, vegetables, and, very commonly, a dessert; which are placed upon the rude tables, and acquaintances, friends, and strangers are hospitably invited to dine with them. This affords a delightful opportunity for chat among friends, and for the gallantry of the young men (to say nothing of widowers who have ceased to be disconsolate) to the ladies.

The Life of a Slave Girl

Harriet Jacobs

This account comes from a remarkable woman, Harriet Jacobs, who was born a slave in Edenton around 1813. She published her *Incidents in the Life of a Slave Girl* in 1861, after escaping to the North in 1842.

During the first years of my service in Dr. Flint's family, I was accustomed to share some indulgences with the children of my mistress. Though this seemed to me no more than right, I was grateful for it, and tried to merit the kindness by the faithful discharge of my duties. But I now entered on my fifteenth year—a sad epoch in the life of a slave girl. My master began to whisper foul words in my ear. Young as I was, I could not remain ignorant of their import. I tried to treat them with indifference or contempt. The master's age, my extreme youth, and the fear that his conduct would be reported to my grandmother, made him bear this treatment for many months. He was a crafty man, and resorted to many means to accomplish his purposes. Sometimes he had stormy, terrific ways, that made his victims tremble; sometimes he assumed a gentleness that he thought must surely subdue. Of the two, I preferred his stormy moods, although they left me trembling. He tried his utmost to corrupt the pure principles my grandmother had instilled. He peopled my young mind with unclean images, such as only a vile monster could think of. I turned from him with disgust and hatred. But he was my master. I was compelled to live under the same roof with him—where I saw a man forty years my senior daily violating the most sacred commandments of nature. He told me I was his property; that I must be subject to his will in all things. My soul revolted against the mean tyranny. But where could I turn for protection? No matter whether the slave girl be as black as ebony or as fair as her mistress. In either case, there is no shadow of law to protect her from insult, from violence, or even from death; all these are inflicted by fiends who bear the shape of men. The mistress, who ought to protect the helpless victim, has no other feelings towards her but those of jealousy and rage. The degradation, the wrongs, the vices, that grow out of slavery, are more than I can describe. They are greater than you would willingly believe. Surely, if you credited one half the truths that are told you concerning the helpless millions suffering in this cruel bondage, you at the north would not help to tighten the yoke. You surely would refuse to do for the master, on your own soil, the mean and cruel work which trained bloodhounds and the lowest class of white do for him at the south.

Every where the years bring to all enough of sin and sorrow; but in slavery the very dawn of life is darkened by these shadows. Even the little child, who is accustomed to wait on her mistress and her children, will learn, before she is twelve years old, why it is that her mistress hates such and such a one among the slaves. Perhaps the child's own mother is among those hated ones. She listens to violent outbreaks of jealous passion, and cannot help understanding what is the cause. She will become prematurely knowing in evil things. Soon she will learn to tremble when she hears her master's footfall. She will be compelled to realize that she is no longer a child. If God has bestowed beauty upon her, it will prove her greatest curse. That which commands admiration in the white woman only hastens the degradation of the female slave. I know that some are too much brutalized by slavery to feel the humiliation of their position; but many slaves feel it most acutely, and shrink from the memory of it. I cannot tell how much I suffered in the presence of these wrongs, nor how I am still pained by the retrospect. My master met me at every turn, reminding me that I belonged to him, and swearing by heaven and earth that he would compel me to submit to him. If I went out for a breath of fresh air, after a day of unwearied toil, his footsteps dogged me. If I knelt by my mother's grave, his dark shadow fell on me even there. The light heart which nature had given me became heavy with sad forebodings. The other slaves in my master's house noticed the change. Many of them pitied me; but none dared to ask the cause. They had no need to inquire. They knew too well the guilty practices under that roof; and they were aware that to speak of them was an offence that never went unpunished.

ஐ *Why the South Fell Behind*

Hinton Rowan Helper

In 1857, when Hinton Rowan Helper of Salisbury published *The Impending Crisis of the South: How to Meet It*, he set the South ablaze with anger. Possession of his book or knowledge of its contents was damaging to any candidate for public office. Yet his ideas reflected the private views of many people in North Carolina, which was among the last southern states to secede from the Union. As the South has looked back at events leading up to the Civil War, many of its leaders and thinkers have conceded that Hinton Rowan Helper, son of a Davie County tenant farmer, was correct in his assessment of the South's situation. This is an excerpt from that assessment.

ஐ It is a fact well known to every intelligent Southerner that we are compelled to go to the North for almost every article of utility and adornment, from matches, shoepegs and paintings up to cotton-mills, steamships and statuary; that we have no foreign trade, no princely merchants, nor respectable artists; that, in comparison with the free states, we contribute nothing to the literature, polite arts and inventions of the age; that, for want of profitable employment at home, large numbers of our native population find themselves necessitated to emigrate to the West, whilst the free states retain not only the larger proportion of those born within their own limits, but induce, annually, hundreds of thousands of foreigners to settle and remain amongst them; that almost everything produced at the North meets with ready sale, while, at the same time, there is no demand, even among our own citizens, for the productions of Southern industry; that, owing to the absence of a proper system of business amongst us, the North becomes, in one way or another, the proprietor and dispenser of all our floating wealth, and that we are dependent on Northern capitalists for the means necessary to build our railroads, canals and other public improvements; that if we want to visit a foreign country, even though it may lie directly south of us, we find no convenient way of getting there except by taking passage through a Northern port; and that nearly all the profits arising from the exchange of commodities, from insurance and shipping offices, and from the thousand and one industrial pursuits of the country, accrue to the North, and are there invested in the erection of those magnificent cities and stupendous works of art which dazzle the eyes of the South, and attest the superiority of free institutions! . . .

In one way or another we are more or less subservient to the North every day of our lives. In infancy we are swaddled in Northern muslin; in childhood we are humored with Northern gewgaws; in youth we are instructed out of Northern books; at the age of maturity we sow our "wild oats" on Northern soil; in middle-life we exhaust our wealth, energies and talents in the dishonorable vocation of entailing our dependence on our children and on our children's children, and, to the neglect of our own interests and the interests of those around us, in giving aid and succor to every department of Northern power; in the decline of life we remedy our eye-sight with Northern spectacles, and support our infirmities with Northern canes; in old age we are drugged with Northern physic; and, finally, when we die, our inanimate bodies, shrouded in Northern cambric, are stretched upon the bier, borne to the grave in a Northern carriage, entombed with a Northern spade, and memorized with a Northern slab! . . .

All the world sees, or ought to see, that in a commercial, mechanical, manufactural, financial, and literary point of view, we are as helpless as babes; that, in comparison with the Free States, our agricultural resources have been greatly exaggerated, misunderstood and mismanaged; and that, instead of cultivating among ourselves a wise policy, of mutual assistance and coöperation with respect to individuals, and of self-reliance with respect to the South at large, instead of giving countenance and encouragement to the industrial enterprises projected among us, and instead of building up, aggrandizing and beautifying our own States, cities and towns, we have been spending our substance at the North, and are daily augmenting and strengthening the very power which now has us so completely under its thumb.

It thus appears, in view of the preceding statistical facts and arguments, that the South, at one time the superior of the North in almost all the ennobling pursuits and conditions of life, has fallen far behind her competitor, and now ranks more as the dependency of a mother country than as the equal confederate of free and independent States. Following the order of our task, the next duty that devolves upon us is to trace out the causes which have conspired to bring about this important change, and to place on record the reasons, as we understand them.

And now that we have come to the very heart and soul of our subject, we feel no disposition to mince matters, but mean to speak plainly and to the point, without any equivocation, mental reservation, or secret evasion whatever. The son of a venerated parent, who, while he lived, was a considerate and merciful slaveholder, a native of the South, born and bred in North Carolina, of a family whose home has been in the valley of the Yadkin for nearly a century and a half, a Southerner by instinct and by all the influences of thought, habits and kindred, and with the desire and fixed purpose to reside permanently within the limits of the South, and with the expectation of dying there also—we feel that we have the right to express our opinion, however humble or unimportant it may be, on any and every question that affects the public good; and, so help us God, "sink or swim, live or die, survive or perish," we are determined to exercise that right with manly firmness, and without fear, favor or affection.

And now to the point. In our opinion, an opinion which has been formed from data obtained by assiduous researches, and comparisons, from laborious investigation, logical reasoning, and earnest reflection, the causes which have impeded the progress and prosperity of the South, which have dwindled our commerce and other similar pursuits, into the most contemptible insignificance; sunk a large majority of our people in galling poverty and ignorance, rendered a small minority conceited and tyrannical, and driven the rest away from their homes; entailed upon us a humiliating dependence on the Free States; disgraced us in the recesses of our own souls, and brought us under reproach in the eyes of all civilized and enlightened nations—may all be traced to one common source, and there find solution in the most hateful and horrible word, that was ever incorporated into the vocabulary of human economy—*Slavery*.

Levity among the Lawmakers

L. S. Gash

In good times and bad, life among North Carolina state legislators has its lighter moments, as in this scene from the General Assembly of March 1, 1867. The Civil War had ended, leaving North Carolina destitute. Even as a vindictive Congress prepared to impose a harsh Reconstruction plan (enactment of which came the next day), the state's lawmakers found occasion to party. The following account is from a letter Senator L. S. Gash of Buncombe County wrote to his wife in Asheville. It appeared in "The Correspondence of State Senator L. S. Gash, 1866–1867," edited by Otto H. Olsen and Ellen Z. McGrew for the July 1983 issue of the *North Carolina Historical Review*.

The "exchange" was Raleigh's Exchange Hotel, owned by John M. Blair, formerly of Asheville. The hotel burned the day after this letter was written. The Judge Battle referred to was William Horn Battle, a justice of the state supreme court. The Treasurer Battle was Kemp Plummer Battle, later president of the University of North Carolina. It should also be noted that the Senate's drunken debate occurred before the seating of the Reconstruction legislature.

☙ The news from Washington have excited our people considerably So much that we got on a drunk on yesterday. The House gave way about twelve and the Senate failed about one o clock. It is positively disgraceful; some of those rich old colts from the East gave a general treat on the East Portico of the Capital furnishing the very best liquor—Ice, Lemons and sugar, and before we old fogies Knew that anything was wrong the whole Capital was in an uproar. The House soon gave way and crouded in the senate chamber. And many Senators like old uncle jimmy Johnson being drunk themselves that not only the senate but the capital itself was drunk; one fool motion after another was put and appealed from or another made before the first could be decided, some clamouring for adjournment To the delight and disgust of the whole senate. Those in a Jovial mood seemed to think it the smartest senate that ever sat and they themselves in the lead, whilst another class who had not caught the spirits thought it a disgrace to the state and that those who thought themselves the smartest were of all men the greatest fools. Your humble servant never opened his mouth one way or the other just looked on. I got up to reply to a gentleman but on looking around and seeing his condition I sat down without opening my mouth.

At three o clock I partook of a sumptuous dinner at the exchange by invitation of Mr. Blair; it was a rich affair. Judges Reid & Battle of the supreme Court, Col Bamford and Col. somebodyelse of the U.S. Army, Col. Pulliam & M. Patton of Ashville, and ex. Gov. Clark and myself surrounded one table; the acting state officials Gov. Worth, Treasurer Battle & Secretary Best & others surrounded the next one to us. There was four tables on each side of the dineing room and I think there was not a drunk man on our line, whilst if the other line had an entire sober man on it I failed to see him. Mr. Blair conducted us to our seats, his regular boarders retaining generally their usual seats, and it was my fortune (being with Mr. Patton) to get a seat on the sober side, but many men unused to public drunkness got considerably foozeled.

❧ *Promoting Progress in North Carolina*

The twentieth-century industry hunting that has attracted many people to North Carolina from northern and midwestern states had its origins in the 1870s and 1880s. As the entrepreneurial spirit of the New South infected increasing numbers of North Carolinians, they encouraged outsiders to move to the state and bring with them their business skills and investment capital. This editorial, from the September 8, 1886, issue of the *New York Tribune*, was a commentary on that promotion. The movement was not an immediate success, as North Carolina remained predominantly rural until well into the second half of the twentieth century and still possessed one of the largest native populations of any state in the Union.

❧ A large number of citizens of North Carolina, not natives of the State, have prepared and signed a circular addressed "to all citizens of Northern birth in North Carolina." The object of the circular is to induce those whom it may reach "to join with us (the signers) in inviting all Northern people who are contemplating immigration to meet us in convention at Raleigh, October 26, that they may hear from us of the superior advantages this State offers to industrious and thrifty settlers." The signers add after their names the States from which they emigrated to North Carolina, and nearly every one of the sister States of the Union is thus represented. They name October 26 and Raleigh as the date and place of the convention because then and there the annual fair of the North Carolina State Agricultural Society is to be held, and they rely upon the fair to aid them in illustrating "the resources of every county from the coast to the mountain."

The scheme is an excellent one. It proves that North Carolina is wide awake, enterprising, seeking for progress and prosperity in a thoroughly practical way. Like the rest of the South, one of her chief needs is population. She possesses a rich and varied soil, a wealth of mineral and timber land, valuable water privileges, good harbors, an agreeable climate and many other advantages calculated to appeal strongly to those who have the world all before them where to choose to settle but have not yet reached a decision. . . . Every such movement [the convention] is deserving of and receives the heartiest encouragement at the North. But if it is to meet the wishes and expectations of its projectors, it must be made to appear beyond a proud venture to men prospecting for homes that if they cast in their lot with the people of North Carolina they will be perfectly secure in all their political rights and privileges. Everybody knows that in portions of the South unless one swears by the Democratic party the community in which he resides will make it unpleasant for him. He may not be positively maltreated, but he will be let alone in an emphatic manner.

We rejoice at the assurance that comes to us that North Carolina has set her face against this un-American, suicidal policy; that she welcomes alike Republicans and Democrats and proposes that they shall have equal rights. Inviting immigration in this spirit and offering superior inducements, there is no reason why she should not increase and multiply.

✎ Life in the Cotton Mills

Jacquelyn Dowd Hall et al.

The New South spirit that brought tobacco factories, furniture plants, and cotton mills to North Carolina also brought a new way of living for the state's people. This excerpt from *Like a Family: The Making of a Southern Cotton Mill World*, by Jacquelyn Dowd Hall, Robert Korstad, James Leloudis, Mary Murphy, Lu Ann Jones, and Christopher B. Daly, reflects that change in lifestyles.

✎ When southern farmers left the land and took a cotton mill job, they called it "public work." The phrase gained currency during the Great Depression as government programs put thousands of the unemployed on federal payrolls, but for at least two generations southern millhands had used it to describe their encounter with factory labor. Men and women who had once tilled the soil left their plows and mules and set out to earn an hourly cash wage—most for the first time in their lives. Despite a long history of small-scale textile manufacturing in the South that left in place scattered survivors from the antebellum years, most mill owners and workers were novices in a new industrial world. Both groups had much to learn, about machines and about each other.

The principal investors in early mills—successful merchants, planters, and professionals—had little knowledge of the manufacturing techniques necessary to operate their factories. Their business skills were essential to the financial health of the companies, but profitable manufacturing also required technical know-how and the ability to organize a work force. The successful manufacturer soon learned that it paid to know the business in all its details. Added to the pressures of buying cheap and selling dear was the need to employ capital and labor efficiently. Only slowly, through trial and error, did industrialists succeed in combining self-confidence and business acumen with the skillful management of people and machines.

Their command of capital gave manufacturers a free hand in designing the physical environment of the mill, but they never held full sway over the shop floor. Millhands themselves helped fashion the social world of work in a way that blunted the shock of their encounter with bosses and machines. Workers who migrated from nearby farms found themselves in unfamiliar circumstances. Instead of feeding and clothing their families directly through their own efforts, they offered their labor for wages to buy the things they needed. But the value of labor could not be measured by cash alone. Millhands also expected work to provide a measure of self-esteem and a feeling of accomplishment. . . .

With a work force in place, manufacturers had assembled the human and technical resources needed to manufacture yarn and cloth. Yet each component of this industrial enterprise presented problems. The river might be too high or too low to power the mill; the cotton fibers might be too short for spinning; badly adjusted looms might produce too many "seconds." But no ingredient was more challenging than the human element. In a business sense, workers were like any other factor of production—a commodity to be purchased as cheaply and used as efficiently as possible. But experience proved that millhands could not be "driven." Owners depended on workers to master their jobs and labor cooperatively with supervisors and with one another. Otherwise, goods could not be produced, profits could not be realized, and wages could not be paid. Manufacturers held the upper hand, but both sides had to acknowledge the other's needs in shaping life on the shop floor.

First-generation workers in southern mills had more to learn than just the mechanics of a new job. On the farm they had chosen and ordered their tasks according to their needs and the demands of their crops. Now they drove themselves to the continuous pace of a machine. Whereas most men, women, and children had once worked together and enjoyed the fruits of their own labor, now they were "hands," working under a boss's orders and for someone else's profit. Farm work, to be sure, had been hard, but mill work took a different toll. Millhands rose early in the morning, still tired from the day before. For ten, eleven, or twelve hours they walked, stretched, leaned, and pulled at their machines. Noise, heat, and humidity engulfed them. The lint that settled on their hair and skin marked them as mill workers, and the cotton dust that silently entered their lungs could eventually cripple or kill them. At best, mill work was a wrenching change.

Chester Copeland came from a long line of farmers and carpenters in rural Orange County, North Carolina, and he remained a devoted farmer except for brief, and unhappy, sojourns in the mills. To him, mill work was "nothing but a robot life. Robot-ing is my word for it—in the mill you do the same thing over and over again—just like on a treadmill. There's no challenge to it—just drudgery. The more you do, the more they want done. But in farming you do work real close to nature. There's always something exciting and changing in nature. It's never a boring job. There's some dirty jobs in farming, but there's nothing you get more pleasure out of than planting, growing, and then harvesting. In other words, you get the four seasons just like there are in a person's life—the fall and winter and spring and summer."

Despite this loss of control, most workers stayed with the factory because it provided a steady income and the work seemed easier than farming, at least to some. Forrest Lacock found farming "a very satisfactory job—you've got no boss man." "But," he continued, "the trouble with what we call one-horse farming, you can't have an income sufficient to take care of all your bills. A public job is more interesting because you can meet your bills." Dewey Helms's father had another reason for coming to the mill. "He wasn't worried about the income he made on the farm; he made as much as he cared about. He wanted to get rid of the harder work. Working in the cotton mill was not as hard work as running one of them mountain farms." Mill work was not for everybody, but the majority of those who came to the factories "never did want to live on the farm no more. They learned how to work in the mill."

◆ A Boy's Exposure to Religion

Erskine Caldwell

Author Erskine Caldwell achieved international fame with novels about poor southern families haunted by fundamentalist religion. He gained his insight into that religion quite naturally, as he relates in this story, condensed from his 1966 memoir, *Deep South: Memory and Observation*.

◆ Being a minister's son in the Deep South in the early years of the twentieth century and growing up in a predominantly religious environment was my good fortune in life.

The experience of living for six months or a year or sometimes longer in one Southern state after another, in cities and small towns and countrysides, and being exposed to numerous varieties of Protestant sects which were Calvinist in doctrine and fundamentalist in practice proved to be of more value to me than the intermittent and frequently-curtailed secular education I received during the first seventeen years of my life.

This fortunate destiny of birth and circumstance could otherwise have been tragic and unrewarding if both my mother and my father had not been wise and tolerant and, consequently, made it possible for me to seek an understanding of life beyond the confines prescribed by prevailing religious beliefs and prejudiced attitudes of mind.

My father was the Reverend Ira Sylvester Caldwell, a North Carolinian, an Associate Reformed Presbyterian ordained minister, a veteran of the Spanish-American War, and a graduate of Erskine College, Erskine Theological Seminary, and the University of Georgia. My mother, Caroline Bell Caldwell, was a Virginian, a teacher, and a graduate of Mary Baldwin College and the University of Georgia. I had neither a brother nor a sister.

Until I was twelve years old, I called my father Bud and my mother was Tarrie. My name for my mother had been derived at an early age from Carrie, which I had been constantly hearing as a diminutive of Caroline. Likewise, by that time, Bud had come to sound to me as befitting and authentic as my own name. Neither parent at any time had ever asked or demanded of me that I call them by names other than Bud and Tarrie.

Aside from the customary formal title of Reverend, my father was known to many of his acquaintances as Ira. In the informal atmosphere of barbershops and on fishing trips with friends it was not unusual for him to be called Preacher.

However, my father's brothers and sisters and other relatives always called him Bud, probably because he was the elder of his parents' six children. Feeling just as closely related to him as anyone else, it had always seemed to me the natural thing to call him Bud, too.

As it happened, though, on my twelfth birthday one of my aunts said it was shocking and disrespectful for me to call my parents Bud and Tarrie, and I was coerced and bribed to promise never again to call them by those names. The bribe I received was a glossy blue bicycle with a bell on the handle-bar and a tyre pump clamped to the frame. I soon became accustomed to saying Mother or *Mère* instead of Tarrie but, while not forgetting the promise I had made, I was never able to think of my father actually having the name Father or *Père*. . . .

My father never objected even in later years to my calling him either Ira Sylvester or I.S. and, when I saw him look at me with a blinking of his eyes and an unmistakable smile, it was as if my aunt had never offered to give me a bicycle. However, he undoubtedly realized that it was inevitable that a boy at my age who wanted a bicycle as much as I did would promise anything within reason in order to have one. . . .

At the time I was twelve years old my knowledge of religion and the evidence of its emotional appeal was confined to what I had heard and seen within only the A.R.P. denomination. This was meagre knowledge for a minister's son in those years and, besides, although I had been christened in a religious ceremony at my birthplace in Coweta County in west Georgia, I had never had the experience of being baptized. And more than that, purposely or not, I had never been asked or ordered to attend Sunday-school. When I did go to Sunday-school, it was because my playmates attended and I wanted to be with them.

It was not surprising to me, since it was in keeping with the privilege of being permitted to learn about life as I lived it, that it was not my own father, but a Jewish storekeeper in Charlotte, North Carolina, who made me aware that religious faiths other than that of the A.R.P. existed in the world and that it was possible for human compassion to cross existing religious boundaries. The storekeeper's name was Mr. Goldstein and he owned a family clothing and shoe store on Trade Street in the business centre of Charlotte.

I was riding my bicycle along the street in the summer afternoon and looking for tin foil in discarded cigarette packs. I had already salvaged enough tin foil to make a ball about the size of a small cantaloup and hoped to get enough to be paid a quarter for it when I sold it to a junk dealer in an alley behind Tryon Street.

I stopped in front of Mr. Goldstein's clothing and shoe store to pick up a crumpled cigarette pack from the gutter and he came out to the kerb and asked me if I wanted a job delivering shoes for him. It was the first time I had ever been offered a job in the business world and I must have been too surprised to say anything. He put his hand on my shoulder and gripped it as if afraid I would leave and not take the job. Then again he asked me if I would work for him. He said he would pay me two dollars a week for working every afternoon except Saturday and Sunday.

The certainty of earning two dollars a week was much more appealing than the uncertainty of finding enough tin foil on the streets to earn twenty-five cents occasionally and I eagerly agreed to take the job. Mr. Goldstein took me into the store, handed me a box of shoes, and wrote the delivery address on a slip of paper. I pedalled my bicycle for what seemed like several miles and finally got to the address on Statesville Avenue near the city limits.

After delivering the shoes to the customer, I went back downtown, but it was already becoming dark and Mr. Goldstein had locked the door of his store and gone away. I was late for supper when I got home and I fully expected to be scolded and told that I could not keep my job. However, my parents said that since I had agreed to work by the week for Mr. Goldstein, I should keep my part of the agreement, and so I went back to the store the next afternoon promptly at one o'clock.

The following Friday afternoon, the end of my first week working for Mr. Goldstein, and pay-day, I was given two boxes of shoes to deliver at the same address and instructed to collect two dollars for one pair and to bring the other pair back to the store. Mr. Goldstein explained that the shoes were in two sizes for a boy about twelve years old and that the boy's mother would keep the pair that fitted best.

When I got to the address on South Boulevard where the shoes were to be delivered, I immediately recognized the small, unpainted, weather-greyed house that was in the same neighbourhood where I lived.

It was the home of two of my playmates and I had often gone there to play with them in the back yard. Their mother was a widow and she did sewing and ironing by the day whenever she could find work in the neighbourhood. The three of them lived in the two-room house with little furniture other than two beds, some chairs, and a large oilcloth-covered table in the rear room. The frail, dark-haired woman was a member of the A.R.P. church where my father was the temporary pastor and she attended services almost every Sunday morning. The two boys, however, had not been to Sunday-school for two months or longer.

While the older boy, whose name was Floyd, was in the house trying on the shoes, his brother Pete and I went to the back yard and played with the train and fire engine they kept in a shed they had built with sides of wooden packing-cases and pieces of tin roofing.

In a little while their mother called me to the rear porch and handed me two dollars and one of the boxes of shoes. Then she said that the larger pair fitted Floyd and that I would see him at the picnic the Sunday-school was having in a park the next afternoon. When I asked if Pete would be at the picnic, she said he would have to stay at home because she could buy only one pair of shoes and did not want him to go to the Sunday-school picnic barefooted.

I took the money and the box of shoes and started to get on my bicycle to go back to the store on Trade Street. It was then that I saw Floyd come to the porch wearing his new pair of shoes, and I looked around at Pete. All I could think of was that Mr. Goldstein would give me two dollars in pay when I got back to the store and that the smaller size of shoes would probably fit Pete because he was a year younger than his brother. I went to the porch and put the box of shoes on the steps and then I got on my bicycle and pedalled up South Boulevard as fast as I could.

When I got back to the store, I gave Mr. Goldstein the two dollars I had collected and then began trying to explain why I had not brought back the other pair of shoes as he had told me to do. Before he could say anything, I told him that I wanted him to keep the two dollars he had agreed to pay me and to use it to pay for the shoes I had left for Pete to wear to the Sunday-school picnic the next afternoon.

Mr. Goldstein sat down on a stool and said nothing for a long time. It was late in the afternoon then, and there were no customers in the store. Presently he looked up and beckoned to me with a motion of his head. When I came closer, he pointed for me to sit down on the counter near him.

First, he asked what church I attended, and then he asked what my father did for a living. After that he looked up at me and shook his head back and forth with a solemn expression on his face.

There was a long silence. Then Mr. Goldstein said he would never be able to understand as long as he lived how Christians and gentiles ever made a living in business and kept from going bankrupt. Turning around and looking up at me, he told me that Jewish people were just as kind-hearted and sentimental and human as Christians, but that Jews had learned long ago to earn money first and then give some of it away later for a good cause. He said that I ought to keep that in mind if I expected to make a living in business and keep out of bankruptcy courts when I grew up.

It was closing time for the store. Mr. Goldstein got up from the stool, talking aloud to himself, and began turning out the lights. I could not hear anything he was saying, but just before he was ready to lock the front door, he handed me a dollar. As he did that, he said he owed me two dollars for a week's salary and that I owed him two dollars for the shoes I had given away and that the only thing to do about it was for each of us to contribute a dollar for Pete's shoes.

When I went home and told my father what had happened, he said it proved that a man did not have to be a Presbyterian or a Baptist or a Methodist or anything else, in order to be blessed with the goodness of humanity. Then Ira Sylvester said he had needed a new pair of shoes for a long time and that he was going to Mr. Goldstein's store the first thing Monday morning and buy a pair.

❧ Cyclone Mack in Burke County

Edward W. Phifer, Jr.

From North Carolina's earliest settlement, its ruralism, poverty, illiteracy, and fundamentalism made it a hotbed of evangelistic religion. George Whitefield and Francis Asbury preached in the state in the eighteenth century, drawing great crowds and inspiring many imitators. So did Sam Jones, Billy Sunday, and Mordecai Ham in the late nineteenth and early twentieth centuries. Among their imitators was Baxter Franklin McLendon, popularly known as "Cyclone Mack." A native of Little Rock, South Carolina, he grew up in the Carolinas and Georgia and failed at a variety of occupations—including preaching. Then, abandoning conventional churches and traditional appeals, he adopted a "tent-meeting" style. This account of his successful Burke County crusade in August and September 1920 was written by Dr. Edward W. Phifer, Jr., a Morganton surgeon and historian. It was excerpted from "Religion in the Raw: Cyclone Mack in Burke County, August–September 1920," in the July 1971 issue of the *North Carolina Historical Review*.

❧ Impulsive, emotional, a poor organizer, financially naive, a bit of a mystic—such was the man who came to Morganton to preach in August, 1920.

A considerable amount of skepticism, and rain-drenched, red clay roads got Mack's meeting off to a slow start, but this did not last for long. Nine days after his arrival, "His big tent . . . estimated to hold more than four thousand," was "full every night. . . ."

A week later it was stated that "Interest in the meeting has been increasing all the time" and people from surrounding areas were "attending in record-breaking numbers." On the previous Sunday the attendance was estimated at "between six and seven thousand." . . . Many families had perfect attendance at the night meetings, and a number of these, to do so, traveled six or eight miles in a mule-drawn wagon. By the third week, at least one baby had been named for Mack, and many additional namesakes were to follow. People went about town whistling or humming "Love Lifted Me" (or John-Three-Sixteen), which apparently was the theme song of the meeting. Manufacturers lent their full support: Alpine Cotton Mill employees were urged to attend; and the management arranged for Mack to preach to the workers in the loft of the Burke Tannery at the noon hour. At one night meeting, the Ku Klux Klan attended in a body, dressed in full regalia, hoods and all. The meeting ultimately gained the enthusiastic support of almost all the clergy of the county and the tacit support of the remainder. Over a thousand conversions were claimed and almost $9,000 was contributed—about $220 of this by Negroes. "I never saw so many one dollar bills in my life," recalls a local merchant who helped count the money. To top it all off, Mack was given three fine coon dogs, which he shipped to Bennettsville. It appears that Cyclone Mack loved dogs as well as people.

Why the McLendon meeting drew such crowds and had such great impact is surely worthy of consideration. Certainly his unconventional techniques—techniques which were unique—had their effect. That is to say, they were unique in Burke County but were not unique in what Wilbur J. Cash termed "orgiastic religion"; the earlier evangelists had used the detailed organizational and promotional methods, so deftly utilized by Mack's administrative apparatus; and even Fife had realized the psychological advantages of the big tent. The pulpit mannerisms, particularly the hyperactivity and extensive use of the "slangy invective" that Mack affected, had been initially introduced by others and had been perfected by Billy Sunday. Nonetheless, Mack gave the studied impression that these actions were dazzling improvisations, arising spontaneously and without prior design, as it were, from his very nature. . . .

True it was that, to some degree, he furnished excitement and amusement for the cynical and the curious. The country folk, and to a slightly lesser extent, the townspeople, lived pedestrian lives. In 1920 fewer than 17 percent of the national population had the equivalent of a high school education and less that 8 percent went to college. Most people were functionally illiterate and read but little. They were, in the main, too poor to travel. Radio, just appearing on the national horizon, was nonexistent in Burke County, movies were of poor quality, facilities for participation in sports were grossly inadequate. Courtroom antics, an occasional circus, or a summer stock company, provided most of the organized amusement. To some, the McLendon meeting fell into this category. At any rate, it was carefully stage-managed. Mack's sermons were punctuated with gyrations, impersonations, and unexpected witticisms; his extreme candor was engaging. "I believe there is a devil," he was wont to say, "first, because the Bible says so, and second, I've had plenty of personal dealings with him." Or, he would warn his listeners: "Don't pass judgment until all the evidence is in." And on being original: "I resolved that I was going to be original or nothing, and soon found out I would be nothing if I kept it up." Any object or person, including himself, was in his eyes derisible, if it suited his purpose. He characterized the graduates of theological seminaries as being "uniform as bologna sausages, all the same size and stuffed with the same thing."

His image was that of a virile, aggressive male, a man of action, a true frontier type who had trafficked in Sin in all its ramifications, struggled with it in all its enormities, persevered until he had conquered it through sheer will, and now presented himself as a skilled clinician who knew the "sin business." Gentle and consecrated church people, some of them ministers, many of whom covertly disapproved of his mannerisms in the pulpit, openly supported McLendon's campaign because they felt he influenced individuals who had never responded through normal church channels. "He reached people no one else could touch," said one observer, "and increased the attendance of every church in town." Others, simply because they were loyal members (and even though they resented the stridency, the sense of exaggerated urgency, and the uncouthness with which Mack's sermons were presented), faithfully followed in the wake of their minister and their church just as they might have voted for an unpalatable political candidate if he were on the "right" ticket. And still others, representing a moral position of the loftiest order, sincerely felt that Mack "brought out Christ so plain" to them that they were forcibly drawn to the altar.

But far and away the majority came because Mack told them what they believed and what they wished to hear. . . . Which is to say that from birth Mack's environment and experience in daily life had been much the same as that of his potential following in Burke County. Insofar as anything can be judged as typical, this county was in 1920 a fairly typical rural and semirural southern community. Certain attitudes and opinions were so deeply ingrained that change was a virtual impossibility. City dwellers and "foreigners" were regarded with distrust, and "too much education" seemed to encourage attempts at modification of fixed values and cherished institutions. Mack took the position that his pronouncements were unassailable. He equated himself with God and was defiant of anyone who doubted his edicts. He stood before the people of Burke County as the last great bulwark against false prophets, and preached the Gospel according to Mack. "On these matters," said a local admirer, speaking in retrospect, "he asked no quarters and he gave none. He asked nobody's opinion about anything." Actually, few of his preachments were at variance with orthodox theology, his biographer admits. His sermons stress "the inspiration [and inerrancy] of the Bible," "the authenticity of the Virgin birth," "redemption by means of the blood shed on Calvary," "regeneration through the Holy Ghost," original sin and atonement. His discourses depended on his own interpretation of the basic fundamentalist doctrines. He was, in truth, controversial only in his style of delivery and the validity of his many digressions. But Mack did not cling for long to abstruse dogmas; he constantly preached about "sin" and its consequences. "Let us [the preachers] stand on the wall as God's watchman and describe the state of the heart, the character of life and the peril of the soul and preach hell hot, life short, death certain and eternity long," he frequently urged his audiences in fiery tones. The sins he discussed were personal—largely confined to vice and intemperance; these were "sins" that he had committed himself, and he described them not only graphically and vividly, but with considerable artistry.

ᗰ Fighting the Old Enemy

Robert Mason

North Carolina's ruralism and religious fundamentalism also inclined it toward prohibition, which grew out of the temperance movements of the 1870s and 1880s. This account of prohibition and its age-old war against moonshine was written by Robert Mason, an Alamance County native who later edited the *Norfolk Virginian-Pilot*. It was excerpted from his 1986 memoir, *One of the Neighbors' Children*.

ᗰ Whether North Carolina might join the parade of states ratifying the Twenty-first Amendment to the U.S. Constitution, repealing Prohibition, was the big issue in the November 1933 election. The *Sanford Herald's* position was soaking wet.

Toward the end of October I wrote an editorial chiding preachers and deacons for teaming up with bootleggers to campaign for, in the name of the "Noble Experiment," crime and disorder. Mr. Paul Barringer, a Sanford leader of the United Dry Forces, replied with a letter upbraiding the *Herald* for bedding down with an unprincipled industry that would encourage wife-beating, furniture breaking, debt-defaulting, and great suffering among little children. He went at us pretty hard.

W. E. Horner, the *Herald's* publisher, was stung. "You've got to come back with something a damsight smarter than you wrote the first time," he told me. I had been writing the editorials since midsummer. "There was the time," he raged on, "when the *Greensboro Daily News*, I think it was, said a candidate for something or other, governor maybe, wasn't fit to be a dogcatcher. The candidate threatened to sue for libel. So the *News* said that, on second thought, it believed the candidate would make a splendid dog-catcher and ought to run for that instead of governor. Now you write something sharp like that."

Whatever I produced extended no journalistic lore. It did not even persuade me that I, having turned twenty-one in September, should go to the courthouse and register to vote. For I did not wish to remember the rest of my life that the first ballot I ever cast was a disappointment to my Presbyterian-elder father.

If I ignored my editorial advice, my readers gave it shorter shrift still. On election day a choir of ladies from the Baptist church, dressed in white and carrying candles to light the spiritual way, marched along the streets singing "Yield Not to Temptation" and "Where He Leads I Will Follow." Sanford and Lee County voted overwhelmingly against the proposition of calling "a convention to consider the proposed amendment to the Constitution repealing the Eighteenth Amendment." So did the State of North Carolina—by more than two to one.

But the results were academic. Prohibition as a national policy collapsed early the following month when Utah became, by one convention vote, the thirty-sixth state to go wet, providing the necessary three-fourths majority to alter the Constitution.

Neighboring Virginia the next year created a system of state liquor stores. Their wares soon seeped into North Carolina as an illicit alternative to white lightning. In 1935 North Carolina introduced, on a limited local-option basis, stores like Virginia's. Sanford waited thirty more years to opt for legal liquor sales.

Clearly, then, the *Herald's* wet stand in 1933 was bold. That was not lost on me. Liquor had been illegal in North Carolina since 1909, a full decade before the nation outlawed it. I was born in 1912 and was a senior at Chapel Hill when Congress modified the Volstead Act to permit the manufacture and sale of 3.2 beer. Thus my generation was unique, and remains so, for having grown up in a period when all intoxicating beverages were jail bait.

Prohibition and defiance of it were visible in Sanford almost constantly in the thirties. No issue of the *Herald* appeared without mention of a still-busting raid or an arrest for moonshining, blockading (also known as rum-running), or bootlegging. The taxis operating from a midtown stand delivered more "bootlegger pints"—12 ounces—of stumphole than they did passengers. One day Rob Seymour, a tinsmith self-taught in copper, came to the office and asked me to address his paper for the next month in care of a general store a dozen or so miles down the road. "I'm going to be in the woods down there sugar-heading," he explained.

I was getting a haircut not long afterwards when a deputy sheriff entered the barbershop and addressed the customer in the chair next to mine. The dialogue went something like this:

"That your Studebaker out there?"

"What's left of it. A fender fall off or something?"

"Naw, not that. But it's squattin' kinda low on the springs, ain't it?"

"Got a load of stovewood in there for mama. She's been burnin' bark and fussin' for a month."

"I know what you got in there. I done pulled out the back seat and looked."

The customer was silent for a long moment, then he sighed: "Oh, goddam, goddam. Peas and onions for supper."

The county jail was a poor feeder. . . .

The chief deputy was more likely than the high sheriff to root out stills and sweet mash. Church people complained that the sheriff courted moonshiners' votes. But he couldn't restrain the chief deputy without giving him good cause to run against him in the next election. Some of the sheriff's friends, admitting he showed little stomach for still-busting, said he simply wasn't hypocrite enough to suck up to the dry establishment.

For it was well known that the sheriff had wrestled hard, from time to time, with the Old Enemy. He claimed to have won, and that earned him some support, especially among good women who admired repentant men. The sheriff was a widower, a lean and handsome man with graying hair, a penchant for dressing well, and courtly manners.

Yet the church gossip that he was soft on moonshiners bothered him some. He had been elected narrowly and knew that his next race would be harder than the last. He had to campaign all the time. . . .

There were four deputies, counting the chief deputy. One of them suggested to me that I join a still-raiding party the chief deputy would lead. I readily accepted. But when I chanced to mention the prospect to Judge Thomas J. McPherson, who presided over county court, he warned me that the operation might be in essence a snipe hunt—that I should expect to be led quickly to an idle still with no one about, which the raiders would then attack with axes, only to flush from nearby bushes a din of shouts and shotgun firing and leaf rattling. Lawmen delighted in scaring hell out of greenhorns, the judge warned me.

So I had my guard up. Nevertheless, I was surprised when the high sheriff himself asked me to go into the woods with him. I told him, fine!

He and I rode in his car down to the Fayetteville highway and onto a dusty road. Near a plank bridge he pulled into the edge of some piney woods. We got out and followed the branch that the bridge spanned. Soon we came upon a small pot still partly covered with brush. The cap and worm were missing.

"There's a house pretty near here," said the sheriff. "We'll just go back to the car and ride there."

The house was small but sturdy and pleasant. In its neat yard were magnolia and dogwood trees and shrubs and flowers. The outbuildings were in good repair.

The sheriff parked in the driveway near the house. He got out and called. A woman came onto the porch. She was almost pretty, forty-five or so, about the sheriff's age.

We went on up. "Hidy, Miss Martha," said the sheriff. "He here?"

"Sheriff," responded the woman. Then, giving herself time to take in the scene before her—the familiar form of the county's top law-enforcement officer and a perfect stranger—she asked, "He?"

"Yes'm," said the sheriff. "He. Him."

"Well, him then," replied the woman. "Him and his brother, they're at their daddy's, helping out today. Left early in the morning. Their daddy's poorly."

"I'm sorry to hear that," said the sheriff. He removed his hat in a gesture of sympathy. Then he jammed it back on his head and spoke in a businesslike way:

"Well tell him then, soon as he gets home, tell him he should come see me. It's Friday today. Tell him the sooner the better. Monday will do. Tell him, too, I found that mess of his by the branch."

The woman's face remained expressionless. "I don't know about any mess," she said.

"No, I wouldn't expect you to," the sheriff answered, kindly. "But tell him just the same I found it, and tell him I want him to come see me and get right when he does. Just that.

"Now, you understand, there ain't one thing I can do about that mess, long as nobody was there. But this man with me here, that makes it another story. He's a federal agent, and under the United States Fresh Path Act, he can make an arrest where the path leads to, and that's to right here. He says he's got to get back to Greensboro this evening. Him and I will talk. We'll have us a talk.

"So you tell him, soon as he comes from his daddy's, I want him to come see me. Monday's fine."

We returned to the car and left. I said, "Sheriff, I want you to know I don't appreciate being used like that. She was a nice-looking lady, and the idea of her hating my guts for nothing I've done doesn't suit me. I know you've got to do your politicking, and I wish you well. But I don't like being used."

The sheriff drove on. "If I was you," he said at length. "I don't believe I'd say what you don't like or anything else. I believe I'd just keep my mouth shut about the whole thing. I'll remind you that it's against the law to impersonate a federal officer."

I couldn't believe my ears. Before I could think of anything to say, the sheriff added, in a drawling sort of way:

"And remember, I've got me a witness back there."

Dead Tired Barning Tobacco

Mary A. Hicks and Edwin Massingill

For more than a century, tobacco was eastern North Carolina's largest cash crop. But growing, harvesting, and curing tobacco was a demanding, labor-intensive enterprise, as this vignette reveals. It is the story of Frances Carson, who lived on a farm near Smithfield in 1939, as North Carolinians struggled through the dying days of the Great Depression. The narrative was recorded by Mary A. Hicks and Edwin Massingill of the Works Progress Administration Writers' Project and published by the University of North Carolina Press in a 1978 book, *Such As Us: Southern Voices of the Thirties*, edited by Tom E. Terrill and Jerrold Hirsch.

Ransome Carson, tall, emaciated, and quivering with nervous energy, was busy stripping the green leaves from waist-high tobacco stalks. He had no time to talk but he straightened for a moment and stared at his visitor.

"Go on up to the barn where the women are," he spoke shortly. "We'll be in after we get this slide full." As soon as he had spoken these few words he returned to his task.

All of the men were barefoot, paying no attention to the hot sand. They wore straw hats with frayed brims and most of them were as dark as Indians.

The women at the barn were laughing and joking. They had strung the last slide of tobacco and were resting, some sitting in the barn door, some on the empty slide, and some on nail kegs. Most of them were barefoot and the loopers wore aprons made from worn oilcloth. Many of them wore blue overalls and blue homespun shirts open at the throat. Some of them wore perky little bonnets; some, straw hats, and the old ladies wore big dark bonnets that covered their necks. Ransome's wife wore blue overalls and a blue homespun shirt. She also wore a ragged straw hat and was barefoot.

"I'd ought to go up to the house and see about Jean," she said. But the tobacco slide appeared. "Oh, I can't go now because there's the slide and I'll have to go on stringing."

"I'd never think of leaving a nine-months-old baby in a house alone for half a day," Granny scorned. "Poor little thing'll never learn to talk or act sensible in its life. It stays by itself all the time. Suppose the house catches on fire or suppose the child swallows something and gets choked to death. Why, suppose it crawls up on a chair and falls and breaks its little neck. There's a hundred things could happen to her. I wouldn't leave none of mine that way."

Frances laughed. "I don't think anything will happen to her. Everybody else leaves their younguns at the houses. Mrs. Creech ties her baby to the table leg with a hemp rope because she's scared it'll get in mischief or swallow something that'll choke it. I left mine in the yard once but it eat sand, chicken manure, and strings, so I decided to leave her in the house and take a chance on her eating buttons. If I left the 'backer every hour or two and went to the house to see about her, Ransome would raise the devil."

The women and children worked rapidly and the green leaves disappeared from the slide quickly. A visitor arrived and started to hand tobacco, but Frances called her over to one side and whispered, "Ruby's crawling with lice; you'd better stay away from her."

The girl gave a shriek and went and sat in the barn door. Frances returned to her hoss and continued stringing tobacco. Now and then the twine broke and the looper gave vent to his feelings in impatient little exclamations, such as "Oh, there," or "Oh, damn." When the sticks were full there were calls of "Stick off," "Get this stick," or just "Stick." One little towheaded boy removed sticks from all four hosses, and he was the busiest person present. A three-year-old clung to her mother's apron, bawling lustily. Small boys wrestled under the barnshed or amused themselves by running straws through the bodies of long green tobacco worms. One boy had perhaps a dozen of them on one straw. Frances joined in the laughter and the jokes, but her brown eyes often looked wistfully toward the weather-beaten, four-room house where her baby stayed alone.

Before the slide was empty another had arrived and then the work went on. The laughing ceased and only occasional exclamations broke the stillness.

Ransome came with the next slide. When he was near enough to be heard he stormed, "Damn it, what have you been doing that you can't keep trucks in the field? I told Johnny that if it was his fault I'd skin his god damned hide. If you damned women wouldn't jabber so much you'd git done sometime." He walked up to Frances and, white-faced, she shrunk back.

"If you don't git a move on I'll git a 'backer stick," he muttered, holding her tightly by the collar. Her eyes dilated and her lips quivered. Then he let go of her and walked hurriedly back towards the field. Frances said nothing but rushed more and more, and she almost entreated the others to hurry. Nobody talked and nobody stopped for anything, and the slide was empty before the next one arrived. They did not get behind again, and at eleven o'clock Ransome returned and ordered Frances to the house to prepare dinner for all the help.

The girl didn't open her mouth but handed her apron to another girl and hurried to the house. She ran in, lifted the baby, and hugged it. It was dirty, but a glance at the floor and at the child's wet clothes explained it. The beds were unmade; clothing lay in heaps on the bed, the table, the chairs, and the bureau. There was no rug on the floor, and the dingy white curtains at the window were ragged and tied in big knots. There were no shades at the windows.

When Frances had suckled the child she built a fire in the stove and set her pots of beans, potatoes, and tomatoes, that she had cooked before dawn, on to warm. She ran into another room and changed to a clean but faded print dress before she made biscuits. She boiled a dozen eggs for salad and made a huge pot full of coffee and sliced a six-layer chocolate cake before twelve o'clock.

The help came up to the well and drew water to wash up. Frances carried soap and towels to them and then hurried back to the kitchen to slice tomatoes and cucumbers. The men, women, and children rubbed their hands with sand first and then scrubbed them with washing powder and washed them in the washtub. Most of the gum was off by this time, but they washed again with toilet soap and then rinsed with clean cold water.

Ransome didn't wait for the others. He washed ahead of the women and hurried to the table. Frances looked embarrassed and tried to reprove him gently.

"Ain't a man got a right to set down at his own table when he pleases?" he bellowed at her.

She said no more and the men filed in and seated themselves on kegs, rickety chairs, and almost bottomless chairs. They ate their food and scarcely spoke until they were in the yard again. The women went tiredly to the table as soon as Frances had washed the dishes and set them on the table again. They ate slower and talked a little, and when they were through eating, Jane Creech helped Frances wash the dishes and Granny put them in the old-fashioned safe.

"I'm tired enough to die," Frances remarked. "I hate 'backer barning, but I know we have to do it. We're off now till two o'clock, though, to let the mules rest. Thank God we've got mules to work or Ransome would work me to death. He's right good to the mules, but he does cuss them and if they make him mad he beats them, too. Think I'll stretch out here on the bed and rest a little.

"I hadn't ought to be so tired. I've worked like this all my life. Papa was a farmer and he made us work so hard that we didn't go to school half of the time. We had to stay at home in the fall and grade 'backer and pick cotton, and in the spring we had to stay out to plant it. That's why I never got out of the fifth grade. I went a little higher than the other six, too." Tears were rolling down her cheeks.

"I'll tell you what's so: tenant farming ain't no pleasure at all. My papa done it and Ransome ain't never done nothing else. We make mighty little after working ourselves near 'bout to death and we move just about every year. I've heard folks say that there was good landlords and bad ones. I ain't never seen neither one. They're all alike, looking for every cent they can, and landlords was born without hearts. I always thought so while I lived at home, and since I married Ransome, I know it.

"I married when I was sixteen and didn't care a snap that he drunk and fought and had been in jail a time or two. I thought he'd stop it when I married him, but he got worse. He drunk and stayed away two or three days and nights at the time. He still does, even in barning season, and I have to set up with the barn all night by myself and then work in the 'backer the next day. When he comes home from being gone so long and I ask him where he's been, he tells me it's none of my damned business, and that's all I ever know about it. He keeps his jug of liquor in the kitchen and drinks when he pleases. If he wants to beat me or the children, he does, and that's all there is to it. He ain't got no mercy on nothing but mules and dogs. He don't think that I need clothes and, do you know, I love him better than most women love their husbands. I reckon women do love bad husbands better than they do good ones. I ain't got nothing, but I'm happy when Ransome's nice to me and the children.

"The little boy's five years old and the baby's nine months old. I ain't never been sick much, not even when they was born. I was up cooking and washing dishes the third day and when the last one was born I milked the cow on the third day. I felt pretty fainty, but there won't nobody else to do it. We had the doctor both times and that's the only times we've had a doctor in eight years.

"I don't hardly ever get out and go nowheres. I don't go to church, and I don't go to town once every six months. I ain't got no near neighbors and I don't care a straw about visiting nohow. I don't take no interest in reading and voting. I don't want to do nothing when I ain't working except rest. I'm tired all the time lately and I reckon I've got a right to be. We're trying to tend seven acres of 'backer, four of cotton, and twenty of corn, besides the garden and peas and 'tater patch. We're not going to make nothing like we done last year.

"Last year we farmed on another place and after we bought a second-hand Model-A Ford we didn't have enough left to buy any winter clothes. We've still got the old car, but we ain't had no money to buy numbers this year. When Ransome goes to town he catches a ride. Sometimes he goes on Saturday and comes back on Tuesday or Wednesday. I never know what to expect and that keeps life interesting. I manage all the year pretty well except during 'backer barning season and then I stay dead tired. Just look at the mess this house is in and you can see that I don't have time to keep it right. Well, anyway, after the barning is over I'll git a little rest, but grading ain't much rest. When you raise the stuff it's really 'backer all the time, pretty near all the year around."

◈ My Grandfather Gets Doused

Fred Chappell

Living in lofty isolation, North Carolina's flinty mountain people hold fast to the ways of their fathers—in music, in language, in politics and religion. All, that is, except Canton poet Fred Chappell's grandfather, who in these stanzas breaks with Methodist precedent and allows himself to be immersed as a Baptist. The poem is from Chappell's 1981 collection, *Mid-quest*.

◈

He hedged his final bet.
The old man decided, to get saved
You had to get *all* wet.

An early April Sunday he braved
Cold river and a plague
Of cold Baptist stares. He waved

And nodded. I saw his wounded leg
Wince at the touch
Of icy stream-edge.

Righteous clutch
Of the preacher dragged him farther in.
Maybe now he didn't want it much,

But ringed by mutely sniggering men
And contraltos making moues,
He managed a foolish unaccustomed grin

And plunged to his knees in ooze
And rush of Pigeon River.
What a bad black bruise

Of reputation! Never
In a thousand thousand thousand years
Had Davis or Clark turned hard-believer

Baptist. Weeping wormy tears
His Methodist fathers screamed
In paid-for plots. My uncles' sneers

Rose like spiritual kites. Who dreamed
Heresy lurked in his slick Sibelius-like head?
It was not seemly what he seemed.

Dead,
And grounded like a hog or horsefly, would
Be better than raving Baptist. No one admitted

It, but to be good
Was to be Methodist.
And everybody should.

Man, were they ever pissed!
He'd taken the habit of laying down laws,
So now this exhibitionist

Apostasy didn't sit so well.
And they all felt sneaky-content because
There went *his* ass to hell.

They'd togged him out in white,
And he rose from the water with a look
As naked and contrite

As a fifth-grader caught with a dirty book.
Was he truly saved at last?
Before he could take it back

They said the words so fast
And hustled him to dry ground
And shook his hand with ungracious haste.

If his theology was unsound,
At least he had a healthy fear
Of dying. . . . He frowned

When he saw me gaping. A double tear
Bloomed at the rim of his eye.
In a yellow-green willow a finch sang clear

And high.
Silence seized us every one,
Standing bemused and dry.

Now O pitiful he looked. The sun
Cloud-muffled, a cold wind-stir
Brought us to compassion.

They fetched his clothes from the car;
Still expostulating,
The preacher led him to a laurel thicket where

He changed. *And changed again.* Waiting
In numb wonder, we heard his voice go
Grating.

Baptized he was. But now
He decided to be *un*baptized. Pale
Pale the preacher grew;

I thought his heart would fail.
"No, Mr. Davis, no, no, no." It couldn't be.
Baptism was all or not at all,

Like virginity.
He'd have to stay washed white,
Baptist through eternity.

"Well, that's all right,"
He said. "But I had no notion it *took* so quick."
His voice glared unworldly light.

Grasped his walking stick,
And saddling his armpit on his crutch, he strode,
Dragging the dead foot like a brick.

At the side of the narrow road
He turned to watch the river driving east.
(Was West Fork Pigeon *really* the Blood

Of the Lamb?) A shadow-creased
Scowl huddled his face
When a thought bubbled up like yeast:

The water that saved him was some place
Else now, washing away the sins
Of trout down past McKinnon Trace.

And now he hoisted his stoic limbs
Into the home-bound Ford. "What damn difference
Will it make?" he said. "Sometimes
I think I ain't got a lick of sense."

∾ Fishing in the Cold Gray Sea

Robert Ruark

From the time the first white explorer set foot in North Carolina, fishing has been an important source of food and recreation. Few people have written about fishing as well or as warmly as Robert Ruark, a best-selling author and nationally syndicated newspaper columnist who grew up on the bays and marshes around Wilmington and Southport. This account of fishing with his grandfather is excerpted from *The Old Man and the Boy*, a 1953 book now considered a classic of American sport.

∾ Now the summer was completely gone, and all the memories of the summer. The time of year I liked better than any other had started. You could tell in so many ways that the summer was finished—your legs didn't sweat the crease out of your Sunday pants any more, and there was just a little nip in the evening air. The dogs that had been listless and shedding hair in the sticky heat got into condition again without being dosed, and began to look hopefully at the tin Liz, like maybe a ride was indicated.

The milky smell of summer was all gone out of the air, and had been replaced by the smell of leaves burning and the tart odor of the last of the grapes. You could feel your blood sparkling inside you, no longer heavy with the summer lethargy. A hot breakfast—pancakes and sausage and eggs busted and mixed into the grits—tasted just fine. The leaves were beginning to crinkle a little on the edges, and the first norther that brought the marsh hens flapping up from flooded marshes had already come and gone. A few ducks—teal, mostly—were beginning to drop in.

I don't know if you remember clearly the unspoken promise of excitement that early autumn brings, just before frost comes to grizzle the grasses in the early morning; before the chinquapins are ripe in their burry shells, before the persimmons lose the alum taste that twists your mouth. It's sort of like the twenty-third of December—Christmas isn't quite here, but it's close enough to ruin your sleep.

This was the time when we went fishing seriously on the week ends—fishing in the cold gray sea that always carried a chop except in the long, smooth sloughs; fishing in the inlets, and fishing off a long pier that went away out into the ocean. It was called Kure's Pier, if I remember right, and it cost something, ten cents or two bits, to fish off it. I used to see a couple of hundred fishermen casting off the pier, and there was so much fishing courtesy around in those days that when a man hung into a real big channel bass all the fishermen on his side would reel in and let him work his fish to the shore.

But by and large there weren't many big ones snagged off Kure's Pier. The stuff ran little—two-pound blues and an occasional sea trout, the old puppy drum and a whole lot of whiting, which we called Virginia mullet. The Old Man and I didn't crave company very much; we went farther down the coast from Carolina Beach past Kure's to old Fort Fisher, where the big guns used to be aimed against the Civil War blockade runners.

Down there we had the peculiar kind of solitude the Old Man loved and which I loved then, without ever knowing why we loved it. Oh, but that was a scary, desolate beach, the offset currents cutting great sloughs where the big fish lay. The silver-sandy beach came down from steep dunes as high as mountains, with just a fringe of sea oats. There weren't any houses as far as you could see. The bush was warped and gnarled by the winds that never stopped, the myrtle and the cedars and the little hunchbacked oaks twisted and tortured and ever buffeted. The thin screech of the wind was always there, and the water was cold. The rafts of sea ducks looked gloomy, and the birds always screamed louder there than on any other beach I can remember. The general air of age was heightened by the fact that you were always stumbling over an old cannon ball or a rusty saber, and the ghosts flew thick at nightfall.

We used to stop off at Kure's Pier once in a while, just to swap lies with fishing friends. We were an odd bunch, I'm forced to admit. The one I liked best was Chris—Chris Rongotis, or some such name as that—a flat-necked Greek who owned a café, naturally, in town. Chris lived to fish. The restaurant was strictly side-bar. Chris always had a joke for me, or a slab of "oppla pie" or "peenoppla pie" or "strumberry tsortcake" he'd fetched from the restaurant, and a thermos of the hottest coffee in the world. He would tell me what it was like back in Greece, and I learned three bars of the Greek national anthem. Chris just about died laughing at my Greek accent.

There were also a doctor and a dentist and a World War hero with most of himself shot loose. There were a Portygee and a Frenchman and a big blowsy old woman who wore pants and hip boots and cussed worse than anybody I ever heard when she lost a fish. I reckon it was my first real taste of the international set—except none of these internationals could have bribed their way into a parlor. The Portygee even wore big gold earrings and shaved every other Fourth of July.

If you snapped a rod or threw your last leader or ran plumb out of cut bait, somebody would come along and lend you a hand without appearing to be doing you a favor.

What I'm trying to do is tell you how nice it was in the fall, in late October and early November, when the big blues ran close ashore to feed off the minnows and the sand fleas. Looking back, I can't think of any real big fish we caught, or any lives we saved, or anything poetic or fancy. But this I do remember—an infection I caught which, if the good Lord is willing, I never aim to get cured of. That is the feeling of wonderful contentment a man can have on a lonesome beach that is chilling itself up for winter, sort of practice-swinging to get ready for the bitter cold that's coming.

We had a little weathered gray shingle-and-clapboard cottage rented for the fall fishing. It stuck up on a high bluff just between Carolina and Kure's Beach. If you stepped too spry off the front piazza, you would tumble right down onto the brown mossed-over rocks, which weren't so much rocks as case-hardened sand. There was a rough board step—more of a ladder, actually—that you had to climb up from the beach, about fifty yards straight up.

It wasn't very grand, I must say. It had a toilet and a ramshackle stove and a bedroom and sitting room and a fireplace. The fireplace was what made it. This fireplace drew so hard that it dang near carried the logs straight up the "chimbley." That was how I pronounced "chimney" until I was about grown, and I still think "chimbley."

This place was home, castle, sanctuary. I mind it so clear, coming in off that beach in the black night. The surf would be booming spooky and sullen, sometimes wild and angry and spume-tossing when the wind freshened. Your feet in the heavy black rubber boots sank down into the squishy sand, and you had to pull them out with a conscious effort as you walked up from the firm, moist sand at the water's edge and slogged through the deep, loose sand to the first steep rise of bluff. You would naturally be carrying a heavy surf rod and a heavy reel and a tackle box, and were generally dragging a string of fish that started out about the size of anchovies and wound up weighing more than a marlin before you got 'em home.

There would be an ache all through your shoulders from casting that heavy line with the four-ounce sinker and the big slab of cut mullet. There would be an ache in the back of your legs from wading in and then walking backward to reel in the fish. There would be cramps in your cold, salt-water-wrinkled red fingers, and your nose would be pink and running. If anybody had snapped you on the ear, the ear would have fallen off. Your feet were just plain frozen inside those clammy rubber boots, and you were salty and sandy from stem to stern.

Somehow you wrestled your gear and yourself up the steep steps in the dark, and the door would open when you moved the wooden latch. The first fellow in lit the lamps, old smoky kerosene lamps, and there wasn't any quarrel about who fixed the fire. Among the Old Man's assorted rules was one unbreakable: you never left the house unless the dishes were washed, dried, and stacked, the beds made, the floor swept and—this above all—a correct fire laid and ready for the long, yellow-shafted, red-headed kitchen match to touch it into flaring life. The Old Man said you couldn't set too much store by a fire; that a fire was all that separated man from beast, if you came right down to it. I believe him. I'd rather live in the yard than in a house that didn't have an open fireplace.

One of the chores I never minded was being the vice-president in charge of the fire detail. I loved to straggle off in the mornings, with the sun still warm and bright before the afternoon winds and clouds chilled the beach, just perusing around for firewood. We had wonderful fire-wood—sad and twisted old logs, dull silver-gray from salt, big scantlings and pieces of wrecked boats, and stuff like that, all bone-dry and wind-seasoned. The salt or something caused it to burn slow and steady with a blue flame like alcohol burns, and the smell was salt and sand and sea grapes and fire, together. All you needed under it was a few tight-crumpled, greasy old newspapers that the bait had been wrapped in and a lightwood knot or two, and when you nudged her with the match she went up like Chicago when the old lady's cow kicked over the lantern.

With that fire roaring you could cut out one of the lamps, because the fire made that wonderful flickering light which will ruin your eyes if you try to read by it but which, I believe, was responsible for making a President of Honest Abe. You backed up to her and warmed the seat of your pants, with your boots still on, and then turned and baked a little cold out of your chapped, wrinkled hands. Only then did you sit down and haul off the Old Man's boots, with one of his feet seized between your legs and the other in your chest, and then he helped you prize your boots off the same way.

It's funny the things you remember, isn't it? I remember a pair of ankle slippers made out of sheepskin, with the curly wool inside. I would set 'em to toast by the fire as soon as I came through the door. When I popped my bare feet into 'em, they were scorching and felt like a hot bath, a cup of coffee, and a pony for Christmas. Then some hot water on my hands, to wash off the salt and the greasy fish and the dirt. Now I started out to do the supper.

The Old Man said that in deference to his advanced years he had to take a little drink of his nerve tonic, and the least a boy could do would be to lay the table and set up the supper. I liked that, too—the Old Man sitting sprawled in a rocker in front of the fire, his feet spread whopper-jawed out toward the flames, puffing on his pipe and taking a little snort and talking kind of lazy about what all had happened that day. Shucks, getting supper wasn't any trouble at all.

You just started the coffee in the tin percolator and got the butter out of the food safe and sliced off a few rounds of bread and dug up the marmalade or the jelly. We had an iron grill that we slid into the fireplace as soon as she began to coal down into nice rosy embers, and it didn't take a minute to lay the halves of yesterday's bluefish or sea trout onto the grill. About the time the fish started to crumble and fall down through the grill I'd stick a skillet full of scrambled eggs over the fire, and in about two shakes dinner was served.

Full as ticks, we'd sit and talk over the second cup of coffee, and then the Old Man would bank the fire and blow out the lamp. We'd reel off to bed, dead from fatigue and food and fire.

These trips were only on week ends, of course, because there was that business about education, which meant I was bespoken five days a week.

But from Friday afternoon until Monday morning early, when the Old Man dragged me out of bed before light in order to check my fingernails and cowlick for respectability, I was a mighty happy boy.

◢ Unrest among the Branchhead Boys

Roy Wilder, Jr.

North Carolina's rural life has greatly enriched its daily language and political idiom, as documented by this story by Roy Wilder, Jr. The vignette was taken from Wilder's 1984 book, *You All Spoken Here*.

◢ When W. Kerr Scott campaigned to become Governor of North Carolina he appealed strongest to voters whose roots were in the soil. "Branchhead boys," he called them, farmers and townspeople who knew the bust of day, coffee that's saucered and blowed, folks who made a good stagger at honest toil and plowed to the end of the row. Scott campaigned to get the farmer out of the mud, he said, so farm families could get to church and farm children to school.

Soon after taking office he astonished the state by proposing a $200,000,000 bond issue, big money in 1949, for a secondary road program. He would pave farm-to-market roads in each of the 100 counties. The bonds would be amortised by a gasoline tax. The proposal was revolutionary, the reaction mixed. Debate was heated and families were split and friendships were jeopardized.

In this seething setting a branchhead boy in Montgomery County came one day to the crossroads store where he traded and loafed. Some of his peers sat about the wood stove and spat in the spit box and berated Governor Scott and deplored the bond issue and the tax levy. They were in ferment.

"Well," one of the group said, taunting the newcomer, "what do you think of your man Scott now?"

Shifting his cud and eyeballing his questioner, the branchhead boy replied:

"Anything my dog trees, I'll eat."

❧ Basketball Bug Bites Dixie

Harry T. Paxton

In the thirty years after World War I, North Carolina became a breeding ground for baseball. Nearly every town and mill had its own team, and many players went on to play in the major leagues. But after World War II, interest in baseball was overtaken by basketball mania, for reasons evident in the following story by Harry T. Paxton, published in the March 10, 1951, issue of the *Saturday Evening Post*.

While North Carolina State University's coach, Everett Case, introduced North Carolinians to an exciting new style of play, the school's William Neal Reynolds Coliseum set a new standard for indoor arenas, since emulated and even exceeded by other institutions and communities.

❧ Around Raleigh, North Carolina, on the night of December twenty-seventh [1950], there was a cold, driving rainstorm, turning toward morning into sleet and ice. "Don't drive!" radio stations were warning motorists the next day. "The roads are covered with ice."

As far as a good many people were concerned, these admonitions were strictly a waste of breath. That afternoon the North Carolina State College basketball team, pride of Raleigh and a considerable portion of the state, was playing its opening game in the Dixie Classic Tournament. Some 11,000 people doggedly made their way to the school's vast William Neal Reynolds Coliseum by game time, with tow trucks standing by on the parking lots to give aid to floundering vehicles. In the evening there was a crowd of 9,000 to watch some of the other contending teams. In three days the tournament drew a total of 58,000 spectators.

Such outpourings have become routine since 1946, when North Carolina State imported Everett Case, an Indiana coaching expert, to bring big-time basketball to the school. His Wolfpack squads quickly won national recognition, and this part of the South—a section not ordinarily associated with the basketball fever—has got the bug in a large way. Home attendance last season was 230,000. Big? It was the biggest of any college in the country.

Signs of the fever are everywhere, not only in Raleigh, which has a population of just 65,000, but throughout the area. New high-school gyms keep springing up, and home backboards sprout out on garages and barns. You can see small boys working out on them at any season of the year. Sporting-goods stores were unable to meet the demand for this equipment last Christmas.

In towns sixty, eighty and a hundred miles from Raleigh, people who a few years ago didn't know the difference between a tip-off and a pick-off—and didn't care—now regularly make the long drive over for the games. Newspapers and radio stations give heavy coverage to basketball. There are play-by-play broadcasts of both home and away games.

Says Ray Reeves, a veteran announcer on Raleigh's WRAL, "Wherever I go on speaking dates, even at football banquets, people want to ask me questions about State College basketball." The success of North Carolina State has had the effect of stimulating Southern Conference basketball activity generally.

At the beginning of the basketball boom, while awaiting construction of the present Coliseum, North Carolina State was playing home games, as it had for many years, in its venerable Frank Thompson Gymnasium. This was a building designed to seat 1,200. The accommodations usually were ample, before World War II, to take care of the students and the few outsiders who wanted to watch the games.

After the war, however, the college's enrollment swelled from around 2,500 to more than 5,000 men. Then Everett Case's first Wolfpack squad, built around a dozen freshmen from the Midwest and East, began burning up the courts during the 1946–47 season. It became increasingly difficult to take care of the students, let alone admit any of the general public. Temporary seats were added, but the demand rose even faster.

The bursting point was reached with the last home game of the season, featuring the University of North Carolina, State's bitterest traditional rival. State had barely managed to beat North Carolina in a previous meeting, winning 48–46 in overtime. Supporters of both schools were passionately eager to see the return engagement.

They turned out in numbers far exceeding the capacity of the hall. When all available space had been filled, the doors were locked. That didn't hold back the throng outside. They tore down the doors and poured into the gym, swarming around the side lines and overflowing onto the playing floor. Officials made several appeals to spectators to get off the court so play could begin. Nobody was willing to leave. Finally authorities gave up and canceled the game. It never was played. However, the teams did eventually meet again in the finals of the Southern Conference Tournament a couple of weeks later. The Wolfpack won another close one, 50–48.

The next year was just as stormy. During the off-season, the college somehow managed to wedge a total of 4,000 seats into the gymnasium. The student body, now at an all-time high of 5,300, was divided into two groups of 2,650, and admitted on alternate home dates. But the balance seldom was sufficient even to meet the needs of the alumni, the faculty and student guests. When an extra-large gathering showed up for a game with Duke on January 17, 1948, some city building inspectors showed up too. They pronounced the building unsafe for crowds in excess of 2,500 due to insufficient fire exits, and forthwith called off the proceedings.

After this false start, State got in one last game in the gymnasium the following week—behind locked doors, to insure compliance with the building inspectors' ruling. Only newspapermen and college officials were admitted. Then the Wolfpack moved to Raleigh's Memorial Auditorium—a frying-pan-into-the-fire proposition, since the auditorium holds only 3,600 for basketball. Not until the Coliseum was finally opened in time for the 1949–50 season did the seating problem ease off. And even the Coliseum's 12,498 seats aren't always enough.

The North Carolina State story is one of the most vivid illustrations of a truth the colleges have been learning in recent years. Basketball offers a much quicker, easier and cheaper route to athletic prominence than football. Here is a school which for years has put money and effort into football—notably in the mid-30's, when Hunk Anderson was coach—and has very little to show for it. State has come up with good clubs from time to time, yet never became a magic name in football. And now, in the space of five years, its basketball team is solidly established as a national power.

The college makes no bones about how this came to pass. They went out and got a basketball coach and some basketball players. North Carolina State was one of the few schools—some of them very small potatoes in sports—which frankly announced that they were not complying with the Sanity Code of the National Collegiate Athletic Association, even before that somewhat noble experiment was abandoned this January. State College authorities say they made a sincere effort to obey the key provision of the Sanity Code—that athletes could be given free tuition, but must work for their room and board. It proved impossible, they testify, for boys to carry their studies and sports and still earn their way on legitimate jobs. So North Carolina State openly reverted to the long-established Southern practice of giving full athletic scholarships—tuition, room, board and fifteen dollars a month for miscellaneous living expenses. They believe in going that far, they say, but no further.

The school's basketball ambitions began to crystallize in 1943, when ground was broken for the present Coliseum. The building was planned partly as a college auditorium—the school no longer had a place big enough for assemblies of the entire student body—and partly as an exhibition hall for state agricultural shows and the like. However, the basketball possibilities were obvious.

Shortly after the end of the war, the college's Athletic council, under the chairmanship of Dr. H. A. Fisher, head of the mathematics department, formally decided to go big time in basketball. The first problem was to get a good coach. Doctor Fisher and others inquired around, and were advised to consult Chuck Taylor, an old pro who serves as "ambassador to the world of basketball" for a rubber-shoe manufacturer, calling each year on hundreds of coaches around the country.

Taylor had played high-school basketball in Columbus, Indiana, in 1919 under a nineteen-year-old coach named Everett Case. He had kept abreast of Case's subsequent career, which included winning 726 out of 801 games in Indiana's red-hot high-school competition, and fifty-six out of sixty-one with Navy service teams. Taylor told the North Carolina State people, "The best basketball coach in the country is a lieutenant commander in the Navy. His name is Everett Case. If you want him, you'd better not waste any time, because some other colleges have been after him to coach for them when he gets out."

This was in March of 1946. Negotiations were begun, and on July first, after his release from the Navy, Case came to North Carolina State.

The next step was to get some playing talent. If it is true that Southern colleges often must recruit boys from other sections to have good football teams, because of the spotty supply of athletes from the local high schools, this is even more true in basketball.

For his first Wolfpack squad, Everett Case reached chiefly for boys he had spotted as likely prospects in service basketball. There was Dick Dickey, from Alexandria, Indiana—"he almost beat my team when he was at St. Mary's Preflight," Case says. Dickey was to score a total of 1,644 points in a four-year career at North Carolina State, establishing a Wolfpack record which has been broken this year by State's Sam Ranzino. Then there were men like Joe Harand, from New Jersey; Warren Cartier, from Wisconsin; Eddie Bartels, from New York; and Jack McComas, from Indiana.

The next year's freshmen included three men who are now the senior stalwarts of the current Wolfpack team—Forward Ranzino, Center Paul Horvath and Guard Vic Bubas. Each year North Carolina State has taken on fresh talent. The college is proud to state that the great majority of its out-of-state recruits have gone all the way through school and qualified for diplomas, or are in the process of so doing.

Coach Case did not promise immediate results, but he got them. He introduced a modern, fast-moving style of play not previously seen very often in the South. His very first year North Carolina State went to the National Invitation Tournament in New York. All told, Case's squads have earned national-tournament bids every year except the 1948–49 season, when they won a mere twenty-five out of thirty-three games. Last year North Carolina State placed third in the NCAA tourney.

The over-all record during the four seasons preceding this one was 107 wins and only 22 losses. Every year the Wolfpack topped the Southern Conference standings, losing a total of only five league games, and every year they won the postseason Southern Conference Tournament, staged among the top eight teams to determine the conference champion.

This season's squad, sometimes referred to as Case V, is another strong one. The scoring leader, Sam Ranzino, was named on several All-American teams last year—as was Dick Dickey. Ranzino is only six-feet-one, but he is an elusive operator who shoots well with either hand both from outside and close up. When he has an off night, the scoring slack usually is taken up by six-foot-seven-inch Paul Horvath, a skilled performer around the backboards. Another old reliable is Vic Bubas at guard, a smooth playmaker and defensive man. These three men, the only seniors on the team, are all heavy-duty performers. Almost everyone else on the fourteen-man squad sees frequent action, including Bobby Speight, Paul Brandenburg, Lee Terrill and Bill Kukoy.

But there are a lot of winning teams in basketball. North Carolina State's rise has meant more than just the emergence of another good ball club. It has transformed the sports picture in an entire area.

North Carolina in general, and Raleigh in particular, had basketball long before the modern Wolfpack, of course. The city even took a mild pride in the fact that, beginning in 1933, the Southern Conference Tournament was staged in the Raleigh Memorial Auditorium every year, with Chamber of Commerce blessing. Yet there were years when many of the 3,600 seats went begging, and civic-minded merchants bought up blocks of excess tickets and distributed them to friends and patrons in order to make a respectable showing at the gate.

In 1947, however, as the first of the new Wolfpack teams neared the end of a great season, there were twice as many applications for tournament tickets as there were seats. The tourney had to be shifted at the eleventh hour to Duke University's 9,000-seat field house in nearby Durham. This year, with the new Coliseum now functioning, the tournament returned to Raleigh.

Raleigh is one of the more cosmopolitan cities in North Carolina. It has very little manufacturing. It functions as the state capital, as an educational center—there are three women's colleges and two Negro colleges in addition to North Carolina State—and as the trading and distribution center for a predominantly agricultural county.

"Until this basketball thing came along, there was very little local pride in the school among the townspeople, outside of those who were our own alumni," testifies a North Carolina State faculty leader. "People would be more interested in Duke and North Carolina and Wake Forest than they were in us. Now even the ones who went to the other schools seem to put us no worse than second."

❧ *Youth and Innocence in Spring Hope*

Class of 1951, Spring Hope High School

The end of World War II brought a new era to education in North Carolina. Young people who were born in the depression and raised during the war began graduating from high schools—many of them from newly consolidated high schools offering a comprehensive curriculum. For the first time in the state's history, large numbers of high school graduates began going to college.

It was before television, before rock-and-roll music, before the glut of cars in high school parking lots, before the advent of drugs, before the rise in teenage pregnancies. It was a moment of innocence, as reflected in this "Last Will and Testament" from *Memoirs, 1951,* the yearbook of Spring Hope High School.

❧

Last Will and Testament

We, the class of 1951, in the town of Spring Hope, the county of Nash, and the state of North Carolina after four years of exposure in these stately halls of wisdom during which time we have added new crevices to our brains by wading through "Macbeth," "Silas Marner," Einstein's Theory of Relativity, and a thousand and one themes, and still being of sound body and excellent mind, do hereby declare this our last will and testament to be executed in the following order.

Article I. To the Faculty

Item I

To the principal, Mr. Parrish, the arbiter of all participants in acts of violence in said school, we leave a certificate, giving him the authority, if at such time he should have the desire, to preach at least two and not exceeding three sermons a year in chapel. We also leave him a can of wax polish and all our hopes that he may add more polish to the school staff.

Item II

To Miss Herring we leave the school building so that during the summer vacation she can fulfill her desire to act as principal.

Item III

To Miss Shuler and Mrs. Smith we leave a mediator so that all their disputes with and among the junior class can be settled in record time.

Item IV

To Mr. King we leave all our hopes that his next year's teams will be as successful as this year's.

Item V

To Mrs. Coleman, our beloved Math teacher, we leave our hopes of better years to come and the calmness which always follows a storm.

Item VI

To Mr. Stevens we leave a more co-operative group of F.F.A. boys that will back him up at F.F.A. meetings.

Item VII

To Mr. Smith we leave a new joke book so he won't tell the same jokes next year.

Item VIII

To Mr. Waters we leave a Glee Club that can sing "Purty Decent."

Item IX

To Mrs. Strickland and Miss Starr, our senior advisers, we leave a book which we have compiled during our last year in school which is entitled *How To Do It All* telling them how to publish an annual at almost no cost, to publish a school paper properly, to read 50 themes and 50 budgets, to give a senior play, to finish class night and graduation, and to still find time to get to their classes without acquiring too many grey hairs during the process.

Article II. To the School Board

To the School Board we leave our very kindest regards and our sincere gratitude for their unfailing kindness and gratitude.

Article III. To Our Parents

To our Parents, who have made this day possible, we bestow all our love and affection for all their efforts and sacrifices.

Article IV. The School Building

To our dear old school building itself, we leave the peaceful quiet caused by our absence and any apple cores, wads of gum, or crumpled notes we may have left behind.

Article V. To the Classes

We give and bequeath to the Jr. Class, our rightful heirs, our self-satisfaction, our importance, and our wisdom, all of which we possess in enormous quantities, and we hope said gifts will be of use in overcoming their present state of inertia. We also leave the Jr. Class any notebooks, pencils, fountain pens, unfinished business and debts, and any boys or girls we may have left behind in our haste to depart. We leave all our examination questions we have been given during the past year for we believe an examination, like history, repeats itself. The answers, never owned in entirety, have long since been mislaid by us and are not included in this legacy.

To the Sophomore class we bequeath our love for argument so when they become Juniors they can compete with their teachers. We also leave the Sophomore Class their first taste of freedom which, we are sure, will be very agreeable to them.

To the young and unsophisticated eighth grade we leave a map of the school building, so that they will not get lost and roam about in everybody's way looking for their classrooms. We include with this map our little book entitled, "How To Tell Teachers," a pamphlet compiled by us after four years of arduous study. The legatees will notice their book is not what to tell the teachers but how to tell them. It tells who your favorite authors must be to stand well in the English department, which teacher is fond of Napoleon, and what questions to ask to make the science teacher forget the lesson and be interesting. This information is invaluable to any wishing to make his grades in the subjects mentioned.

It will be noticed, although we have left bequests to the Junior class, soon to be seniors, to the Sophomores and to those who will in the fall become freshmen, we have made no mention of the present Freshmen class which will be known as the Sophomore class next fall. We have left them nothing, because by that time their self-valuation will have attained such heights that nothing in our possession would be regarded by them as worthy of their distinction.

⌘ Testing the Family Faith

Doris Betts

As more of North Carolina's youths went away to college, they sometimes came home with shocking ideas, such as atheism, as in this story, "All That Glisters Isn't Gold." The piece comes from *The Astronomer and Other Stories*, by Statesville native Doris Betts, a writer of fiction and English professor.

⌘ When I was a little girl, before the term "babysitter" had been invented, I used to stay with Miss Carrie whenever my parents were going places. Now that I think about it, I wonder where they went and what they did—but I never wondered then. Certain days I would be taken to Miss Carrie's house on Ingram Street. About the time all the possibilities of her house, yard, and possessions had been exhausted, my mother would arrive to take me home.

There was an odor in Miss Carrie's house, hard to identify. If you put your face close to a plate of cold leftover biscuits and breathed in deeply . . . Not exactly that odor, but it would be close enough. When I came home I would stand in the hall and try to discover the smell of my own house, but I never could.

With Miss Carrie lived her twenty-three-year-old nephew Granville, whom she had reared like a son for family reasons. Miss Carrie worried about Granville, who had gone off to the university in Chapel Hill and learned to be an atheist. She worried out loud and in his presence. I worried silently, because I loved Granville and I wasn't sure love was permitted atheists.

All the time Granville kept arguing religion with my mother and his Aunt Carrie. Anybody could tell by their voices his arguments were better than theirs.

My mother might say, her tone defensive, "You been to college and can *talk* good, but the Lord looketh on the inner man!"

The talk would go on and on: Granville speaking and explaining and making his points, and my mother quoting. And Granville asking long, serious, involved questions; and my mother reciting.

If Granville was uptown in his new insurance office, my mother would comfort Miss Carrie and give her advice. "Don't you argue with Granville your own self. You let the Lord do that. That's why we've got Scripture."

I lay on my stomach under the bed. Even the dust on the linoleum was cold.

"I want you to know, even a little child can ask some hard questions!" my mother sighed. I smiled proudly and let my finger travel the long closing spiral of the bedspring overhead.

It was not necessary that I listen to Mother's side of these planning sessions with Miss Carrie. Long since I'd heard all these things. By now I could say great chunks of catechism and memory work, could duplicate my mother's faith in the mirror of repetition. I had been taught all the references available to doubters. I knew the way to open a good Christian discussion with any atheist was to announce, "In the beginning was the Word, and the Word was with God, and the Word . . ." Some days I hoped this made more sense to atheists than it did to me.

So it was not necessary that I listen to the two women as they ran through their review, in preparation for Granville's test. Those words lay in me so precise and long familiar I never thought of them any more than I noticed my fingernails. I found a hairpin under the bed and began to scrape old dirt from between the boards in the corner.

I knew everything my mother and Miss Carrie would say; but where did Granville learn *his* words? In what class had those strange verses been taught? Sharp words, hostile ones, words that built up some sort of idea tower and then toppled it down like Babel, keen words—yet for all their edge they fell from him lightly, as if it were not hard work to blaspheme.

Each of his words was like a splinter and each slid invisibly inside me. There was a sore spot wherever one had penetrated; soon there were bruises all over my religion it was not safe to touch. I preferred the soreness from those splinters to the painful operation of having them removed.

My mother sometimes complained that if Granville was home when I spent the day at Miss Carrie's I later had a restless night and tended to fever; but I think she only said this so she could add, obliquely, "By their fruits ye shall know them." And nudge my daddy, who was Granville's friend.

︽ *The Vertical Negro Plan*

Harry Golden

Court-ordered desegregation in North Carolina schools and colleges raised social and political tensions in the 1950s, moving Charlotte editor-essayist Harry Golden to offer this wry suggestion for overcoming opposition to seating black and white students in the same classroom. The commentary is taken from his best-selling 1958 book, *Only In America.*

︽ Those who love North Carolina will jump at the chance to share in the great responsibility confronting our Governor and the State Legislature. A special session of the Legislature (July 25–28, 1956) passed a series of amendments to the State Constitution. These proposals submitted by the Governor and his Advisory Education Committee included the following:

> (A) The elimination of the compulsory attendance law, "to prevent any child from being forced to attend a school with a child of another race."
> (B) The establishment of "Education Expense Grants" for education in a private school, "in the case of a child assigned to a public school attended by a child of another race."
> (C) A "uniform system of local option" whereby a majority of the folks in a school district may suspend or close a school if the situation becomes "intolerable."

But suppose a Negro child applies for the "Education Expense Grant" and says he wants to go to the private school too? There are fourteen Supreme Court decisions involving the use of public funds; there are only two "decisions" involving the elimination of racial discrimination in the public schools.

The Governor has said that critics of these proposals have not offered any constructive advice or alternatives. Permit me, therefore, to offer an idea for the consideration of the members of the regular sessions. A careful study of my plan, I believe, will show that it will save millions of dollars in tax funds and eliminate forever the danger to our public education system. Before I outline my plan, I would like to give you a little background.

One of the factors involved in our tremendous industrial growth and economic prosperity is the fact that the South, voluntarily, has all but eliminated Vertical Segregation. The tremendous buying power of the twelve million Negroes in the South has been based wholly on the absence of racial segregation. The white and Negro stand at the same grocery and supermarket counters; deposit money at the same bank teller's window; pay phone and light bills to the same clerk; walk through the same dime and department stores, and stand at the same drugstore counters.

It is only when the Negro "sets" that the fur begins to fly.

Now, since we are not even thinking about restoring Vertical Segregation, I think my plan would not only comply with the Supreme Court decisions, but would maintain "sitting-down" segregation. Now here is the Golden Vertical Negro Plan. Instead of all those complicated proposals, all the next session needs to do is pass one small amendment which would provide *only* desks in all the public schools of our state—*no seats*.

The desks should be those standing-up jobs, like the old-fashioned bookkeeping desk. Since no one in the South pays the slightest attention to a Vertical Negro, this will completely solve our problem. And it is not such a terrible inconvenience for young people to stand up during their classroom studies. In fact, this may be a blessing in disguise. They are not learning to read sitting down, anyway; maybe standing up will help. This will save more millions of dollars in the cost of our remedial English course when the kids enter college. In whatever direction you look with the Golden Vertical Negro Plan, you save millions of dollars, to say nothing of eliminating forever any danger to our public education system upon which rests the destiny, hopes, and happiness of this society.

My White Baby Plan offers another possible solution to the segregation problem—this time in a field other than education.

Here is an actual case history of the "White Baby Plan To End Racial Segregation":

Some months ago there was a revival of the Laurence Olivier movie, *Hamlet*, and several Negro schoolteachers were eager to see it. One Saturday afternoon they asked some white friends to lend them two of their little children, a three-year-old girl and a six-year-old boy, and, holding these white children by the hands, they obtained tickets from the movie-house cashier without a moment's hesitation. They were in like Flynn.

This would also solve the baby-sitting problem for thousands and thousands of white working mothers. There can be a mutual exchange of references, then the people can sort of pool their children at a central point in each neighborhood, and every time a Negro wants to go to the movies all she need do is pick up a white child—and go.

Eventually the Negro community can set up a factory and manufacture white babies made of plastic, and when they want to go to the opera or to a concert, all they need do is carry that plastic doll in their arms. The dolls, of course, should all have blond curls and blue eyes, which would go even further; it would give the Negro woman and her husband priority over the whites for the very best seats in the house.

While I still have faith in the White Baby Plan, my final proposal may prove to be the most practical of all.

Only after a successful test was I ready to announce formally the Golden "Out-of-Order" Plan.

I tried my plan in a city of North Carolina, where the Negroes represented 39 per cent of the population.

I prevailed upon the manager of a department store to shut the water off in his "white" water fountain and put up a sign, "Out-of-Order." For the first day or two the whites were hesitant, but little by little they began to drink out of the water fountain belonging to the "coloreds"—and by the end of the third week everybody was drinking the "segregated" water; with not a single solitary complaint to date.

I believe the test is of such sociological significance that the Governor should appoint a special committee of two members of the House and two Senators to investigate the Golden "Out-of-Order" Plan. We kept daily reports on the use of the unsegregated water fountain which should be of great value to this committee. This may be the answer to the necessary uplifting of the white morale. It is possible that the whites may accept desegregation if they are assured that the facilities are still "separate," albeit "Out-of-Order."

As I see it now, the key to my Plan is to keep the "Out-of-Order" sign up for at least two years. We must do this thing gradually.

Patton Let It All Out

Ronald Green

Since the turn of the century, sports enthusiasts in North Carolina have increasingly enjoyed playing golf, especially after the development of Pinehurst as a golf resort in the 1920s. In addition to famous golf courses, North Carolina has produced many famous golfers. Here is sportswriter Ronald Green's profile of one of them, reprinted from the *Charlotte Observer* of May 11, 1986.

Of all the people in sports with whom I have crossed paths over the years, most of whom I admired and enjoyed and some of whom became my friends, my favorite remains and will almost certainly remain Billy Joe Patton.

I almost added, "a golfer from Morganton," but that no more describes Patton than "a writer from Missouri" describes Mark Twain.

The time and place of our most frequent encounters undoubtedly has something to do with the joy that Patton's name evokes, as it did these past few days when, at age 64, he was playing in the N.C. Senior Amateur at Charlotte Country Club.

The time would be the years between the mid-1950s and mid-1960s when he was in full flight as our most exciting and colorful amateur golfer, and the place would be Pinehurst, where he had some of his finest moments.

There are two reasons I mention all of this now. One is that the North & South Amateur, which Patton won three times, begins Monday in Pinehurst. That brings gushing back memories of the sweet days covering the North & South in the softness of springtime with its sunshine and soft perfume from blossoming shrubs, and the longleaf pines and the elegance of that lovely village.

The second is that a young man who appeared to be in his mid-20s dropped by the office a few days ago to talk some golf and when I mentioned the name of Billy Joe Patton, he said, "Yes, I've heard of him."

Heard of him, that's all? Well, of course. The years slip by so rapidly, we often forget that a generation has passed and that visions that are still so vivid in our minds are not shared by the young.

Patton is a treasure that ought to be preserved, so let me tell you about him. But how, in so little space and time?

First, let's get the numbers out of the way. Patton won three North & South Amateurs (one of the country's most highly regarded amateur tournaments), two Southern Amateurs and several lesser tournaments. He won 20 consecutive matches at Pinehurst against stiff opposition at one stretch. He played on five Walker Cup teams and six other international teams. He twice led the U.S. Open after 36 holes, finishing as low amateur in both, and was twice low amateur in The Masters. He is in two halls of fame and in 1982 won the Bobby Jones Award presented by the U.S. Golf Association in recognition of distinguished sportsmanship in golf.

But that is relatively lifeless information.

This was Billy Joe:

In 1954, he led The Masters after one round, was tied for the lead after two, fell five shots back after three but then played himself back into it early in the final round with some brilliant golf, including a hole-in-one at the sixth. But he was a daring player whose fast swing and go-for-broke attitude regularly put him in the honeysuckle and behind trees throughout his career. (Nothing he couldn't handle, usually, because he had marvelous imagination and an ability to extract himself from peril that I've never seen equaled.)

He chanced reaching the green in two on the par-five 13th hole on that final round at The Masters, when he was galloping neck-and-neck with no less than Ben Hogan and Sam Snead, and found water. He walked off the 13th with a double bogey. As he went to the next tee, he noted the dejection in his huge gallery and said, "Let's smile again."

Another visit to water after a long-odds gamble on the 15th did him in, and he finished one shot behind Hogan and Snead, who tied for the championship and played off the next day, Snead winning.

Playing Labron Harris in the semifinals of the U.S. Amateur at Pinehurst, Patton found himself two down at the 13th. He had about a 6-foot putt for birdie to win the hole. To snap himself out of the doldrums into which his game had fallen, he went into his golf bag, pulled out a pair of bent-up glasses that looked like he had sat on them, which he had, and a beat-up cap, and put them on. Then he holed the putt.

He won the next hole to even the match but then, his game being like the wind, he hit an awful shot, lost the hole and eventually the match.

Once in the North & South, playing extra holes, Patton found his tee shot on the second hole, which runs alongside a road, in a downhill lie in heavy rough. He had no chance to reach the green with his next shot.

As he dug in to whack at the ball, a car stopped nearby and a woman asked one of the spectators if he knew where she could find a room.

Patton, hearing this, never looked up.

"Just wait a few minutes and you can have mine."

After he had won the Southern Amateur on the same Pinehurst course in 1965 at the age of 43, when he knew twilight was settling over his days of glory (it was his last significant victory), he climbed into his convertible and began the drive back to Morganton with the top down, alone.

"My wife thought it was just another tournament I had won," he said. "My kids felt about the same way. But that victory did something to me. I was alive.

"After I accepted my trophy, I got in that car and drove out of Pinehurst. When I got on the highway and there was just me and the pine trees shooting by, I let out the damnedest yell you ever heard. I kept shouting and driving. I let it all out."

Let it all out. That was always Patton's way. Smashing long drives, finding them in the trees, studying what seemed to be a solid wall of lumber in front of him and then ripping twisting, climbing shots through the trouble, onto the green and knocking in the putt for a birdie. He played swashbuckling golf, happy golf, splendid in its result; golf that substituted soul for mechanism, golf that had dramatic uncertainty to it, golf to which bystanders could relate.

His saving grace was a putter that loved him. He has often said that back when he was young, nobody could handle a 6-footer the way he could. He just didn't think he could miss.

Once in the North & South, his approach to the 18th hole sailed over the green and came to rest on asphalt near the clubhouse, a good 100 feet from the hole. He chose a putter, rolled it along the asphalt, through a swale, onto the green, six feet from the hole. And made it to save the match.

Along the way through his glory days, down all the fairways and through all the brambles and brush, he chatted amiably with the gallery. He loved crowds. They ignited him. Ken Venturi once said of The Masters, where Patton played 13 times and almost always finished well, "If they locked the gates and didn't let anybody in, Billy Joe couldn't break 80."

And the galleries loved him, as much at that time, I believe, as they would later love Arnold Palmer.

There was a joy to his game that few playing at the upper level of golf could equal.

All of it—his scrambling, his nerve, his down-home gabbing with the spectators, his passion, his grace, his humor—all of it made him the most delightful and endearing person I've ever come across in sports.

At this time of the year, I always think of him and feel good for having been there when he was.

❧ The Last American Hero

Tom Wolfe

Auto racing has been a popular pastime among North Carolinians since the 1910s, when wooden race tracks were built in several cities and in others drivers competed in over-the-road race courses. Revived after World War II, the sport soared to great popularity on dirt ovals and tree-lined straightaways. With the building of super-speedways in the 1960s, racing attracted a whole new social cult and grew into a billion-dollar business. This excerpt from journalist Tom Wolfe's 1963 profile of Junior Johnson reflects the building of that cult.

Ten o'clock Sunday morning in the hills of North Carolina. Cars, miles of cars, in every direction, millions of cars, pastel cars, aqua green, aqua blue, aqua beige, aqua buff, aqua dawn, aqua dusk, aqua aqua, aqua Malacca, Malacca lacquer, Cloud lavender, Assassin pink, rake-a-cheek raspberry, Nude Strand coral, Honest Thrill orange, and Baby Fawn Lust cream-colored cars are all going to the stock-car races, and that old mothering North Carolina sun keeps exploding off the windshields. Mother dog!

Seventeen thousand people, me included, all of us driving out Route 421, out to the stock-car races at the North Wilkesboro Speedway, 17,000 going out to a five-eighths-mile stock-car track with a Coca-Cola sign out front. This is not to say there is no preaching and shouting in the South this morning. There is preaching and shouting. Any of us can turn on the old automobile transistor radio and get all we want:

"They are greedy dogs. Yeah! They ride around in big cars. Unnh-hunh! And chase women. Yeah! And drink liquor. Unnh-hunh! And smoke cigars. Oh yes! And they are greedy dogs. Yeah! Unh-hunh! Oh yes! Amen!"

There are also some commercials on the radio for Aunt Jemima grits, which cost ten cents a pound. There are also the Gospel Harmonettes, singing: "If you dig a ditch, you better dig two. . . ."

There are also three fools in a panel discussion on the New South, which they seem to conceive of as General Lee running the new Dulcidreme Labial Cream factory down at Griffin, Georgia.

And suddenly my car is stopped still on Sunday morning in the middle of the biggest traffic jam in the history of the world. It goes for ten miles in every direction from the North Wilkesboro Speedway. And right there it dawns on me that as far as this situation is concerned, anyway, all the conventional notions about the South are confined to . . . the Sunday radio. The South has preaching and shouting, the South has grits, the South has country songs, old mimosa traditions, clay dust, Old Bigots, New Liberals—and all of it, all of that old mental cholesterol, is confined to the Sunday radio. What I was in the middle of—well, it wasn't anything one hears about in panels about the South today. Miles and miles of eye-busting pastel cars on the expressway, which roar right up into the hills, going to the stock-car races. In ten years baseball—and the state of North Carolina alone used to have forty-four professional baseball teams—base-ball is all over with in the South. We were all in the middle of a wild new thing, the Southern car world, and heading down the road on my way to see a breed such as sports never saw before, Southern stock-car drivers, all lined up in these two-ton mothers that go over 175 m.p.h., Fireball Roberts, Freddie Lorensen, Ned Jarrett, Richard Petty, and—the hardest of all the hard chargers, one of the fastest automobile racing drivers in history—yes! Junior Johnson.

The legend of Junior Johnson! In this legend, here is a country boy, Junior Johnson, who learns to drive by running whiskey for his father, Johnson, Senior, one of the biggest copper-still operators of all times, up in Ingle Hollow, near North Wilkesboro, in northwestern North Carolina, and grows up to be a famous stock-car racing driver, rich, grossing $100,000 in 1963, for example, respected, solid, idolized in his home-town and throughout the rural South, for that matter. There is all this about how good old boys would wake up in the middle of the night in the apple shacks and hear a supercharged Oldsmobile engine roaring over Brushy Mountain and say, "Listen to him—there he goes!", although that part is doubtful, since some nights there were so many good old boys taking off down the road in supercharged automobiles out of Wilkes County, and running loads to Charlotte, Salisbury, Greensboro, Winston-Salem, High Point, or wherever, it would be pretty hard to pick out one. It was Junior Johnson specifically, however, who was famous for the "bootleg turn" or "about-face," in which, if the Alcohol Tax agents had a roadblock up for you or were too close behind, you threw the car up into second gear, cocked the wheel, stepped on the accelerator and made the car's rear end skid around in a complete 180-degree arc, a complete about-face, and tore on back up the road exactly the way you came from. God! The Alcohol Tax agents used to burn over Junior Johnson. Practically every good old boy in town in Wilkesboro, the county seat, got to know the agents by sight in a very short time. They would rag them practically to their faces on the subject of Junior Johnson, so that it got to be an obsession. Finally, one night they had Junior trapped on the road up toward the bridge around Millersville, there's no way out of there, they had the barricades up and they could hear this souped-up car roaring around the bend, and here it comes—but suddenly they can hear a siren and see a red light flashing in the grille, so they think it's another agent, and boy, they run out like ants and pull those barrels and boards and sawhorses out of the way, and then—Ggghhzzzzzzzhhhhhhggggggzzzzzzzeeeeeong!—gawdam! there he goes again, it was him, Junior Johnson!, with a gawdam agent's si-reen and a red light in his grille!

I wasn't in the South five minutes before people started making oaths, having visions, telling these hulking great stories, and so forth, all on the subject of Junior Johnson. At the Greensboro, North Carolina, Airport there was one good old boy who vowed he would have eaten "a bucket of it" if that would have kept Junior Johnson from switching from a Dodge racer to a Ford. Hell yes, and after that—God-almighty, remember that 1963 Chevrolet of Junior's? Whatever happened to that car? A couple of more good old boys join in. A good old boy, I ought to explain, is a generic term in the rural South referring to a man, of any age, but more often young than not, who fits in with the status system of the region. It usually means he has a good sense of humor and enjoys ironic jokes, is tolerant and easygoing enough to get along in long conversations at places like on the corner, and has a reasonable amount of physical courage. The term is usually heard in some such form as: "Lud? He's a good old boy from over at Crozet." These good old boys in the airport, by the way, were in their twenties, except for one fellow who was a cabdriver and was about forty-five, I would say. Except for the cabdriver, they all wore neo-Brummellian wardrobing such as Lacoste tennis shirts, Slim Jim pants, windbreakers with the collars turned up, "fast" shoes of the winkle-picker genre, and so on. I mention these details just by way of pointing out that very few grits, Iron Boy overalls, clodhoppers or hats with ventilation holes up near the crown enter into this story. Anyway, these good old boys are talking about Junior Johnson and how he has switched to Ford. This they unanimously regard as some kind of betrayal on Johnson's part. Ford, it seems, they regard as the car symbolizing the established power structure. Dodge is kind of a middle ground. Dodge is at least a challenger, not a ruler. But the Junior Johnson they like to remember is the Junior Johnson of 1963, who took on the whole field of NASCAR (National Association For Stock Car Auto Racing) Grand National racing with a Chevrolet. All the other drivers, the drivers driving Fords, Mercurys, Plymouths, Dodges, had millions, literally millions when it is all added up, millions of dollars in backing from the Ford and Chrysler Corporations. Junior Johnson took them all on in a Chevrolet without one cent of backing from Detroit. Chevrolet had pulled out of stock-car racing. Yet every race it was the same. It was never a question of whether anybody was going to *outrun* Junior Johnson. It was just a question of whether he was going to win or his car was going to break down, since, for one thing, half the time he had to make his own racing parts. God! Junior Johnson was like Robin Hood or Jesse James or Little David or something. Every time that Chevrolet, No. 3, appeared on the track, these wild curdled yells, "Rebel" yells, they still have those, would rise up. At Daytona, at Atlanta, at Charlotte, at Darlington, South Carolina; Bristol, Tennessee; Martinsville, Virginia—Junior Johnson!

And then the good old boys get to talking about whatever happened to that Chevrolet of Junior's, and the cabdriver says he knows. He says Junior Johnson is using that car to run liquor out of Wilkes County. What does he mean? For Junior Johnson ever to go near another load of bootleg whiskey again—he would have to be insane. He has this huge racing income. He has two other businesses, a whole automated chicken farm with 42,000 chickens, a road-grading business—but cabdriver says he has this dream Junior is still roaring down from Wilkes County, down through the clay cuts, with the Atlas Arc Lip jars full in the back of the Chevrolet. It is in Junior's blood—and then at this point he puts his right hand up in front of him as if he is groping through fog, and his eyeballs glaze over and he looks out in the distance and he describes Junior Johnson roaring over the ridges of Wilkes County as if it is the ghost of Zapata he is describing, bounding over the Sierras on a white horse to rouse the peasants.

A stubborn notion! A crazy notion! Yet Junior Johnson has followers who need to keep him, symbolically, riding through nighttime like a demon. Madness! But Junior Johnson is one of the last of those sports stars who is not just an ace at the game itself, but a hero a whole people or class of people can identify with. Other, older examples are the way Jack Dempsey stirred up the Irish or the way Joe Louis stirred up the Negroes. Junior Johnson is a modern figure. He is only thirty-three years old and still racing. He should be compared to two other sports heroes whose cultural impact is not too well known. One is Antonino Rocca, the professional wrestler, whose triumphs mean so much to New York City's Puerto Ricans that he can fill Madison Square Garden, despite the fact that everybody, the Puerto Ricans included, knows that wrestling is nothing but a crude form of folk theatre. The other is Ingemar Johansson, who had a tremendous meaning to the Swedish masses—they were tired of that old king who played tennis all the time and all his friends who kept on drinking Cointreau behind the screen of socialism. Junior Johnson is a modern hero, all involved with car culture and car symbolism in the South. A wild new thing—

◈ The Education of Terry Sanford

Terry Sanford

North Carolina has had many governors who championed education: David L. Swain of Asheville, Edward B. Dudley of Wilmington, Charles B.

Aycock of Goldsboro, Cam Morrison of Mecklenburg, and J. C. B. Ehringhaus of Pasquotank. Terry Sanford of Fayetteville joined their number in 1960, when he called for "A New Day" in North Carolina education. He not only led a movement for better schools but became the leader of the liberal wing of the Democratic party, a position he continued to hold as president of Duke University and as a U.S. senator.

This excerpt from his 1966 book, *But What About the People?*, offers an insight into his commitment to public education.

~ The December wind was biting through my wool sweater, and I was wishing that I had never left home to look for a Christmas tree. My older brother, ten years of age and bigger than I, was carrying the ax slanted across his shoulder like a soldier's rifle. Our father was setting the pace, which was a little too brisk for me. I wanted a warm fire. I wanted to be inside.

Then around the curve in the wooded trail there it was, looming like the Promised Land. An unpainted shanty was all it was and the front door had even fallen off, but there was a thriving column of smoke surging from the chimney. Inside, the flaming glow rivaled the magnificence of the midday summer sun, and it was obvious that the door hadn't fallen off at all. It was being used as firewood.

Presiding over this warming utopia, in an otherwise empty room, was a little man with a red face and a strange odor on his breath. The odor, in later years I was to learn, was canned heat, which in those days of prohibition was about as handy a source of drinking alcohol as you were likely to find.

He welcomed us in and we crouched around the fireplace until the door was all consumed. It wasn't very long. When the fire burned out he went his way, his World War I overcoat almost dragging the ground.

My daddy knew him. He called him Johnny and they exchanged some small talk about how cold it was, and how good the fire felt, and how it was only a short time until Christmas. I wanted to ask him what he was doing, and where he was going, and who was he anyhow. But I didn't. I waited and asked my daddy, after he had gone.

What was Johnny up to? My daddy said, "No good, I'm afraid." What did he do? "Nothing, most of the time." Where did he live? "Wherever he can beat somebody out of rent."

His name was Johnny Randolph. I knew his boys at school. One of them, Honey, was about my age, ragged, dirty, a troublemaker by the teachers' standards, profane at the age of six, thief of ten-cent-store items at the age of seven, one of those who came to school most of the time without any lunch bag.

Honey wasn't unique. There were many like him at school. They didn't do well, and ultimately they drifted away, or their families moved maybe, or they just weren't there any more. I hadn't heard of the word "dropouts," but that is what they were.

I remember hearing another story about Honey. He couldn't have been fourteen years old, maybe only twelve. In his way he was already a colorful character. One deputy sheriff was pleased to sit around the courthouse lawn and tell about the time he took Honey to the reformatory. That is how I knew he had been caught breaking into a store. With great guffawing, the deputy described how Honey entered the admission office. He pushed back the two deputies with both of his scrawny little arms and yelled, to the delight and entertainment of the reformatory staff members, "Clear the damn way! Here comes John Dillinger the Second!"

The next time I heard his name I was sitting in the Governor's chair, talking to a lawyer. He wanted commutation for a young prisoner who had been studying to get a high school diploma in our prison school system. The plea had some merit. The name was totally unfamiliar to me until the lawyer said, "You may remember his father, Honey Randolph. He was killed by a train several years ago down in South Carolina."

Into my mind flashed this cycle of tragedy and failure. The burning door, the army coat, the canned heat odor, the school dropout, the pathetic braggadocio at the reformatory, the manslaughter conviction of the third generation.

Somehow this boy, born into a house of despair, with incomplete education and no skill, killing a friend in a drunken brawl, was an instantaneous revelation of both the erosion and the repair of the human spirit.

The helping, encouraging, sympathetic hand extended by an enlightened prison system had been grasped by the third generation of ignorance and poverty. True, he hadn't proved himself, but the spirit, while badly mangled, was still alive. We could take him by the hand; we could lead him to self-respect and productivity. Or could we?

If we could not, then it was certain that yet another generation of ignorance and poverty would be visited upon us. If we could redeem this boy, his children could move to brighter opportunities.

Could we break this cycle of poverty? Could we break it for the Randolph boy, and for tens of thousands like him, both in and out of prison, both on and off relief rolls, both black and white, all born into poverty which breeds ignorance and ignorance which breeds poverty?

This young prisoner and his father and his grandfather were pitiful examples of the erosion of human resources from generation to generation. This was proof of neglect. This was our failure to protect the greatest of America's assets, her people, all of them.

In Honey Randolph's boy, the tragedy was sharply in focus. But what about the others? What about the high school valedictorian who started in the first grade with Honey? He is now very respectable and not at all in prison, but his abilities have not been fully used because funds for a college education were not available. This is an equally tragic waste of America's human resources. And what about all the boys and girls between these two extremes—those who drop out of school, those who never learn to read, those who can but do not learn a skill, those with superior academic or artistic talents never uncovered? Like silt in a great river washing out to form a useless marshland, this potential for the development of North Carolina, and America, has been swept away in wasted lives.

Education develops human resources. Human resources, in turn, make a nation whatever it is to be. It seemed to me, when I pondered running for governor of North Carolina, that education must of necessity be our primary concern. In the first place, we were behind in the comparative ratings with other states. This meant our children, generally speaking, started life with a competitive disadvantage.

Furthermore, education in the formal sense was not reaching enough people in any state, so even if we provided huge additional sums of money we would not be doing the job of total education. Even in those states and areas where comparative per pupil expenditures were high far too many children were not benefiting very much.

I decided I would make it my business to improve our system of developing human resources. I decided I would run for governor and make education the star by which we would sail.

&. A Crusader for the Right

Elizabeth Drew

Like Furnifold Simmons and O. Max Gardner before him, Jesse Helms went to Washington to become the brain trust, money raiser, and ideological leader of conservative forces in North Carolina politics. Like Simmons, Jesse Helms made his base the U.S. Senate. This profile of his personality, background, methods, and views was written by Elizabeth Drew and published in the July 20, 1981, issue of the *New Yorker* magazine.

❧ Jesse Helms, the Republican senior Senator from North Carolina, has, within a brief period of time, established himself as a power in the land by working at it doggedly, by establishing alliances with determined groups, and, most important, by inventing a new form of politics. Other senators have worked hard, but few as hard as Helms has. Other senators have established connections with outside groups and developed constituencies that reach beyond their states, but none to the extent that Helms has. And no other member of Congress has ever put together a political apparatus of the scale and nature that Helms has. His persistent efforts to determine the national agenda, and to influence the personnel and the policies of the Reagan Administration, have effect because of the power that Helms has methodically built. He is not just another senator, he is a force—and he represents a new political phenomenon. He and his extensive network of aides and allies have figured out how to tap some very old strains in American politics through a cool use of some of the most modern, sophisticated, and original political techniques.

Soon after he was first elected to the Senate, in 1972, Helms became known as someone who was constantly offering amendments on the Senate floor, and while he was being widely dismissed by his Senate colleagues as an aberration or a joke, or a nuisance, he was building something that they did not notice until it was already in place. He and his associates constructed a network of organizations—including tax-exempt foundations and Helms' own political-action committee, the second-largest raiser and spender of "independent" funds in the 1980 elections—which constitutes a revolution in politics. They made a new combination of the instruments that were lying about. Helms' persistent offering of amendments and increasingly successful efforts to define the national agenda, his position as one of the nation's most effective fundraisers, his attempts to shape the Administration are all of a piece. The amendments help raise funds to defeat those who do not agree with the amendments (and elect those who will), and they help him build his national constituency and alliances with like-minded groups, and that helps him shape the national agenda.

Helms is an ordinary-looking man. There is nothing exceptional about his speaking style or his intellect. He is gray: tall, slightly stoop-shouldered, with graying, thinning hair, and he tends toward gray suits. His large eyes peer through horn-rimmed glasses that rest slightly low on his nose—giving an appearance that suggests he might not be too bright. (The glasses have become his signature; one of his political advisers once discouraged him from changing them.) But Helms' colleagues have come to recognize him as intelligent enough for the role that he has assumed, and as a clever and crafty man. When I asked one conservative Republican senator how shrewd Helms is, he paused and then replied, "Very—in terms of being able to plot out a given course and achieve a certain result." Says another conservative Republican, "He has an innate craftiness and cleverness that's stunning to watch. You can't box him in—he'll defang you when you get close. Anyone who sells him short is going to lose—and has. He's amazing and formidable."

Now fifty-nine years old, Helms was born in the small town of Monroe, North Carolina. He is soft-spoken, talkative, and affable. He is a grandfather: he and his wife, Dorothy, have two daughters and adopted a nine-year-old boy whom they read about in the papers around Christmastime eighteen years ago—an orphan who had cerebral palsy. "He's been a blessing to us," Helms told me. Helms leads a quiet, serious life focussed primarily on his work. He is a devout Baptist—he has served as a deacon of his church and as a Sunday-school teacher—and in his politics he has attached himself to the fundamentalist-Christian movement. He presents himself as a modest and humble man, and yet much of his adult life has been built around the power of publicity and the use of his ability to arouse, if not inflame, people on his issues. He is uncommonly polite: he will bow when greeting a woman, and leap to open a door for her; he will swoop Capitol Hill tourists into a "Senators Only" elevator with a grand gesture. A word that is often used to describe Helms is "courtly"; his is an elaborate courtliness, an exaggerated throwback to a particular Southern political style. Behind Helms' courtliness is a man who has played a very rough form of politics. His courtly, self-deprecating, easygoing style contributes to his power. . . .

When Helms first got to the Senate, he did two important things: he made himself an expert on the Senate rules, and he started offering his amendments. His amendments were, like his commentaries, his opinions—in a new form, and in more socially acceptable terms. Few senators bother to master the intricacies of Senate procedures—those who have done so have tended to be Southerners—but knowledge of the rules can be very handy. Helms' arena has been the Senate floor rather than the committees or the back rooms. His interest has been in taking issues to the floor—using his knowledge of the procedures to advantage—and forcing his colleagues to go on the record on all manner of questions that they would prefer to avoid. His amendments had to do with prohibiting busing, prohibiting abortion, permitting prayer in the schools; with sex education; with cutting off aid to countries he found offensive. Often, his amendments had a surface appeal that made it difficult for senators to explain a vote against them—even though they felt them to be bad policy or bad precedent. Says one conservative senator, "When you vote against one of Jesse's amendments, it takes a page-and-a-half letter to explain why. I voted against one of Jesse's amendments on sex education and my mother called me up to complain. Jesse offers the kind of amendments that make your *mother* call you up." The amendment on sex education would have required that parents be notified and give their consent before students participated in sex-education programs in public schools. Most senators believed that this was not the business of the federal government, and the amendment was rejected, sixteen to seventy-three. Helms is often defeated, but that is not the point; he has larger purposes. His amendments gave him a kind of publicity that was useful, firmed up his relationships with a cluster of "New Right" groups, helped him raise money, and provided material with which he and his allies could try to defeat opponents. The money-raising mailings that go out from Helms' organization, as well as from its allies, stress the issues that Helms has raised, and focus the attack on certain senators who are up for reelection. One very conservative Republican senator says, "He'll push some doggy amendment and go right over the cliff with it. But when he does that he's trying to make a point to his following, and that's very shrewd of him. They all say, 'Ah, Jesse, a man of principle.' "

Loading Crabs at Wanchese

William Least Heat Moon

Fishing may be a sport for many Tar Heels, but along the long, jagged coast it is a livelihood for others, as in this scene from William Least Heat Moon's 1982 best-seller, *Blue Highways*.

In 1584, Philip Amadas and Arthur Barlowe, the leaders of Raleigh's first colonial exploratory expedition, returned to London from Roanoke with tobacco, potatoes, and a pair of "lustie" Indians to be trained as interpreters. Their names were Manteo and Wanchese. The Virgin Queen and the courtiers in their lace ruffs were fascinated by the red men. Months later when the Indians returned to the sound, Manteo, the first man baptized by the British in America, was on his way to becoming a proper English gentleman. But Wanchese, after seeing London, came back an enemy of "civilized" society. Four hundred years later, the towns carrying their names, sitting at almost opposite ends of the island, still show that separation.

Wanchese, smelling of fish and the sea wind, was on the lower tip of Roanoke. For generations the trawlers had passed through Oregon Inlet of the Banks to tie up at the little stilt piers of Wanchese. They still did, although the fleet worked out of here only in winter. The boats, maybe a hundred and fifty strong, came from the north—Massachusetts and Rhode Island, New York and New Jersey—to work the milder waters, where they trawled for flounder and dragged the mud for hibernating hardshell crabs. In spring, they followed the fish north, and the summer party-boats and a few yachts motored in.

The town had a craft shop now, but mostly it was splintered pilings and warped gangways and fish barrels. The small houses, built by seamen used to working in limited quarters, were made even smaller by the expanse of marsh weed and scrub loblolly stretching away to the sound. Rusting boilers and winches and broken hulls bobbed up like buoys from the waving grass; on lawns, under the crimson violence of camellias, fishermen had set admiralty anchors rusted to fragility or props painted red, white, and blue. From any home the boatmen could look to the wharf and see the white wheelhouses trimmed only in black, and the booms with lines and nets dripping like kelp.

The sun was just gone, the time Carolinians call "day down." I walked the wharf and read names of the trawlers: *Country Cousin, Brother's Pride, Blue Chip*. I came to a wooden shed with two windows gleaming like cat eyes in the night. A sign above the door: JAMES GRIGGS WHOLESALE. As I passed, a low, dusky whisper slipped from the side of the building, and a shadowy arm hooked me. "Hey, sport. You be here to help load?" It was a small, compact black man without age. He fixed me with his left eye while the milky right one shone like a moonstone.

Then a rasp from the shed: "Bring him in, Balford, and let's git the hell movin'." Balford motioned for me to follow inside. He stood behind me in the doorway and said, "Here, Griggs."

The room, a glowing of yellow bug lights and redolent with fish and diesel fuel, was stacked with crates of hardshell crabs. The crabs clacked their bony claws and reached through the slats at my eyes. Griggs, a white man, took a good pull on a can of beer. "Our third man ain't comin'. Kin you work? For money." Why not, I thought. I told him I could. "You a strong boy?"

"Lift my own weight with two men helping."

"How much you weigh, topper?"

"About one-thirty-five."

"Fancy that. These here crates weighs one thirty-five. Some's a tot heavier."

So we started. The truth was they all were a tot heavier. Balford and I slid crates to the scales, I weighed them, Balford in a slow and uncertain hand wrote down the number, and we hoisted them to Griggs on the truck.

There were more crabs than crates, and the critters kept hopping out of the overfilled boxes like popcorn in a hot skillet. The floor crawled with their oblique scuttles for the nearest dark underside. They scrabbled and clacked, and we crunched them into an agony of yellow ooze as we heaved on the crates. I started shuffling to avoid stepping on them. Balford got mad. "Pull on that drawhook, sport. They's crabs, not custard pies." A jimmy reached up and clamped onto my pant leg and slid back and forth across the floor with me until we finished. I had to break its claw to free my cuff.

The pickup, loaded beyond the legal maximum, listed to port. I asked Griggs how far he had to take them. "Over to Belhaven, couple hours away." He gave Balford and me a beer, relieved himself against the shed, and fished up his wallet. His fingers fumbled among the bills and drew out a five. He said, "There you be."

From the darkness, a man with legs like masts and arms like spars and great blue-ebony lips walked up. Griggs called him Big Man. Never had I heard speech like his. "We bean oat since yahstudy. Got mebbee leven hunred pounds o' blues."

He had missed his regular truck and wanted Griggs to take his crabs. Griggs pointed to the crates stacked high on the pickup. "Be money for me could I haul them, but surely I cain't."

Big Man said he would have to take his blues out in the sound and dump them. "It gone hurt me someten good."

Griggs was sorry. "See if the fish house can put them on ice." He gave Big Man a beer. The diesel engines of Big Man's trawler mumbled at the wharf, and Griggs' crabs clacked and chattered in the crates, and the men looked for a solution. Then Big Man went off to the fish house, Griggs and Balford to Belhaven, and I walked to my truck.

Later that night, just before I fell asleep, I heard Big Man's boat pull out, and I knew he was heading for open water to dump a half ton of blue crabs. He had said, "Most, day nebba make it to da bottom what da big fish eatem." For me, it had been one fine day.

✒ *Seeking Inspiration from History*

H. G. Jones

Shamed by a persistent poverty and ruralism, North Carolinians have tried to compensate by safeguarding evidence of their past glories. In doing so they have become leaders in national movements to preserve public records, promote the writing of state and local histories, and identify and save historic sites. R. D. W. Connor, North Carolina's first public archivist, went on to become the first U.S. archivist.

This résumé of the state's preservation efforts appeared in the July 1985 edition of the Raleigh *News and Observer*, celebrating the four-hundredth anniversary of the Roanoke colonies. It was written by H. G. Jones, curator of the North Carolina Collection in the Wilson Library at the University of North Carolina at Chapel Hill.

✒ When John Spencer Bassett, a Trinity College professor, complained in 1899 that no more than 20 North Carolinians were concerned enough with their heritage to support an active historical organization, he misread the yearnings of a people still trying to recover from the effects of a civil war.

What Bassett failed to recognize was that discouraged people often seek inspiration from history. Accomplishments of the past serve as confirmation that they can influence the course of the future.

The foundation for a surge in historical interest had been laid with the introduction of rudimentary history courses at Trinity College and the University of North Carolina and with the publication of a monumental series of colonial records under the editorship of the crippled secretary of state, William L. Saunders. These newly printed documents, coupled with sources contained in a state records series compiled by Walter Clark, provided grist for the literary mills of a tiny coterie of historians who, along with well-read laymen, began turning out revealing monographs and articles on North Carolina's past.

These publications were eagerly read not so much by the plain citizens of the state as by their leaders. The formation in 1900 of the State Literary and Historical Association, therefore, did not come from a grassroots movement; rather, the founders and early leaders of the organization were from among the state's political and social elite. Of its first five presidents, one was a governor, two were justices of the supreme court and two were college presidents. The association thus started out with credibility and prestige.

It needed both, for North Carolina was without any statute, agency or mechanism for preserving and promoting use of its historic resources. No wonder, then, that the new organization's first emphasis was upon literacy and books. It pledged to assist in the establishment of schools, libraries and literary clubs, and to work for the collection, preservation, production, and dissemination of the state's history and literature.

"Lit and Hist," as the association was affectionately called, compiled a phenomenal record in its early years. Some of the accomplishments—establishment of schools and libraries, for instance—fitted perfectly into Gov. Charles B. Aycock's educational program for the state. Others were more easily achieved through a new state agency, the North Carolina Historical Commission, created by the General Assembly in 1903 at the bidding of the Literary and Historical Association.

Even with only a minuscule state appropriation, the commission joined the association in producing an impressive number of publications, historical markers and public ceremonies. As secretary of the commission, Robert Digges Wimberly Connor inaugurated a program that would develop into one of the leading state archival and historical agencies in the nation and propel himself into the position of first Archivist of the United States.

Meanwhile, "Lit and Hist" remained the public relations arms for cultural interests, encouraging spinoffs of special-interest groups such as the folklore, art, music, archaeological, antiquities, and genealogical societies. This birthing of new organizations inevitably led to a draining of financial support from the Literary and Historical Association, which in 1985 is struggling for its very existence while its cultural children flourish.

The ferment of history early in the century was not limited to the capital city. In fact, Connor's missionary zeal spread to the University of North Carolina and Trinity College, where Joseph G. deRoulhac Hamilton and William Kenneth Boyd gathered in private manuscripts while Connor gave primary attention to public records. As source materials became more conveniently available, the number of publications multiplied and something of a patriotic fervor swept the state.

It was natural for the North Carolina Historical Commission, as an official state agency, to assume major responsibility for historical matters. It soon amassed a huge archives of public records and private manuscripts, inaugurated a distinguished publications program, coordinated public ceremonies and commemorative markers, took over operation of the state museum of history and established a legislative reference department. In 1924 Albert Ray Newsome started the *North Carolina Historical Review*, today a leading state journal, and in 1935 he lobbied through the legislature a model bill giving the commission responsibility for the protection of all public records.

The most dramatic expansion of the agency came under Christopher Crittenden, a sound, fun-loving UNC historian who traded places with Newsome in 1935 and served as director for a third of a century. The broadening of the commission's program led in 1943 to a change of its name to the State Department of Archives and History and in the next three decades to a standing as one of the largest and most comprehensive state historical departments in the country. In 1968, the new Archives and History-State Library Building was occupied on Jones Street.

The State Archives took on an administrative function following World War II. To assist public officials in managing their mounting quantities of records, archivists conducted inventories of the records of each agency and established time periods for their retention or disposition.

Courthouses, too, were bulging from the "paper explosion" of the postwar years, and local officials groaned under the burden of voluminous records. Furthermore, fires in courthouses or buildings housing local records occurred all too frequently, and the resulting losses of vital records—deeds, mortgages, wills, estates papers, and marriage, divorce, and tax records—created havoc.

To provide for a security copy of essential local records, the Department of Archives and History in 1959 launched a bold new program that even today is unmatched by any other state. At a cost of $5 million over the next 25 years, the staff inventoried the records of all 100 counties, established retention and disposition schedules for them, and microfilmed the permanently valuable books and papers.

The resulting statistics were staggering: 110,376 bound volumes containing about 55 million pages, along with large quantities of unbound manuscripts, were microfilmed on 47,873 reels; duplicate copies of the film were placed in the State Archives for use by researchers, and the master negatives were stored in a specially-designed vault; 1,335,718 pages of deteriorating local records were restored through the Barrow process; 3,100 volumes were rebound; more than 5,000 volumes and several thousand cubic feet of "loose papers" were transferred to the State Archives.

J. G. deRoulhac Hamilton made Chapel Hill the center for research in Southern history by so thoroughly scouring the region for private manuscripts that he earned for himself the nickname "Ransack" and for his department an official designation as the Southern Historical Collection. In 1984 the collection contained an estimated 9.4 million items with a monetary value of $45 million. Historians, of course, do not place dollar values on original source materials; the figure was drawn up for the Department of Insurance.

At Durham, Boyd and his successors also brought in Southern materials; but they spread their net farther afield. Duke's manuscript department, therefore, is not limited by geography and contains more than seven million items.

After World War II, other institutions joined these elite manuscript repositories, and now researchers find their way to East Carolina, Wake Forest, UNC-Charlotte and more than 100 other collections, most of them small in comparison.

Manuscripts, of course, are but the raw materials for books and articles. The Department of Archives and History took the lead in publishing state historical materials, including documentaries, pamphlets and leaflets.

Observances of anniversaries—such as the Carolina Charter tercentenary, Civil War centennial, Revolution bicentennial and the current commemoration of the 400th anniversary of the Roanoke colonies—sparked publication programs that fell to the department for completion, including a new colonial records series.

After its founding in 1922, the University of North Carolina Press joined in producing books about the state and by North Carolinians, and its success spurred the entry into the field by private publishers such as John Fries Blair of Winston-Salem.

The North Carolina Collection at UNC-Chapel Hill dates to 1844, but it was organized officially in 1917 and grew into the most comprehensive library of printed state materials, its holdings numbering nearly 200,000 cataloged items alone.

Recognition of North Carolina authors began in 1905 with the presentation by President Theodore Roosevelt of the Patterson Cup to John Charles McNeill. The Mayflower Society Cup for nonfiction and the Sir Walter Raleigh Award for fiction replaced the Patterson Cup later in the century.

They, like several others, are awarded annually during the traditional gathering of cultural organizations, simply called "Culture Week," an intellectual and social extravaganza unique to North Carolina.

When the Hall of History was transferred from the Department of Agriculture to the Historical Commission in 1914, its longtime curator went along with it. Already a legendary packrat and raconteur, "Colonel" Fred A. Olds was as much a curiosity to two generations of children as the artifacts that he showed them.

Today the Museum of History draws nearly 200,000 visitors a year, is bulging at the seams with about 350,000 artifacts, and is seeking expanded quarters.

Nearby the State Capitol, restored during Gov. Robert W. Scott's administration, is a sort of museum in itself; it attracted nearly 130,000 visitors last year; 60,000 more trekked through the Executive Mansion, also given a new lease on life.

Since World War II, other museums have opened in the state, such as the Mint Museum of History in Charlotte, Museum of the Albemarle, Greensboro Historical Museum, New Hanover County Museum, and the special-interest Museum of Early Southern Decorative Arts in Winston-Salem.

As in the case of archives, publications and museums, the Department of Archives and History took the lead in the preservation of historic and archaeological sites. More than 1,200 highway historical markers alert motorists to sites associated with historic events or personages, and since 1955 the department has designated 21 properties as state historic sites. They range from Tryon Palace and Brunswick Town in the east to the Duke Homestead and Alamance Battleground in the Piedmont and to the Vance Birthplace and Thomas Wolfe Memorial in the mountains. Altogether, they draw nearly a million visitors annually, with the highest visitation figures at Fort Fisher, the Elizabeth II and Reed Gold Mine. Historic Fort Macon is still administered as a state park.

Five historic sites are operated by the federal government—Fort Raleigh, Guilford Battleground, Moores Creek Battleground, the Carl Sandburg home and the Wright Brothers Memorial. Historic properties are occasionally acquired and operated by county and municipal governments through local historical commissions, and Biltmore is the most popular privately operated historic site.

The North Carolina Society for the Preservation of Antiquities, founded in 1939, stimulated historic preservation in the private sector. By the 1960s, considerable activity was under way in saving local landmarks, often with small challenge grants from the General Assembly or the Smith Richardson Foundation. Several local historical commissions were created to carry on community projects.

The most profound leap in historic preservation, however, followed passage of the National Historic Preservation Act of 1966. Three years later North Carolina received its first federal grant—a puny $4,181—to begin a statewide survey of historic properties for the purpose of nominating significant sites to the National Register of Historic Places.

Only 47 sites were admitted to the register the first year, but as federal and state funds were increased, nominations rose; today the register lists about 1,000 North Carolina properties, and the survey has identified 25,000 more sites possessing some degree of historic, archaeological, or architectural value.

The impact of this survey was enormous: local citizens began to show pride in what previously they simply called "old buildings"; an increasing number of organizations and individuals got into the act of saving structures; federal and state governments provided more (though still modest) challenge funds; and tax laws were amended to provide incentives for the restoration and adaptive use of historic properties.

The old antiquities society was transformed into the Historic Preservation Foundation of North Carolina, which administers a revolving fund by which properties are purchased and resold on condition that the new buyers restore and preserve them.

Once an activity of "little old ladies in tennis shoes," historic preservation has become fashionable socially and economically, and this new acceptability of things old has reinvigorated formerly decaying neighborhoods such as Oakwood in Raleigh. It also is transforming the face of North Carolina.

John Spencer Bassett failed to recognize the utility of history as a powerful force in motivating the citizenry. He earned a national reputation as a historian and left his native state in disgust. R. D. W. Connor, on the other hand, knew that an understanding of the past could furnish the yeast needed to leaven a lethargic people. Connor—and Hamilton, Crittenden and others—stayed. North Carolinians of 1985 are the beneficiaries of their faith and of their leadership in preserving our heritage.

❧ Why We're Called Tar Heels

William S. Powell

Among North Carolina's many blessings is its colorful nickname, the Tar Heel State. What is a Tar Heel and how did the term originate? Both are questions that puzzle newcomers and natives alike. Here is a carefully researched response from William S. Powell, retired University of North Carolina professor and the state's foremost authority on North Carolina history. It is reprinted from the March 1982 issue of *Tar Heel* magazine.

❧ We all have had to deal with the problem at one point or another, particularly when we go abroad (more than two states away) and declare our state of residence.

"Oh, that's such a beautiful state," folks respond, before pausing. "But why are you called Tar Heels?"

The *why* comes easily, but *when* it all started takes explaining. In fact, history shows that North Carolina residents have taken an albatross from around their necks and pinned it on their chests like a badge of honor.

The moniker is rooted in the state's earliest history, derived from the production of naval stores—tar, pitch and turpentine—extracted from the vast pine forests of the state. Early explorers from Jamestown pointed out the possibilities for naval stores production along the Chowan River. Eventually Parliament offered a bounty for their production, and North Carolina became an important source of tar and pitch for the English navy. For several years before the American Revolution, the colony shipped more than 100,000 barrels of tar and pitch annually to England.

The distillation process for tar and pitch was messy and smelly. Rich pine logs were stacked, covered with earth and burned. The tar ran out through channels dug on the lower side of the pile. Because of this product, so extensively produced in North Carolina, the people of the state were called "Tarboilers," according to the first volume of the *Cincinnati Miscellany*, an Ohio journal published in 1845. Forty-three years later, the poet Walt Whitman also recorded that the people of North Carolina were called "Tar Boilers." In both cases the name clearly was applied in derision. In May 1856, *Harper's Magazine* mentioned someone who "lost his way among the pine woods that abound in that tar and turpentine State," while an 1876 book on the Centennial Exposition described someone who "spent his youth in the good old 'Tar and Turpentine State.'"

A story that at best must be considered folklore states that when Lord Cornwallis's troops forded the Tar River in early May 1781 en route to Yorktown, they emerged with tar on their feet. This marked their passage through North Carolina as tar heels. The tar reputedly had been hastily dumped into the river to prevent the British from capturing it. This story cannot be traced beyond the 20th century and may have been made up to suggest the naming of the river.

But *when*, beyond doubt, did the term Tar Heel begin to be applied to North Carolinians? Clearly during the Civil War. In the third volume of Walter Clark's *Histories of the Several Regiments from North Carolina in the Great War, 1861 to 1865*, published in 1901, James M. Ray of Asheville records two incidents in 1863 that suggest the nickname's original application. In a fierce battle in Virginia, where their supporting column was driven from the field, North Carolina troops stood alone and fought successfully. The victorious troops were asked in a condescending tone by some Virginians who had retreated, "Any more tar down in the Old North

State, boys?" The response came quickly: "No; not a bit; old Jeff's bought it all up." "Is that so? What is he going to do with it?" the Virginians asked. "He is going to put it on you'ns heels to make you stick better in the next fight."

After the Battle of Murfreesboro in Tennessee in early January 1863, John S. Preston of Columbia, S.C., the commanding general, rode along the fighting line commending his troops. Before the 60th Regiment from North Carolina, Preston praised them for advancing farther than he had anticipated, concluding with: "This is your first battle of any consequence, I believe. Indeed, you Tar Heels have done well."

Similarly, sometime after North Carolina troops had fought particularly well, Gen. Robert E. Lee is said to have commented: "God bless the Tar Heel boys." Like the Cornwallis story, however, the exact occasion has not been noted.

A San Francisco magazine, *Overland Monthly*, in its August 1869 issue, published an article on slang and nicknames. The author cited a number of terms used in the Old North State. "A story is related," he wrote, "of a brigade of North Carolinians, who, in one of the great battles (Chancellorsville, if I remember correctly) failed to hold a certain hill, and were laughed at by the Mississippians for having forgotten to tar their heels that morning. Hence originated their cant name 'Tarheels.' "

A piece of sheet music, "Wearin' of the Grey," identified as "Written by Tar Heel" and published in Baltimore in 1866, is probably the earliest printed use of Tar Heel.

On New Year's Day, 1868, Stephen Powers set out from Raleigh on a walking tour that in part would trace in reverse the march of Gen. William T. Sherman at the end of the Civil War. As a part of his report on North Carolina, Powers described the pine-woods of the state and the making of turpentine. Having entered South Carolina, he recorded in his 1872 book, *Afoot & Alone*, that he spent the night "with a young man, whose family were away, leaving him all alone in a great mansion. He had been a cavalry sergeant, wore his hat on the side of his head, and had an exceedingly confidential manner."

"You see, sir, the Tar-heels haven't no sense to spare," Powers quotes the sergeant as saying. "Down there in the pines the sun don't more'n half bake their heads. We always had to show 'em whar the Yankees was, or they'd charge to the rear, the wrong way, you see."

As in this particular case, for a time after the Civil War, the name Tar Heel was derogatory, just as Tar Boilers had been earlier. In Congress on Feb. 10, 1875, a black representative from South Carolina had kind words for many whites, whom he described as "noble-hearted, generous-hearted people." Others he spoke of as "the class of men thrown up by the war, that rude class of men I mean, the 'tar-heels' and the 'sand-hillers,' and the 'dirt eaters' of the South—it is with that class we have all our trouble. . . ." The name also had a bad connotation in an entry in the 1884 edition of the *Encyclopedia Britannica*, which reported that the people who lived in the region of pine forests were "far superior to the tar heel, the nickname of the dwellers in barrens." *The New York Tribune* further differentiated among North Carolinians on Sept. 20, 1903, when it observed that "the men really like to work, which is all but incomprehensible to the true 'tar heel.' "

At home, however, the name was coming to be accepted with pride. In Pittsboro on Dec. 11, 1879, the *Chatham Record* informed its readers that Jesse Turner had been named to the Arkansas Supreme Court. The new justice was described as "a younger brother of our respected towns-man, David Turner, Esq., and we are pleased to know that a fellow tar-heel is thought so much of in the state of his adoption." In Congress in 1878, Representative David B. Vance, trying to persuade the government to pay one of his constituents, J. C. Clendenin, for building a road, described Clendenin in glowing phrases, concluding with: "He is an honest man . . . he is a tar-heel."

In 1893, the students of the University of North Carolina founded a newspaper and christened it *The Tar Heel*. By the end of the century, Tar Heel—at least within the state—had been rehabilitated. John R. Hancock of Raleigh wrote Senator Marion Butler on Jan. 20, 1899, to commend him for his efforts to obtain pensions for Confederate veterans. This was an action, Hancock wrote, "we Tar Heels, or a large majority of us, do most heartily commend." And by 1912, it was a term of clear identification recognized outside the state. On August 26 of that year, *The New York Evening Post* identified Josephus Daniels and Thomas J. Pence as two Tar Heels holding important posts in Woodrow Wilson's campaign.

So there it was in 1912, the stamp of credibility on Tar Heel. Surely an august institution such as *The New York Evening Post* would never malign two gentlemen of the stature of Daniels and Pence, no matter how bitter the Presidential election campaign. The badge of honor stuck, and, in a manner of speaking, North Carolina residents have sat back on their heels ever since, happy to be Tar Heels. Who'd want to be a Sandlapper, anyway?

❧ Sources

Environment: Physical, Historical, Attitudinal

"A Sailor's First Impressions," by Arthur Barlowe, from Richard Hakluyt, *Principal Navigations* (London, 1589), 728–33.

"The First Permanent Colony," from John Lawson, *A New Voyage to Carolina*, ed. Hugh Talmage Lefler (Chapel Hill: University of North Carolina Press, 1967), 69–70.

"Hereditary Nobility in the Carolinas," by C. Wingate Reed, from *The State*, May 27, 1961, 15–16. Reprinted with permission from *The State* magazine and Shaw Publishing, Inc.

"A Land of Opportunity," by William Tryon, from William S. Powell, ed., *Correspondence of William Tryon and Other Selected Papers*, vol. 1 (Raleigh: Division of Archives and History, 1980), 136, 139–40. Reprinted with the permission of the North Carolina Division of Archives and History.

"Benighted in the Wilds of America," from Janet Schaw, *The Journal of a Lady of Quality*, ed. Evangeline W. Andrews and Charles M. Andrews (New Haven: Yale University Press, 1939), 146–49. Reprinted with permission.

"A Visit by President Monroe," from Lemuel Sawyer, *Auto-Biography* (New York: published by the author, 1844), 21–22.

"North Carolina's Languishing Condition," by James Seawell, "Report of the Committee on Internal Improvements," *Legislative Documents*, 1833, from Charles L. Coon, ed., *The Beginnings of Public Education in North Carolina: A Documentary History, 1790–1840*, vol. 2 (Raleigh: North Carolina Historical Commission, 1908), 228–29. Reprinted with the permission of the North Carolina Division of Archives and History.

"The Poorest State in the Union," from Frances Anne Kemble, *Journal of a Residence on a Georgian Plantation in 1838–1839*, ed. John A. Scott (New York: Alfred A. Knopf, 1961), 18–28. Copyright © 1961 by Alfred A. Knopf, Inc. Reprinted by permission of the publisher.

"Early Industries," by Porte Crayon, from *Harper's New Monthly Magazine*, March 1857, 437–41, and April 1857, 741–46.

"A Tight Boot," by Charles W. Chesnutt, *Cleveland News and Herald*, January 30, 1886.

"The Civil War on the Home Front," from Catherine Ann Devereaux Edmondston, *"Journal of a Secesh Lady": The Diary of Catherine Ann Devereaux Edmondston, 1860–1866*, ed. Beth G. Crabtree and James W. Patton (Raleigh: Division of Archives and History, 1979). Reprinted with the permission of the North Carolina Division of Archives and History.

"On the Eve of Reconstruction," by Jonathan Worth, from J. G. de Roulhac Hamilton, ed., *Correspondence of Jonathan Worth*, vol. 2 (Raleigh: North Carolina Historical Commission, 1909), 1040–41. Reprinted with the permission of the North Carolina Division of Archives and History.

"A Blackjack Bargainer," from O. Henry, *Whirligigs* (New York: Doubleday and Company, 1907), 5–21.

"Charlotte and Her Neighbors," from Isaac Erwin Avery, *Idle Comments* (Charlotte: Stone Publishing Company, 1912), 20–23.

"The Downfall of Fascism in Black Ankle County," from Joseph Quincy Mitchell, *McSorley's Wonderful Saloon* (New York: Duell, Sloan, and Pearce, 1943), 229–38. Reprinted with permission.

"Greensboro, or What You Will," from Gerald W. Johnson, *South-Watching: Selected Essays by Gerald W. Johnson*, ed. Fred Hobson (Chapel Hill: University of North Carolina Press, 1983), 45–50. Copyright © 1924 by the *Reviewer*. Reprinted with permission.

"Half across the Mighty State," from Thomas Wolfe, *Of Time and the River* (New York: Garden City Books, 1935), 25–27. Reprinted by permission of the estate of Thomas Wolfe.

"In Defense of North Carolina," by Clyde R. Hoey, from *Addresses, Letters and Papers of Clyde Roark Hoey, Governor of North Carolina, 1937–1941* (Raleigh: Council of State, 1944), 340–41. Reprinted with the permission of the North Carolina Division of Archives and History.

"A Piece of Luck," from Frances Gray Patton, *A Piece of Luck* (New York: Dodd, Mead and Company, 1944), 237–48. Reprinted with permission.

"In the Great Pine Forest," from Jack Kerouac, *The Dharma Bums* (New York: Viking Press, 1958), 135–37. Copyright © 1958 by Jack Kerouac, renewed, 1986 by Stella Kerouac and Jan Kerouac. Reprinted by permission of the publisher, Viking Penguin, a division of Penguin Books USA Inc.

"Warrenton Was a One-Street Town," from Reynolds Price, *Kate Vaiden* (New York: Atheneum, 1986), 104–6. Copyright © 1986 Reynolds Price. Reprinted with permission of Atheneum Publishers, an imprint of Macmillan Publishing Company.

People

"Tar Heels All," by Jonathan Daniels, from Federal Writers' Project, comp., *North Carolina: A Guide to the Old North State* (Chapel Hill: University of North Carolina Press, 1939), 3–7.

"A Well-Shaped, Clean-Made People," from John Lawson, *A New Voyage to Carolina*, ed. Hugh Talmage Lefler (Chapel Hill: University of North Carolina Press, 1967), 174–76.

"An Unquieted Passion for Adventure," by Robert E. Lee, from William S. Powell, ed., *Dictionary of North Carolina Biography* (s.v. Blackbeard the Pirate), vol. 1 (Chapel Hill: University of North Carolina Press, 1979), 163–64.

"Tar on Daniel Boone's Heels," by Joe Knox, from *Greensboro Daily News*, February 29, 1976. Reprinted with permission from the *Greensboro News & Record*.

"A Roaring, Rollicking Fellow," from Robert V. Remini, *Andrew Jackson* (New York: Twayne Publishers, 1966), 13–25. Copyright © 1966. Reprinted with permission of Twayne Publishers, a division of G. K. Hall & Co., Boston.

"Rejecting a Pernicious Custom," by Michael G. Martin, Jr., from William S. Powell, ed., *Dictionary of North Carolina Biography* (s.v. Barker, Penelope), vol. 1 (Chapel Hill: University of North Carolina Press, 1979), 95–96.

"The Best, Wisest, and Purest," from R. D. W. Connor, *Makers of North Carolina History* (Raleigh: Alfred Williams and Company, 1930), 146–57. Reprinted with permission.

"A Prophet without Honor," by Noel Yancey, from *The Spectator*, September 1, 1988, 45. Reprinted with permission.

"Poetry Buys a Slave His Freedom," by Martha McMakin, from *Goldsboro News-Argus*, April 24, 1966. Reprinted with permission.

"The Inseparable Twins," by Darryl Traywick, from William S. Powell, ed., *Dictionary of North Carolina Biography* (s.v. Bunker, Chang and Eng), vol. 1 (Chapel Hill: University of North Carolina Press, 1979), 269–70.

"Vance Fought Yankees, Confederates," by Richard Walser, from *Greensboro Daily News*, April 3, 1966. Reprinted with permission from the *Greensboro News & Record*.

"At the Center of Turmoil," from William C. Harris, *William Woods Holden: Firebrand of North Carolina Politics* (Baton Rouge: Louisiana State University Press, 1987), 1–3. Copyright © 1987 by Louisiana State University Press. Reprinted by permission of Louisiana State University Press.

"A New South Pioneer," by Brent D. Glass, from William S. Powell, ed., *Dictionary of North Carolina Biography* (s.v. Cannon, James William), vol. 1 (Chapel Hill: University of North Carolina Press, 1979), 320.

"She'll Serve Humanity," by James D. Pendleton, from *Charlotte Magazine*, July–August 1974, pp. 42, 62–65. Reprinted by permission.

"Charles Aycock's Soaring Quality," by Edwin Alderman, from *The North Carolina Historical Review* 1 (July 1924): 243–50. Reprinted with the permission of the North Carolina Division of Archives and History.

"A Pioneer in Educating Blacks," by A. M. Burns III, from William S. Powell, ed., *Dictionary of North Carolina Biography* (s.v. Brown, Charlotte Hawkins), vol. 1 (Chapel Hill: University of North Carolina Press, 1979), 242–43.

"Buck Duke: Philanthropist or Robber Baron?," by Jonathan Daniels, from Jonathan Daniels, ed., *Tar Heels* (New York: Dodd, Mead and Company, 1941), 105–20. Reprinted by permission of the four daughters of Jonathan Daniels.

"The Mother of Good Roads," by Jeffrey J. Crow, from *American Public Works Association Reporter*, November 1977, 4–5. Reprinted by permission of the author.

"Brother Exum Takes Her Seat," from *Asheville Citizen-Times*, May 8, 1960. Copyright, Asheville Citizen-Times Publishing Co. Reprinted with permission.

"Breaching the Savage Ideal," from W. J. Cash, *The Mind of the South* (New York: Alfred A. Knopf, 1941), 328–35. Copyright © 1941 by Alfred A. Knopf, Inc., and renewed by Mary R. Maury. Reprinted by permission of the publisher.

"Waynesville Wonder Makes All-American," from *The State*, December 9, 1933, 18. Reprinted with permission from *The State* magazine and Shaw Publishing, Inc.

"Senator Sam Tells Stories," from Sam J. Ervin, Jr., *The Humor of a Country Lawyer* (Chapel Hill: University of North Carolina Press, 1983).

"One of Smithfield's Favorites," by Karl Kohrs, from *Parade Magazine*, January 3, 1954. Reprinted with permission.

"Dr. Frank's Radiant Spirit," by Tom Wicker, from the *New York Times*, February 20, 1972. Copyright © 1972 by The New York Times Company. Reprinted by permission.

"Ed Murrow's Inquiring Mind," by Charles Kuralt, from *North Carolina Historical Review* 48 (April 1971): 161–70. Reprinted with the permission of the author and the North Carolina Division of Archives and History.

"Andy Griffith Makes People Laugh," by Lillian Ross and Helen Ross, from *The Player: A Profile of an Art* (New York: Limelight Editions, 1984). Copyright © 1962 by Lillian and Helen Ross. Reprinted with permission.

"A Power in the East," by Rob Christensen, from Raleigh *News and Observer*, June 25, 1978. Reprinted by permission of the News and Observer Publishing Company of Raleigh, N.C.

"The Mellowing of Billy Graham," from Frye Gaillard, *Race, Rock and Religion: Profiles from a Southern Journalist* (Charlotte: East Woods Press, 1982). Reprinted by permission.

"A Buttoned-Down Boat-Rocker," by Luisita Lopez, from *Charlotte Observer*, December 10, 1972. Reprinted by permission of the *Charlotte Observer*.

Events

"George Washington Visits Salem," from Adelaide Fries, ed., *The Records of the Moravians*, vol. 5 (Raleigh: North Carolina Historical Commission, 1941), 2324–25. Reprinted with the permission of the North Carolina Division of Archives and History.

"A Vote to Unite the State," from Burke Davis, *The Southern Railway: Road of the Innovators* (Chapel Hill: University of North Carolina Press, 1985), 113–15.

"War Ends at Bennett Place," from Burke Davis, *Sherman's March* (New York: Random House, 1980), 250–63. Reprinted with permission.

"The Hanging of Tom Dula," from Manly Wade Wellman, *Dead and Gone: Classic Crimes of North Carolina* (Chapel Hill: University of North Carolina Press, 1954), 172–85.

"A Visit from General Lee," from Charles Bracelen Flood, *Lee: The Last Years* (Boston: Houghton Mifflin Company, 1981), 232–37. Copyright © 1981 by Charles Bracelen Flood. Reprinted by permission of Houghton Mifflin Company.

"Ringing in a New World," from Phillips Russell, *The Woman Who Rang the Bell: The Story of Cornelia Phillips Spencer* (Chapel Hill: University of North Carolina Press, 1949), 147–50.

"Walter Hines Page Attacks the Mummies," by Walter Hines Page, from Raleigh *State Chronicle*, February 4, 1886.

"A Voice in the State Capital," from Josephus Daniels, *Editor in Politics* (Chapel Hill: University of North Carolina Press, 1941), 85–92.

"The Illegal Play That Saved Football," by Jack Claiborne, from *Charlotte Observer*, September 10, 1988. Reprinted by permission of the *Charlotte Observer*.

"George White's Farewell to Congress," from the *Congressional Record*, January 29, 1901.

"The Wright Brothers Learn to Fly," from Harry Combs with Martin Caidin, *Kill Devil Hill: Discovering the Secret of the Wright Brothers* (Boston: Houghton Mifflin Company, 1979; Englewood, Colo.: TernStyle Press, 1986), 202–20. Reprinted by permission of TernStyle Press and Harry Combs.

"The Camels Are Coming," from Nannie M. Tilley, *The R. J. Reynolds Tobacco Company* (Chapel Hill: University of North Carolina Press, 1985), 211–13.

"The Babe's First Homer," by Elizabeth Simpson Smith, from *Tar Heel: The Magazine of North Carolina*, March/April 1979. Reprinted with permission.

"Defeating the Monkey Law," from Willard B. Gatewood, Jr., *Preachers, Pedagogues, and Politicians: The Evolution Controversy in North Carolina, 1920–1927* (Chapel Hill: University of North Carolina Press, 1966), 130–46.

"Justifying the Sales Tax," by J. C. B. Ehringhaus, from David Leroy Corbitt, ed., *Addresses, Letters, and Papers of John Christoph Blucher Ehringhaus, Governor of North Carolina, 1933–1937* (Raleigh: Council of State, 1950), 26–27. Reprinted with the permission of the North Carolina Division of Archives and History.

"The Indians Scalp the Klan," from Wyn Craig Wade, *The Fiery Cross: The Ku Klux Klan in America* (New York: Simon & Schuster, 1987), 303–4. Copyright © 1987 Wyn Craig Wade. Reprinted by permission of Simon & Schuster, Inc.

"Founding the Research Triangle," from Luther H. Hodges, *Businessman in the Statehouse* (Chapel Hill: University of North Carolina Press, 1962), 203–9.

"The Sit-Ins Begin," from William H. Chafe, *Civilities and Civil Rights: Greensboro, North Carolina, and the Black Struggle for Freedom* (London: Oxford University Press, 1980), 99–120. Copyright © 1980 by Oxford University Press, Inc. Reprinted by permission.

Social Fabric

"A Bucolic Society," by William S. Price, Jr., from *The North Carolina Experience: An Interpretive and Documentary History*, ed. Lindley S. Butler and Alan D. Watson (Chapel Hill: University of North Carolina Press, 1984), 83–86.

"An Indian Path to Salvation," by William Byrd II, from William K. Boyd, ed., *William Byrd's Histories of the Dividing Line betwixt Virginia and North Carolina* (Raleigh: North Carolina Historical Commission, 1929), 198–202. Reprinted with the permission of the North Carolina Division of Archives and History.

"Quarrels among the Baptists," from Robert M. Calhoon, *Religion and the American Revolution in North Carolina* (Raleigh: Division of Archives and History, 1976), 50–53. Reprinted with the permission of the North Carolina Division of Archives and History.

"Engage in Domestic Employments," by Thomas Ruffin, from J. G. de Roulhac Hamilton, ed., *The Papers of Thomas Ruffin* (Raleigh: North Carolina Historical Commission, 1920), 342–44. Reprinted with the permission of the North Carolina Division of Archives and History.

"Tavern Life among Lawyers," from Robert Strange, *Eoneguski, or, the Cherokee Chief: A Tale of Past Wars* (Washington, D.C.: Frank Taylor, 1839), 2 vols., 1:210–12.

"Services at a Country Church," from George Higby Throop, *Bertie: Or, Life in the Old Field, a Humorous Novel* (Philadelphia: A. Hart, 1851), 180–85.

"The Life of a Slave Girl," from Harriet Jacobs, *Incidents in the Life of a Slave Girl*, ed. L. Maria Child (Boston: published for the author, 1861).

"Why the South Fell Behind," from Hinton Rowan Helper, *The Impending Crisis of the South: How to Meet It* (N.p.: Ayer Company, 1857), 12–15.

"Levity among the Lawmakers," by L. S. Gash, from Otto H. Olsen and Ellen Z. McGrew, eds.,"The Correspondence of State Senator L. S. Gash, 1866–1867," *North Carolina Historical Review* 70 (July 1983): 360–61. Reprinted with the permission of the North Carolina Division of Archives and History.

"Promoting Progress in North Carolina," from *New York Tribune*, September 8, 1886.

"Life in the Cotton Mills," from Jacquelyn Dowd Hall, James Leloudis, Robert Korstad, Mary Murphy, Lu Ann Jones, and Christopher B. Daly, *Like a Family: The Making of a Southern Cotton Mill World* (Chapel Hill: University of North Carolina Press, 1987), 44–45, 52–53.

"A Boy's Exposure to Religion," from Erskine Caldwell, *Deep South: Memory and Observation* (Athens: University of Georgia Press, 1980), 1–8. Copyright © 1966, 1968 Erskine Caldwell. Reprinted with permission.

"Cyclone Mack in Burke County," by Edward W. Phifer, Jr., from "Religion in the Raw: Cyclone Mack in Burke County, August–September 1920," in *North Carolina Historical Review* 48 (July 1971): 234–38. Reprinted with the permission of the North Carolina Division of Archives and History.

"Fighting the Old Enemy," from Robert Mason, *One of the Neighbors' Children* (Chapel

Hill: Algonquin Books, 1986), 43–49. Copyright © 1987 by Robert Mason. Reprinted by permission of Algonquin Books of Chapel Hill, a division of Workman Publishing Company, Inc.

"Dead Tired Barning Tobacco," recorded by Mary A. Hicks and Edwin Massingill of the WPA Writers' Project, from Tom E. Terrill and Jerrold Hirsch, eds., *Such As Us: Southern Voices of the Thirties* (Chapel Hill: University of North Carolina Press, 1978), 94–98.

"My Grandfather Gets Doused," from Fred Chappell, *Midquest: A Poem* (Baton Rouge: Louisiana State University Press, 1981), 30–33. Copyright © 1981 by Fred Chappell. Reprinted by permission of Louisiana State University Press.

"Fishing in the Cold Gray Sea," from Robert Ruark, *The Old Man and the Boy* (Harrisburg, Pa.: Stackpole Books, 1953), 69–75. Copyright © 1953, 1954, 1955, 1956, 1957 by Robert C. Ruark. Copyright © 1985 by Harold Matson, Paul Gitlin and Chemical Bank. Reprinted by permission of Henry Holt and Company, Inc.

"Unrest among the Branchhead Boys," from Roy Wilder, Jr., *You All Spoken Here* (New York: Viking Penguin, 1984), 56–57. Copyright © 1984 by Roy Wilder, Jr. Reprinted by permission of the publisher, Viking Penguin, a division of Penguin Books USA Inc.

"Basketball Bug Bites Dixie," by Harry T. Paxton, from *Saturday Evening Post*, March 10, 1951, 31, 111. Copyright © 1951 The Curtis Publishing Co. Reprinted with permission.

"Youth and Innocence in Spring Hope," from *Memoirs* (yearbook of Spring Hope High School, Nash County, North Carolina), 1951. Reprinted with permission.

"Testing the Family Faith," from Doris Betts, *The Astronomer and Other Stories* (New York: Harper and Row, 1965), 95–97. Reprinted by permission of Doris Betts.

"The Vertical Negro Plan," from Harry Golden, *Only in America* (Cleveland: World Publishing Company, 1958), 121–23. Reprinted with permission.

"Patton Let It All Out," by Ronald Green, from *Charlotte Observer*, May 11, 1986. Reprinted by permission of the *Charlotte Observer*.

"The Last American Hero," from Tom Wolfe, *The Kandy-Kolored Tangerine Flake Streamline Baby* (New York: Farrar, Straus, and Giroux, 1965). Copyright © 1965 Tom Wolfe. Reprinted by permission of Farrar, Straus, and Giroux, Inc.

"The Education of Terry Sanford," from Terry Sanford, *But What About the People?* (New York: Harper & Row, 1966), 1–4. Copyright © 1966 by Terry Sanford. Reprinted by permission of Harper & Row, Publishers, Inc.

"A Crusader for the Right," by Elizabeth Drew, from *New Yorker*, July 20, 1981. Reprinted with permission.

"Loading Crabs at Wanchese," from William Least Heat Moon, *Blue Highways: A Journey into America* (Boston: Little, Brown and Company, 1982), 59–61. Copyright © 1982 by William Least Heat Moon. Reprinted by permission of Little, Brown and Company.

"Seeking Inspiration from History," by H. G. Jones, from Raleigh *News and Observer*, special edition commemorating the four-hundredth anniversary of the Roanoke colonists, July 1985. Reprinted by permission of the author.

"Why We're Called Tar Heels," by William S. Powell, from *Tar Heel*, March 1982. Reprinted with permission.